CADOGAN guides

Scotland's Highlands and Islands

Richenda Miers

Cadogan Books plc
Letts House, Parkgate Road, London SW11 4NQ

The Globe Pequot Press
6 Business Park Road, PO Box 833, Old Saybrook, Connecticut 06475–0833

Design by Animage
Maps © Cadogan Guides, drawn by Thames Cartographic Ltd

Proof-reading: Lorna Horsfield
Indexing: Ann Hall
Production: Book Production Services
Mac Help: Typography 5

Editing: Robert Snedden
Managing: Vicki Ingle
Series Editors: Rachel Fielding and Vicki Ingle

ISBN 0–947754–86–5

A catalogue record for this book is available from the British Library

Library of Congress Cataloging-in-Publication-Data available

The author and publishers have made every effort to ensure the accuracy of the information in this book at the time of going to press. However, they cannot accept any responsibility for any loss, injury or inconvenience resulting from the use of information contained in the guide.

Printed and bound in Great Britain by the Lavenham Press, Lavenham, Suffolk, on Jordan Opaque supplied by McNaughton Publishing Papers Ltd. CRC by Cooling Brown

Acknowledgements

I would like to thank the staff of the Scottish Tourist Boards and of the various Area Tourist Boards who have given me much valuable help advice and information: especially Anne Burgess, Kevin Howett, Helen McGregor and John Walter. Most of all I would like to thank my editor, Robert Snedden.

The publishers would like to thank Alex, Horatio and Kicca, Lorna and Charles.

About the Author

Richenda Miers is a novelist, freelance journalist and travel writer. Part English and part Scottish, she divides her time between the two countries, and has spent many years living 'north of the border'.

She has many ties to the country she loves: her husband served in a Highland regiment; her son was born in Inverness; two of her daughters went to school in Aberdeen; and two of her children studied at Scottish universities.

The Miers family share a home in the Outer Hebrides.

Contents

Maps

O Caledonia! stern and wild,
Meet nurse for a poetic child!
Land of brown heath and shaggy wood,
Land of the mountain and the flood,
Land of my sires! what mortal hand
Can e'er untie the filial band
That knits me to thy rugged strand!

Sir Walter Scott

Introduction

When Scotland was divided into its present regions in 1975, Highland region encompassed the northern two-thirds of the country but excluded Perthshire and Argyllshire, both of which belong to the 'Highlands' in their true sense. Children used to be taught that the Highlands was the land north and west of a line drawn from Helensburgh, to the north of Glasgow, across the country to Stonehaven, south of Aberdeen. In fairness, this line should be allowed a slight curve to include Perth and a dip to the southwest to take in the Kintyre peninsula and the island of Arran, but as a rough and ready Highland divide it is as good as any.

The juxtaposition of stark mountains, luxuriant glens, bleak moorland, peat-dark lochs, cascading rivers and magnificent coasts gives the Highlands and Islands of Scotland a landscape that cannot be rivalled. Vast areas of it are virtually inaccessible, except on foot or by single-track roads and this has helped to preserve a rich natural heritage that includes many rare species of flora and fauna. Some 790 islands, only 130 of them inhabited, lie off the coast of Scotland. Only a handful lie south of the Highland line.

Main roads are excellent, but it is often necessary to drive long distances to navigate around lochs and mountains. Many of the minor roads are single track with passing places—infuriating in the caravan season.

Until relatively recently the Highlands and Islands were so isolated geographically that few outsiders ventured into them. Impassable mountain ranges and huge tracts of water made communication between remote communities arduous. It was only after the first Jacobite rising in 1715 that General Wade's road system, devised for the purpose of controlling the rebellious Highlanders, allowed travellers such as Doctor Johnson to discover this previously untapped source of purple prose.

The Battle of Culloden that ended the 1745 Jacobite rebellion also brought about the end of the clan system and contributed to the mass exodus from the Highlands that took place over the following hundred years or so. Tumbled stones are all that remain to mark where crofting communities once squeezed a living from the poor soil, subsisting under the protection of their clan chief.

Agriculture, fishing and tourism are the main occupations of today's highlanders. In the remote parts, not much has altered in the last century. It would be no surprise to find a live sheep wandering into a crofter's kitchen. The advent of television has brought some superficial changes, and there may now be modern hotels with pile carpets and en suite bathrooms, but round the back there may be a dozen discarded vehicles peacefully rusting away. The beautiful countryside is often littered with rusting beer cans, tattered polythene and empty bottles, most of it abandoned by locals rather than being left behind by careless tourists.

In the western Highlands, particularly in the islands, there are still old bards and tellers of tales, singing and reciting the songs and stories that have been passed down by word of mouth over the centuries. You will find the best fiddlers and pipers in those areas that were untouched by the Reformation and by the Calvinists' stern suppression of fun and gaiety.

Highland games are a popular summer diversion and those held in the remoter parts are generally less showy than the smarter gatherings around Royal Deeside. In the past the games were often organized with a serious purpose, giving clan chiefs an opportunity to do some talent-spotting for men fit for their armies.

Whatever sort of holiday you want, you'll find it in the Highlands. You can climb in the Cuillins with crampons and ropes, go skiiing in Glenshee or the Cairngorms, reel in a salmon as it thrashes about in the Spey, or sail among the islands on the west coast at the helm of a sturdy ketch and anchor for the night in a sheltered sea-loch, falling asleep to the eerie wailing of seals. You can explore the blanket bog of the Flow Country, spotting rare birds and insects and carnivorous plants. You can sit in a croft-house kitchen, pungent with acrid peat-smoke, and listen to Gaelic songs and stories of the past that have been passed down by word of mouth over many generations. If you are a gourmet, you can dine on smoked salmon or local oysters, followed by a succulent lobster, fresh from the Minch, or an inch-thick Aberdeen Angus steak, and finish off with raspberries from the Carse of Gowrie. And for your picnic lunch, you can buy scampi off one of the fishing boats, boil them up in a billycan over your camp fire, and eat them still warm with wholemeal bread. You can go north and look for that elusive cosmic stunt, the Aurora Borealis (Northern Lights), when shafts of coloured lights, mostly green and red, flash across the sky like a pageant of searchlights. If none of these attractions are to your taste, you can rent a bothy on a remote island and curl up in front of a peat fire with a glass of whisky and your favourite companion.

While in the Highlands let yourself be guided by the philosophy of the people—*ùine gu leòir* is Gaelic for 'time enough', and *uisge beatha*, 'water of life', has given us our word 'whisky'. With all the Highlands and Islands have to offer, what more could anyone want?

This book is dedicated to the memory of my mother-in-law, Honor Capel Miers.

Sorrow and silence are strong
and patience and endurance is godlike

from *Evangeline*, by Henry Wordsworth Longfellow

Travel

James Boswell & Samuel Johnson
on their tour of the Hebrides in 1773

Getting There

By Air

Scheduled flights serve Scotland from all over the world, *some* direct, some via London.

From the US, there are direct services with Northwest Orient to Prestwick Airport, 30 miles (48km) south of Glasgow. Free coaches connect with frequent trains to Glasgow.

From Canada, Air Canada flies from Toronto and Halifax to Prestwick.

European airlines with direct scheduled services to Scotland include: British Airways, from Milan, Paris, Frankfurt, Dusseldorf, and Munich; Air UK, from Amsterdam, Bergen, Copenhagen, Oslo, Stavanger; KLM Royal Dutch Airline, from Amsterdam; SAS, from Copenhagen, Oslo and Stavanger; Lufthansa, from Dusseldorf; Scandinavian Airways, from Oslo, Stavanger and Copenhagen; Icelandair Airways, from Copenhagen and Reykjavik. Visitors from other countries must travel via England.

From England

British Airways and **British Midland Airways** fly direct to Edinburgh and to Glasgow (Abbotsinch), from London Heathrow. British Airways also flies to Inverness via Glasgow. **AirUK** flies to both cities from Gatwick. Flights take just over an hour and there are frequent buses and plenty of taxis into Edinburgh or Glasgow. All airlines offer economy fares with conditions, such as having to book and pay ahead, with no cancellation refund. For example, British Airways offers non-refundable return fares, London to Edinburgh or Glasgow, booked at least two weeks in advance, for from £107 (full fare £218, standby £148) and London to Inverness £120 (full fare £244, standby £142). Offers change frequently so it is always worth checking. There are also many special 'package' offers, some of which include return fare, self-drive car, insurance and a tank of petrol.

Heathrow Airport, ✆ 081 759 4321
British Midland, ✆ 071 589 5599
British Airways, Inverness, ✆ 0463 232471
British Airways, ✆ 0345 222111
Air UK, ✆ 0293 517654

By Train

British Rail runs regular train services from London to Scotland from Kings Cross and Euston stations. The inter-city trains are modern and comfortable and it is a good idea to book seats in advance during the tourist season. The journey to Edinburgh or Glasgow takes from four to five hours and there are at least 15 trains a day to both cities. Special-offer tickets, with all sorts of extras such as free parking, a free dram and free breakfast, are frequently available. London to Edinburgh/Glasgow: Superapex, booking at least 14 days ahead, £29 return; Supersaver, not travelling on a Friday, £59 return; normal return, £69. London to Inverness, Supersaver, £72; normal return, £80. These prices are only a guide.

In addition, there are direct trains to Scotland from several other towns and cities, and convenient connections from Edinburgh and Glasgow. Overnight sleeper connections from London and Bristol operate to Edinburgh, Glasgow, Dundee, Perth, Aberdeen and

Inverness. A second-class sleeper costs £25 (first-class costs £30 but you must then have a first-class ticket). During the holiday season you should book sleepers well in advance.

Kings Cross Station, London, ✆ 071 837 4200

Euston Station, London, ✆ 071 387 9400

Waverley Station, Edinburgh, ✆ 031 556 2451

Buchanan Street Station, Glasgow, ✆ 041 332 9811

Central Station, Glasgow, ✆ 041 204 2844

Aberdeen Station, ✆ 0224 594222

Inverness Station, ✆ 0463 238924

By Bus or Coach

Several coach companies operate between London and Scotland, usually running at least one day coach and one overnight. The journey from London to Edinburgh or Glasgow takes about six hours, with an hour's stop at a service station. The coaches are reasonably comfortable, with toilets. Some have a snack service and show a film. Prices vary and there are often special offers. Average midweek return, London to Edinburgh or Glasgow, costs from £24.

Eastern Scottish Coaches, Victoria Coach Station, London, ✆ 071 730 0202

Scottish City Link, Victoria Coach Station, London, ✆ 071 730 0202 and Glasgow, ✆ 041 332 9191

By Car

An excellent network of motorways means that you can drive comfortably from London to Edinburgh in 7 hours, sticking to the 70 mph limit. The M1, A1(M) and A68 is the quickest route to Edinburgh, and the M1, M6 and A74, to Glasgow.

Specialist Tour Operators and Special-interest Holidays

Tour operators offer many travel-inclusive packages: golfing holidays, fishing holidays, historic trails, scenic tours, etc. Consult your travel agent for details.

in the US

Abercrombie and Kent, ✆ 800 323 3602, runs tours through lovely Highland scenery in The Royal Scotsman, a restored steam train.

Caravan Tours, ✆ 800 621 8338, offers a 15-day holiday for Americans which includes the air fare from New York, escorted motorcoach tours of Scotland and Ireland, free entrance fees, evening entertainment and first-class hotels.

in the UK

Alternatively, there are package tours arranged from all over Britain, ranging from luxury coach tours with scheduled itineraries and first-class accommodation, to cheaper tours with less ritzy accommodation.

Alfa Travel, 6 Golden Hill Lane, Leyland, Lancs PR5 2NP, © (0772) 621 622, runs luxury coach tours and arranges accommodation.

Clansman Monarch Holidays, Central Reservations, St Andrews Square Bus Station, Edinburgh EH1 3DU, will arrange coach tours and accommodation.

Hi-Line, © 0253 290431, runs a holiday advisory service and can tell you everything you want to know about a holiday in the Highlands and Islands. Staff will also make all bookings for you.

National Holidays operates from all over the country an extensive choice of tours, © 0924 383838 (West Yorks) or 0942 44246 (Lancs).

The Scottish Tourist Board publishes a free brochure, *Scotland*, with details of over 300 good-value holidays, all of which can be booked at an ABTA Travel Agent.

Special-interest Holidays

If you like to build your holiday round a theme or particular activity, the **Scottish Tourist Board** publishes an excellent free brochure, *Adventure and Special Interest Holidays in Scotland*, with details of dozens of ideas for 'different' holidays, and addresses to contact. Write for a copy to the Scottish Tourist Board, PO Box 15, Edinburgh EH1 1UY. You can, for example, go on an archaeological holiday. For creative people there are arts and crafts courses offering instruction as well as relaxation. Subjects range from painting and music to woodcraft, silversmithing and stone-cutting. Outdoor holidays include: birdwatching, camping, canoeing, climbing and walking, cross-country and downhill skiing, cycling, diving, fishing, gardening, geology, gliding, golf, riding, shooting and stalking, swimming and watersports.

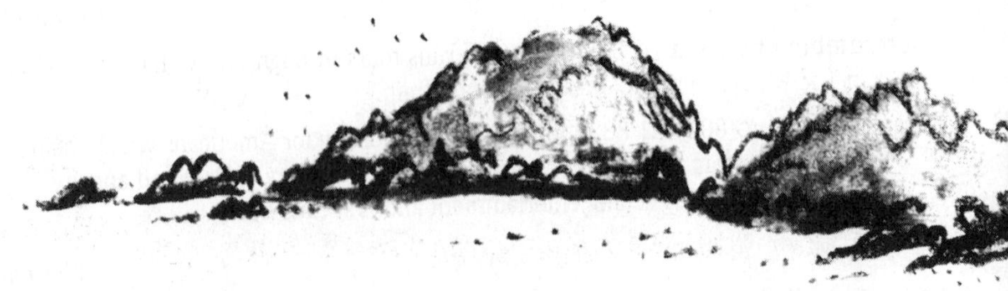

There are also holidays for those who prefer a more cerebral break—English language courses, for example, with outdoor activities laid on, such as **English Écosse**, run by Fiona Wyllie, Arduaine, Oban, Argyll, ✆ 085 22227. Or, if you really want to stretch yourself, the **College of Sabhal Mor Ostaig**, in Skye, runs short courses in Gaelic and in piping at all levels, as well as courses in fiddle, clarsach, accordion, song and dance, ✆ 07414 373.

cruising holidays

If you want to see the west coast of Scotland from the sea, haven't got your own boat, and prefer an experienced hand on the helm, try **STA Schooners**, ✆ 0705 832055. They run week-long voyages in the *Malcolm Miller*, a 300-ton topsail schooner, and part of the experience is that you are one of the crew—a pleasure for which you pay quite a lot. There are many more, smaller and mostly cheaper:

Sinbad Charters, ✆ 0346 842247, or **Yacht Corryvreckan**, ✆ 0631 64371.

Western Isles Sailing & Exploration Company, ✆ 0208 851457, operates out of Oban. Its *Marguerite Explorer* is a beautiful gaff-rigged ketch with a highly competent crew who are only too happy to teach passengers the complexities of sailing as they cruise in some of Scotland's most beautiful waters.

Hebridean Island Cruises, ✆ 0756 701338, offers cruises on the western seaboard in the *Hebridean Princess*, a floating luxury hotel with a crew of 30 serving 40 passengers. If you are lucky with the weather and can afford luxury prices, this is an ideal holiday for hedonists.

There are plenty of opportunities for a 'run ashore'. **Serenissima**, ✆ 071 730 9841, does a cruise in MS *Caledonian Star*, starting from Edinburgh and going up the east coast to Orkney and back down the west coast via the Outer Hebrides to Greenock.

outdoor holidays

For an outdoor activity holiday try **Garry Gualach Country Holidays**, Invergarry. In a relaxed family atmosphere, you can do a variety of things including pony-trekking, sailing and windsurfing, fishing and field sports. There are boys' and girls' dormitories, and two family rooms, and the rates are cheap. Holidays here are unique and never forgotten. Contact Jane Isaacson, © 08092 230.

touring holidays

Touring holidays range from luxury transport and accommodation to spartan. Try **Landrover Expeditions**, © 03552 30385, which gives a good selection of Scottish scenery and attractions and a choice of hotel, farmhouse and camping accommodation. Other tours include Scottish Heritage tours of castles and historic sites, whisky tours—where someone else drives you home—and scenic tours.

working holidays

There are 'working' opportunities, such as Farmhouse Holidays where you can help with anything from peat-cutting to cheese-making: try **Hi Line House**, © 0349 63434. Or go on a conservation project, learning drystone walling, fencing, tree-planting and lots more, © 0786 79697. For impoverished students, a fruit-picking holiday in Perthshire can be fun. With free accommodation and acres of strawberries and raspberries to pick, there are worse ways of making holiday money, © 0250 3707.

Getting Around

By Air

British Airways and Loganair operate services around the mainland and out to the islands.

Loganair

Aberdeen Airport, © 0224 723306

Glasgow Airport, Abbotsinch, © 041 889 3181

Inverness Airport, © 0463 62332

Kirkwall Airport, Orkney, © 0856 3457

Lerwick Airport, Shetland, © 059 584 246

Stornoway Airport, Lewis, © 0851 3067

British Airways

Aberdeen Airport, © 0224 722331

Edinburgh Airport, © 031 333 1000

Glasgow Airport, Abbotsinch, © 041 887 1111

Inverness Airport, © 0463 232471

Wick Airport, © 0955 2215

By Train

As well as the main inter-city routes, branch lines run through the very best of highland scenery. Trains run as far as Thurso and Wick via Inverness and Lairg, in the far northeast, and to Oban, Fort William, Mallaig and Kyle of Lochalsh in the west. Aberdeen–Inverness, Glasgow–Stranraer, Glasgow–Oban and Perth–Inverness are all very attractive journeys. The **Kyle Line** runs from Inverness across Scotland to Kyle of Lochalsh, a lovely stretch of country which links up with the five-minute ferry crossing to Skye. The famous **West Highland Line** from Glasgow to Fort William and on to Mallaig is worth doing just for the beauty of the journey, and the trains themselves—beautifully preserved locomotives and coaches. **British Rail** offer all sorts of excellent bargain tickets; check at any station.

Freedom of Scotland Rover tickets allow you to travel anywhere in Scotland: 15 days costs about £100. There are other travel passes worth enquiring about. North Americans can buy a Brit Rail Pass through their travel agents. There is also a motor-rail service to the main cities.

By Bus

Buses serve most of Scotland. In very rural areas there is usually a 'postbus' service in the mail mini-bus—an experience often memorable for the social outing as much as for the transportation. Enquire locally or at tourist information centres.

By Car

Car hire firms operate from the airports and stations, and there are always local firms: the more rural, the better the bargain usually. A car is essential for anyone wishing to explore the larger islands,and can usually be hired locally at fairly reasonable rates. Arnold Clark are very reasonable, from about £16 a day. You drive on the left in Scotland, as in the rest of the British Isles, and it is law in Britain for drivers and all passengers to wear seat belts. Road signs are similar to those in Europe. There is a mandatory speed limit of 70mph on all motorways. Parking in towns is usually restricted to parking meters and car parks. A single yellow line by the kerb means you can't park by day; a double yellow line, and zigzag lines by pedestrian crossings, mean no parking at any time.

Main roads are generally good, although many are not dual carriageways. In rural areas there are many single-track roads with passing bays. These should not be used for parking; they are also for slow cars to pull into, to allow faster ones to overtake. When touring in the far north, remember there are not many petrol stations and some close on Sundays.

Hitch-hiking

It is neither more nor less chancy to thumb a lift in Scotland than anywhere else. In populated areas, be extremely wary. In the islands, however, locals will invariably stop and offer a lift without being thumbed; it is part of their instinctive hospitality.

Scotland has 130 inhabited islands, most of them around its west coast. This area is served by **Caledonian MacBrayne** ferries, and rail links connect with many of the services. All crossings except the very shortest must be booked in advance. Return fares work out cheaper than singles if you are able to plan your trip to take advantage of these. Car fares are calculated according to the length of the vehicle. MacBrayne's, or CalMac as it is known, also offers economy Island Hopscotch tickets, and Island Runabout tickets for unlimited travel over a set period, both of which offer considerable savings. It publishes a comprehensive brochure with details of schedules, prices and special offers, some of which change seasonally as well as annually. Contact Caledonian MacBrayne Ltd, The Ferry Terminal, Gourock, PA19 1QP, ✆ 0475 650100 for details.

Orkney and Shetland are served by **P&O Scottish Ferries** sailing out of Aberdeen. It offers cruises and inclusive holidays to the islands. For its comprehensive brochure, write to PO Box 5, Jamieson's Quay, Aberdeen AB9 8DL, ✆ 0224 57 2615.

Links between the islands are operated in Orkney by **Orkney Islands Shipping Co Ltd**, Head Office, 4 Ayre Road, Kirkwall KW15 1QX, ✆ 0856 872044; and in Shetland by Shetland Islands Council, Shetland Islands Tourism, Market Cross, Lerwick ZE1 0LU, ✆ 0595 3434.

Detailed information on how to reach a particular island destination is given with that island's entry in the book. For sailors there is nowhere in the world more beautiful (and often challenging) than the waters around Scotland's islands and there are many sheltered anchorages from which to explore.

Practical A–Z

eating out

You can choose between *haute cuisine* that will satisfy any gourmet, good plain cooking at a reasonable price, and fast-food. In the cities, meals are served at fairly flexible hours, but in smaller places you should aim to have lunch between 12.30 and 2pm, and dinner between about 7 and 9pm. If you know you will be late it is wise to make arrangements in advance. 'High tea' is an alternative to dinner, usually served between 4.30 and 6.30pm, and is an extremely sustaining meal consisting of a main course (usually fried) followed by bread, cake, biscuits, etc., washed down by cups of tea—a very British meal. Some of the country's best restaurants are to be found tucked away in out-of-the-way places. These are mentioned in the relevant sections within this book.

national dishes

Fair fa' your honest, sonsie face,
Great chieftain o'the puddin'-race!
Aboon them a' ye tak your place,
Painch, tripe, or thairm:
Weel are ye wordy o' a grace,
As lang's my arm.

from 'Address to a Haggis', by Robert Burns

Scotland has an unmatched reputation for salmon, both fresh and smoked. The development of fish farming has increased the availability but it has to be said that 'wild' salmon is usually nicer than that which has been reared in a farm. Apart from the salmon, national dishes include trout, sea fish, shellfish, game, beef and lamb. Almost without exception you should go for these served simply in the traditional ways. Poached salmon with mayonnaise, new potatoes and cucumber; a freshly caught mackerel, fried so that its skin is crisp and curling, with wedges of lemon and watercress; an Aberdeen Angus fillet steak, medium-rare, an inch thick, with a green salad of lettuce, chives and a hint of garlic; well-hung roast grouse with game chips, fresh petit pois, fried breadcrumbs, bread sauce, and gravy. These will linger on the taste buds as well as in the memory long after any dish wrapped up in an exotic sauce and given a pretentious name.

Everyone should try haggis—if only once. It is made of the heart, liver and lungs of a sheep, mixed with suet, oatmeal and onion, highly seasoned and sewn into the sheep's stomach. Traditionally, it is eaten with 'bashed neeps' (mashed turnip; turnip, in Scotland, is what the English call swede) and washed down with neat whisky. Try black pudding, too: its unusual flavour is strangely addictive.

the celebrated haggis
Fair fa' your honest, sonsie face,
Great cheiftain o' the pudden race

Arbroath smokies are fresh haddock, dry salted and smoked in pairs; a delicate, mild flavour makes them particularly delicious and the best way to eat them is cold, with brown wholemeal bread and butter, a generous squeeze of lemon juice and plenty of freshly ground black pepper.

Porridge is no longer a national habit but you can always get it in hotels. The popular myth that Scotsmen eat their porridge with salt, standing up or walking about, is quickly disproved when you discover how many of them sit down and tuck into it heaped with sugar and cream and sometimes even black treacle.

Scottish cheeses are worth pursuing. Crowdie is unique to Scotland, a creamed cottage cheese, made from skimmed milk. Dunlop cheese, originally made in an Ayrshire village of the same name, is now also made in Orkney, Arran and Islay. Caboc is a rich double-cream cheese rolled in pinhead oatmeal. Galic and Hramsa are both soft cream cheeses flavoured with wild garlic and herbs.

Oatcakes are unsweetened biscuits made with oatmeal, best eaten with cheese, honey or marmalade. Brand-named oatcakes can be dull compared with delicious local and home-made varieties that crumble and melt in the mouth. Shortbread originated in Scotland and is known all over the world. You will find many local variations.

Soups include cock-a-leekie, made with chicken and leeks; Scotch broth, made with mutton stock and barley; cullen skink—delicious—made with smoked haddock, and partan bree, made with crab.

Scotch pies are to be found all over the country; small round pies made of hot-water pastry filled with minced meat, eaten hot. Bridies are pies made with a round of pastry folded over, filled with meat, sometimes padded with potatoes and vegetables.

Cranachan, if properly made, is memorable; double cream, and sometimes crowdie, is mixed with toasted oatmeal, sweetened and eaten with fresh soft fruit, preferably raspberries—another of Scotland's specialities.

The Scottish Tourist Board brings out a *Taste of Scotland* booklet every year offering details of over 200 hotels and restaurants specializing in good Scottish cooking.

drink

Inspiring, bold John Barleycorn!
What dangers thou canst make us scorn!
Wi' tippenny, [ale] we fear nae evil;
Wi' usquabae, [whisky] we'll face the devil!

from 'Tam o' Shanter', by Robert Burns

Among the myths that need to be taken with a pinch of salt is the whisky myth. The average canny Scot will go for the two bottles of cut-price blended whisky that he can get for the price of one bottle of vintage malt. On the whole, except among the rich, malt whisky is kept for special occasions, bought as presents for other people—or exported. There are over a hundred malts and every connoisseur will swear to the unquestionable superiority of his particular fancy. However, experiments involving the transfer of a 'favourite' malt into a bottle with a rival label will often prove that it is the eye rather than the taste buds that dictate preference. Most of the distilleries are on Speyside, northeast of Aviemore, in the north, or on the islands of Islay and Jura and a large number of them run guided tours lasting about an hour, complete with a free dram, showing the process of whisky making. The Malt Whisky Trail, on Speyside, is a 70-mile (110km) voyage of discovery, taking in eight distilleries. Tourist information centres will provide details.

Traditionally, malt whisky should be drunk neat or with a little water—any other additions spoil the flavour. No other country in the world has the essential ingredients for that unique taste that makes Scotland's whisky so special: a blend of snow melt, peaty water and carefully malted barley. A Scotsman will never ask for 'Scotch'—unless he is abroad and in danger of being served with a foreign imposter.

Drambuie is a whisky liqueur, very drinkable for those who enjoy 'stickies'. Gingermac or whisky-mac is a mixture of whisky and ginger wine which slips down easily on cold days.

Scotsmen prefer to drink seriously, in bars, though wine bars and English-type pubs are mushrooming in the towns. You may hear, in a true bar, someone ordering 'a pint of heavy and a chaser'. This will be a pint of bitter and a dram of whisky—the accepted way to spin out the precious *uisge-beatha*—the 'water of life'. Often the dram is not sipped and savoured, but tossed down in a single reviving gulp. In the old days, when the licensing laws were restrictive, there was no time for leisurely drinking. Now, licensing laws in Scotland permit public houses to stay open for 12 hours a day, or longer with special extensions, but not all of them choose to do so. Generally, a bar will be open from 11am to 2.30pm, and from 5pm to about 11pm, with reduced hours on Sunday. Most city centre bars will stay open till at least midnight and residents in licensed hotels can buy drinks at any time. Children under 18 may not be served drink in a public house or restaurant, nor may they be sold alcohol in a shop. Some establishments provide special family rooms where children can join their parents, but they must not drink alcohol here. Landlords risk losing their licences if they break the law in this respect.

Slàinte (pronounced slahn-tchuh) is Gaelic for 'health' and is often heard as a toast.

Historic Scotland

Historic Scotland is a division of the Scottish Office Environment Department, responsible for the care and upkeep of many of the country's historic ruins, buildings and sites. Some castles and historic houses open to the public are privately owned and each has its own opening times and admission charges. Wherever possible, this book gives an idea of opening dates but these change from year to year and should be checked in advance. There is an 'open to view' ticket which entitles you to free entrance to 563 places of historic interest: castles, abbeys, stately homes, famous gardens, etc., in Scotland, England, Wales and Northern Ireland. These can be bought from major tourist information centres. Many castles, historic houses and smaller museums close for the winter.

Doors Open Day is Scotland's contribution to 'Heritage Days', two weekends every

September when Europe's finest buildings are open free to the public. You can explore historic churches, towers, country houses, breweries, power stations and many more. Find out dates and details from local tourist information centres

Maps

Good maps are essential if you are to enjoy your holiday to the full. Bartholomew's half-inch maps are good but you need many of them and they are expensive. There is a very adequate *Ordnance Survey Motoring Atlas,* 3 miles: 1 inch (Scottish Highlands and Islands, 7 miles: 1 inch), available from most garages and bookshops. A 'tourist map' of the whole of Scotland, marking special attractions, is useful. Maps of each region are obtainable from the relevant tourist information centre. If you plan to walk or climb then you should get the appropriate Ordnance Survey sheets, scale 1:50000.

National Trust for Scotland

Many of Scotland's historic buildings and conserved land are under the care of the National Trust for Scotland (NTS), a charity formed in 1931 to promote the preservation of the country's heritage. Over a hundred properties, including castles, small houses, islands, mountains, coastline and gardens come under the protection of the NTS. Most are open from April to October, and admission charges vary. Annual membership admits one person free to all NTS properties, and to all National Trust properties in England, Wales and Northern Ireland. Write to the National Trust for Scotland Head Office, 5 Charlotte Square, Edinburgh EH2 4DU, © 031 226 5922.

Packing

Because of the unpredictability of the weather, sweaters and waterproof clothing are essential all year round if you are to enjoy the country to the full, as are comfortable, sturdy shoes. Remember Scotland is famous for its woollen industry so if you intend to buy Fair Isle, Shetland, Cashmere and tweed, pack the minimum. Rubber boots are useful but uncomfortable for walking long distances—they are cheap to buy locally if wet weather looks relentless. Go prepared for rain and cold; the chances are you will have hot sunshine and drought. Scottish waters are cold, but if the sun shines you might regret not bringing bathing things.

Public Holidays

New Year's Day is the only statutory public holiday in Scotland. Bank Holidays are mainly for banks only and include: 2 January, the Friday before Easter, the first Monday and last Monday in May, the first Monday in August, 30 November (St Andrew's Day), 25 December (Christmas Day), and 26 December. Most towns and districts have local public trades' and other holidays which vary from place to place and from year to year. It is worth asking at one of the Area Tourist Board Information Centres for the annual leaflet, *Public Holidays in Scotland.*

Shopping

tweed and wool

As well as the tourist-traps, there are sheds and cottage parlours where weaving is still done on hand looms, mostly in the islands and parts of the highlands. They are invariably signposted from the road. Hardwearing Harris tweed is acclaimed all over the world: to be authentic it should be woven in the home of the crofter on a hand loom with Scottish wool (but not necessarily wool from Harris). Perhaps the most tempting of the first-class woollen establishments is Campbells of Beauly, Inverness-shire.

glass and pottery

Some Scottish glass is beautiful. At Caithness Glass in Perth, Oban and Wick, factory tours show all the processes of glass-blowing, moulding and engraving, and there are shops selling the finished products. Potter's workshops can be found all over Scotland.

hoots memorabilia

Traditional accessories to Highland dress, set with cairngorms and amethysts, in wrought silver and gold, can be bought from most jewellers. Jewellery made from local stones can be found in workshops and craft shops throughout the country. With such a large deer population, both decorative and functional objects carved from horn are made all over Scotland. Take home a shepherd's crook, called a *crommach*, with a handle carved from ramshorn or, if your luggage isn't designed to take something of five feet or more in length, go for a horn salt spoon or drinking bowl.

food and drink

Try and squeeze a side of smoked salmon into your suitcase but make sure it is well wrapped. It isn't cheap for good quality. Buy shortbread, oatcakes and Dundee cake, in tins. They are a good reminder of a Scottish holiday. In the duty-free shop at the airport your choice lies between the malt whisky you have adopted as your 'special' (if in doubt, Glenmorangie won't let you down) and Drambuie, Scotland's whisky liqueur.

Sports and Activities

canoeing

This is possible all round the coast and on many of the rivers, where the fast flow is often ideal for 'white water' canoeing. There are many water-sport centres. The Scottish Sports Council, 1–3 St Colme Street, Edinburgh, ✆ 031 225 8411, runs outdoor training centres where courses include canoeing.

climbing and walking

From the gentlest stroll to the toughest climb, Scotland, small as it is, has as much to offer as any country and a lot more than most. The scenery is unbeatable, the terrain everything from easy to dangerously challenging. The choice is endless. The one drawback may be the capricious weather. A day that begins in brilliant sunshine can end in freezing rain.

Unfortunately there are still a number of people who don't take the dangers of climbing and hill walking in the Highlands and Islands seriously. They set out ill-equipped and with insufficient skills and knowledge of the terrain and almost inevitably get into difficulties. Frequently it falls to the brave men and women of the mountain rescue services to extricate these foolhardy people, often at the risk of their own lives.There are a few simple rules that, if observed, could save lives, money and tempers:

Get a weather forecast for the area in which you intend to walk or climb. Watch the weather the whole time you are out and be prepared to turn back if conditions become dangerous, for example if visibility decreases, the wind gets up, or the temperature falls dramatically.

Plan your route carefully, remembering that rivers and burns can fill quickly after a rainstorm and cut you off, and peat bogs and rocks can be exhausting to walk over.

Tell someone where you are going, when you expect to return, and how many there are in your party. Leave a clearly visible note in your car with this information. And don't forget to tell your informant that you've come back! It's not unknown for such forgetfulness to send rescue services out on a wild goose chase looking for someone who is happily propping up a bar.

Take appropriate clothing and equipment: even in summer a sweater and waterproofs are essential. On any serious hillwalk or climb take gloves, hat, waterproof and windproof jacket and trousers. Wear proper walking boots with good ankle support and a sole with a good grip. Take enough food and drink to see you through a crisis: high energy rations such as chocolate and dried fruit are useful. Take a torch, a first-aid kit, whistle and survival bag. These precautions could save your life.

Always carry a map—Ordanance Survey maps are ideal—and a good compass, ideally with a protractor, and be sure you know how to use them properly. It is easy enough to find your way when you can see where you have been and where you are going, but if the mist or a blizzard closes in, as they frequently do, you could spend the rest of a short life wandering around in small circles feeling extremely unhappy. On mountain routes take an ice axe and crampons and don't set out unless you know how to use them.

It would be impossible to list the literally thousands of walks and climbs in the Highlands and Islands. There are 279 peaks over 3000 feet (914 metres) in height (seven of them over 4000 feet–1230 metres) in Scotland. These are called Munros after the mountaineer Sir Hugh Munro who first listed them. Munro bagging, as it is called, is a popular pastime and most of them are reasonably accessible, often within easy reach of public roads.

The Cuillins, in Skye, have provided a testing training ground for some of the world's top mountaineers. The Arrochar Alps, the peaks northwest of Loch Lomond, particularly the Cobbler, 2891ft (867m), and the Trossachs are both popular and accessible, as is Ben Vorlich, 3231ft (969m), near Lochearnhead. North of Loch Tay, Ben Lawers, with its exceptional alpine flowers, is another Munro at 3984ft (1195m), looked after by the National Trust for Scotland. Perthshire has a number of hills, including Schiehallion, 3554ft (1066m), near Loch Rannoch. The hills around Glen Lyon are also good and Glencoe has a variety of challenging peaks. Further north, Ben Nevis, 4406ft (1322m), is Scotland's highest mountain, with several routes up including a well-marked tourist route. There are a number of other high hills in Lochaber. To the northwest, the highest peaks of the Grampians are truly arctic in the winter, but splendid for experienced climbers. The eastern edge of the Grampians, around Glen Clova, and the Lochnagar area, accessible from Deeside, are also popular. North of the Great Glen, Torridon, in the west, offers spectacular rock scenery, equalled only by the peaks of the Inverpolly Nature Reserve north of Ullapool, including the distinctive Stac Polly, 2009ft (603m), Canisp, 2779ft (834m) and Guilven, 2399ft (720m). Ben Hope, southwest of Tongue, is Scotland's most northerly Munro, at 3042ft (913m).

There are coastal footpaths, nature trails, woodland trails and long-distance footpaths, including the **West Highland Way**, which runs for 95 miles (150km) from Milngavie on the outskirts of Glasgow to Fort William on the south end of the Great Glen. It includes a marvellous range of lowland and highland scenery, on the old drove roads, forestry tracks, an old military road and a railway track bed.

The **Speyside Way** runs for 30 miles (48km), from Tugnet to Ballindalloch, then a further 15 miles (24km) to Tomintoul, with splendid and very varied scenery along the route.

Ski lifts for walkers are available at Cairngorm, Glencoe and Glenshee. These chair-lifts are open for hill walkers out of season only and give easy access to the higher terrain.

Scotland: Walks and Trails gives details of a selection of walks which need no special equipment and are suitable for children. *Scotland: Hillwalking* gives details of over 60 more difficult, higher-level walks. Both can be obtained from **Scottish Holidays**, Telelink, 56 Belhaven Road, Wishaw M12 7BN. *Great Walks in Scotland*, by Hamish Brown, Rennie McOwan and Richard Mearns, published in paperback by Ward Lock, is also highly recommended. **The Wayfarers**, Brayton, Asputria, Cumbria CA5 3PT, © 06973 22383 (or 172 Bellevue Avenue, Newport, RI 02840, USA, © 401 849 5087), organize excellent walking holidays in Mull and Iona. Everything is laid on for you, luggage is moved forward every day, the accommodation is excellent, and the walks are well planned. Look in *Walk Scotland*, a free publication available from the Scottish Tourist Board, for details of other companies offering similar schemes.

Useful addresses

The Scottish Sports Council, Caledonia House, South Gyle, Edinburgh EH12 9DQ, © 031 317 7200.

The British Mountaineering Council, Crawford House, Precinct Centre, Booth Street House, Manchester M13 9RZ, © 061 273 5835.

The Mountaineering Council of Scotland, 71 King Street, Crieff PH7 3HB, © 0764 4962.

Winter Road Check: Highland, © 0898 654610; Grampian, © 0898 654620.

curling

Scotland's traditional winter game is usually played on indoor rinks these days. It has been played in Scotland for over 450 years and is described as 'a sort of bowls on ice'. For information on where you can go to watch or participate contact the **Scottish Sports Council,** 1–3 St Colme Street, Edinburgh, © 031 225 8411.

diving

The wonderful clarity of the sea around the coast, full of highly coloured sea animals and plants, makes Scottish waters among the best in the world for diving. There is a wide choice of good places where you can dive. The places listed here are outstanding. In the north there is Scapa, in Orkney. Four ships of the sunken German fleet, scuttled at the end of the First World War, lie untouched below the clear waters of this huge anchorage and offer marvellous scope for wreck diving. You can charter boats and get air from several places around the coast. On the west coast the waters around Oban are excellent, with a good air supply and boats to charter in Oban. The Sound of Mull is littered with wrecks, and there is sub-aqua cliff scenery. Ailsa Craig and the Firth of Clyde are also good diving sites. The Summer Isles, in the northwest, are also ideal for diving. For more information contact the **Scottish Sub-aqua Club**, 16 Royal Crescent, Glasgow, © 041 332 9291.

Lord, suffer me to catch a fish,
So large that even I,
When talking of it afterwards,
May have no need to lie.

'A Fisherman's Prayer', Anon

In the first half of the 19th century southern fishermen began making the stagecoach trek to Scotland to ply for salmon with rod and line. The industrial revolution had begun to pollute England's great salmon rivers, and was to wipe the salmon out in many of them by the turn of the century. The Scottish lairds had been accustomed to sending forth their 'sealgairs' (hunters) to procure fish and game for them, frequently disdaining such activities themselves. They were amazed and delighted to be paid by these newcomers for the right to dangle their baits in the water.

Much has changed since Scotland made its name as the world's best fishing venue. The night-time revellers who hunted spawning salmon in their breeding places with lamps and pronged spears have been replaced by fishermen and women throwing out high-tech fishing lines with rods made of supremely light, flexible and strong new materials. Where once the huge bulk of Scottish salmon was caught by estuary nets, now salmon nets (challenged by the low price of farmed salmon) are becoming uneconomic; many have fallen into disuse, or been bought up and laid to rest by the rod angling fraternity. The silver king of the river is chiefly valuable as a game fish, and the value of fishing rentals to Scotland, apart from the benefits fishing brings to many sideline economies, is enormous. The capital value of salmon fishing in Scotland has been calculated at close to £1 billion. It is no exaggeration to say that in the valleys of some of the great rivers like the Spey and Tay, the way of life is chiefly determined by the fishery. Fishing hotels and lodges occupy strategic positions above the precious waters, and ghillies' and water bailiffs' houses are never far from the fish that sustains their livelihood. In many villages on rivers the focal point is the tackle shop, trading not only in fishing paraphernalia, but also in gossip about pools in which fish have been caught and the flies that have caught them. The news of big hauls is particularly influential with trout fishermen, and round any little loch in which someone has struck lucky, large concentrations of anglers are to be observed days later, trying in vain to repeat an individual's one-off glory.

The joy of a river is that its course connects contrasting parts of the country. The sources of many of Scotland's great rivers are swampy spring-fed patches in hanging valleys high in the mountains, or even springs in the floors of lochs. Many Scottish rivers can be fished from the mountain burns near the headwaters right through to the wide sleepy stretches flowing through farmland nearer the coast. In some places fishermen use rod and line to spin for migratory fish in the sea off the river mouths, usually for seatrout. Seatrout are the members of the native brown trout family which choose to migrate to sea, but unlike the Atlantic salmon, which forage as far as the Greenland shelf to feed, seatrout winter offshore, generally returning in spring and early summer. In seeking enjoyment from duping fish many methods have been devised to balance the challenge of a catch with applications of physical dexterity and manual skill. Fishing is an outwitting art, and man delights in playing the deceiver.

Salmon fishing in Scotland is classically associated with the wet fly, a contraption of feathers and other titbits which need bear no resemblance to any known insect or creature, but for certain well-tested reasons rouses fishes' aggressive urge. On the bigger rivers spinning is practised in slow, wide pools; but fly fishing is in the ascendancy, and spinning increasingly frowned on. The ancient practice of worming, which is suited to the tails of deepening pools where the worms twirl enticingly in the current, is discouraged even more.

Dapping is a technique developed for catching seatrout and brown trout in windy conditions on lochs. By deploying a loose silky cord from a pole-like rod the fly can be made to dance over the surface like an insect blown from land and trying unsuccessfully to rise. Nymph fishing employs a wingless body in imitation of the fly at larval stage. When a trout takes a nymph it is capitalizing on the momentary opportunity offered by a fly as it rises from the river-bed prior to hatching on the surface. Dry fly, like nymph, is imitative, and although in most Scottish salmon rivers the water is too cold for dry fly to be successful, trout fishermen use it productively on warm evenings on the lochs, when the puffed-up wings of the dry fly keep it popped up on the surface.

The water surface to all fishermen is a hypnotic thing, always moving, always changing with the shifting light in the sky. Cunliffe Pearce has written evocatively of 'the top of the water, that magic looking-glass through which trout and man mysteriously make acquaintance with each other'. In Scotland there is the extra factor of supreme scenery. The Highland lochs—Loch Lomond, Loch Awe—are famed for beauty, yet also loved in a different way by the connoisseurs for the fishing they offer. Some of the far north rivers—Helmsdale, Brora, Naver, Dionard—open out through heather moorland, and become faster as they drop through rocky passages before entering the sea. The outer isles have magnificent salmon and seatrout fishing, and it is on the magical Grimersta, where running fish can stream by in a seemingly endless flow, that the British record catch by one man in a day was recorded—52 salmon. Some of the most exciting trout lochs are those gem-like bodies of water in the far north, famous for being dour and unco-operative in one mood, then exploding into action the next. A hundred fish in a day to two rods is not unimaginable.

Scottish salmon fishing is not, as is sometimes said, the preserve of rich tenants on famous water. There are thousands of miles of fishing in Scotland, and many opportunities for those who seek them out. The game fishing magazines, *Trout and Salmon* and *Salmon Trout and Seatrout*, advertise plenty of rentable fishing, and once embarked on the salmon fishing circuit, chances spring up for keen fishermen through contacts made along the way. Some local councils own water, and many rivers are open to day-ticket fishermen either through angling associations, fishing hotels, local river boards, or private riparian owners. Salmon fishing permits start at around £10 per day. Trout fishing is available in greater supply than is ever utilized, particularly in the far north and west of Scotland, and some of the famous fishing hotels have access to numerous remote lochs which never see a fisherman year-round. A boat on a loch costs around £10 a day, bank fishing around £8. Tourist information centres circulate fishing information, and details of self-catering accommodation which is accompanied by trout fishing. The more expensive salmon fishing possibilities are marketed through the main sporting agencies, and often sold in exclusive packages based in neighbouring fishing lodges.

The salmon fishing season varies from river to river, starting from January in some places and as late as March in others. Trout fishing is from 15 March to 6 October. Sea fishing is extensive, with such a length of coastline. Porbeagle shark, halibut, cod, bass, hake, ling, skate and turbot are but a few of the many species of fish you can expect to find. There is never a shortage of charter boats or, in most places, of experienced locals to take you out. There is no closed season: weather and availability are the only limitations. Again, ask at your hotel, or in the tourist information centre.

Useful Addresses for Fishermen

Central Scotland Anglers Association, 53 Fernieside Crescent, Edinburgh, ✆ 031 664 4685.

Scottish Anglers National Association, 307 West George Street, Glasgow, ✆ 041 221 7206.

Scottish Federation for Coarse Angling, TighnaFleurs, Hill o' Gryfe Road, Bridge of Weir, Renfrewshire, ✆ 0505 612580.

The Scottish Federation of Sea Anglers, 18 Ainslie Place, Edinburgh, ✆ 031 225 7611.

Scottish Sports Council, 1–3 St Colme Street, Edinburgh, ✆ 031 225 8411.

golf

The monarch in these parts is **Gleneagles**, in the lee of the Ochils. The Kings and the Queens are as fine a pair of courses as you will come across in a day's march, and the combination of great golf and good living is hard to beat, if you can afford it.

Golf in the Highlands is concentrated around the east coast. Aberdeen boasts 11 courses of which **Royal Aberdeen** and **Murcar** stand out, both classic links and right next door to one another. **Cruden Bay** is a splendid seaside course and, were it a little longer and more accessible, could be a great test for a full-blown professional tournament. From **Fraserburgh**, the fanatic could have a fortnight of golf before he got to Inverness, without ever playing the same course twice. While Fraserburgh is a pure links and great fun, Banff sports a couple of titled courses in **Royal Tarlair** and **Duff House Royal**. Neither are really links courses but should not be bypassed if the itinerant golfer is taking his time about sampling all the delights of Highland golf.

In Morayshire, **Moray (Lossiemouth)** and **Forres**, both next to the sea, are the pick, together with **Elgin** some 12 miles (19km) inland. Still moving west, at **Nairn** there is a highly regarded links course, which on more than one occasion has played host to the Scottish Championships. **Boat of Garten**, in the Spey Valley, is a relatively short course, but a joy to play. James Braid designed it, and there are superb views—making it a must!

North of Inverness, **Fortrose and Rosemarkie**, **Muir of Ord** and **Strathpeffer Spa** all offer a pleasant 18 holes, but **Tain** is the choice if time is short. A new bridge at Tain has cut an hour from the journey north to **Royal Dornoch** and made this magnificent links more accessible. But for its location, Dornoch would be the choice for the most important championships and indeed the Amateur Championships were played there for the first time in 1985.

Golf on the islands should not be ignored. **Arran** has seven courses of which **Blackwaterfoot**, **Lamlash** and **Brodick** are the pick. Then there is **Machrihanish** on the **Mull of Kintyre** and the **Machrie** on **Islay**. Islay has just the one course and eight distilleries, so care is needed with your priorities if the golf is to be enjoyed.

Back up the coast from Irvine, **Gourock** and **Largs** are fine courses, while the sheer volume of courses close to Glasgow almost defy selection.

Golfing Holidays

A number of tourist organizations organize specialist holidays. The Scottish Tourist Board, 23 Ravelston Terrace, Edinburgh, © 031 332 2433, will send full details.

gliding

Gliding is possible in some areas and most clubs offer temporary membership and instruction. Consult the **Scottish Sports Council**, 1–3 St Colme Street, Edinburgh, © 031 225 8411.

pony trekking

This is a pleasant way of seeing the country and you don't have to be an experienced rider. There are lots of pony-trekking centres, offering a choice of day trekking or trekking and camping. The local tourist information centres will give you addresses: most tourist maps mark them with a horseshoe. The Scottish Tourist Board publishes a leaflet called *Pony Trekking and Riding Centres in Scotland.*

sailing

Sailing off the west coast of Scotland and among the western and northern islands is so beautiful that it makes cruising among the admittedly warmer and more glamorous locations further south, such as the Greek islands, something of an anti-climax. The weather can be tricky, of course, but this should not deter experienced sailors and there will be many fine days to enjoy. Experience is also necessary to navigate the rocks, currents and whirlpools that make these waters such a challenge. Proper maritime charts are essential. Those less certain of their abilities should stick to the lochs and inshore waters.

Once you are afloat with a good skipper and navigator there could be no better way of exploring this incomparable coastline. Seen from the sea the scenery is somehow even more magnificent than it appears from the land, and you will be able to explore sealochs that are virtually inaccessible by overland routes. As well as dozens of harbours and official moorings there are innumerable sheltered anchorages far from any human habitation. Here you can drop anchor and swim in the cold waters with only seabirds and sheep to see you, before going ashore to enjoy a supper of freshly caught mackerel cooked on an open fire as you listen to the eerie sound of seals calling to each other.

There are marinas and sailing centres around the coast from the Clyde to Ullapool, and on many of the larger lochs. If you haven't got your own boat you can charter from a variety of places, either a fully manned boat or one to crew yourself. *On the water in Scotland* is a directory of watersports facilities in Scotland. It lists names and addresses of firms that hire boats of all categories, for all uses, together with information about slipways, chandlers, moorings, canals, and so on. It is available from the Scottish Tourist Board, 23 Ravelston Terrace, Edinburgh EH4 3EU, ✆ 031 332 2433.

Useful Addresses

Royal Yachting Association (Scotland), Caledonia House, South Gyle, Edinburgh EH12 9DQ, ✆ 031 317 7388.

North of Scotland Yachting Association, 18 Crown Avenue, Inverness IV2 3NF.

shinty or shinny

Scotland's version of Irish hurling is said to derive from cries used in the game: shin ye, shin t'ye. It's like hockey, with a leather ball and curved sticks.

shooting and stalking

The terrain is ideal, with farmland, mixed woodland and moorland, and Scotland has a long tradition of good game management. The estuaries and marshes provide excellent scope for wildfowlers, and there are plenty of deer. Stalking, for the uninitiated, involves spending all day wriggling through wet undergrowth until your prey is within range and then, at a signal from the keeper, missing it, or wounding it and spending the night following it to administer the *coup de grâce*. Stalking with a camera instead of a rifle can be infinitely more rewarding. Game-shooting species include pheasants, snipe, grey partridge, woodcock, grouse, capercaillie and ptarmigan. Permitted wildfowl species include many varieties of duck and geese. Rough shooting is for wood pigeon, rabbit and hare. Deer species include red deer, roe, fallow and sika. All other species of wildlife, both bird and mammal, are strictly protected in Scotland by the Wildlife and Countryside Act. No game shooting is allowed on Sundays and a certificate is required by anyone owning or using either a rifle or a shotgun. Before you shoot game you must get a game licence, which is available in all main and branch post offices throughout the country. Some hotels will arrange shooting and stalking and local tourist boards will advise on contacting estates and on shooting seasons.

skiing

There are five ski centres in the Highlands: Glencoe, the Nevis Range (Aonach Mor), Cairngorm, Glenshee and the Lecht. All have excellent runs and lift networks, as well as equipment hire and ski schools. First timers should note that the picture-postcard conditions often found in the Alps are not so common in Scotland. At times only the most enthusiastic of skiers will enjoy their sport here, when the slopes are icy, balding and pitted with rocks and tree stumps and a piercing wind cuts through even the best thermal clothing. But on the many good days' skiing in Scotland is good fun amongst some of the most beautiful scenery in the world.

Ski Hotline Scotland gives information on road and snow conditions and weather forecasts. Ski Call Scotland is the Meteorological Office's service for skiers. Numbers for both services are given with each entry below.

Glencoe is situated on the A82 about 95 miles (150km) north of Glasgow and 25 miles (40km) from Fort William. The centre is open five days a week from Thursday to Monday inclusive during the season, and every day over the Easter period. There are 15 runs, including a particularly easy one called Mugs' Alley!, and six lifts. There is a log cabin restaurant and a Museum of Scottish Skiing and Mountaineering.

Ski Hotline: ✆ 0891 654 658
Ski Call: ✆ 0891 500 795
Ski School: ✆ 0397 750825

The **Nevis Range** is 125 miles (200km) from Glasgow and 5 miles (8km) north of Fort William off the A82. The access road, sighposted Aonach Mor, is seldom affected by snow. The centre is open throughout the season, which can last from as early as October to as late as May. There are 18 runs of all standards and nine lifts. There is also a 250-foot (75-metre) dry ski slope. A crèche for three to seven-year-olds is open from 9 to 12am and from 1 to 4pm. The Snowgoose Restaurant and Bar seats over 200 and there is also a snack hut.

Ski Hotline: ✆ 0891 654 660
Ski Call: ✆ 0891 500 799
Ski School: ✆ 0397 705825

Cairngorm is situated off the A9, 135 miles (215km) from Edinburgh, 28 miles (45km) from Inverness and 9 miles (15km) from Aviemore. Thre are plans for a £15 million re-development, but there are already plenty of good runs of all categories. There is a day-lodge with licensed restaurant, shop and ski hire, and snack bars on the slopes.

Ski Hotline: ✆ 0891 654 655
Ski Call: ✆ 0891 500 797
Ski School: ✆ 0479 810336 or 810310

Glenshee is 80 miles (130km) from Edinburgh, 105 miles (170km) from Glasgow, 40 miles (65km) from Perth and 12 miles (20km) from Braemar on the A93. Spread over three valleys, it has the widest selection of runs in Britain, 38 in all ranging over all categories. There are 26 lifts. There is a licensed restaurant and cafés, ski schools, shop and a crèche in high season.

Ski Hotline: ✆ 0891 654 656
Ski Call: ✆ 0891 500 798
Ski School: ✆ 03397 41331 or 025085 216

The Lecht is 100 miles (160km) from Glasgow, 50 miles (80km) west of Aberdeen and 7 miles (11km) from Tomintoul on the A939. It has 12 lifts and 17 runs of varying degrees of difficulty. There is a summer ski slope and night skiing on three of the runs. Facilities include a licensed day lodge, shop and ski hire, and a crèche. Glen Mulliach, 4 miles (6km) north of the Lecht, is the centre for Nordic Cross Country Skiing, ✆ 0807 580 356.

Ski Hotline: ✆ 0891 654 657
Ski Call: ✆ 0891 500 796
Ski School: ✆ 09756 51440

surfing

Surfing in Scotland hardly conjures up images of Hawaiian shores and hot weather, but the north of Scotland can lay claim to some of the best surfing waves in Europe. In fact, the European Amateur Surfing Championships were held in Thurso in 1981. Any exposed part of Scotland's long coastline has the potential for excellent waves; but the northernmost section, from Bettyhill almost to John O'Groats, has a reputation for the most consistent swells and variety of breaks. There are waves to suit everyone, from gentle beachbreaks to massive reefs, point breaks and river mouths. This is wild-frontier surfing against stunning back-drops of mountains and castles.

The water is a slightly off-putting brown, but don't be alarmed because it's only coloured by peat washed down from the hills. There are very few local surfers but those there are are really friendly.

water sports

Water sports are available all over the country, including sailing, windsurfing, waterskiing and swimming. Coastal resorts invariably have sailing clubs where you can get tuition and hire boats and equipment. There are a large number of inland water sport centres on the lochs. For full details get the *Scotland Holiday Afloat* booklet from the Scottish Tourist Board or call ✆ 0382 21555 or 0577 62816.

Tourist Offices

For tourism purposes, Scotland is divided into regions covered by **Area Tourist Boards**; each has its own **Tourist Information Centre** and publishes its own free brochure with local information and a fully comprehensive accommodation guide. Readers are strongly advised to use these brochures to supplement the recommendations made in this book. Information centres will also advise on routes, sporting permits and local events, and will book accommodation.

The Scottish Tourist Board's Scottish Travel Centre, 19 Cockspur Street, London SW1 5BL, ✆ 071 930 8661 (open Mon–Fri throughout the year) provides a full range of information, advice and literature. It also helps with route planning, and has a travel agency where you can make reservations for accommodation and book for events such as the Edinburgh Military Tattoo.

Also in London is the **British Travel Centre**, 12 Regent Street, Piccadilly Circus, W1, ✆ 071 730 3400 (open daily, no telephone service on Sundays). Here, the British Tourist Authority, British Rail, American Express and Roomcentre combine to provide a comprehensive booking service covering rail, air and sea travel, sightseeing tours, theatre tickets and accommodation. They also change currency.

For drivers using the M6 route north, **Southwaite Tourist Information Centre**, in the Southwaite Service Station, a few minutes south of the border near Carlisle, offers full information on all areas in Scotland, and accommodation services.

The main Tourist Information Centre for the whole of Scotland is **Edinburgh Marketing** in Waverley Market, 3 Princes Street, Edinburgh (open daily, except Sundays, Oct–May, personal callers only). Run in partnership with American Express and Europcar, it offers advice to tourists in all areas, accommodation and travel booking, route planning, a Scottish bookshop, currency exchange and car hire. The head administrative office of the Scottish Tourist Board is at 23 Ravelston Terrace, Edinburgh, EH4 3EU, ✆ 031 332 2433.

Tracing Your Ancestors

For many reasons, not least the Highland Clearances in the 17th and 18th centuries, a large number of exiled Scots, and descendants of exiled Scots, return to the land of their origins hoping to trace their family history. Write to the Keeper of the Records of Scotland, **Scottish Record Office**, Her Majesty's General Register House, Princes Street, Edinburgh EH1 3YY, ✆ 031 557 1022. Send all the information you have on your ancestors. Many clans have their own clan historian/library and will give advice. Alternatively, try a good researcher, such as **Census Searches**, The Lady Teviot, The Knoll, Stockcroft Road, Balcombe, West Sussex RH17 6NG, ✆ 044 4811 654.

Where to Stay

The choice of accommodation in Scotland is enormous, ranging from (a few) superb, luxury hotels to simple bed and breakfasts, or self-catering. The price is not always a reliable guide. The accommodation guides in the local brochures give full details of price and facilities. This book gives only a very small selection and tourists should always try to get one of these publications for each area they want to visit.

As little as £10 a night can buy bed and breakfast in a clean house, with a warm welcome and a thumping good breakfast. £120 can buy a night in a four-poster bed or £150 a suite with a jacuzzi. You can rent a whole house or cottage from as little as £60 a week to over £600. Prices often vary seasonally: single rooms are usually more expensive, per head, than double. You can get good value in a hotel for as little as £15 a night in some areas.

A static caravan costs from £40 a week upwards, and campsites charge from about £3 a night for visiting caravans. Campsite facilities vary enormously. Some are good, others not, but often the scenery makes up for primitive plumbing. The one at Braemar is excellent.

Many bed and breakfast places serve an evening meal and all hotels provide full service. In the more rural areas, and indeed in the towns, don't be put off by the lack of en suite bathrooms in the smaller hotels. What they lack in modern facilities is invariably made up for in the friendly hospitality of the staff. Very often 'public bathroom' means sole use of a bathroom across the passage.

prices

Prices change frequently. In this guide accommodation is loosely graded into three categories, based on the price of bed and breakfast for one person in a single room—double rooms are almost always cheaper per person—as charged in 1994. Many hotels do special bargain breaks, so it is well worth enquiring about these.

expensive You won't see much change from £60 at the bottom end of this range, and the ceiling is out of sight.

moderate About £30–50 should buy you a comfortable night.

inexpensive As little as £10 a night, if you are lucky, up to about £30 and some of the cheapest are often surprisingly good.

Scottish Tourist Board accommodation gradings

An impartial team of inspectors visits hotels, guest houses, bed and breakfast and self-catering establishments, to assess their quality. They award classifications ranging from 'Listed' to five crowns, and gradings from 'Approved' to 'Highly Commended', depending on the standard and facilities. Full details can be obtained from the **Scottish Tourist Board**, 23 Ravelston Terrace, Edinburgh EH4 3EU, ✆ 031 332 2433. Visitors should be aware that these awards are based on a set range of standards and facilities such as: TV, shoe-cleaning kit, full-length mirror, trouser press, luggage stand, hospitality tray, etc. , as well as the more obvious requirements such as heating and towels. They do not apply to character and soul. It is therefore possible to opt for a Highly Commended, five-crown hotel only to find yourself in a sweltering, double-glazed bedroom crammed with gadgets and electric goodies, totally lacking in atmosphere. Equally, an old-fashioned, slightly shabby ex-shooting lodge, as full of highland character and hospitality as you could ever wish for, with blazing log fires instead of central heating, pure cotton sheets, early-morning tea brought to you, and delicious home cooking, may be excluded from the Scottish Tourist Board's list because of its lack of tangible 'facilities'.

As well as the individual publications you can get free from area tourist centres, the Scottish Tourist Board publishes a number of useful brochures covering the whole country, with details of accommodation, sports, special holidays, etc.

youth hostels

There are 80 youth hostels in Scotland, marked on most maps by a triangle. They fall into three grades, A, B and C, some having central heating, hot showers, carpets, etc., and all offering dormitory accommodation and self-catering facilities. Anyone over the age of five may use a youth hostel. The one on Loch Lomond is very high class and so is Carbisdale Castle, near Bonar Bridge. For full details, you can write to **SYHA**, 7 Glebe Crescent, Stirling FK8 2JA, ✆ 0786 72821.

History

From the Ice Age to Christianity

The Ice Age eradicated evidence of any previous habitation in Scotland. **Stone Age** settlers, at least 7000 years ago, were the first to leave clues to their existence. Burial sites and middens (rubbish heaps) from those times have thrown up enough to tantalize archaeologists, but not enough to leave more than a shadow of the identity of those nomadic tribes. They came from Asia and Europe, through England and Ireland, wave after wave of them, creeping up the coast in dug-out canoes, settling for long enough to leave traces of their culture and way of life, before vanishing into obscurity. They lived off deer and wild boar, fish and crustaceans. Some only stayed a short time, living in caves. An excavated house in Grampian dates from 7000 BC, a round stone building about 25 feet (8m) across. Later, farmers came from the Continent and introduced agriculture. People settled for longer periods, burning forests and enriching the land with potash.

After the hunters and gatherers came the **Beaker People**, who laid beakers in the tombs of their dead. They were skilful engineers and historians puzzle over their mysterious stone circles and monoliths, and over the true purpose of their brochs (massive stone towers built near the sea in the far north, about 2000 years ago). Metal was introduced about a thousand years before Christ, and with it the sword and shield. Scotland, on the trade route between Ireland and Scandinavia, was able to barter food and hides for bronze and copper. During this millennium the Celtic-speaking Britons arrived, a sturdy, fair-haired race, combative and quick to attack in order to acquire precious land. The local people built defensive forts, with ditches and ramparts, such as the ones on Barry Hill and Finavon, and skirmishing became part of life.

The Romans arrived in AD 82 and with them came the first record of Scottish history, written by the historian **Tacitus**. Tacitus describes how his father-in-law, **Agricola**, defeated an army of tall, red-haired men on an unidentified hillside in the northeast, in the **Battle of Mons Graupius**. The exact location of this battle is debatable, but it was somewhere in today's Grampian, so called from a misprint of 'Graupius' by a 16th-century chronicler. Roman remains were found as far north as the Moray Firth and Tacitus recorded that they 'discovered and subdued' Orkney.

The Romans called their victims *picti*, the painted ones, from which the name 'Picts' is thought to derive, and failed to subdue them. Highly trained legionnaires could not compete with hostile tribes who faded into the mountains, forests and marshes, refusing to fight army-to-army, preferring to lay cunning ambushes for their aggressors. The Romans fell back having, it has long been believed, lost the entire Ninth Legion in a savage massacre. In fact, evidence of their having been merely posted elsewhere was unearthed recently when traces of their later existence were found around the Danube.

Four races dominated Scotland, then called Alba, or Alban in the years after the Romans withdrew. The **Celtic Picts** were the most powerful, occupying the land from Caithness to the Forth; the **Teutonic Angles**, or **Anglo-Saxons**, occupied Bernicia, south of the Forth; the **Britons**, another Celtic race, occupied the western lands south of the Clyde. Finally there were the **Scots**: Celts who had come over from Ireland during the 3rd and 4th centuries and settled north of the Clyde, establishing the **Kingdom of Dalriada** and eventually giving their name to all Scotland. **St Ninian** founded the first Christian centre at Whithorn, near the Solway Firth, in 397, and started the daunting task of converting the pagans. Then came **Columba**, a clever man of royal birth, who was exiled from Ireland and arrived in Scotland in 563. He established himself on the island of Iona, continuing St Ninian's work, and sent missionaries to the mainland and to the other islands. They penetrated further and further into Pictland. Columba's influence was political as well as religious and he did much to consolidate the strength of the Scots.

By the end of the 7th century the four kingdoms of Alban were nominally converted to Christianity—a Celtic Christianity, not yet in line with that dictated by Rome.

The Birth of Scotland

At the end of the 8th century Norsemen began to attack from the north, conquering Orkney and Shetland, the Western Isles, Caithness and Sutherland, while the four kingdoms continued to fight amongst themselves, weakening their resistance to outside attack.

In 843 **Kenneth Macalpine**, King of the Scots, achieved some sort of union between Scots and Picts, making himself king over all the territory north of the Forth and Clyde, which then became Scotia. The Picts, who had been dominant for more than 1000 years, vanished for ever. They remain an enigmatic people whose history is unrecorded and unknown; an elusive ghost-race who will perhaps never be fully understood. It was not until 1018, however, that **Malcolm II** defeated the Angles and brought Bernicia, or Lothian, into the kingdom. He was succeeded in 1034 by his grandson **Duncan I** who already ruled the Britons, and so the four kingdoms were finally united into one Scotland, except for those parts occupied by the Norsemen. The country was divided into seven main kingdoms, of which Fife was the strongest, plus a few smaller ones, each ruled by a *mormaer*. The *Ard Righ* or High King was their overlord—King of the Scots, but not of Scotland, for each *mormaer* owned his land. In those days, under a remarkable clan system in which no one was subservient and each played an important part, Scotland was truly democratic.

Duncan I was killed in 1040 by **Macbeth**, the last Celtic king, whose 17-year reign was chronicled as a time of plenty. He was killed by Duncan's son, **Malcolm Canmore**, with the help of the English, in 1057. *Ceann Mor* is Gaelic for big head, referring to Malcolm III's status rather than any anatomical defect, or conceit.

Malcolm Canmore's second wife, **Margaret**, brought in English clergy and established an English court, transforming Scotland into a kingdom similar to Norman England. The Lowland clans gave up their democracy: *mormaers* became earls and established a feudal system, while the Highlands and Islands retained the old, patriarchal clans. David I, ninth son of Malcolm Canmore, inherited the throne in 1124. He had been brought up in England and gave large Scottish estates to his Anglo-Norman friends. The Highlanders took little notice of these southern interlopers.

Malcolm IV was 13 when he inherited the throne from his grandfather David I. Known as Malcolm the Maiden, he was nevertheless a brave young man, whose courage inspired many of his followers. Gentle and religious, he ruled for only 12 years before he died, to be succeeded by his brother, **William the Lion**, who launched an ill-conceived expedition into Northumberland in 1174. It failed and William was captured. He was forced to sign the humiliating **Treaty of Falaise**, placing Scotland under feudal subjectiion to England.

Alexander II succeeded to the throne in 1214, and directed his attention to the Western sles, whose lords gave their allegiance to Norway. It was his son, **Alexander III**, however, who managed to expel the Norsemen from the Hebrides. He did this by defeating old **King Haakon IV** of Norway in the **Battle of Largs** in 1263. The Hebrides became part of the Kingdom of Scotland again, though the Lords of the Isles paid little heed to any authority but their own.

When **Edward I** of England declared himself to be overlord of Scotland there were several claimants to the throne, the strongest being **John Balliol**, son of the regent, and **Robert the Bruce**. Edward insisted that Scotland should contribute to English defence costs and join with them in an invasion of France. Rather than do this the Scots instead formed an alliance with France in October 1295. The **Auld Alliance**, as it became known, was between two independent kingdoms, rather than being forced by a stronger state on a weaker one, as England had sought to do to Scotland. Edward saw it as practically a declaration of war.

In 1296, Edward's army progressed through Scotland, compelling nobles and lairds to sign the **Ragman Roll** acknowledging him to be their king. He then returned to England, taking with him what he thought to be the Stone of Destiny, brought from Ireland seven centuries earlier and believed to embody special powers of sovereignty. It had always been used in the coronation of Scottish kings. Edward was convinced he had finally conquered Scotland.

Robert the Bruce, grandson of John Balliol's rival,became Guardian of Scotland, alongside Balliol's nephew, **Red John Comyn**. Bruce resigned the guardianship in 1302 and went over to Edward's side. In 1306 Bruce and Red Comyn met at Greyfriars Kirk, in Dumfries. They quarrelled and Bruce killed Comyn, possibly because of his refusal to help Bruce in a campaign for the Scottish throne. Seizing the initiative,Bruce went to Scone and had himself crowned King of Scotland in March 1306. Edward hurried north and defeated Bruce, a month later, at Methven. Outlawed, his friends and allies dead, Bruce went into hiding but returned to Scotland in 1307, overcame all other claimants to the throne and defeated Edward I's successor, Edward II, at **Bannockburn** in 1314.

Bruce was succeeded by his young son, **David II**, with **Thomas Randolph, Earl of Moray**, as regent. The 42 years of David's reign were troubled times for Scotland. He was captured by the English at the **Battle of Neville's Cross** in 1346 and spent the next 11 years in England as a captive. Following his ransom and release in 1357, David was offered easier terms for the ransom's repayment if he would name Edward III or one of his sons as his successor. Not surprisingly, the Scottish parliament rejected this notion. David reigned until his death in 1371, to be succeeded by his steward, Robert.

The Stewarts

The Stewarts took their name from their hereditary position as stewards to the kings of Scotland. Robert, the first Stewart king, was better as regent than monarch. Anarchy, rebellion and internal squabbles disturbed the peace he strove for. Robert II died in 1390 and was succeeded by his son, **Robert III**. Crippled by a kick from a horse, Robert was in poor health and much of the responsibility of government passed to his brother, the **Duke of Albany**. The ailing Robert III sent his son and heir, **James I**, to France in 1406, fearing Albany had plans to remove him from the succession, but the young prince was captured by pirates and handed over to the English. Robert died a month later, leaving Albany in full power for 18 years while James was held hostage. Powerful nobles seized the opportunity to consolidate their strength. They expanded their estates and built up private armies, many of them becoming as powerful as kings. Most notable among them was the **Douglas** family, whose lands and subjects rivalled those of the king. Meanwhile, in the northwest, the Lords of the Isles allied themselves with the English and continued to live their own lives with little regard for central government.

James I returned to his throne in 1424, aged 29, to find his country in turmoil. His first step was the execution of the Albany family in 1425 and the seizure of their considerable estates. In 1427 he summoned the Highland chiefs and arrested 40: Alexander of the Isles retaliated by burning Inverness. Further rebellion from the west was subdued and James redressed the balance of power in the Lowlands by annexing many of the earldoms that had threatened his supremacy. His policies earned him many enemies and in 1437 three of them stabbed him to death, leaving his six-year-old son **James II** as his heir.

James II came to his throne in 1449 at the age of 19. He continued the reforms so dear to his father, but was threatened by an alliance between the Douglases, Crawfords and John of the Isles. James was killed in 1460 when a cannon exploded during the siege of Roxburghe.

James III was nine when his father died and so Scotland was once more ruled by regents, until his accession at the age of 19. He married the King of Norway's daughter, whose dowry included Orkney and Shetland. James was an intellectual, better fitted for academic life than a crown. He survived one attempt to dethrone him but six years later his son led a successful coup against him, becoming James IV in his place. James III was killed in mysterious circumstances at the decisive battle of Sauchieburn, a parliamentary inquiry recording simply that the King 'happinit to be slane'.

James IV, most popular of the Stewart kings, was 15 when he came to the throne. He was clever and charming, a good leader, pious and energetic, generous, flamboyant and sensual. The arts and education blossomed and James led the way. He authorized the building of palaces and churches. His court was elegant and cultured and the country was peaceful and prosperous. But the peace was not absolute: on the doorstep the Lords of the Isles continued to live as they always had, fiercely patriarchal, their loyalties rooted in their clans and chieftains. James, who had learnt Gaelic, decided to visit the Western Highlands and Islands, hoping to win the friendship of the clans. His attempts were viewed with suspicion, so he desisted and appointed overlords to rule them. This resulted in an uprising of the Macdonalds and Macleans who stormed and burned Inverness in 1503.

In that same year James married 12-year-old Margaret Tudor and signed a Treaty of Perpetual Peace with England. But in 1511, his brother-in-law, Henry VIII of England, joined the Pope, the King of Spain and the Doge of Venice in a Holy League against France. James passionately desired a united Europe. Determined to maintain a balance of power, therefore, he renewed the Auld Alliance with France and tried, in vain, to mediate. In 1513, threatened from all directions, France appealed to Scotland for help. James in turn appealed to Henry, who replied with insults.

Against advice, in August 1513, James led a Scottish army across the Tweed, to **Flodden Field**, where they were massacred by the superior forces of the English. The king, his nobles and most of Scotland's best men were killed in a battle as pointless as it was valiant: it was perhaps Scotland's greatest tragedy. The country was left leaderless, its army slain, its new king **James V**, a toddler and its regent, Margaret Tudor, with divided loyalties.

There followed a period of more turmoil until the king was old enough to take office and try to restore order. His second wife, **Marie de Guise-Lorraine**, bore him two sons, both of whom died, and a daughter, Mary, Queen of Scots, only a few days old when her father died after his army was defeated at Solway Moss by Henry VIII in 1542.

Henry VIII, determined to absorb Scotland, proposed a marriage between Mary and his delicate son, Edward, but the Scottish parliament rejected such a proposal and renewed instead the Auld Alliance with France. Mary, aged five, was sent to France for safety, where she stayed for 15 years, marrying the French Dauphin. While she was away, Protestantism was gaining power in Scotland. In 1554, Marie de Guise-Lorraine replaced Arran as Regent. The presence of many French officials in the Regent's government greatly upset the Scottish nobility. Several of them, calling themselves 'The Lords of the Congregation', declared their support for the Protestant religion. In 1559, **John Knox**, a powerful Reformer, delivered a fiery sermon in Perth, denouncing the Church of Rome.

The Stone of Destiny

Traditionally, the Stone of Destiny was the pillow on which Jacob laid his head when he dreamt about the ladder of angels reaching from earth to heaven. Its subsequent history is shadowy. It floated round the world carrying mystical powers of sovereignty until it arrived in Ireland, whence it was brought to Dunadd by early missionaries and used as a throne in the coronation of Scottish Kings.

In those days, *mormaers* owned their kingdoms and the High King was their overlord, King of the Scots but not of Scotland. At the coronation, each *mormaer* filled a shoe with earth from his kingdom and poured a little into a footprint carved into a rock. The King sat on the Stone of Destiny and put his foot over this cocktail of Scottish soil.

From here the Stone was moved to Dunstaffnage. In the 9th century, Kenneth Macalpine took it to Scone where it continued to be a coronation throne for the united Scots and Picts. Edward I, believing firmly in its mystical powers, pinched what he thought to be the Stone of Destiny during one of his ravages of the north and whisked it off to become part of the Coronation Chair in Westminster Abbey. It has been there ever since, except for a brief hiatus in 1950 when Scottish Nationalists kidnapped it and hid it for about three months in Arbroath. The canny Scots had almost certainly hidden the original stone—the one in London, a rather dull lump of plain sandstone, is not ever a replica, because the true stone was intricately carved, It is safe, in a secret cavern, and will be brought out by its hereditary guardians when the time is right.

Replica of the Stone of Scone

Mary's French husband died at the end of 1560 and she returned to her country as queen in 1561—no longer Mary Stewart, but Mary Stuart, the French form of her name which was adopted in England. A devout Catholic, she had no desire to tangle with the Protestants and merely wished to be allowed to practise her own religion in peace. This horrified John Knox and his followers, who found her light-hearted ways obnoxious.

In 1567 an ill-advised marriage to the earl of Bothwell sparked off an inferno of protest from both Catholics and Protestants. Mary was imprisoned and Bothwell forced into exile. Humiliated, Mary was forced to abdicate in favour of her baby son, **James VI**. Her half-brother, **James Stewart, Earl of Moray**, bastard son of James V, was proclaimed Regent. Mary fled to England and threw herself on the mercy of her cousin, Elizabeth I. Elizabeth, without an heir, could not forget Mary's claims to the English throne. Mary was imprisoned for 20 years, and then beheaded.

James proclaimed himself king in 1585 and found himself head of a country divided between Catholics and Protestants. He aspired to impartiality, incurring the animosity of both factions. A Protestant in name, if not belief, James had no wish to antagonize his Protestant cousin Elizabeth of England and spoil his chances of inheriting her throne. He concluded an alliance with England and made no more than a formal protest when Elizabeth agreed to the execution of his mother in 1587.

The Protestant religion in Scotland now presented problems. It was divided between the extreme Presbyterians, who wanted a religion of the purest simplicity with equality of ministers and no bishops or elaborate ritual, and James' English form of Protestantism, with bishops appointed by the Crown and a formal liturgy. He tried to impose his will on the Kirk, but failed. In 1603, Elizabeth I died, appointing James her heir. Thus, he became James VI of Scotland and I of England. He hurried to London and only returned to Scotland once, preferring the magnificence of the English court, and the ritual of the Church of England. But he still tried to foist Episcopacy on his northern subjects and re-instate formal worship. He died in 1625 and his son, **Charles I**, succeeded him.

Charles had no love for the Kirk. When he went north for his Scottish coronation, his subjects were scandalized by the 'Popish' practices he brought with him. Thousands flocked to Greyfriars Kirk in Edinburgh in February 1638 to sign the **National Covenant**, condemning all Catholic doctrines and upholding the 'True Religion'. The Covenant, however, was somewhat ambivalent: its signatories swore, not only to uphold the True Religion, but also to be loyal to a king who demanded the Episcopacy they shunned. Thus, loyal subjects of the Crown found themselves torn between obedience to the king and obedience to their new religion.

When civil war broke out in England, the Covenanting Scots agreed to help the English Parliamentarians. In 1649, Charles I was defeated by Cromwell and executed. The Scots grasped this opportunity to advance their quest for stability and invited his exiled son, **Charles II**, to Scotland as king, on condition that he supported the Covenant. Furious, Cromwell invaded Scotland. Charles went back into exile and Cromwell ruled both countries until he died in 1658. The **Restoration** in 1660 brought Charles II to the throne. He ignored the promises he had made, and sought to reintroduce Episcopacy. This rekindled the fervour of the Covenanters, who fled to the hills and worshipped in secret 'Conventicles'. In 1670, these conventicles were declared treasonable, and there followed the **Killing Times**, when thousands of Covenanters were slaughtered.

Charles II died of apoplexy in 1685 and was succeeded by his brother, **James VII/II**, Scotland's first Catholic sovereign for 120 years. James tried unsuccessfully to introduce tolerance for all religions. He was deposed in 1688 by his Protestant daughter Mary and her Dutch husband, William of Orange. He fled to France and **William and Mary** were crowned King and Queen. Some Scots, mostly Highlanders, remained true to James. The **Jacobites**, as they were called, rose, under **Graham of Claverhouse** and almost annihilated William's army in a savage battle at **Killiecrankie** in 1689. But Claverhouse was killed, leaving them leaderless, and they lost heart and returned to their Highlands.

The government, uneasy about the rebellious Highlanders, issued a proclamation, ordering all clans to take an oath of allegiance to the Crown by the first day of 1692. Circumstances prevented **Alisdair MacIain of Clan Donald** from taking the oath until after the deadline. This provided the government with a chance to intimidate the Highland clans. A company of Campbell soldiers, commanded by a relation of MacIain's, **Captain Robert Campbell of Glenlyon**, billeted themselves on the MacDonalds in Glencoe. They rose at dawn and slaughtered their hosts. The barbarity of the Massacre of Glencoe produced public outcry, not so much because of the number killed—38 out of about 150—but because of the abuse of hospitality. The king denied all foreknowledge: as a gesture, he sacked his Secretary of State, the Master of Stair, who had instigated the deed.

Union and Enlightenment

Between 1698 and 1700 Scotland's economy was shattered by an unsuccessful attempt to colonize the Darien coast on the isthmus of Panama. Scotland, bankrupt, and plunged into political crisis, was forced to accept the **Treaty of Union**, in 1707, uniting the parliaments of England and Scotland. This carefully worded document brought advantage to both countries, giving Scotland a badly needed boost to her economy and the right to Presbyterianism, and removed the threat of further war between the two countries.

The signing of the Treaty of Union forced the Scots to accept a Hanoverian succession, but Jacobite loyalties still prevailed in the Highlands. **James Edward Stuart**, son of the deposed James VII/II, was regarded by many as Scotland's king. The Old Pretender, as he was called by the Hanoverians, made three unsuccessful attempts to regain his throne. (Pretender is from the French *prétendre*—to claim, not from the English word for make-believe.) His expedition from France in 1708 only got as far as the Firth of Forth. In 1715, the Earl of Mar, upset by his treatment at the hands of the Hanoverian George I, raised the Pretender's banner and proclaimed James king. The rising looked promising but following the inconclusive battle at **Sheriffmuir**, support for it fell away. The Old Pretender put in a brief appearance in Scotland but soon returned to France. In 1719, a final attempt was made, backed by the Spanish; but the supporting fleet was lost in a storm and the Highlanders dispersed.

Stringent measures were taken to quell the clans. Between 1726 and 1737 General Wade built military roads and forts, opening up the Highlands and linking strategic strong points, at Fort William, Fort Augustus and Fort George. He raised a regiment of clansmen loyal to the Whig government, the Black Watch, whose duty was to keep order among the resentful clans.

George I was an unattractive German who disliked the British as much as they disliked him. When he died, his son, **George II**, equally Germanic and unsuitable to rule over Highlanders who still clung to their Jacobite dreams, gave them excuse enough. Exiled in Rome, the Old Pretender's son, **Prince Charles Edward Stuart**, was a brave young man with charisma and magnetism. He pawned his mother's rubies, set sail for Scotland and landed in Eriskay on 23 July 1745, determined to win the crown for his father.

At first his reception was daunting: Macdonald of Boisdale told him to go home. 'I am come home', he retorted. MacLeod, and Macdonald of Sleat, refused to help, but Macdonald of Clanranald stood by him. Cameron of Lochiel was reluctant to encourage what he believed to be romantic folly, but he was won over and on 19 August the standard was raised in **Glenfinnan** and the Old Pretender proclaimed King James VIII/III, with Prince Charles as his regent. Subsequent events are well known. The prince picked up support as he advanced on Edinburgh but his army probably never exceeded 8000 men. Capturing Perth on the way, he held glorious court at Holyrood, defeated General Cope's soldiers at **Prestonpans** and gathered enthusiastic support.

On 1 November Prince Charles led his motley army south, hoping to attract more Jacobites on the way, with the intention of taking London. Meeting little resistance, but picking up little support, they reached Derby, only 127 miles from their target, on 4 December. At this point Charles's prudent advisers insisted that to go further was madness. On 6 December he agreed reluctantly and the Highlanders turned round to march in an orderly retreat back to Scotland.

On 17 January 1746, the Jacobites won their last battle, defeating Cope's successor, General Hawley, at Falkirk. Hearing news of the advance of the Duke of Cumberland's army from England, the Prince took his army back into the Highlands, capturing Inverness on 21 February. On 16 April, Cumberland marched towards Inverness, his forces meeting the Jacobite army on Drummossie Moor, south of **Culloden**. Out-numbered and out-gunned, the Jacobites were soon defeated. Defeat turned into a rout in which Cumberland's men showed no mercy to their opponents.

The Prince escaped, with a price of £30,000 on his head, and spent the next five months in hiding in the Western Highlands and Islands. Aided by brave **Flora Macdonald**, he escaped eventually to Europe, where he lived in squalid exile for the rest of his life, dying in Rome in 1788.

The English and the Lowland Scots were determined to squash the rebellious Highlanders for ever. They enforced the **Act of Proscription** in 1747, banning Highland dress and the bearing of arms. Jacobites who had not died at Culloden were either executed or transported. The old way of life was dead. The act was repealed in 1782, but by this time it was no longer relevant; the **Highland Clearances** had begun. Between 1780 and 1860, thousands of crofters were evicted from their homes in the Highlands and Islands to make way for sheep. Many others emigrated voluntarily, to escape persecution, to Canada, America, New Zealand and Australia. In the mid-19th century Ireland's potato famine reached the Highlands, resulting in appalling hardship and causing further emigration. By the end of the 19th century, the rural Highlands and Islands were almost deserted.

A flourishing cotton industry collapsed in the 1860s when the American Civil War cut off supplies of raw cotton and heavy industry developed instead. Glasgow, once the biggest tobacco importer in Britain, led the world in shipbuilding. Expanding industries meant expanding labour forces; there were concentrations of population in industrial areas, fed by refugee Highlanders and Irish.

Shipbuilding and engineering developed rapidly from the mid-19th century until, by the beginning of the 20th century, some 100,000 jobs were related to Clydeside shipbuilding alone. The Steel Company of Scotland, founded in 1871, replaced iron, and the entire economy of west and mid-Scotland depended on Glasgow's heavy industry. The First World War took its toll of Scottish manhood, but it needed a constant supply of arms and ships and machinery and there was more than enough work for those left behind. It was the Great Depression in the 1920s and 1930s that dealt Scotland a mortal blow. After the Wall Street Crash in 1929, the global wave of economic disaster washed over Clydeside and by 1936 the output from the shipyards had fallen from three-quarters of a million tons to less than 60,000, with at least two-thirds of the workforce unemployed. In order to try to increase efficiency and generate more trade, firms merged and pruned their labour forces still further, resulting in more job losses. Not surprisingly, socialism flourished, passionately fuelled by leaders like James Maxton and Emmanuel Shinwell. Public opinion favoured the plight of the workers and by the end of the 1930s, things were beginning to look up. The Second World War brought with it a fresh demand for armaments and ships: Clydeside boomed and Scotland grew prosperous again. But after the war, competition from abroad began to steal trade. Shipyards, steelworks and factories closed. Less coal was needed so coalmines closed. The oil boom in the 1970s brought new prosperity for a while but this was short-lived affluence.

A new generation of enterprising minds, particularly from Glasgow, is turning the tide of apathy. Diversification has spread a rash of light industry throughout the country and workers are more inclined to negotiate for rights than to cripple their livelihood with strikes. Politically, Scotland leans to the left and juggles with nationalism. Those in favour of autonomy hold that they are the poor relations of politicians at Westminster, whose survival-of-the-fittest policies make no allowance for Scotland's circumstances. But when, in 1979, they were invited to vote for Devolution, over 36% didn't bother to vote and the Nationalists lost through the nation's apathy. There were further stirrings of nationalist feeling prior to the General Election of 1992 when it seemed likely that the Conservative Party's 13-year grip on government would be loosened. The opposition parties were united in offering greater or lesser degrees of autonomy to the Scottish people but these promises came to nothing when the Conservatives, although winning a mere 11 of Scotland's 72 seats in Parliament, were once again returned to power in the south.

Genetically proud and independent by nature, Scotland bides its time. Who can say when the Stone of Destiny will be brought from its hiding place?

Topics

Climate

A popular postcard shows someone sitting in a deck chair under an umbrella in pouring rain, with the caption 'Having plenty of weather here in Scotland'. In fact, with a bit of luck, you can return from a holiday in Scotland with a tan not entirely inflicted by wind, and photographs showing idyllic blue skies and brilliant sunshine. Unpredictability is the main drawback and it is common to get wide contrasts in one place in one day. When the weather is good, there is no country better. When the weather is bad and people struggle against piercing winds and relentless rain and a damp chill pervades to the marrow, Siberia would be preferable. It is worth remembering that places in the north of the country have an average of 18 to 20 hours of daylight in the summer, and resorts on the east coast are noted for their hours of sunshine. In the far north, in the middle of the summer, it is never completely dark. In spite of the Gulf Stream, whose warm waters are alleged to lick the western shores of Scotland, the sea is gelid.

In general, the west is wettish, and mild enough in some coastal regions to support palm trees and tropical vegetation. The east is drier with a more bracing climate and colder winds. Winter in the Highlands, when the precipitation is mainly snow, can be very beautiful, with clear skies and sun, though temperatures may seldom rise above freezing.

An unfortunate side-product of the moist, mild weather in the west is the 'midge', a particularly virulent breed of gnat unequalled in persistence anywhere else in the British Isles. Grown men have been reduced to gibbering wrecks under their vicious attacks. They are at their worst in warm, humid conditions; they hide when it is windy and sometimes, though not always, in very bright sunshine. Anyone contemplating camping or picnicking during the midge season should have lots of the strongest possible repellent. In truth, midges can completely ruin an outdoor holiday; even the natives retreat indoors when they are marauding. The only good thing about them is they won't follow a boat off-shore.

Religious Differences

In the Highlands and Islands, where communities tend to be slow to change, there are predominantly Catholic areas, where they rejected the Reformation and reconverted, while others, following the laird, became Protestant. On the whole, Catholics and Protestants live together perfectly happily with few of the sectarian problems experienced in Ireland. Sometimes there is a conflict with the strict Sabbatarian beliefs and practices of a few Presbyterians, and invariably the media will manage to stir up an 'incident'.

In the Outer Hebrides, South Uist, Eriskay and Barra are almost entirely Catholic. In their belief God belongs to every day and Sunday is for celebration, both in church and out. North Uist, Harris and Lewis are Presbyterian and the most rigid Protestants in Britain.

Their interpretation of the Fourth Commandment is stringently enforced by the Lord's Day Observance Society, who exert moral, social and political pressure. Sunday is for long sermons in church, full of the threat of damnation; for reading the Bible and holy tracts; for dark clothes and solemn faces. No work must be done, not even cooking; the washing must come in off the line; the fishing boats must lie at anchor and swings are padlocked.

Until recently, no ferries ran to the islands on Sundays. Then Caledonian MacBrayne announced a changed schedule including some Sunday sailings. The uproar was clamorous. There were huffings and puffings and threats of barricades. Running in tandem with this dispute, there was friction over a new £12 million school, built at tax-payers' expense, on the island of Benbecula, mid-way between the Catholic south and Protestant north and serving both. The predominantly Protestant Western Isles Council would not employ supervisory staff on Sundays, so no one could use the school's leisure facilities—swimming pool, cafeteria, games hall, library, etc. Catholics protested that their beliefs allowed them to have fun on Sundays and they saw no reason why Sabbatarian rules should prevent them from doing so. The situation was satisfactorily resolved in the end, but not without lasting damage to the hitherto dignified, *laissez-faire* attitudes that enabled such extreme creeds to live side by side in harmony.

The majority of Scots belong to the Established Church of Scotland, or Presbyterian Church and its many breakaway sects. The Episcopal Church, with its bishops, is the equivalent of the Church of England. The Free Presbyterian Church of Scotland (Wee Frees) is a tiny, fundamentalist sect who believe that the Pope is 'Antichrist' and the Mass 'the most blasphemous form of religious worship that Satan ever invented; an offence unto God and destructive of the souls of men.' In 1989, Britain's Lord Chancellor, Lord Mackay of Clashfern, a member of this strict sect, was castigated by fellow members of his congregation because he attended Requiem Masses for two of his Catholic friends. The Free Church Synod suspended him from his position as a senior Elder of the Kirk, and from Communion. Lord Mackay, who once said his Church gave 'the most tender love that has ever been described', was forced to resign from it.

Clans and Tartans

The Scottish clan system was once an integral part of the Highlands and Islands. Every member of the clan bore the name of the chief, whether related by blood or by allegiance, and each was an equal member of the clan family (Mac means son of). The chief was the father, ruler and judge and the strength of the clan lay in his justice, kindness and wisdom, and in the loyalty of the members of the clan, to him and to one another. Rents were mostly paid in kind or man-rent, and in return for his patronage and protection, the chief could call on his people at any time to form an army and fight for him.

It is known that Highlanders wore some sort of brightly coloured, striped and checked material as far back as the 13th century, though whether the designs, or 'setts', were related to clans or to territories is not known for certain. The Suppression of the Highlands after Culloden in 1746 broke up clans, forbade tartan and highland dress to all civilians, and led to the death of the clan system. During the 36 years Highland dress was banned, many of the old setts were lost or forgotten.

The highland regiments were exempt from the ban so it is through them that the kilt survived. The early regiments all wore the Government, or Black Watch, tartan, sometimes introducing coloured overstripes to differentiate one regiment from another. It was not until Hanoverian George IV appeared at Holyrood in 1822 in an astonishing Highland outfit, that the fashion for tartan was revived. In a wave of enthusiasm, a large number of tartans were hastily designed, and adopted by clans who had for many years been kindred in name only. They were also keenly worn by Lowlanders whose ancestors would have died rather than be seen in Highland dress. It is these relatively modern patterns that make up most of today's enormous range of tartans, which can be seen all over the world, not only in cloth but also adorning luggage, footwear and a staggering range of knick-knacks. The average Scotsman doesn't stride over his native hills swathed in tartan. On the whole, kilts are kept for ceremonial or formal occasions, or for 'Sunday best', and a great many Scotsmen don't even own one.

Clan feelings still run strong, especially in the veins of expatriates, but the clan name is now no more than an umbrella for museums, annual gatherings and ceremonial, with the chief as a figurehead, in a tartan costume redolent of moth balls. The mystique that has grown up round clan tartans is put into perspective by the apocryphal story of the irate chieftain, towering over one of a coach party, visiting his ancestral castle:

'By what right are you wearing my tartan, my man?'
'By the ri' o' purrchis, at fifteen pounds a yard, my lord.'

See also 'Clans and Families' at the end of the guide.

The Highland Clearances

The Clearances are an emotive subject and it has to be remembered that the first emigration ship sailed out of Fort William as early as 1773, almost 20 years before *Bliadhna nan Caorachd*—the year of the sheep. There were several reasons for the depopulation of the Highlands after Culloden. Some Jacobites who had escaped execution found it expedient to go abroad for a few years; others were transported. Many Catholics, unable to practise their religion publicly at home, sought liberty across the ocean. The suppression of the Highlands and the breaking up of the clan system deprived chiefs of their hereditary status as patriarchs, and many drifted south to become London Scots. Away from the womb of the clan and the benefits of feudality, however, they felt the pinch financially. Vast, infertile estates in the north, overpopulated by impoverished peasants, brought in little or no revenue. Rents paid in kind were of little use to those trying to keep up with society in fashionable assembly rooms or pay off gambling debts in gentlemen's clubs. Sheep farmers from the south offered good rent for sheep-runs in the north but they wanted land free of people. Highland landowners, desperate for money, began to evict their tenants. Some built resettlement towns and villages for them and established new livelihoods such as fishing; some merely served eviction notices and employed agents to enforce them; some offered to assist with fares to new countries. Hundreds of crofting communities—those which relied entirely on their smallholdings for a living—broke up and scattered. Those who didn't emigrate flocked to the cities in the hope of finding work or to settlements, mainly on the coast, where the land was unsuitable for sheep.

Meanwhile, in the islands, landlords basked in a false prosperity from the kelp industry. Seaweed, of which there was a seemingly inexhaustible supply, was collected after each tide, burned in kilns, processed into valuable fertilizer and exported. All that was needed was a huge labour force to cut, carry and burn it. Island proprietors with an eye to the main chance offered tiny plots of land to dispossessed crofters from the mainland. They charged high rent and deliberately ensured each tenant had not enough land for self-sufficiency, forcing them to work at the kelp. By 1812 the islands were crammed with people entirely dependent on kelp for their living . After the Napoleonic Wars, import duty was abolished and cheap foreign kelp flooded the market: prices plummeted; people starved. Proprietors and politicians, faced with the problem of destitute multitudes, offered inducements to encourage emigration and many people went. The final blow came in 1846. The potato famine, which had already decimated Ireland, drifted across the sea in wind-born spores and descended on Scotland, half of whose population lived on potatoes. For the already starving Highlanders and Islanders, the effect was catastrophic. Many of those who had managed to stay on, often surviving several evictions, were now forced to join their compatriots in Canada, America, Australia and New Zealand. By the end of the 19th century, the rural Highlands and Islands were almost deserted.

Gaelic

Gaelic is still the first language in the Outer Hebrides, but even there, with an influx of non-Gaelic speakers and television, the children are growing up speaking English among themselves. Elsewhere it is no longer a living language, though many people are trying to revive it and there are many great Gaelic scholars. Sabhal Mor Ostaig, in Skye, is a popular and very successful Gaelic college; television and radio have a lot of Gaelic slots. It is taught in schools and in adult classes and there are a large number of Gaelic publications. It is an almost impossible language to 'pick up' by ear and eye because the spoken word bears little resemblance to the written. Recently, a crop of new notices appeared in some of the islands, proclaiming placenames in Gaelic. They must have cost a fortune: local people don't need them, and visitors can neither understand, nor pronounce them.

Gaelic, which is much older than English, stems from the Goidelic branch of Celtic languages, which were an offshoot from the earlier Indo-European language. Scottish Gaelic became a distinct dialect separate from Irish around the 13th century, and there are still many similarities. With the revival of Gaelic has come a revival of Gaelic culture. Groups like Runrig and Capercaillie who perform modern style Gaelic music are enormously popular and an important part of the Scottish music scene.

Crofting

Since the Highland Clearances, croftland tenure has been strictly controlled to protect the rights of the tenant. A croft is a smallholding in the Highlands, with a few acres, as many sheep as the land will support, and sometimes cows and poultry. If there is arable land it will be tilled. In the old days, *feannagan*, or inappropriately named lazy-beds, were dug for potatoes, involving much hard work, deep digging and the carting of heavy creels of seaweed for fertilizer. Some of the work on the croft is still done communally—sheep-dipping and shearing for instance, and cutting the peat and haymaking. Peat is still used as fuel in some areas. Composed of partially rotted vegetation, compressed in waterlogged conditions in temperate or cold climates, it takes 3000 years to form a depth of one foot, so peat-bogs are getting scarce. It is cut in the spring in oblong slabs with a special digger and stacked *in situ*, on end like miniature wigwams, until dry. In a wet summer the peat can still be lying late into the year. Once dry, it is built into neat beehives. As recently as the 1970s, hay was cut with scythes, and it is still turned with pitchforks until dry.

The family dwelling is the croft-house—often mistakenly called the croft. Less than 50 years ago, many Highlanders still lived in a *tigh dubh* or black house, now almost extinct except as a folk museum or byre. It had thick, double walls, about 6 feet (1.8m) high, made of local stone and packed with earth and rubble. Unlined on the inside, it had rounded corners, no gables, and a reed- or heather-thatched roof anchored by boulders tied to ropes of plaited heather. Inside, the furniture was functional: a dresser, box-beds, a bench, stools, rat-proof meal chests, coffers and a spinning wheel. A peat fire was laid on a stone slab on the earthen floor in the middle of the room, the smoke escaping out of a hole in the thatch. In earlier times, light came from a *crùisgean*—a lamp fuelled with fish liver oil burning on a wick of plaited rushes. Even within this century, in some island communities the beasts shared the family house, penned at one end with the floor sloping down towards them and the effluent running out through holes in the wall.

The crofter is the owner or tenant of the croft. Most crofters have a subsidiary job as well: fishing, building or public works. Since the Clearances, the Crofting Commission has kept very careful control of crofters' rights.

Céilidh

Céilidh (pronounced kayly) is a Gaelic word meaning visit. In winter, when nights were long, crofters used to gather in one of the houses when darkness fell, packed in round the central fire. One of the older members, often a bard or musician, acted as the master of ceremonies and everyone was expected to contribute to the entertainment. The women knitted or spun, men repaired fishing nets or whittled wood; everyone listened. Stories, songs, poems, proverbs and legends were recited, passing their history, folklore and tradition from one generation to the next. Their music stirred the soul: mouth-music, straight from the heart; Gaelic songs; pipe, harp and fiddle music. Children grew up steeped in the past and could tell you who their great-great-great-grand-uncle was and whose sweetheart he had run off with. The practice is dying now, thanks to television, and *céilidhs* tend to be commercial shows, staged in halls and hotels.

Piping

Two kinds of bagpipes are played in Scotland these days, the 'warm wind' and the 'cold wind'. The Highland bagpipe, being mouth blown, is 'warm wind'; the Lowland or Border bagpipe is blown by a bellows operated by the piper's right elbow, hence 'the cold wind pipes'. The Highland bagpipe is designed to be played out of doors; the Lowland is essentially an indoor instrument. Recent improvements in the manufacture of the Highland bagpipe along with the higher standards now being demanded by audiences have altered the tone of the instrument until it can be listened to with pleasure indoors, where the most prestigious piping events are held. The Highland bagpipe no longer 'skirls'. The 'Small Music' of the Highland bagpipe includes marches and dance tunes in differing tempi; the *ceòl mor*, the 'Great Music' (usually anglicized as 'pibroch' from *pìobaireachd*, meaning piping) comprises tunes constructed on a theme followed by up to ten variations.

Pibroch pieces date from the late 15th century and their names commemorate great events in Highland history. Pibroch is listened to in silence. It is unwise for the visitor to interrupt, even by a whisper. The Lowland pipes are intended to accompany social events indoors and fit in well with the folk music groups now popular in Scotland and beyond. Their tone is sweet and mellow and the repertoire includes the ancient Border ballads from the days of the cross-border raids and feuds as well as a wide range of dance music and song airs. Both instruments are taken seriously in Scotland, for their own sake as well as for their traditional connotations. Derogatory comment is not appreciated, especially if voiced in the accents of south Britain. The pipes were never specifically proscribed by the Disarming Act of 1747, but it would have been a brave piper who would have played within earshot of a Government post. The oldest thesis on pipe music was written during the proscription and there are several pibroch pieces that were composed while the Act was still in force.

Sorcerers and Superstition

Communities lived in terror of Devil-worshippers and sorcerers, whom they believed could control the elements and cause plague, famine, drought, miscarriages and crop failure. In the Middle Ages, fertile Celtic minds were fed by inherited paganism, folklore, ignorance and religion. This was particularly so in Galloway and the Highlands, where remote communities were separated by vast tracts of moor, hill and loch, far from urban influence, schools and the steely eye of the Church. Every act, from pre-birth to death was vulnerable and the power of evil had to be propitiated. Offerings of food, herbal potions, benisons, gestures, talismans and rites were employed in the hope of warding off supernatural ills. Curiously shaped stones had magic properties. Certain lakes and wells were thought to be especially efficacious. Pilgrims brought their sick and their petitions and tied votive offerings to trees and bushes. People still go to some of the *Clootie Wells* as they are called. There is one at Culloden where coachloads of people arrive on or around May Day, the Celtic Beltane, and throw money into the well. Superstition or not, when the Highland Division was being pounded on the beaches of St Valery-en-Caux, in the summer of 1940, the Culloden Clootie Well attracted throngs of petitioners. Another, on a back road in Ross-shire, is so festooned with squalid old rags it looks like a tinkers' tip, yet even today, no one removes them for fear of reprisals from the god of the well.

It was by no means just ignorant peasants who believed in sorcery. Macbeth's encounter with the three witches was not a figment of Shakespeare's rich imagination. His source for the story was Holinshed, the 16th-century chronicler, who describes 'three women in strange and wild apparell, resembling creatures of eldritch world', who 'vanished immediatlie' having delivered their prophecies. The last execution for witchcraft in Scotland was believed to be in Dornoch in 1727, when a mother was found guilty of riding upon her daughter, who had been transformed into a pony and shod by the Devil. She was burned in a barrel of pitch having first warmed her cold feet at the fire that was to consume her.

Seers

The second sight, *taibhsearachd* in Gaelic, goes hand in hand with sorcery and among the many seers who emerged from the Celtic mists were Thomas the Rhymer and the Brahan Seer. Thomas, born in 1220, lived for nearly 80 years, and earned himself the title 'True Thomas'. He predicted the death of Alexander III and the Battle of Bannockburn. Traditionally, he had a passionate affair with the Fairy Queen and went off to live with her for three years in Elfland, deep in the Eildon Hills.

The Brahan Seer, Còinneach Odhar, is an enigmatic figure from the 17th century, known for the uncanny accuracy of many of his prophecies about the Highlands, some of which are still to be fulfilled. He fell asleep, so it is said, on an enchanted hillside: when he awoke he was clutching a stone with a hole in it, through which he could see the truth and the future. Among the events he foretold that have already happened are the depopulation of the Highlands, the demise of crofting, the arrival of rich landowners, and the making of the Caledonian Canal. He said that when it was possible to cross the River Ness in Inverness dryshod in five places, a terrible disaster would strike the world. There were four bridges over the Ness until a fifth was erected to replace one about to be demolished. This was opened at the end of August 1939: on 1 September Hitler marched into Poland.

The Brahan Seer met his death by antagonizing his patroness, the Countess of Seaforth. The Earl visited France, soon after the Restoration of Charles II in 1660, and had not returned. The Countess sent for the Brahan Seer and asked what her husband was doing. When he was reluctant to say, she pressed him until he revealed that the Earl was in a sumptuous gilded room, grandly decked out in velvet, silk and cloth of gold, with a voluptuous lady on his lap. The Countess was furious, accused him of malice and ordered him to be burnt in a barrel of tar at Fortrose. Before he died he predicted the downfall of the Seaforth Mackenzies, whose line came to an end after a dramatic chain of events, precisely following the prophecy, in 1815.

Bonnie Prince Charlie

Charles Edward Louis John Casimir Silvester Severino Maria Stuart, better known as Bonnie Prince Charlie and as the Young Pretender (from the French *prétendre*—to claim), was born in Rome on 31 December 1720. He was brought up to believe that his father, James, the Old Pretender, was the rightful heir to the British throne and that he himself was the heir apparent.

James, born in 1688, was the only son of James VII/II by his second wife, Mary of Modena. Both England and Scotland wanted a Protestant king and James VII/II was staunchly Catholic, so he was removed from the throne and replaced by Mary, his eldest daughter by his first marriage to Anne Hyde, and her unattractive husband, William of Orange, in 1689. They were succeeded by Mary's sister Anne in 1702, and on her death in 1714 the throne passed to George I, great-grandson of James VI/I through his daughter Elizabeth, to preserve the Protestant line. He was an unpleasant man who disliked the English as much as they disliked him. He was succeeded by his son, George II, in 1727.

The Old Pretender, recognized and funded by the Pope as the legal king of Britain, made several abortive attempts at claiming his throne. He married Clementine Sobieska who bore him two sons, Charles and Henry (born 1725). He believed that his sons should mix with Protestants as well as Catholics and saw to it that they did so. Charles grew up in an atmosphere of intrigue, finding himself courted as Prince of Wales and heir apparent to the throne of Great Britain. He had a natural charm that would win support in the future.

In 1743, the French decided that an invasion of Scotland, with Prince Charles Edward Stuart as its leader, would confound the English and install a pro-French Jacobite on the throne. Having instigated the plot, the French were not over-generous in their support but Charles raised the necessary funds and in July 1745 set sail for Scotland in the *Du Teillay.*

Off the Lizard the Prince's escort ship *Elisabeth* was involved in an engagement with HMS *Lion.* Both ships were badly damaged and Elisabeth was forced to retreat to France, carrying with her most of the invading force's arms and stores. The Prince continued north to Scotland. Eighteen days after leaving France he went ashore on ther tiny island of Eriskay in the Outer Hebrides. Legend has it that seeds of a pink convolvulus carried on his shoes from France fell and germinated where he walked. True or not, the flower still grows on Eriskay and nowhere else in the Hebrides.

His reception was not wholehearted. Macdonald of Boisdale advised him to return home. 'I am come home, sir,' retorted the Prince. Landing on the mainland at Loch nan Uamh, in Arisaig, he was faced by the reluctance of the clan chiefs to support him. Eventually, however, he won the reluctant support of the Macdonalds and Cameron of Lochiel and on 19 August 1745 he raised his father's standard at Glenfinnan. The Old Pretender was proclaimed King James VIII of Scotland and Charles appointed his Regent. His supporters numbered just 1200 ill-equipped clansmen, mostly Macdonalds and Camerons.

The Highlanders marched first to Invergarry, collecting support on the way and on to Blair Atholl, by which time their number had reached 2000. From Blair Atholl they carried on to Perth where the Prince heard that General Cope was planning to take the Government army from Inverness to Edinburgh to defend the capital. The Prince arrived at Edinburgh on 16 September and the Government troops stationed there fled in disarray. The Highlanders took control of the city in the name of King James VIII.

General Cope arrived at the outskirts of Edinburgh and was famously beaten by the Highlanders in the fifteen-minute Battle of Prestonpans on 21 September. With the benfit of local knowledge of the terrain, the Prince's men were able to overwhelm the enemy with the sheer speed and ferocity of their attack.

The outcome of this battle so boosted the Prince's morale that he came to believe he and his army were invincible, in spite of the fact that many of the Highlanders deserted after the battle. A recruiting campaign brought his army up to about 5500 and in November they set off for London, beliving that the Prince's brother Henry was to come to their aid with a considerable French army.

By 4 December the Highlanders had reached Derby, just 127 miles from London. Charles was confident of going on to take the capital but his staff thought otherwise. They had found little support for their cause in England and had no way of knowing that almost nothing lay between them and the capital, nor that the French were close to launching their invasion of the south coast. Reluctantly, the Prince agreed to retreat to Scotland.

The Highlanders' retreat was an orderly one and by 20 December, just six weeks after his campaign had begun, Charles was back in Scotland. On 17 January 1746 the Highlanders won their last battle, defeating Cope's successor, General Hawley, at Falkirk. Lack of fire-power prevented the Highlanders from taking Stirling Castle and, knowing the Duke of Cumberland's army to be heading north, they carried on to Inverness.

On 16 April 1746 Charles' army of 6000 faced the 9000-strong army of the Duke of Cumberland on Drummossie Moor near Culloden, five miles from Inverness. Within an hour the Jacobite rebellion was finally over. Over 1000 Highlanders were slaughtered by the better disciplined and equipped English army; on Cumberland's orders many more were butchered as they lay wounded and helpless.

Charles escaped to begin five months of hiding in the Highlands and Islands with a price of £30,000 on his head. During all that time no one betrayed him. Famous among his exploits was his trip 'over the sea to Skye' from South Uist, disguised as Flora Macdonald's serving woman 'Betty Burke'. On 19 September Prince Charles Edward Stuart sailed from Borrodale, never to return. He spent the rest of his life in France and Italy, drowning his bitterness in habitual drunkenness. He died in January 1788 of a stroke, leaving his legend behind him.

Johnson and Boswell

When Dr Samuel Johnson, English critic, poet and lexicographer, aged 63, and his companion 32-year-old James Boswell, Scottish writer and Johnson's biographer, set off on their journey to the Hebrides in 1773, the first emigrant ships had already sailed and the Highlands were rapidly losing the character Dr Johnson wished to observe. The Act of Proscription imposed after the 1745 Jacobite Rising had virtually wiped out the clan system and everything that went with it.

What they found was a wild land, totally foreign to Johnson's experience. A fierce supporter of the underdog, whether slave or victim of the Clearances, Johnson's account of their journey, read in parallel with Boswell's, gives a graphic picture of the Highlands in the latter part of the 18th century.

Boswell was a well-born snob who 'collected' Johnson some ten years before they set out on their journey. Whether he actually liked Johnson or not is disputable. After their first meeting in 1763, he described him thus: 'Mr Johnson is a man of most dreadful appearance. He is a very big man, is troubled with sore eyes, the palsy and the King's evil (scrofula). He is very slovenly in his dress and speaks with a most uncouth voice. Yet his great knowledge and strength of expression command vast respect and render him very excellent company.'

The unlikely pair set off on their journey—the frighteningly literate Johnson, dogmatic and irascible, susceptible to female charms and careful of his health, accompanied by Boswell, intelligent but largely self-taught, sensitive to the opinions of others, punctilious, and randy as a goat. They left Edinburgh on 18 August 1773 and travelled via St Andrews and Montrose up the east coast to Aberdeen. From here they visited Slains Castle. Johnson was intrigued by the architecture and by the local features. Boswell was more concerned with the discomfort of his room and the smell of his pillow.

As they continued through Forres they both record a mention of Macbeth. Johnson noted that they were approaching 'a prelude to the Highlands, leaving fertility and culture behind with nothing ahead but a great length of road, nothing but heath.' At Nairn they saw their first peat fires and first heard the Gaelic language.

In Inverness Boswell was embarrassed by Johnson's espousal of the benefits gained by Scotland following the the Act of Union in 1707 and worried about what people who didn't know him might think. From Inverness they took to horses and rode down Loch Ness. Passing a Druid's temple Johnson commented, 'To go and see one druidical temple is only to see that it is nothing, for there is neither art nor power in it; and seeing one is quite enough.'

They visited an old woman in a bothy, where Johnson first discovered the primitive conditions in which the peasants lived. He was interested to know where the old crone slept but she suspected his motives and he withdrew. Boswell was less tactful and inspected her humble sleeping area by the light of a taper.

From Fort Augustus they travelled west. On this part of their journey Johnson noted that the country was 'totally denuded of its wood, but the stumps both of oak and firs, which are still found, shew that it has been once a forest of large timber'. They passed a party of soldiers to whom they gave 'two shillings to drink'. The soldiers turned up at the pub in Glenmorison where Boswell and Johnson had put up for the night. The travellers clearly sat up with them and their hangovers the following morning were attributed to the poor quality of the whisky. Their host during this visit bemoaned the fact that the rent for his farm had gone up to 20 pounds from 5 pounds in 20 years.

As they progressed into the 'bosom of the Highlands' Johnson recorded that they now had 'full leisure to contemplate the appearance and properties of mountainous regions, such as have been, in many countries, the last shelters of national distress, and are everywhere the scenes of adventures, stratagems, surprises and escapes.' He was amazed to see snow on the peaks and to learn that it might stay there until added to by the following winter's snows.

As they passed Bernera Barracks near Glenelg, Boswell thought wistfully of the hospitality they might have had from such a place, but the barracks was manned by only a seargeant and a few soldiers and they passed on to an inn at Glenelg. Here they were shown to a room that was 'damp and dirty, with bare walls, a variety of bad smells, a coarse black greasy fir table, and forms of the same kind'. Johnson slept in his clothes on a bundle of hay. Boswell 'being more delicate, laid himself sheets with hay over and under him and lay in linen like a gentleman'.

They then crossed to Armadale in Skye where they were welcomed by Sir Alexander Macdonald and entertained by bagpipes. They encountered the beginnings of the island winter of wind and rain, in contrast to the Highland winter of snow and ice. On the island of Raasay they were lavishly entertained by the laird, Mr Mcleod, and his family of three sons and ten daughters. They dined and danced and listened to Gaelic songs. While exploring the island Bowell discovered the ruins of Castle Brochel, complete with inside lavatory, a facility rarely found in the houses of Scotland at the time. 'Sir,' he said to his host, 'you take very good care of one end of a man, but not the other.'

From Raasay they made their way anti-clockwise around Skye and called on Macdonald of Kingsborough and his wife, Flora. She, renowned for her part in the escape of Bonnie Prince Charlie after the failure of the '45, so impressed Johnson that he wrote of her: 'Flora Macdonald, a name that will be mentioned in history and if courage and fideltiy be virtues, mentioned with honour.'

On they went to Dunvegan where they found 'Lady Macleod, who had lived many years in England ... who knew all the arts of southern elegance and all the modes of English economy.' Johnson found Dunvegan so comfortable that Boswell had to prod him into continuing their journey.

As they travelled on Johnson noted details of the agriculture and the Highlands generally, while Boswell noted the hangovers that resulted from over-indulgence in bowls of punch. A storm during their crossing to Coll frightened Boswell more than Johnson, who retired to his berth and ignored it. Bad weather kept them on Coll longer than either of them found amusing.

They sailed for Mull on 14 October. Travelling across the island put Johnson in a bad humour, partly because his horse was too small for him and could hardly bear his weight and partly because he lost the oak stick he had brought from London. They crossed to Iona by moonlight. Johnston said, 'if this be not roving among the Hebrides, nothing is'. Both men were deeply moved by 'treading that illustrious island which was once the luminary of the Caledonian regions whence savage clans and roving barbarians derived the benefits of knowledge and the blessings of religion.' They spent the night in a barn and the next day explored the monastery, abbey and other buildings. Boswell was disappointed to find it all so broken down and was unimpressed by the uninscribed gravestones of the kings. He had expected marble monuments such as those found in Westminster Abbey.

They returned to Mull where they were entertained by the Laird of Lochbuy, described by Boswell as a 'bluff, comely, noisy old gentleman, proud of his hereditary consequence and a very hearty and hospitable landlord'. Johnson was not pleased to be offered cold sheep's head for breakfast. They inspected the castle and Johnston recorded a general description of castles in the Highlands and Islands.

From Mull they crossed to Oban on the mainland, somewhat relieved to be not so much at the mercy of the elements. They were amused to read in a newspaper that they were thought to be still weather-bound on Skye. At Inverary, they were entertained by the Duke of Argyle, whom Boswell knew, and were well pleased with his hospitality. Continuing on horses supplied by the Duke they crossed the Rest and Be Thankful and descended to Loch Lomond.

The remainder of their journey took them out of the Highlands, south to Ayrshire and so back to Edinburgh. Boswell recorded that Johnson had told him that the time he had spent on his journey was the pleasantest part of his life.

Highland Wildlife

The relative remoteness of the Highlands and Islands has guaranteed that they have remained largely unspoiled, with a range of wildlife unparalleled elsewhere in Britain. Keen eyes will spot rare birds almost anywhere in the Highlands. A good pair of binoculars and a willingness to walk away from the crowds are your only requirements.

Go to Shetland, Orkney, St Kilda or the Western Isles for seabirds such as skuas, puffins and gannets. Aviemore is a good centre for inland birds, including crested tits, crossbills, golden eagles and capercaillie. The extraordinary sawing sound of the corncrake, now almost extinct in the rest of Britain, can still be heard in the Western Isles. The mudflats of Findhorn Bay, the mouth of the River Lossie, and the shingle and lagoons around the Spey estuary attract geese, waders, terns and many more, including the osprey, once extinct in Scotland. Loch Garten has a closed-circuit television trained on an osprey eyrie. Lochs in the peatlands of Sutherland and Caithness are good for red- and black-throated divers. Perhaps the most rewarding place for birdwatchers is Fair Isle, staging post for a vast number of migratory birds. There is a lodge you can stay in, © 03512 258, open from April to October.

Where to Watch Birds in Scotland by Mike Madders and Julia Welstead, published by Helm at £11.99, is a useful book for birdwatchers.

The mammal life of the Highlands and Islands includes species rarely seen in more populated parts of Great Britain. Deer are, if anything, too numerous here and can often be seen near roads and habitations in winter. Polecats are becoming a menace, devastating domestic poultry; pine martens, red squirrels, wildcats and otters can be seen more and more frequently and there are still some feral goats. Mink farms flourished in Scotland in the 1950s and many escaped or were let loose into the wild. Seals, dolphins, porpoises and whales are not uncommon around the coasts and can often be seen from boats and sometimes from the land, especially around the Western Isles, the Grampian coast, the Moray Firth and the Cromarty Firth.

Adders and the harmless slow worm, actually a legless lizard, not a snake, may be spotted sunning themselves on rocks or in heather. Other species of lizard may also be seen.

Among the rarer butterflies to be seen in woodlands and elsewhere are several varieties of argus, fritillary and skipper. The emperor moth, magpie moth and northern eggar are conspicuous on moorland.

Scotland is famous for its salmon, trout and sea trout. Other river and loch fish include brook lamprey, pike, eel, three-spined stickleback, minnow and the rare Arctic char, a relic of the ice ages.

Botanists come a long way to see the rich variety of plants that grow in profusion throughout the Highlands and Islands, in spite of pressures from grazing sheep, cattle and deer. The machair of the Outer Hebrides, especially South Uist, produces carpets of rare wild flowers, including orchids. The blanket bog peatlands of Caithness and Sutherland are particularly noted for their sphagnum mosses, which keep the surface moist and acid, slowing the decay of plant remains. Here, sundews, butterworts and bladderworts trap and digest insects. The native woodland that once covered Scotland has almost all been destroyed. The birch survives, together with pines, oak, alder, ash, hazel, rowan, aspen, wych elm and willow.

Strathclyde

Strath means 'broad valley' but Strathclyde is much more than just the valley of the Clyde. When the regional divisions were drawn up in 1975 Strathclyde embraced large chunks of lowland Scotland and equally large parts of areas that had previously been considered as parts of the Highlands. Even today people who live in Argyllshire prefer to use Argyll as their postal address in preference to Strathclyde.

Glasgow lies at its industrial heart, astride the Clyde and surrounded by a straggle of satellite towns, not beautiful but vibrant with character. Yet the highland parts of Strathclyde are remote and wild, with serpentine sea lochs eating into the land to form long peninsulas and narrow isthmuses. Moor, hill and forest are fringed by miles of beaches, with many islands lying off the coast, like stray pieces of a jig-saw. The eastern boundary of Strathclyde cuts through Loch Lomond, an over-popular beauty spot, perhaps. In rural Argyll fishing, farming and tourism are the main occupations.

The ancient Dalriada Scots from Ireland settled in Argyll and formed their powerful kingdom. Here, Columba landed to spread the Christianity Saint Ninian had introduced at Whithorn, more than one and a half centuries earlier. Welsh Celts moved up and occupied the land south of the Clyde. As well as dozens of prehistoric burial mounds, stones and cairns, Strathclyde's coast is punctuated with the remains of fortresses and watch-towers, built to defend the land from invasion by sea.

Tourist Information

Tourist Information Centre, 35–39 St Vincent Place, Glasgow, © 041 227 4880.

Dunoon and Cowal Tourist Board, 7 Alexandra Parade, Dunoon, © 0369 3785.

Garrison House, Millport, Isle of Cumbrae, © 0475 530741.

Isle of Arran Tourist Board, Brodick, Isle of Arran, © 0770 2140/2401.

Isle of Bute Tourist Board, Rothesay, Isle of Bute, © 0700 2151.

Mid-Argyll, Kintyre and Islay Tourist Board, The Pier, Campbeltown, Argyll, © 0586 52056.

Oban, Mull and District Tourist Board, Information Centre, Oban, © 0631 63122.

There is also a number of seasonal tourist offices, which are usually open from April to October.

Loch Lomond

Oh, ye'll take the high road,
An' I'll take the low road,
An' I'll be in Scotland afore ye,
But me an' my true love will never meet again
On the bonnie, bonnie banks o' Loch Lomond.

The song 'Loch Lomond' was composed in Carlisle jail by Donald MacDonald of Keppoch, a Jacobite awaiting a trial that ended in brutal death after Culloden. The English were capricious in their distribution of justice: some prisoners were arbitrarily sent to the gallows, others were set free and told to walk home. MacDonald, fairly sure of his fate, wrote that his spirit would get back to Scotland on the low road of death faster than his living companions on the high road.

The route north from Glasgow takes you along the A82 via Dumbarton. A new road gives views across the loch with its islands and anchorages, to the hills on the far side. This is particularly beautiful in the early morning when there is little traffic and mist clings to the glassy water as the sun rises over Ben Lomond. Bluebells carpet the ground under oak woods. The loch is 24 miles (38.5km) from north to south, its southern end as much as 5 miles (8km) wide, narrowing to a long, thin neck in the north. The largest inland loch in Scotland, Loch Lomond is one of the most beautiful, though being so accessible it is also one of the most popular.

Balloch, at the south end of the loch, is a holiday resort with a marina. **Balloch Castle Country Park** (open daily: free; visitor centre open Easter–Sept) is 200 acres of woodland, park and gardens on the shore of Loch Lomond. You can drive up the east side of the loch as far as Balmaha from where you can climb Ben Lomond.

Luss on the west side is a popular village with a kilt shop. All this part of the country is owned by the Colquhoun family, whose former home Rossdhu is being converted into a country club with golf courses.

A number of cruise boats operate on the loch. The small islands scattered over the south end are steeped in history. **Inch Cailleach** (Island of the Old Women) was the burial place of the fierce MacGregor clan. It belongs to Scottish Natural Heritage and has trails and woodland paths. Ruined **Lennox Castle**, on Inch Murrin (Isle of Spears), was where the Duchess of Albany retired, after James I slaughtered her family in 1425.

There are plenty of places to launch small boats and a number of boats for hire from the many marinas, holiday parks and water-sport centres lining the shore.

Helensburgh

An alternative route north from Dumbarton is the A814 via Helensburgh and Loch Long. This route is narrow and twisting in some parts, clinging to the water most of the way and keeping company with the railway.

Helensburgh, at the mouth of the Gare Loch, 8 miles (13km) northwest of Dumbarton, is a resort built on a grid of wide streets, the town sloping up from the Clyde. Ferries cross the river to Gourock and pleasure cruises run from the pier. This is sailing territory, the water usually speckled with craft of all sizes. There are good shops, plenty of places to stay and lovely views across the Clyde. Helensburgh was the birthplace of John Logie Baird, one of the inventors of television.

The Hill House, overlooking the Clyde in Upper Colquhoun Street (open daily: adm), was designed by Charles Rennie Mackintosh for the publisher W. W. Blackie in 1902 and is his finest domestic work, demonstrating his flair for simplicity of line. Owned by the National Trust for Scotland, its gardens are being restored to Mackintosh's original design and an audio-visual programme describes his life.

Glen Fruin, within easy walking distance of Helensburgh, is surrounded by beauty and solitude, serenaded by the clatter of streams flowing down from the hills. Climb **Ben Chaorach** and look down into the glen. You may hear the echo of war cries and pleadings for mercy. In 1603 there was a battle between the Colquhouns (pronounced Ka'hoon) and the MacGregors, arising from boundary disputes and accusations of cattle pilfering. The MacGregors slew not only the Colquhoun men, and their families who had been shut away in a barn for safety, but also a party of schoolboys who had been taken to watch the fun. The clan was proscribed in punishment.

Rhu, a mile (1.5km) west of Helensburgh, is another boating mecca, with woodland and lovely shrubs at **Glenarn Gardens** (open Mar–June: adm).

The two routes meet at Tarbet where the A82 goes north past the hulk of **Ben Vorlich** into Central Region. The Strathclyde route goes west to the Cowal Peninsula, through Glen Croe on the A83.

expensive

Buchanan Highland Hotel in Drymen, © 0360 60588, is an excellent place with good food.

moderate

Ardlui Hotel, © 03014 243, is a small country hotel on the northern tip of Loch Lomond, with moorings. It is a delightful, friendly place. **The Inverbeg Inn** at Luss, © 0436 86678, also overlooks Loch Lomond and runs a fleet of self-drive motor cruisers, with sleeping accommodation for from two to 12 people. Prices on request. **Rosslea Hall Hotel**, Rhu, © 0436 820684, overlooks the Gare Loch and the Firth of Clyde. It has good food and wine, pony trekking from the hotel and a free dram on arrival. **Duck Bay Hotel and Marina** on Loch Lomond, © 0389 52789, is a lively spot for boating people. **Salmon Leap Inn** in Drymen, dating from 1759, is a lively place with good bar meals.

inexpensive

Tarbet Hotel, © 03012 228, is a Scottish baronial-style mansion overlooking Loch Lomond, with a comfortable modern interior, friendly staff and reasonable food. What it lacks in elegance is made up for by the position. The **Lomond Youth Club** on Loch Lomond is a particularly grand youth hostel.

The Cowal Peninsula

The Cowal Peninsula attracts many climbers, sailors and holidaymakers in the summer. The drive west from Tarbet through Glen Croe on the A83 is spectacular. The distinctive shape of **The Cobbler**, 2891 feet (890m), looms to the north of the road as it twists and climbs up the shoulder of **Beinn Ime** to **The Rest and Be Thankful**—which speaks for itself. The views from the car park here are worth stopping for. A stone commemorates the completion of this military road in 1750, part of a network constructed to try to keep order in the Highlands after the Jacobite risings. Known as the **Arrochar Alps**, the hills round here offer excellent climbing for experts. Apart from The Cobbler and Beinn Ime, there are Beinn Narnain, Ben Vane and Ben Vorlich marching away to the northeast—all 'Munros' over 3000 feet (923m).

The Cowal Peninsula stretches to the south, part of Argyll's misshapen lobster claw, washed on either side by Loch Long and Loch Fyne. **Carrick Castle** is a 14th-century ruin on a promontory in fjord-like Loch Goil. The Glen Mhoir approach down the B828 from The Rest and Be Thankful is dramatic, the road dropping from 1000 feet (308m) to sea level in 3 miles (4.5km). This was where the Argylls kept their documents and their prisoners. A remote enough place in those days, the great shell of the keep is still impressive, even with its rash of water-sport enthusiasts nearby. The road ends here but you can just see where the loch joins up with Loch Long, to the southeast. The area within the triangle formed by The Rest and Be Thankful, Loch Long and Loch Goil is known as **Argyll's Bowling Green**. A more unlikely name would be hard to find. Measuring 8 miles by 4 (13 by 6.5km), it includes 10 major summits and is only accessible on foot. Fantastic views can be had from the tops of the hill; a jigsaw of moor and hill, each irregular piece linked by a gleaming sliver of water.

The motorist must retrack to where the road branches, 3 miles (4.5km) north of Lochgoilhead.

The award-winning **European Sheep and Wool Centre**, at Lochgoilhead (open daily, Apr–Oct: adm), is the first of its kind in Europe. There are 19 different breeds of sheep, demonstrations of shearing and a shepherd and his dog working the sheep (three shows daily, at 11am, 1pm and 3pm: Sat by prior arrangement only). There is a shop and a coffee shop. Adjacent is **Drimsynie Leisure Complex**, with a heated swimming pool, jacuzzi, sauna, 9-hole golf course and a restaurant. In the winter (Nov–Mar), Drimsynie is converted into a four-lane **curling rink**.

The B839 then runs northwest through **Hell's Glen**, a steep hanging valley overlooking Loch Fyne at its far end.

Loch Fyne is renowned for sea fishing and oysters. A string of villages line the loch: Cairndow, St Catherines and Strachur. Much of this area is covered by the Argyll Forest Park.

From Strachur, the A815 runs south down forest-fringed Loch Eck. Branch left at the Whistlefield Hotel and take the long way round, down Glen Finart—more lovely views—to **Ardentinny**, a picturesque village with a sandy beach on Loch Long. The road hugs the shore to Strone Point and back northwest along Holy Loch. The loch is said to have been so named when a ship, carrying earth from the Holy Land intended as foundations for Glasgow Cathedral, foundered in a storm as it tried to get round the corner into the sheltered Clyde and finished up in this appendix of the river.

Younger Botanic Garden (open daily, April–Oct: adm) is barely 2 miles (3km) north of the head of the loch. In May and June the gardens blaze with yellow, orange, flame and crimson azaleas, and rhododendrons ranging from white to deep maroon. There is a splendid avenue of sequoias (giant Californian Wellingtonias).

Dunoon and Around

Dunoon is 5 miles (8km) south of the junction with the A815 and is the chief resort on the Cowal Peninsula. It was just a village until early in the 19th century, when rich merchants built villas and developed it into a resort. The long, low sprawl of the town, washed by the Firth of Clyde, is backed by a crescent of blue-green tree-covered hills. Two ferry companies operate a service across the Clyde between Gourock and Dunoon—a 20-minute crossing. Dunoon is an ideal holiday centre on the threshold of some of the finest walking and climbing country. It is also at the heart of idyllic sailing water. For those who prefer to let someone else take the helm, there are cruises on the Firth of Clyde in the summer.

The Cowal Highland Gathering is one of the town's highlights, on the last Friday and Saturday in August. Over 150 pipe bands compete, drawing huge crowds. It also stages World Highland Dancing Championships.

Dunoon Castle, of which only a trace remains, dates from the 13th century. It was built on the site of an earlier fort, with a colourful history that kept it bouncing back and forth between English and Scottish hands like so many of the strongholds of Scotland. Edward I took it; Robert the Bruce retook it; then Edward Balliol, who was ousted by Robert II. In 1471 the Earls of Argyll were made Honorary Keepers by James III, on condition they paid the Crown a fee of a red rose, whenever demanded. When Queen Elizabeth II visited Dunoon in 1958, she was presented with a red rose without having to demand it.

An attractive drive south from Dunoon takes you to Toward Point with a lighthouse on the tip. The track beyond goes only halfway up the east side of Loch Striven.

Lazaretto Point, north of Dunoon on the A815, beyond Hunter's Quay, was the quarantine station for servicemen fighting in the Napoleonic Wars.

To explore the rest of the peninsula take the B836 west from the head of Holy Loch to the head of Loch Striven and on to the A886. Here turn left and take the new road down the east side of Loch Riddon to Colintraive, with views across to Tighnabruaich and the Kyles of Bute. A car ferry runs from Colintraive to Bute (see p.77). The new road then peters out but it is possible to get on down to Strone Point and some way up the west shore of Loch Striven.

Back up to the head of Loch Riddon on the A886, take the A8003 down the west side, high above the Kyles of Bute with views in all directions. **Tighnabruaich** (house on the hill) and **Kames** are two popular resorts looking across the Kyles to Bute. A B road runs on down to Ardlamont Point, the most southern tip of the Cowal Peninsula, rising to 205 feet (63m). The waters of Loch Fyne, Kyles of Bute, Sound of Bute and Kilbrannan Sound meet at the foot of the headland.

From Ardlamont, go north about 4 miles (6km) to Millhouse and then west a couple of miles to **Portavadie**. With deep water offshore, this area was chosen as an oil-platform construction site and £14 million was spent on ground preparation. An enormous dry dock was built. But no one seemed to want any oil-platforms and the place stood unused. Eventually, the sea-wall was breached, the dock flooded and the £14 million washed away.

Back to Millhouse, take the B8000 north, through Kilfinan, a hamlet where the hotel has 16th-century vaults and the church stands on a Celtic site. **Otter Ferry**, 3 miles (4.5km) to the north, takes its name from the Gaelic *oitir* (a sandbank): yachtsmen beware. The sandbank sticks out more than a mile into Loch Fyne, prominent at low tide but easy to trip up on when submerged by the flood tide. The Norsemen who fought in the Battle of Glendaruel in 1100 beached their longships side by side on the sand bar, clambered ashore and marched over the pass into Glendaruel 5 miles (8km) to the east. They were slaughtered by the Scots, who threw their bodies into the river: *ruel* is a corruption of the Gaelic for 'blood flowed'.

expensive

Creggans Inn, Strachur, on the shores of Loch Fyne, © 0369 86 279, is well known for excellence in both food and ambience. They have a very good bar here.

moderate

Ardfillayne Hotel, West Bay, Dunoon, © 0369 2267, looks over the Firth of Clyde and has a good reputation for service, comfort and food. **Hafton Country Club, Hotel and Lodges**, Hunter's Quay, © 0369 6205, is an excellent base for a family holiday, with both baronial-style hotel accommodation and self-catering chalets. Prices include club membership for all the facilities of this lochside complex: swimming pool, snooker and games room, video cinema and video games, table tennis, tennis, putting. For an extra fee, golfers get unlimited play over Cowal Golf Course.

Ardentinny Hotel, © 0369 81 209/275, is on Loch Long, surrounded by rhododendrons. Boats can be hired from the hotel and package holidays include free ferry tickets, and entry to the Younger Botanic Garden and Inveraray Castle. The food is first class.

Kilfinan Hotel is an old coaching inn in a rural hamlet near Loch Fyne. Whitewashed, with 16th-century vaults, it has excellent food and log fires. Among the many hotels overlooking the scenic Kyles of Bute, try **Kames Hotel**, © 0700 811489, on the seafront in Kames. It is comfortable, serves reasonable food and has a friendly atmosphere.

inexpensive

In Dunoon, Esplanade Hotel, © 0369 4070, overlooks the traffic-free West Bay Promenade, a few minutes' walk from the pier. This is a jovial hotel for the gregarious. Abbeyhill Hotel, Dhailling Road, © 0369 2204, has a good view overlooking East Bay Promenade. It is comfortable and well run. Rosscairn Hotel, Hunter Street, © 0369 4344, is in a quiet, residential area next to the 18-hole Cowal Golf Club, and offers free golf in March, April and October. Drimsynie House Hotel and Leisure Complex, Lochgoilhead, © 03013 247/284, is a Victorian mansion, with mock battlements and turrets. It stands in wooded grounds overlooking Loch Goil with a 9-hole golf course, heated swimming pool and jacuzzi, good food and a pool room.

Mid-Argyll: Knapdale and Kintyre

This is walking country where spectacular views unfold at every turn and the best places are inaccessible except on foot.

Loch Fyne, a long narrow arm of the sea, washes the western shore of the Cowal Peninsula. It seems to eat its way into the Highland landscape—a mixture of hill and

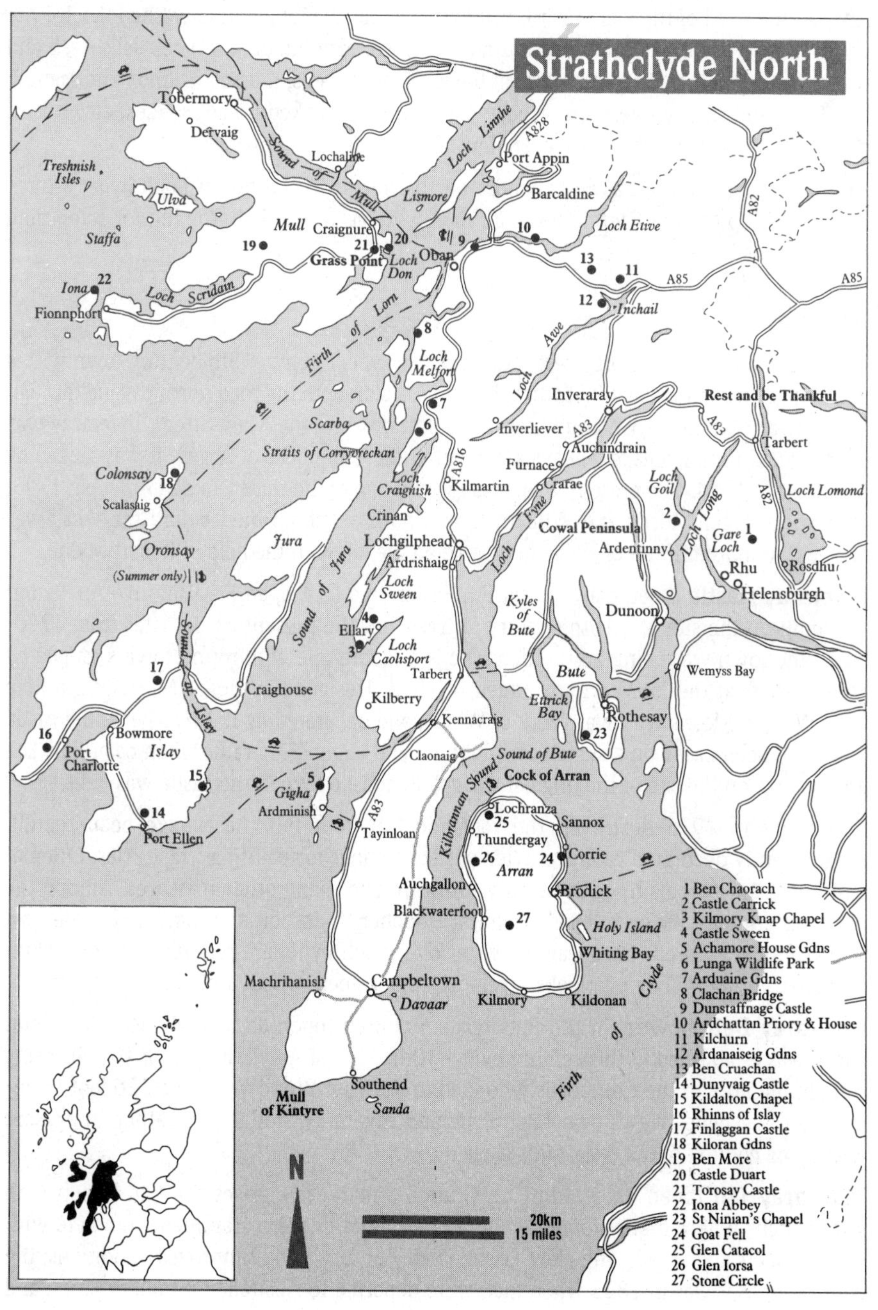

Strathclyde North
Tobermory
Dervaig
Treshnish Isles
Ulva
Staffa
Mull
Lochaline
Sound of Mull
Loch Linnhe
Port Appin
Barcaldine
Lismore
Craignure
Grass Point
Loch Don
Oban
Loch Etive
Iona
Fionnphort
Loch Scridain
Firth of Lorn
Inchail
Loch Awe
Loch Melfort
Inveraray
Rest and be Thankful
Scarba
Inverliever
Auchindrain
Tarbert
Straits of Corryvreckan
Furnace
Colonsay
Scalasaig
Loch Craignish
Kilmartin
Crarae
Loch Goil
Loch Lomond
Oronsay
Jura
Crinan
Cowal Peninsula
Gare Loch
(Summer only)
Lochgilphead
Ardrishaig
Sound of Jura
Loch Fyne
Ardentinny
Loch Long
Rhu
Rosdhu
Helensburgh
Loch Sween
Kyles of Bute
Dunoon
Ellary
Loch Caolisport
Sound of Islay
Craighouse
Tarbert
Bute
Wemyss Bay
Kilberry
Ettrick Bay
Rothesay
Kennacraig
Bowmore
Islay
Port Charlotte
Claonaig
Sound of Bute
Cock of Arran
Gigha
Ardminish
Kilbrannan Sound
Lochranza
Sannox
Tayinloan
Thundergay
Port Ellen
Corrie
Arran
Auchgallon
Brodick
Blackwaterfoot
Holy Island
Whiting Bay
Machrihanish
Campbeltown
Davaar
Kilmory
Kildonan
Firth of Clyde
Southend
Mull of Kintyre
Sanda
A828
A82
A85
A83
A816
N
20km
15 miles
1 Ben Chaorach
2 Castle Carrick
3 Kilmory Knap Chapel
4 Castle Sween
5 Achamore House Gdns
6 Lunga Wildlife Park
7 Arduaine Gdns
8 Clachan Bridge
9 Dunstaffnage Castle
10 Ardchattan Priory & House
11 Kilchurn
12 Ardanaiseig Gdns
13 Ben Cruachan
14 Dunyvaig Castle
15 Kildalton Chapel
16 Rhinns of Islay
17 Finlaggan Castle
18 Kiloran Gdns
19 Ben More
20 Castle Duart
21 Torosay Castle
22 Iona Abbey
23 St Ninian's Chapel
24 Goat Fell
25 Glen Catacol
26 Glen Iorsa
27 Stone Circle

forest, in some parts rising steeply from the water, in others rolling back in sweeps of farmland. At the head of the loch, near Cairndow, look for the long, white-washed 'Loch Fyne Oyster Bar'—a really excellent restaurant in an old farm building. A shop sells fresh and smoked sea food including oysters from the local oyster beds, mussels, salmon and scampi; also fresh and smoked venison, special cheeses, home-baked bread, sauces, etc. It isn't cheap but it's well worth a visit, even if just for the seafood chowder.

At the head of Loch Shira, an appendix off the northwest corner of Loch Fyne, a track leads north up remote Glen Shira to a ruined cottage where Rob Roy hid for some time during one of his adventures.

Inveraray

Inveraray stands on the northwest shore of Loch Fyne, a pretty 18th-century town with a gracious air. It is curiously un-Scottish, built in a T-plan with the road north passing through an archway and the parish church on a mound, dividing the Main Street. Inveraray was once a small fishing village, always a domain of the Campbells of Argyll. It was sacked by Montrose in 1644. The present town was the creation of the third Duke of Argyll, in 1743, employing Roger Morris and William Adam, both of whom died before the work was finished. John Adam, son of William, completed the job with the help of Robert Mylne.

Inveraray Castle (open daily except Fri, Easter–mid-Oct; open Fri also, July–Aug: adm) was built on the site of a 15th-century fortress, but the present castle dates from 1770, when the town was being built. The castle is a square pile with round towers topped by conical roofs at the four corners, added in 1878. Designed by Roger Morris, with help from William Morris who was Clerk of Works, and decorated by Robert Mylne, the castle may have been based on a sketch by Vanbrugh and is imposing rather than beautiful. The grounds are on the site of the original village, demolished when the castle was built.

A bad fire in 1975 destroyed the roof and top floor but these have been rebuilt. Magnificently decorated rooms provide perfect settings for paintings, tapestries, Oriental and European porcelain, 18th-century furniture and many other treasures. Among the paintings are portraits by Kneller, Raeburn, Hoppner, Gainsborough, Batoni, and Ramsay. The grounds, with old trees framing vistas over Loch Fyne, are reminiscent of an 18th-century painting. A folly overlooks Inveraray from a steep, wooded hilltop.

Inveraray Bell Tower, in the Episcopalian church (open daily, early May–late Sept: adm), was established in this century by the 10th Duke of Argyll, its peal of 10 bells being rung in memory of the Campbells who died in the First World War. The 126-foot (39m) granite tower gives views over Loch Fyne and Inveraray though it is rather an eyesore within the context of the rest of this elegant town.

Inveraray Jail (open daily: adm), in Church Square, comprises the Old Prison with ghastly cells where men, women, children and lunatics were crammed, complete with sound effects and smells; the New Prison (19th-century), with improved conditions; the courtroom as it was in 1825 when men were deported to Australia for minor crimes; and many exhibitions, including one on Crime and Punishment with details of medieval punishment—hanging, branding, tongue-boring and burning. You can also see the open-air cages called airing yards where prisoners took exercise. There is a souvenir shop.

Argyll Wildlife Park, 2 miles (3km) south of Inveraray (open daily: adm), is a 60-acre site with European wildfowl, a large owl collection and such unlikely residents as wallabies, which hop about the forest tracks. Wildcats, badgers, Highland foxes, deer, wild goats, soay sheep and many other species can be seen.

Auchindrain Museum (open daily, Easter–30 Sept; closed Sat, June, July and Aug: adm), 6 miles (9.5km) south of Inveraray, is an old West Highland township with 18th- and 19th-century cottages and outbuildings furnished in their original styles. On display are parlours, kitchens with box beds, byres, barns, a smiddy, and all the old utensils. There are demonstrations of the runrig or strip-farming methods prevalent in the Highlands until the end of the 18th century, when villages had communal tenancy of farmland and paid their rent jointly, in this case to the Argylls.

The name of **Furnace**, a couple of miles further on, is an unhappy reminder of the troubled times that reigned during the 18th century. It is so called from the charcoal-burning smelting furnace, established here to utilize trees felled by order of the Hanoverian government, so that rebel Highlanders still clinging to the Jacobite cause would have less cover in which to hide.

Crarae Woodland Garden (open daily: adm), 3 miles (4.5km) south, has azaleas and rhododendrons in season. Walks cross and recross a burn as it cascades over falls and through a gorge among a variety of conifers, hardwoods and shrubs.

Lochgilphead

Lochgilphead, 24 miles (38km) southwest of Inveraray, at the head of Loch Gilp and another appendix off Loch Fyne, is a holiday resort as well as the shopping centre for the area, with good shops around the wide main street that was once the market place. The Mid Argyll Show takes place in Lochgilphead in August. **Kilmory**, once a country house, is the headquarters of Argyll and Bute District Council and the grounds are a public park.

The **Crinan Canal** cuts through from Ardrishaig on Loch Gilp to Crinan on the west coast. It was built at the end of the 18th century, and stretches for 9 miles (14.5km), with 15 locks, through the top of the Kintyre Peninsula. It was designed to cut out the treacherous waters around the Mull of Kintyre that inhibited trade between the west coast and Glasgow, and was much used at first by commercial puffers, fishing boats and passenger craft. With the decline of the herring industry and the introduction of rail and road networks, it lost most of its commercial traffic and is now mainly used by pleasure boats, saving the sailor 130 miles (208km). Going down the canal in a small boat is a peaceful way of passing a fine day, though you have to work the lock gates yourself, straining at the handles that wind up the sluices in the massive wooden gates, and leaning on the great timber arms that swing them open when the water either side is level. In 1847, Queen Victoria sailed down the canal in a decorated barge drawn by horses ridden by postilions dressed in scarlet, on her way to the Western Isles.

Crinan is a hamlet around a sheltered harbour, popular with sailors, with the tidal gate between the canal and the open sea. The Crinan Hotel is one of the best in Scotland, overlooking the island-speckled Sound of Jura.

Knapdale

Knapdale is nearly an island. It runs south from Lochgilphead like a clenched fist, just managing to hang on to the long arm of Kintyre. This part of the west coast, on the Gulf Stream, is unbelievably lush in the summer. Autumn is glorious; a wonderful range of colours shades the hills. So too is spring, when rhododendrons and azaleas are in bloom against the soft new green and the sparkle of water. Perhaps the best time of all, though, is November, when a light dusting of snow covers the last autumn leaves, and the water shows steel-grey against the hills etched in white. It is possible to drive right round the coast from Lochgilphead and across the middle from Inverneil to Achahoish. Along the coast each mile opens up a fresh view to the islands of Jura and Islay in the west, or down through layers of hills to distant lochs and the sea.

The Ormsary Estate on the west coast of Knapdale runs historic holidays, garden holidays and drawing and painting holidays. Each is carefully planned with every attention to comfort, ease and interest. You are transported to places of historic interest or to gardens with an informed guide, the accommodation is first class—both self-catering and full board—and the situation is glorious. The drawing and painting holiday is suitable for beginners and the more experienced. For details, contact Ormsary Estate Holidays, PO Box 7, Lochgilphead, Argyll PA31 8JH, ✆ 08803 222.

Travelling clockwise from Lochgilphead, **Kilberry**, in the southwest corner of Knapdale on the B8024, has a collection of 9th- and 10th-century stones and some from the Middle Ages, gathered up from the surrounding area and housed under cover in a steading, just north of the hamlet, signposted **Kilberry Stones** from the road. Marion Campbell, the archaeologist who collected the stones, lived in Kilberry Castle, a brooding pile which has belonged to the Campbells of Kilberry for centuries.

St Columba's Cave, 12 miles (19km) northwest of Kilberry on the western shore of Loch Caolisport (pronounced Killisport) near Ellary, is an enchanted spot, almost tangibly spiritual. There is an altar on the right with two crosses carved above, a smaller cave, reached by steps, traces of dwellings outside the cave and the ruin of a chapel. As its name indicates, tradition associates this cave with the saint's mission in Scotland. Excavations in the 19th century unearthed evidence that there was a settlement here as far back as 8000 BC, making St Columba comparatively modern.

Unfortunately, there is a private road with a locked gate and it is not possible to go on round the peninsula. You must backtrack via Lochgilphead to explore Loch Sween.

Castle Sween guards the entrance to Loch Sween from the eastern shore. Now alas surrounded by a caravan site, some say it is the oldest stone castle on the Scottish mainland. Dating from the 11th century, it is a great sprawl of a ruin, Norman in style, with buttresses. You can see the old ovens, the well and the original drain and rubbish-chute in the wall of the round tower, down which everything, including sewage, was indiscriminately cast.

The castle was a stronghold of the MacSweens in the 12th and 13th centuries but they lost their lands when they sided with the English in the 14th century. Robert the Bruce besieged it and installed the McNeills of Argyll to maintain it, one of whom married a MacMillan. Thus, Knapdale became MacMillan territory. The castle was destroyed in 1647 by Royalists, fighting the cause of Charles I.

The 13th-century **Kilmory Knap Chapel**, on the southern tip of the peninsula north of Loch Caolisport, contains sculpted stones and **MacMillan's Cross**, elaborately carved in the 15th century, possibly by monks from the monastery at Kilberry.

Kintyre

An isthmus between East and West Loch Tarbert, straddled by the village of Tarbert, joins Kintyre to Knapdale. Here, in the 11th century, Malcolm Canmore struck a bargain with the Norwegian King Magnus Barelegs who was harrassing him. He told Magnus he could claim any western island he could get to by boat with his rudder down. Magnus had his Vikings tow him across the isthmus— and claimed Kintyre as his.

A road circles most of the coast of the peninsula, passing through villages and hamlets, most of which cater for summer visitors. The landscape is similar to that of Knapdale, cut by wooded valleys rising to hilly moorland. The east and west routes meet at **Campbeltown** at the head of Campbeltown Loch, a haven for boats in a westerly gale, and subject of that hopeful song: 'O Campbeltown Loch I wish you were whisky'. It is a holiday town and boating centre, and was once an important herring port, with 33 distilleries, of which two remain open. Although less than 40 miles (64km) from Glasgow as the crow flies, Campbeltown is about 135 miles (216km) by road.

Flora Macdonald sailed to North Carolina from Campbeltown in 1774, emigrating with her family nearly 30 years after her brave actions helped save the life of Prince Charles Edward Stuart. William McTaggart, that great painter of Scottish life and scenery, was born in the town in 1835.

Campbeltown Museum (open daily except Wed and Sun: free) in Hall Street has a demonstration of how vitrified forts were formed.

Davaar Island is a lump of rock with a cave in it at the mouth of the loch, accessible at low tide along a shingle spit on the southern shore. Here in 1887 a man called Archibald Mackinnon secretly painted a picture of the Crucifixion on the rock, inspired by a dream. It is a moving picture after the style of El Greco, lit by a shaft of light that streams into the large cave through an aperture. In 1934, when the artist was 80, he returned to the cave and restored the painting.

Machrihanish, 6 miles (9.5km) west of Campbeltown and fully exposed to the fury of Atlantic gales, is a holiday village with a hotel, golf course, camp site and sandy beaches, as well as an airport.

Mull of Kintyre

Southend, tucked round the corner to the east of the Mull of Kintyre, is another holiday village. There is a golf course and sandy beaches with dunes covered in marram grass, which offer shelter from the wind. Nothing remains today of **Dunaverty Castle**, which once stood above vicious rocks here, shrouded in uncomfortable memories. Three hundred of Montrose's men, fighting the cause of Charles I, were besieged there by the merciless Covenanter General, David Leslie. The Royalists, mostly Irish mercenaries, were forced by thirst to surrender and shamelessly massacred.

Keil, just west of Southend, has a flat rock traditionally regarded as the place where St Columba first landed in Scotland. Keen eyes will spot footprints burnt into the rock where he stood, turning his back on the land that had outlawed him.

From Southend you can hire a boat and go to **Sanda Island**, about 2 miles (3km), where Robert the Bruce hid in 1306 on his way back from Rathlin Island.

The **Mull of Kintyre**, the southern tip of the peninsula, is a rocky extremity with a lighthouse and sheer cliffs. You must walk the final 1½ miles (2.5km) or so to the point. Only 13 miles (21km) from Ireland, it is impressive in westerly gales. The Mull of Kintyre was the subject of a popular song by Paul McCartney, who bought a house close by.

Where to Stay

expensive

Crinan Hotel, © 054683 261, already mentioned, is worth it. It is supplied daily by fishing boats that unload a short distance from the kitchen, and its food is renowned. The views across the water to the islands are marvellous, especially at sunset. Open mid-March to end October.

moderate

Lochgair Hotel, © 0546 86333, near Lochgilphead and the loch, is comfortable.

Stonefield Castle Hotel, Tarbert, © 0880820 836, overlooks Loch Fyne, with moorings, fine gardens, summer swimming pool, good food and service. **Columba Hotel**, Tarbert, © 0880820 808, has a sauna, gym and solarium.

See Knapdale above for **Ormsary Estate Holidays**, ©08803 222, for historic, garden and painting and drawing holidays in marvellous accommodation in a glorious setting.

inexpensive

In Inveraray, **The Great Inn**, © 0499 2466, overlooks Loch Shira and Loch Fyne, close to the castle entrance. Open April to October, this is a family hotel without too many frills. In the middle of the town, **George Hotel**, © 0499 2111, is the most attractive hotel/inn in Inveraray with open fires, panelling, a good atmosphere, nice bar and excellent food. **Fernpoint Hotel**, © 0499 2170, is highly recommended with lovely views. **Stag Hotel**, Lochgilphead, ✆ 0546 602496, in the town centre, has friendly, easy-going staff and comfortable rooms. **The Argyll Hotel**, ✆ 0546 602221, also in Lochgilphead, is old. **Tarbert Hotel**, ✆ 0880820 264, is right on the harbour in this sailing centre, popular for *après* sailing.

In Campbeltown, **Royal Hotel,** Main Street, ✆ 0586 552017, overlooks Cambeltown Loch from the harbour. It is lively. **White Hart Hotel**, ✆ 0586 552440/553356, is a family hotel on a busy corner in the Main Street.

Eating Out

See above for **The Loch Fyne Oyster Bar**. Also good are: **The Smiddy** off Lorne Street in Lochgilphead, where they serve delicious wholefood-type meals at reasonable prices, and **Tayvallich Inn**, an excellent bar and restaurant on the shores of Loch Sween where the seafood is particularly good.

Lorne and Oban

The new A816 runs up the west coast from Lochgilphead to Oban. It flirts with the sea, dipping and rising, pulling away and swooping back again with magnificent views.

Four miles (6.5km) northwest of Lochgilphead is all that is left of **Dunadd Fort**, capital of the kingdom of Dalriada from the 6th to the 9th centuries, a powerful political centre. It was the headquarters of early missionaries, including St Columba, until Kenneth MacAlpine moved the capital to Pictland. A rocky hillock above a meandering river is all that remains, and, if you search carefully, a rock with carvings of a boar, some Ogham inscriptions . . . and a footprint. Historians believe this was the place where kings were crowned and that St Columba crowned Aidan here in 574, using the disputed Stone of Destiny as the throne. The footprint is indisputable and only the most prosaic could resist the urge to stand in it and imagine those ancient ceremonies on this lofty site.

From Dunadd to **Kilmartin** is about 3 miles (4.5km) and packed with well-labelled prehistoric standing stones and burial cairns dating from the Stone Age and Bronze Age. Some of the cists have been reconstructed and you can go inside and see the carvings on the walls. There are also carved stones erected on plinths in the old church at Kilmartin.

Carnasserie Castle, 9 miles (14.5km) north of Lochgilphead, is the ruined home of John Carswell, first Protestant Bishop of the Isles, who in 1597 translated Knox's liturgy into Gaelic. It was the first Gaelic book ever to be published.

Lunga Wildlife Park, on the Ardfern Peninsula, north of Loch Craignish, has indigenous animals and there is experimental white fish farming in the loch.

Arduaine Gardens, just north on Loch Melfort (open daily: adm), has sub-tropical plants as well as magnolias, rhododendrons and azaleas, a water garden and rock garden and many rare trees and shrubs.

Seil is a hook of land west of Loch Melfort—an island joined to the mainland by the much-photographed hump-backed Clachan Bridge, celebrated as 'the only bridge over the Atlantic'. From this bridge a narrow road twists down to Easdale, scarred by old slate-quarry workings, flooded out in a terrible storm and no longer operating. Rows of traditional slate-workers' cottages add atmosphere. There is a large souvenir shop/art gallery manned by a tartan-clad artist. Part of *Whisky Galore* was filmed here, many years ago, transforming the township into a stage set.

Oban

Oban, 37 miles (59km) north of Lochgilphead, is unmistakably a holiday resort in summer, when the streets seethe with visitors and traffic. The town rises steeply from a crescent-shaped bay, its main street fronting on to the harbour. High above stands **McCaig's Tower**, a large circular folly with pillars, built in 1897 by a banker, McCaig, to give work to the unemployed and create a museum and observation tower as a memorial to his family. It was never finished.

The Catholic See of Argyll and the Western Isles has its well-attended cathedral, St Columba's, in Oban, overlooking the harbour. Although this area is predominantly Protestant, there are still communities which were left untouched by the Reformation.

The harbour is a busy boat terminal. MacBrayne's steamers ply between Mull and the Inner and Outer Hebrides, and smaller ferries, fishing boats and pleasure craft create an ever-changing scene. The quays are thronged with cars, people and freight. The town is fringed by hotels and neat villas offering bed and breakfast. Cafés and restaurants are packed and there is a fairly lively night life offering a choice between discos, public *céilidhs*, or family fun shows.

Oban Distillery in Stafford Street, © 0631 62110, is open to visitors on weekdays: ring for an appointment.

World in Miniature, on North Pier (open daily: adm), is a display of miniature rooms, furniture, dioramas, etc, all scaled at one inch to one foot.

Among the many entertainments, the Argyllshire Gathering in August is a great Highland occasion, with lots of piping and dancing and traditional games. In September the Oban Gala Day and Street Fair is a colourful carnival, especially when the sun shines.

Oban Rare Breeds Animal Park is a couple of miles (3km) on past the golf course, with unusual breeds of sheep, cattle, goats, pigs, poultry, ducks, deer, etc. It also has a pets' corner, nature trails, tea-room and shop.

Ganavan Sands, just north of Oban, is a good place to relax if you enjoy company—it tends to become densely populated in good weather. It has a restaurant, bar, coffee shop, car park, play area, putting, donkey rides, watersports and a launching slip.

Oban is a base for sub-aqua divers, with air supplies in the town and good underwater terrain. The Sound of Mull is littered with wrecks and the waters offer a wealth of marine life and cliff scenery. It is also ideal for sailing, with some fairly challenging, breathtakingly beautiful stretches, especially south through the Firth of Lorne to the Sound of Jura, past the infamous Corryvreckan whirlpool (*see* p.83).

Lismore Island

From Oban, a car ferry (taking an hour) runs 6 miles (9.5km) north to Lismore Island in Loch Linnhe. There is also a passenger ferry from Port Appin. This long sliver of rock, overlaid with loam and heather, was the seat of the diocese of Argyll from 1200 to 1507, in the days before Luther stirred up the beginnings of the Reformation. Traces of the miniature cathedral that was once here are incorporated into the parish church, built in 1749. The bishop's dwelling, the 13th-century **Achadun Castle**, is at the southwest end of the island, now a ruin. The overgrown, jagged ruin of **Coeffin Castle**, in the northwest, also dates from the 13th century. The remains of **Broch of Tirefour** stands on the northeast coast, overlooking the mainland.

Bachuil House (open by arrangement, © Lismore 256: free) is on the island and contains the Bachuil Mor, or pastoral staff of St Moluag, the man who converted the island to Christianity in the 6th century. Moluag and Columba are said to have been rivals, the one being a Pict, the other a Celt.

North Argyll and Appin

Dunstaffnage Castle (open daily except Thurs afternoon and Fri, Oct–March: adm) is 4 miles (6km) north of Oban on a rocky promontory guarding the entrance to Loch Etive. A splendid ruin, it seems to grow out of the rock. Parts of it stand over 60 feet (18.5m) high, its massive walls more than 10 feet (3m) thick. Flora Macdonald was held prisoner here for a few days after helping Prince Charles in 1746. Tradition holds that the Stone of Destiny came here from Dunadd, staying until Kenneth Macalpine moved it to Scone in an attempt to draw together his kingdom of Picts and Scots.

The coast road north from Oban and Dunstaffnage crosses the crooked finger of Loch Etive at Connel, where sea and loch are in constant turmoil trying to pour in and out through a bottleneck. It loops round Loch Creran, clinging to the coast in places with more good views. This northern tip of Strathclyde is rugged, mountainous hinterland laced with rivers and cascading burns, cut by Loch Etive.

About a mile (1.5km) north of the Connel Bridge, a minor road to the right runs 5 miles (8km) out to the northern shore of Loch Etive and **Ardchattan Priory** (always accessible: free) founded in 1230. This was the meeting place of Robert the Bruce's Parliament, in 1308, one of the last to be held in Gaelic. Among the remains of the priory, burned by Cromwell's soldiers, some carved stones can still be seen. The gardens of **Ardchattan House** (open April–November: free) are next door.

Bonawe has an impressive iron ore smelter, of great importance during the Napoleonic Wars, well looked after by Historic Scotland.

Port Appin is an attractive little place with a pier and lovely views to the islands. There is a craft shop and an excellent bar/fish restaurant in what was the old ferry house—an excellent place to stop off for lunch.

Castle Stalker (open by appointment, March–Sept: adm, © Upper Warlingham 2768), dating from 1500, has a magnificent setting on an islet at the mouth of Loch Laich. Keep an eye out for seals round here; they bask on the rocks in large numbers, flopping down into the water if disturbed, to pop up and stare balefully at intruders with great velvety eyes. (*See* Ballachulish, for the Appin Murder.)

The A828 goes on north up Loch Linnhe and crosses into the Highland Region.

The A85 east from Connel to Loch Awe is an attractive drive with views of Loch Etive, through the Pass of Brander below the looming bulk of **Ben Cruachan** (3695 feet—1137m). **The Hollow Mountain**, 6 miles (9.5km) beyond Taynuilt, is a great cavern hewn out of Ben Cruachan to accommodate an underground power house (open daily March–Oct: adm). Electric buses run through the tunnel and there is a visitor centre. This glistening subterranean empire is not for the claustrophobic.

Anyone with the time and energy to climb Ben Cruachan will get some of the best views in Scotland from its summit.

Loch Awe is a 23-mile (37km) long serpent of water with thickly wooded shores, many islands, and more than its share of midges clinging to the dense vegetation. The huge Victorian building you see from the road is the **Loch Awe Hotel**, fairly hideous inside and out but with wonderful views from its terrace. **St Conan's Church** on the north shore of the loch is charming with unusual architecture made up of all sorts of bits and pieces.

Kilchurn Castle, on a commanding site at the north end of the loch, dates from 1440. It belonged to the Campbells of Breadalbane until it was taken over by Hanoverian troops in 1746, with the consent of the anti-Jacobite Campbells. The gale that destroyed the Tay Rail Bridge also demolished one of Kilchurn's turrets.

When the level of the loch is low, traces of several *crannogs* can be seen—man-made islands where early settlers built dwellings for protection against attack. Some of the islands were used as clan burial grounds, especially **Inchail**, where there is a ruined chapel dating from the 13th century and several graves of the Macarthur Clan.

There are good walks either side of the loch. On the west side there is an information centre at **Inverliever.**

Ardanaiseig Gardens (open 31 March–31 Oct: adm) are at the north end of the loch, east of the B845. They contain rhododendrons, azaleas, rare shrubs and trees and good views across the loch to Ben Cruachan. There is a hotel with a restaurant, open for coffee, lunch and tea.

White Corries Chairlift (open daily in summer and weekends, Jan–April: adm) is north of Tyndrum on the A82, almost on the border with the Highland Region. The lift climbs 2100 feet (646m) into the hills with glorious views over Rannoch Moor and into Glencoe.

expensive

South of Oban, **Knipoch Hotel**, Kilninver, near Oban, © 08526 251, is open all year except January. It looks across Loch Feochan to a sunset behind the Hills of Lorne. Knipoch stands on the burial route along which the Kings of the Scots (including Macbeth and Duncan) were carried from Scone Palace to Iona. With award-winning food, it caters for 'the more discriminating traveller'.

moderate

In Oban, **The Manor House**, Gallanach Road, © 0631 63053, on Oban Bay, was built by the Duke of Argyll in 1780 as his Oban retreat and later used as a dower house. It has marvellous views, is comfortable and serves good Scottish and French food, expecially seafood. The following are all similar—comfortable, old-fashioned seaside-resort hotels, overlooking the harbour, giving value for money and serving wholesome, if predictable, food: **Alexandra Hotel**, © 0631 62381; **Columba Hotel**, © 0631 62183 and, slightly more lively, **Great Western Hotel**, © 0631 63101.

Loch Melfort Hotel, Arduaine, © 08522 233, open April–Oct, has established a reputation for good service, comfort and excellent food. Yachtsmen of the yellow-boot variety tend to stop off here for a civilized evening out, swapping Force Nine stories in the Chart Room Bar. The main house, built in 1900, gazes out across an island-speckled sea. The six bedrooms are done up like guest rooms in a country house. An adjoining Cedar Wing, long and low, has 20 rooms, each with its own bathroom, balcony and picture window, facing south across the water.

Isle of Eriska at Ledaig, © 063172 371, is a Scottish baronial pile, built in 1884, connected to the mainland by a bridge. Its proprietors, Robin and Sheena Buchanan-Smith, have created a comfortable private-house atmosphere, with log fires and an excellent kitchen. **Invercreran Country House Hotel**, Glen Creran, near Appin, © 063173 414/456, in a sheltered glen surrounded by hills, is a well-run, comfortable hotel, with an excellent dining room. **Ardsheal House**, Kentallen of Appin, Appin, © 063174 227, stands on a peninsula with views over Loch Linnhe to the Morvern hills. Open from April to November, Ardsheal was built in 1760 in 900 acres of woods, meadows and beach. Oak panelling, open fires and antiques give it a country-house atmosphere and the food is excellent. **Airds Hotel**, Port Appin, © 063173 236, overlooking Loch Linnhe, Lismore and Shuna and Morvern hills, is very comfortable, with good food and friendly staff. It is open from March to January with special winter reductions.

Ardanaiseig, Kilchrenan, © 08663 333, stands beneath Ben Cruachan on the shores of Loch Awe, in a garden of rhododendrons and azaleas. It was built in 1834 to designs by William Burn and has a 'country house' atmosphere. It has been the family home of the proprietors since 1964. The food is excellent, and the accommodation very comfortable.

inexpensive

In Oban, try the **Caledonian Hotel**, © 0631 63133 and **Argyll Hotel**, © 0631 62353. There are dozens more.

North of Oban, **Falls of Lora Hotel** at Connel, © 063171, overlooks Loch Etive, 5 miles (8km) from Oban. Another of the old-fashioned-style hotels, it gives good service.

Cuilfail Hotel, Kilmelford, © 08522 274, is an attractive old coaching inn, serving excellent food. **Lorne Inn**, at Ardfern, further south, © 08525 284, is an unpretentious, family-run inn, not over-endowed with mod cons.

Ford Hotel, Ford, © 054681 273, just north of Kilmartin, is good value, as is **Tigh-an-Truish**, Clachan Bridge, © 08523 242.

For very special bed and breakfast, try Mrs McAuslan, Cornaig, Kilmartin, © 05465 224.

Eating Out

For a good bistro-type restaurant, go to **The Cairn Restaurant** at Kilmartin.

The Strathclyde Islands

Cumbrae

Great Cumbrae is so close to the Ayrshire mainland that it hardly counts as an island.

Getting There

It takes just seven minutes to reach in the roll-on, roll-off ferry that runs every 15 minutes from Largs.

Tourist Information

All year, **Largs**: © 0475 673765.
Tourist Information Centre, **Millport**, © 0475 530753, April–Oct.

Less than 4 miles (6km) in length and 2 (3km) in width, the island has a 12-mile (19km) coastal road round it and is ideal for bicycling.

Millport straggles around a wide bay looking south across the Tan to Little Cumbrae. A great many people go to Cumbrae in the summer, so don't expect to 'get away from it all': the beaches are packed on a fine day. There is a National Water Sports Centre on the island and these waters are excellent for sub-aqua diving.

Although Cumbrae is not ideal for the recluse, it has some interesting rock formations and good plant and animal life. The earliest village was at **Kirkton** about half a mile from the old pier in Millport, where the chapel was dedicated to St Columba in 1330 and replaced in 1612. The 'Cathedral of the Isles' in Millport is the smallest cathedral in Britain, designed by the important Victorian architect William Butterfield.

The **Museum** (open Tues and Sat in season: free) shows the history of Millport and Cumbrae over the centuries. Boats run from Millport to Little Cumbrae. The ruined castle there was a residence of Robert II in the 14th century.

Where to Stay

There are a few hotels, guest houses and bed and breakfasts in Millport, but the standard is not high. The **Royal George Hotel**, ✆ 0475 530301, overlooking the bay, is probably the best bet, or **Millerston Hotel**, West Bay Road, ✆ 0475 530480, which is only open April to October.

Arran

The miracle of Arran is that it has clung to its character despite the thousands of holiday-makers attracted every year by its beauty. It is slightly larger than the Isle of Wight, about 20 miles (32km) from north to south, 9 miles (14.5km) across and 56 miles (90km) in circumference. Although hotels, guest houses and chalet settlements ring the island, it is possible to roam inland for miles, and feel totally remote.

Arran was inhabited way back before the dawn of recorded history, as its ancient stones and burial cairns prove. Since then its lovely landscape and mild climate have been put to many uses. The Irish Scots came over and settled in the early 6th century, making Arran part of the Kingdom of Dalriada. The Vikings held it for a time, until they were ousted by Somerled, Lord of the Isles, who was possibly of Norse descent himself. In the 18th century sportsmen established deer here, overrunning the crofts and driving out many of the tenant farmers.

There is so much to do here it would be easier to list what is not available. Sea sports include: swimming, sailing, windsurfing, water skiing, sub-aqua diving and fishing. Land sports include: golf, riding, pony trekking, tennis, squash, bowling, and of course, walking and climbing. Time spent birdwatching will reward you with sightings of rare species and the flora and fauna of the island are diverse.

A holiday atmosphere prevails on the ferry from Ardrossan to Brodick on Arran. For an hour crowds jostle for tables in the bar and lounges. If it is raining at Brodick don't worry; Arran usually manages to show a smiling face for at least some of the day.

Getting there

The car ferry from Ardrossan, with train link from Glasgow, takes about an hour. April–Oct: Claonaig, Kintyre–Lochranza takes half an hour. Further information: Caledonian MacBrayne Ltd, Ferry Terminal, Gourock, Renfrewshire, ✆ 0475 33755 (enquiries)/34531 (reservations).

The Pier, **Brodick,** ✆ 0770 2140/2401.

Brodick

Brodick is a large resort-village with plenty of hotels, guest houses, and bed and breakfast places. It spreads around Brodick Bay overlooked by Brodick Castle.

Brodick Castle (open Mon, Wed, Sat, April and first half Oct; daily May–Sept: grounds open all year: adm) belongs to the National Trust for Scotland. The home of the Dukes of Hamilton, it was built in the 13th century on the site of a Viking fortress. Much of the treasures on display were brought to the castle by Susan Euphemia Beckford, who married the 10th Duke in 1810. She inherited them from her father William Beckford, the reclusive, eccentric collector of fine art, who built Fonthill Abbey in Wiltshire, and wrote *Vathek.* The guidebook to the castle gives details of all the silver, porcelain, paintings and furnishings. The castle is a tall, stately building of red sandstone, facing the sea and surrounded by a range of hills dominated by Goat Fell. The gardens are a surprise—the fabulous colours and pungent scents are exotic enough to to have been part of the rich oriental settings in *Vathek* itself.

The **Isle of Arran Heritage Museum** (open Easter–Oct, Mon–Sat: adm) occupies an 18th-century croft-farm on the edge of Brodick. The smithy, cottage and stable block illustrate changing conditions from the far past to the turn of the century. Rooms in the cottage show nostalgic Victoriana, complete with black kettle on the hob and iron bedstead under the eaves.

The road round the island only loses the sea in a couple of places, while the String Road cuts through the middle from Brodick to Blackwaterfoot. Another road cuts through Glen Scorrodale from Lamlash to Lagg Inn.

Goat Fell, 2866 ft (874m), north of Brodick, dominates Arran. It is best attacked on a clear day; there are several ways up and the views from the top make it all worth while. There won't be any goats— 'Goatfell' comes from *Gaoith Bheinn*, windy mountain, but you might see golden eagles gliding on air currents in a corrie below.

Corrie is about 6 miles (9.5km) north of Brodick. Its white cottages, trim colourful gardens, harbour, quay and beach have made it a favourite with artists.

Walk up into the glens that cut into the hinterland like spokes of a wheel. There are two at **Sannox**—delightful, secret places away from the road, with heather, lichens, mosses and alpine willow, and many rare wild flowers. The **Fallen Rocks**, beyond Sannox, are thought to be the relics of a landslip in the Palaeozoic Age which sent these massive boulders—some as big as houses—tumbling to the beach. This is a popular place for rock climbers. Sannox has a nine-hole golf course. **North Sannox Farm Park** (open Mon–Sat: adm) has small and pet animals, including chipmunks, and play areas for children.

Lochranza, possibly from Loch of the *chaoruinn* (rowan), lies 2 miles (3km) southwest of the northern headland, Cock of Arran. The 13th/14th-century Lochranza Castle (open daily: free) is a romantic ruin on the tidal flats, backed by hills. The castle is L-plan, three storeys high with a pit prison in the vaulted basement. It is said to have been a staging post for Robert the Bruce in 1307, when he returned from his famous encounter with the spider of Rathlin Island. Seen against a flaming sunset, this roofless shell is stunning. Lochranza has a nine-hole golf course.

Heading south from Lochranza down the west side of the island, the road clings to the sea with hills tumbling down almost to the beach. Steep-sided **Glen Catacol** runs inland up into the hills through beech, oak and larch, chestnut and fir, and vivid green ferns. **Thundergay**, 5 miles (8km) south of Lochranza, gets its strange name from *Tor-na-Gaoith* (hill-of-the-wind). Two miles (3km) further south, **Pirnmill** is derived from the bobbin mill that was here in the days when linen was an important industry in the island. The mill has now been converted into holiday flats. **Glen Iorsa** runs northeast through marshy bog land, hemmed in by barren hills. It is a great tract of lonely, waterlogged moor, lying below frowning crags cut by steep ravines and lochans.

The southwest quarter of Arran is rich in prehistoric remains. These include **Auchagallon Stone Circle**, 15 red sandstone blocks which once encircled a cairn; the **Farm Road Stone Circle**, close by (within range of the nine-hole Machrie golf course); the **Machrie Standing Stones**, slim, primeval monoliths whose mysterious purpose is still unknown, and the **Kilmory Cairns**, at Lagg Inn.

King's Caves at Drumadoon, Blackwaterfoot, are where Robert the Bruce is said to have sheltered when returning to free Scotland from the stranglehold of English domination. Legend brings the 3rd-century warrior-poet Fingal (Fionn) MacCumhail here, father of Ossian and leader of the Feinn, who feature in the old sagas. There are rock carvings of typical Pictish hunting scenes and animals in the caves.

A lovely 10-mile (16km) walk takes you up **Glen Scorrodale** from **Sliddery** and along Sliddery Water to Lamlash Bay.

Kildonan, 6 miles (9.5km) east of Sliddery, is a sprawling farming village with two hotels and a sandy beach. There are views from here of Pladda Island Lighthouse and Ailsa Craig, which rises like an iceberg 13 miles (21km) out to sea. Look for a large colony of Atlantic grey seals along the shore towards Bennan Head to the west. Unafraid and curious, they come quite close to the shore to inspect passers-by. The mysterious carcass of a large sea-creature, discovered here in 1981, baffled experts for some time until it was identified, with great disappointment, as a gigantic basking shark. Before the headland, a winding path used by smugglers in the 18th century hugs the cliffs and leads to the road above. **South Bank Farm Park** (open Easter–Oct: adm) has sheep dog demonstrations and rare breeds of farm animals and deer.

Whiting Bay, 5 miles (8km) north of Kildonan, is a popular holiday village. Here, shops and hotels jostle with holiday cottages along the waterfront. There are also craft shops which specialize in leather, pottery and wood carving. A jewellery workshop, signposted at the north end of the village, sells locally made silver and gold jewellery. For evening entertainment, **Nags Bistro** has live music and a disco in the summer. There is an 18-hole golf course with fine views across the Firth of Clyde to the Ayrshire hills. **Glen Ashdale Falls** are signposted from the south end of the village, up a steep, wooded glen to where crystal water cascades down on to glistening rocks. **The Giant's Graves** (signposted) are a stone circle traditionally associated with Fionn MacCumhail.

Lamlash completes the circular tour of the island, 3 miles (4.5km) south of Brodick on Lamlash Bay, which is almost blocked at the mouth by Holy Island. This wonderfully safe anchorage, now a yachtsman's haven, has given shelter to many an important traveller. King Haakon and his fleet took refuge here after they had been defeated in the Battle of Largs in 1263, and in 1548 the ship carrying five-year-old Mary, Queen of Scots to France from Dumbarton sheltered here. Lamlash has annual sea angling competitions, renowned throughout Scotland.

Holy Island, with St Molio's Cave, is not at present open to the public. It is the home of a Buddhist community.

Take home one of Arran's unique blends of mustard, locally made and sold at **Arran Provisions**, The Old Mill, Lamlash. The range is enormous. They also do delicious jams, jellies, sauces, and chutneys. Another local speciality is Arran cheese—a Dunlop cheese made at The Creamery in Kilmory.

Where to Stay

moderate

Auchrannie Hotel, Brodick, ✆ 0770 2234/5, is a 19th-century mansion, five minutes from beach and golf course. Excellent food is served in a conservatory-style restaurant. **Douglas Hotel**, Brodick, ✆ 0770 2155, on the sea front, has live entertainment, dancing, sauna and a beauty salon. **Kinloch Hotel**, overlooking the sea at Blackwaterfoot, ✆ 077086 444, is a comfortable modern eyesore with good food, indoor swimming pool, solarium, sauna and squash court. Not for the recluse.

inexpensive

Arran Hotel, on the sea front in Brodick, ✆ 0770 2265, welcomes children at reduced prices and has a nice garden. Open March to October. **Invercloy Hotel**, Brodick, ✆ 0770 2225, is opposite a safe sandy beach and has balconies in front and a friendly atmosphere.

Lagg Hotel, Kilmory, ✆ 077087 255, is an 18th-century coaching inn set in 10 acres of attractive woodland by the Lagg Burn. The food is first rate.

Eating Out

For an evening out, try **Wishing Well Restaurant**, Lagg, ✆ 0770 87255, in converted stables. Seafood is a speciality, with lobster when available.

Bute

Bute is a holiday island, attracting many people in the summer, including Glaswegians who like to take a trip 'doon the watter'. Rothesay is a town of bright lights and tourist traps, a little run-down at present although great efforts are being made to revive it. There are plenty of hidden corners if you are prepared to walk to some of the less accessible beaches and coves, especially in the northwest. The **Kyles of Bute** are the very beautiful narrow straits separating the island from the mainland in the northwest and northeast. Sailors exploring the coast will find a number of secret bays populated only by seals and sea birds. Mountstuart (not open to the public), an incredible Gothic mansion, is the main home of the Bute family who own the island as well as much else in Britain and have been revered patrons of the arts for generations. They are Scotland's premier Catholic aristocratic family and are responsible for some very important architecture in Britain.

Throughout the season the island plays host to many events, including a Jazz Festival in May, a Folk Festival in July and Bute Highland Games in August. There are also angling competitions and a bowling tournament; three golf courses, tennis, riding, good fishing and every sort of water sport in wonderfully clear water. Nature lovers will appreciate the walking and birdwatching. During the summer there is plenty of organized jollity to while away the evenings and pleasure cruises for the day time.

Getting there

There is a roll-on, roll-off car ferry from Wemyss Bay, which is an hour's drive or train journey from Glasgow. There are frequent sailings daily, lasting half an hour. The roll-on, roll-off car ferry from Colintraive, Argyll, also has frequent sailings daily; the crossing takes 5 minutes. For further information, contact Caledonian MacBrayne, The Ferry Terminal, Gourock, Renfrewshire, © 0475 33755, or 0700 502707.

Tourist Information

15 Victoria Street, **Rothesay**, © 0700 502151, open all year.

Rothesay is the hub of Bute, a town humming with activity and tourist attractions.

Rothesay Castle (open daily except Thurs mornings and Fri, Oct–March: adm) was built in 1098 in the days when Norsemen dominated the islands. It reverted to Scotland after the Battle of Largs, in 1263. Added to over the centuries, it is an impressive fortress with high curtain walls and drum towers enclosing a circular courtyard. King Robert the Bruce captured it in 1313 and it was his great-great-grandson who was first created Duke of Rothesay, a title held by the present Prince Charles. The castle was used as a headquarters when both James IV and James V tried, with little success, to subdue the arrogant rule of the Lords of the Isles. Cromwell battered it badly during the Civil War and it was burned by Argyll in 1685 during the Monmouth Rebellion; it then lay in ruins until restoration began in the 19th century.

The **Bute Museum** is behind the castle (open every day except Sun during April and May; daily June–Sept; Tues–Sat afternoons, Oct–March: adm). There are displays of Bute's geology, ancient history, maritime traditions, culture and natural history.

Winter Garden Visitors' Centre in Victoria Street, in a restored 1920s seaside theatre, contains a heritage centre, cinema and bistro. **Rothesay Pavilion** is a multi-purpose entertainment centre with fun-filled family shows.

Ardencraig Gardens (open daily May–Sept: free), south of Rothesay, supply plants for the whole island. As well as demonstration gardens and fish ponds, there are aviaries with exotic foreign birds. Fuchsias add a vivid splash of colour.

Canada Hill, above the town in the lower middle part of the island, is an easy walk and gives panoramic views of the Firth of Clyde, Argyll and Arran.

St Blane's Chapel, on the southern toe of Bute, is a 12th-century ruin with a Norman arch, built on the site of a monastery founded by St Blane in the 6th century.

St Ninian's Chapel, halfway up the west coast, on a point by a glorious sandy bay, is another early settlement.

Ettrick Bay, further north, has a sandy beach.

Where to Stay

inexpensive

Guildford Court, Watergate, Rothesay, © 0700 3770, is a listed building overlooking the harbour with both hotel accommodation and self-catering suites.

Kingarth Hotel, at the south end of the island, © 070083 662, is comfortable and friendly with a bowling green, near a golf course.

Bayview Hotel, 22 Mountstuart Road, Rothesay, © 0700 2339, is a Victorian house on Craigmore Shore, 10 minutes from the pier with views of Rothesay Bay.

Royal Hotel, Albert Place, Rothesay, © 0700 3044, overlooks the yacht marina, a short distance from the ferry terminus. It has a cabaret every night during the season. Private loch fishing and special terms for golfers can be arranged.

Glenburn Hotel, Glenburn Road, Rothesay, © 0700 2500, stands in six acres overlooking the water. It's a busy place, next door to a heated swimming pool and a golf course, and the food isn't too bad.

Ardencraig, © 0700 4550, has seven cheap self-catering chalets high above the Firth of Clyde, each with one public room and two bedrooms which sleep six.

Gigha

(Pronounced with hard g, 'Ge'a'.)

Gigha is Norse for god, and indeed this is an earthly Garden of Eden, 6 miles (9.5km) long and never more than 1½ miles (2.5km) wide, warmed by the Gulf Stream, with frost almost unknown.

Getting There

Six ferries a day (four on Sundays) run to Gigha from Tayinloan, halfway up the west side of Kintyre. (Fewer in winter.)

For further information contact Caledonian MacBrayne, ✆ 0475 33755.

Tourist Information

West Highland and Islands Tourist Board, The Pier, **Campbeltown**, ✆ 0586 552056.

Gigha has been on the market several times recently. Islands like this suffer from being bought and sold by rich businessmen who see them as toys.

Perhaps the most celebrated of Gigha's residents is Seumas McSporran, a sturdy figure past his half-century with a genial smile almost as wide as his face. He has lived on the island for all but two years of his life and holds some 14 or 15 jobs. 'I have to consult a list to get up to date with them.' They include: sub-postmaster, postman, registrar, Pearl Assurance agent, special constable, fireman, ambulance driver, taxi driver, and undertaker. He and his wife run the general store and he has a uniform or outfit to go with each job.

Achamore House Gardens (open daily Apr–Oct, 10am–6pm: adm) contain a riot of sub-tropical plants and shrubs, all thriving in the mild westerly climate. The gardens were developed by Sir James Horlick, who bought the island in 1944. A lucky combination of the acidic soil, the warm air of the Gulf Stream and Sir James' milk-drink-derived fortune created this paradise of rhododendrons, camellias, and azaleas. There are carpets of bulbs and many exotic blooms to give a vivid foreground to lovely views.

The ruined church at Kilchattan dates from the 13th century. There is a golf course, a visitor centre, a hotel and a Boathouse Bar.

Where to Stay

moderate

Gigha Hotel, ✆ 05835 275, would be a perfect honeymoon retreat on this paradise island. Almost ranch-style, and not a bit grand, it has good local food and lovely views.

Gigha Enterprises have a house and two self-catering cottages, ✆ 05835 254; quite pricey.

inexpensive

Down the scale a bit, but also full of character, **Post Office House**, © 05835 251, has four bedrooms, one public bathroom and a great atmosphere.

Islay

(Pronounced Eyela.)

Islay, the most southerly of the Inner Hebrides, is some 14 miles (22km) off Kintyre, about 25 miles (40km) from north to south and 20 (32km) across at the widest point. Farmland rises to moor transversed by burns; rugged coastline gives way to open sweeps of beach. A favourite holiday island for birdwatchers, naturalists, photographers and artists, it also has much to interest archaeologists; the island has been inhabited since Neolithic times.

Excellent trout and salmon fishing can be found on the rivers Duich and Sorn, and on well-stocked lochs such as Gorm, Torrabus and Ballygrant. Boats can be hired locally for sea-angling, too. Warmed by the Gulf Stream, so they say, miles of sandy beaches offer swimming and sunbathing. The surf is sometimes good. Machrie 18-hole golf course is well known.

Perhaps best known for its distinctive peaty malt whisky, Islay has eight distilleries which scent the air with the pungent smell of smouldering peat. Now and then islanders tangle with conservationists who insist that the special Duich Moss peat, essential for the flavour of Islay whisky, should be preserved for rare Greenland white-fronted geese. At a stormy meeting not so long ago the islanders, furious at Green interference, argued that whisky was more vital to their survival than 'any bloody goose'. The distilleries welcome visitors.

Getting There

Ferries run to both Port Ellen and Askaig from Kennacraig in northwest Kintyre, taking just over two hours.

Loganair fly from Glasgow to the island's airport at Glenegadale. Flights take half an hour.

A local bus service links most of the island communities with extra runs in the summer. There are day tours of beauty spots and places of interest.

Tourist Information

West Highlands and Islands Tourist Board, The Pier, **Campbeltown,** © 0586 552056.

Tourist Information Centre, **Bowmore,** © 049681 254.

Port Ellen is the ferry arrival point at the south of the island. Port Ellen Distillery, built in 1815, dominates the skyline overlooking Leodamus Bay. Closed during the slump of the 1930s, it was then modernized. It was closed briefly again in 1983 due to a 'Whisky Lake'.

The 14th-century **Dunyvaig Castle** is an impressive ruin on a cliff, 3½ miles (5.5km) east of Port Ellen. It was the stronghold of the Macdonalds of Islay in the days when the Lords of the Isles considered themselves to be separate from the authority of the Crown. **Kildalton Cross** beside ruined Kildalton Chapel, 7 miles (11km) further north along this road, is an important survival of Celtic art. It is a 9th-century Celtic cross carved from a single block of blue stone and inscribed with early Christian symbols. Similar to one in Iona Abbey, it is one of the finest in the country. There is a hotel here. **Claggain Bay** beyond the chapel is sandy with rocky pools, backed by Beinn Bheigeir (1612 feet—496m), the highest hill in Islay.

The rugged **Oa Peninsula**, 5 miles (8km) southwest of Port Ellen, was a haunt of smugglers and illicit whisky distillers, who made cunning use of its sheer cliffs honeycombed with caves. One road crosses it but most of the peninsula is only accessible on foot.

Machrie, north of Oa, has an 18-hole golf course on the machair, and borders the sandy crescent of Laggan Bay.

Bowmore, 14 miles (22km) or so north of Port Ellen, was the old capital and administrative centre of the island. It was seat of the Islay Parliament, a sort of feudal court. The village was built by Daniel Campbell the Younger in 1768, on the site of monastic lands and was one of the earliest of Scotland's planned villages introduced by wealthy 'improvers' in the 18th century. The village is crowned by an intriguing, round church, Italian in design. Its shape deprives the devil of any corners in which to lurk.

Bowmore Distillery, established in 1779, claims to be the oldest legal distillery on Islay and is still privately owned.

Brigend is a hamlet among woods at the head of Loch Indaal with good beaches and a hotel. **Islay Woollen Mill** is an old working mill where you can watch tweed being woven and buy the products.

The Rhinns of Islay sticks out from the west side of the island like a great hammerhead. Here there are more wonderful walks and views. Bruichladdich Distillery overlooks Loch Indaal and produces an excellent 10-year-old single malt.

The award-winning **Museum of Islay Life** is in a converted church in **Port Charlotte**, on the southeast shore of the Rhinns (open daily Easter–Oct; Sun afternoons, Nov, Jan–March; closed Dec: adm). Exhibits cover the history of the island, with traditional craft work and tools, a maritime section and domestic artefacts. A lapidarium, below the museum, displays an important collection of carved stones dating from the 16th century.

There is a wildfowl sanctuary at **Ellister** south of Port Charlotte, and an RSPB reserve at **Loch Gruinart** to the north. **Portnahaven** is the southwest tip of Islay, with the green shores of Ireland only spitting distance away.

Ruined **Finlaggan Castle** stands on an islet in Loch Finlaggan, just off the road from Bowmore to Port Askaig. This was the main stronghold of the Macdonalds, Lords of the Isles. The 14 chiefs of the Lordship were summoned to council meetings here, to confer with their overlord. They came from all over the Kingdom of the Isles, many in coracles, accompanied by members of their clans. They were proud men, settling their disputes and problems independently of the Scottish Parliament, often with great wisdom and justice and often with bloodshed.

Port Askaig is the other ferry terminal, and boats run from here to the Isle of Jura. The views across the narrow Sound of Islay to the Paps of Jura are glorious. There is a hotel and a roadless hinterland to the north.

Where to Stay

moderate

Bridgend Hotel, © 049681 212, not only has a private bathroom for each of its 10 bedrooms, but three extra, public ones as well. It has a pretty garden, good food and is open all year.

inexpensive

Port Askaig Hotel, © 049684 245, open all year, looks over the harbour, and is attractive and cosy, with three public bathrooms between nine bedrooms. **Lochside Hotel**, Bowmore, © 049681 265/244, overlooks Loch Indaal, and is old-fashioned, friendly, and ideal for birdwatching. Open all year, with two public bathrooms to seven bedrooms.

Jura

Just off the northeast coast of Islay, Jura has very little tourist accommodation and is far less frequented though more beautiful. Wild and rugged, it is famous for its deer, which are keenly stalked by the owners and guests of the sporting estates of which the island is comprised. Over 20 miles (32km) long and sparsely populated, it has a small village, Craighouse, a distillery and a hotel. Silver and white sandy beaches give way to rugged shingle which teems with wildfowl. Loch Tarbert almost cuts the island in two from the west. The three Paps of Jura rear up at the south end of the island—the highest is 2576 feet (793m). A single-track road runs south from the ferry, and then some way up the east coast. Most of the island is only accessible on foot. The west coast—private land—has some amazing caves, some of which have been adapted for temporary use by shepherds.

Getting There

A car ferry runs frequently from Port Askaig on Islay to Feolin. It is a 10-minute crossing (there are fewer ferries on Sundays).

Tourist Information

West Highlands and Islands Tourist Board, The Pier, **Campbeltown**, © 0586 552056.

Craighouse, the only village, has the island's single hotel, **The Jura**. They will arrange riding, fishing, sea-angling, boating, shooting and water skiing.

The **Corryvreckan Whirlpool** in the strait between Jura and Scarba is notorious to west-coast sailors and can be both lion and lamb. In the right conditions of tide and weather, its mighty maw has been known to suck down whole boats, roaring like an express train. But at slack tide, it can be approached by sea, its satin-smooth water ruffled by tiny eddies that pull gently at the boat without harm.

Seven miles (11km) beyond Ardlussa, on a rough track, lies **Barnhill**, the white farmhouse where George Orwell lived, and wrote *1984*, struggling against the consumption that killed him.

Jura House Garden and Grounds (open all year: adm) at the southern end of the island were laid out around the middle of the last century to exploit the natural features and beauty of the area. There is a lovely walled garden and walks.

Where to Stay

inexpensive

Jura Hotel, Craighouse, © 049682 243, has a relaxed atmosphere in a lovely setting, with good food. It gets very booked up. There is a self-catering house at Craighouse, sleeping five: c/o Mrs Mary Keith, Keills, Craighouse, Isle of Jura, Argyll PA60 7XG, © 049682 214; open April–Oct. Another, a bit more expensive, sleeps six: c/o Mr Renwick, 5 Kelvin Drive, Glasgow, © 041 946 4361. A third **Ardfarnal**, sleeps nine: c/o Mr A. Fairman, 83 James Street, Helensburgh, Dunbartonshire, © 0436 75760.

Colonsay and Oronsay

These two tiny islands, joined at low tide, lie 10 miles (16km) west of Jura, 25 miles (40km) from the mainland. To the west, the only thing between here and Canada is **Du Hirteach Lighthouse**. The landscape is made up of craggy hills, woods and a rocky coastline broken by silver sands. Their names are derived from the Saints Columba and Oran who landed here on their way to Scotland from Ireland. Legend holds that when Columba discovered he could still see the shore of the land from which he had been exiled, he pressed on to Iona; whether from repugnance or sadness is not related. It is also said that he banished snakes from the two islands, as he did on Iona.

Both islands have a high average of sunshine. Over 500 species of wild flowers can be found, including rare purple orchids, sea samphire and marsh helleborine. Bluebells and primroses bloom in the woods, wild irises flower in damp corners, harebells nod on the sand dunes and purple thrift clings to the rocks. Eucalyptus, palm trees and rare shrubs flourish in the mild climate. There are also over 150 different bird species.

Getting There

The car ferry from Oban, three times a week, takes 2½ hours, and in summer, from Kennacraig via Islay, about the same time.

Tourist Information

Tourist Information Centre, **Oban**, Argyll, ✆ 0631 63122.

Colonsay House Gardens (open daily: free) have sub-tropical shrubs and plants, rhododendrons, embothriums, magnolias and palm trees.

Wild goats roam the island, reputedly descended from survivors of a Spanish Armada wreck in 1588. Otters can be seen occasionally and there are lots of grey seals. **Balnahard** is a beach with hundreds of cowrie shells in the coves. When the wind is in the west, **Kiloran Bay** in the northwest offers safe surfing in huge Atlantic rollers. **The Strand** is a beach a mile (1.5km) wide in the south of the island festooned with mussels on the rocks, and prawns in the pools. For about three hours at low tide, the Strand becomes a causeway to Oronsay, an enchanted island populated by sheep and serenaded by skylarks.

St Oran's Chapel, on Oronsay, is a ruined 14th-century priory, named after St Columba's faithful companion. Although the cloisters have collapsed, this is a splendid ruin with gravestones carved with boats and warriors and hunting scenes. A tall, carved Celtic cross stands at the entrance. Excavations revealed that Oronsay was inhabited in the Middle Stone Age. Certainly Norsemen lived here, long before the present chapel was built by Columban monks.

Where to Stay

moderate

Isle of Colonsay Hotel, ✆ 09512 316, is highly recommended, informal, and serves good food. It also has three self-catering chalets, each with two bedrooms and one public room.

inexpensive

There are three bed and breakfast places: **Baleromindobh Farm**, ✆ 09512 305, a farm house with three bedrooms: **Seaview**, ✆ 09512 315, a working croft with three bedrooms; and **Garvard**, ✆ 09512 343, a farmhouse with three bedrooms. There are also a number of cottages to let on Colonsay and flats in Colonsay House.

Mull

Mull, 'isle-of-the-cool-high-bends', is the largest of the Inner Hebrides and merits a whole book to itself. It is shaped like a caricature of the British Isles, its southwestern peninsula kicking frivolously upwards. Encircled by 300 miles (480km) of rugged coastline, it is deeply cut by lochs with many wooded hillsides and secret corners, easily reached by coastal roads. The western seaboard is sprinkled with islands: **Inch Kenneth**, **Ulva**, **Staffa** and, further west, the **Treshnish Isles** with **Coll** and **Tiree** beyond. There are plenty of boat trips to the islands and some of the hotels charter their own boats. In addition, local men will take you fishing or sightseeing. The whole coast is a sailor's paradise. Around the head of Loch Na Keal about halfway down the west coast, there are steep cliffs fringed by sandy inlets. The hinterland is a mass of hills, dominated by **Ben More**, 3169 feet (975m), in the west.

Johnson and Boswell came to Mull during their tour of the Hebrides. Johnson lamented the lack of trees, attributing this to idleness, but applauded the French wine he was given.

There are more red deer on Mull than people: over 3000 roam the island and the smaller fallow deer can be seen in the woods around Gruline and Salen. There are also polecats, weasels, stoats, mink, feral ferrets and otters. Wild white goats can be seen from Grass Point down to the Ross of Mull.

Unlike some other islands, the depopulation of 150 years has been reversed in Mull. With fishing, farming, tourism and building to employ them, fewer young people are seeking the bright lights of the mainland and there are a number of incomers who prefer insular peace and beauty to the materialistic scramble of the cities.

There is a Drama Festival in March, a Music Festival in April, Tobermory Highland Games in July, and also Children's Highland Games. West Highland Yachting Week takes place in early August, Salen Show, which includes a dogshow, is in August and there is a car rally in October.

Getting There

Car ferries run frequently from Oban to Craignure in just under an hour; Oban–Tobermory takes about two hours and Lochaline–Fishnish, a quarter of an hour. There is also a car ferry from Kilchoan to Tobermory, taking half an hour. You can get 'Multi-stop' ferry tickets, much cheaper, if you want to visit several places.

Further information: Caledonian MacBrayne, ✆ 0475 34531, or 0631 62285.

There is an airfield on the island to which charter flights can be arranged from Glasgow. Most roads are single-track with passing places.

island cruises

Inter-island cruises in high-speed charter boats, to Staffa, Treshnish, Coll, Eigg, Muck, can be booked from Richard and Judy Fairbairns, Dervaig, ✆ 06884 223. Or try Turus Mara, ✆ 06884 242/0631/63122. You need to go prepared: take a good picnic and weatherproof clothing as conditions change quickly, and seasick pills—the slow Atlantic swell can be disastrous for uneasy stomachs. You might see whales and dolphins.

The boat from Oban passes **Lady Rock**, an islet off Lismore Lighthouse at the head of Loch Linnhe. In the 16th century, a Maclean of Lochbuie, disenchanted by his wife, tethered her to this rock. Passing fishermen took pity and released her and she fled to her father, Campbell of Inveraray. This irate chief invited Maclean to stay on the pretext of commiserating with him on the death of his wife. At the end of dinner, the 'deceased' wife confronted her husband, and her relatives set on him with broadswords.

Tourist Information

Oban, Mull and District, Oban, Argyll PA34 4AN, ✆ 0631 63122
Tourist Information Centre, **Tobermory**, Isle of Mull, ✆ 0688 2182.

fishing

Wet- or dry-fly trout fishing is available in Mishnish Lochs, Loch Tor and Loch Frisa. Licences, tackle and bait can be obtained from Brown's Ironmongers in Tobermory High Street or the National Forestry Commission's office at the south end of Loch Frisa. You can also hire rods and boats.

Tobermory

Having stopped off at Craignure, the ferry sails up the Sound of Mull to Tobermory —the Well of St Mary—the 'capital' of Mull. Founded as a fishing village in 1789 on the site of an earlier Christian settlement, it has one of the most sheltered harbours in Scotland, tucked round behind a headland. The village clusters round the anchorage. Terraced houses, colour-washed in strong reds, pinks, yellows, blues, ochres, rise from the harbour up a steep, wooded bank. Yachstmen and fishermen jostle for mooring space.

The **Mull and Iona Museum** (open weekdays, May–Sept: adm) is in a converted church in the Main Street, with exhibitions of the island's history. In the bay beyond the harbour lies the wreck of a galleon, the *Florencia*, part of the Spanish Armada, which is still a focus of attention for treasure seekers today. The ship sought shelter here in a storm in 1588. Always hospitable, the islanders treated the Spaniards with courtesy, restocking their stores and entertaining them in grand style. But Scotsmen are thrifty as well as hospitable and when rumour came that the *Florencia* was about to depart without having paid its dues, a local man, Donald Maclean, went aboard to remonstrate. He was locked up in the ship's cell, but managed to escape. In retaliation he blew up the ship, together with the hoard of gold and treasure it was alleged to have been carrying. So far, only a few coins and cannon have been discovered, but the search continues. Divers should note, however, that the wreck is protected and it is forbidden to dive in its area.

Tobermory has a nine-hole golf course, on the northern tip of the island, owned by the Western Isles Hotel. The spectacular views down the Sound of Mull are are apt to distract the players.

Going west on the B8073, look for three small, linked lochs where there is trout fishing. Snake Pass, beyond the last loch, is said to be the home of many adders. This is also the start of a good walk to Loch Frisa.

On the steep hill down into **Dervaig** there is a cemetery at Kilmore, with some of the oldest gravestones on Mull. Filmgoers may recognise this as one of the sets for *Where Eight Bells Toll.* **Mull Little Theatre**, in Dervaig, 6 miles (9.5km) from Tobermory, is in the Guinness Book of Records as the smallest professional theatre in Britain, with 37 seats. Six times a week in the summer, two or more actors from visiting professional companies stage really excellent productions, which should be booked well in advance: ✆ 06884 245. In the winter there are amateur productions. A restaurant and guest house serves dinner before and after the show. Lunch is also served before matinées. Meals should be booked, ✆ 06884 345.

The Old Byre Heritage Centre, a mile (1.5km) beyond Dervaig (open daily, Easter–mid-Oct: adm) is a crofting museum with tableaux showing life at the time of the Highland Clearances with the family and animals round the central fire, busy about their daily lives. A half-hour audio-visual programme illustrates further what life was like.

The west coast road gives views out to the scattering of islands that create such wonderful seascapes, especially when seen against a setting sun. There are good sandy beaches and it is usually possible to find shelter on one of them.

Boats run from Dervaig or Ulva to the **Treshnish Isles** and to **Staffa**, when the weather is fair. A new landing stage on Staffa makes access easier in rough weather and some cruises allow you an hour ashore. You can go into **Fingal's Cave** by boat or walk round the side on a platform. This huge cathedral-like cavern is made up of columns of basalt, some hexagonal, truncated at different levels like organ pipes and of similar construction to Ireland's Giants Causeway. The formation inspired Mendelssohn in 1829 to write the *Hebrides* overture.

Cruises which include **Lunga** in the Treshnish Isles, are especially good during the nesting season. You are advised not to linger too long over the puffins at the start of your tour: they are so bewitching, you may never see the rest of the island. They sit scratching, chatting and popping in and out of their burrows, an arm's length from you. There are also kittiwakes, razorbills, shags and guillemots and lots of black rabbits.

The island of Ulva will be familiar to anyone who knows the poem 'Lord Ullin's Daughter', which tells the tale of 'The Chief of Ulva's Isle' and his lover, fleeing her father's wrath and drowning in the ferry, crossing to the island. Lord Ullin stood helpless on the shore, while: *The waters wild went o'er his child, And he was left lamenting.*

A couple of miles before the Ulva Ferry look for the Eas Forss, a waterfall that cascades over the cliff into a pool and then under a rock, arching into the sea.

The walks and views all down the west coast are good. Much of the coastline is columned basalt with sandy bays and rock coves, with seals, guillemots, oystercatchers and herons in the rock pools. Wild flowers are abundant: orchids, bright pink thrift, yellow irises.

Where the road turns south, before cutting back inland across the Ardmeanach peninsula, you can look out across the entrance to Loch na Keal to Inch Kenneth. This was the burial place of many Scottish kings and was visited by Johnson and Boswell in 1773, as guests of Sir Allan Maclean and his two daughters. Unity Mitford took refuge here with her family after her unfortunate association with Hitler and the Nazis. To the right, **Tragedy Rock** is a huge boulder which crashed onto the cottage of a young local couple on the first night of their married life, 200 years ago, killing them both.

The Ardmeanach Peninsula is owned by the National Trust for Scotland. At Burgh on the southern tip, aptly named The Wilderness, there is a fossilized tree 50 million years old embedded in the shore.

The Ross of Mull is the southwest headland, with softer scenery. **Erraid**, the tidal islet off the southwest tip of the Ross, was once home to Robert Louis Stevenson, and it was here that David Balfour swam ashore from the wreck of the brig *Covenant*, in *Kidnapped.* **Uisken** on the south side, reached by a road from Bunessan, is a lovely beach with lonely crofts, mostly ruined—another village abandoned in the Clearances.

Isle of Mull Wine Co at Bunessan welcomes visitors and will arrange tastings by appointment, © 06817 403. They make the Isle of Mull Vermouth, and The Mull Riveter, a blend of their own vermouth and bitters with vodka. Children will enjoy a visit to the **Angora Rabbit Farm** at Ardtun near Bunessan, where they can see how their clipped coats are made into wool. Further east at Pennyghael, take the road south to Carsaig, a lovely spot where salmon fishermen still work. The amazing Carcaig Arches is a famous geological freak—a natural, jagged archway through the rock.

The A849 goes inland back towards the east coast from the head of Loch Scridain. At Ardura a road turns south to Loch Buie, a lovely drive down past Loch Spelve and Loch Uisg. Moy Castle, at the end, now a ruin, was the ancestral home of the MacLaines of Lochbuie. If you take the track on round the coast for 3 miles (4.5km) you come to **Lord Lovat's Cave**.

Duart Castle (winner of the Castle of the Year award in 1988: open daily, May–Sept: adm) is 15 miles (24km) east of the head of Loch Scridain across great tracts of moor and hill. It is an impressive fortress on a headland guarding the approach to the Sound of Mull. It dates from the 13th century, and was the home of the Chiefs of Maclean, until it was confiscated after the Jacobite rising in 1745. It was bought back and restored in 1912 by Sir Fitzroy Maclean, who was then the chief. He was a gallant Hussar Colonel who had ridden with the Light Brigade in the Crimea and died at the age of 100, affectionately known as Old Man A Hundred. As well as the keep, visitors can see the cell where prisoners from the Spanish galleon *Florencia* were held after it had been sunk in Tobermory, in 1588, by Donald Maclean. There are relics of the Maclean family in the main hall, with many of the gifts presented to the late Chief—who was among many other things, Chief Scout and Lord Chamberlain—during his world tours. There is also an exhibition of scouting throughout the Commonwealth, in the old staff rooms at the top of the castle.

Just south of Duart, the road to **Grass Point**, on Lochdon, was the old drovers' road for cattle and sheep from the outer isles, bound for mainland markets. It was also the landing point for pilgrims going to Iona. The seal on one of the rocks round the bay is of rather a different species to those living in the waters round Mull. It was the handiwork of the eminent sculptor, poet and writer, the late Lionel Leslie. First cousin of Winston Churchill, he and his wife Barbara came to live in the old Drover's Inn, after the last war, building it up from a ruin with their own hands. Boatloads of visitors came over from Oban in the summer to have tea, buy local crafts and listen to the sculptor's stories. Even in his mid-eighties his wit was as sharp as the stone he could no longer see to carve. There are also bas reliefs of a deer, an eagle, fighting swans and horses on the walls of a roofless byre beside the house, in lasting memory of a great artist. The house has been done up as a holiday home.

Torosay Castle (open daily, late April–mid-Oct: adm) is a mile (1.5km) south of Craignure near Duart. This 19th-century Scottish baronial building, with all the embellishments so beloved by the Victorians, was designed by David Bryce. The 11 acres of terraced Italian-style gardens with a statue walk and water garden were laid out by Robert Lorimer. The house contains magnificent paintings of wildlife by Thorburn, Landseer and Peter Scott, and family portraits by Poynter, de Lazlo, Sargent and Carlos Sancha. There are also hunting trophies, a library and an archive room with photographs and scrapbooks going back over 100 years. In the high season boats run from Oban direct to Torosay. A **miniature railway** runs from Craignure Pier, a mile and a half, to the castle, the only passenger train service in the Hebrides.

The roofless, ruined church by the cemetery at **Salen** is unlikely to be restored. A wicked Maclean of Duart was buried here many years ago and the consequence was the roof blew off. Three times they put it back and three times it blew away, unable to settle over the remains of such a villain. Sadly, the first-century statue of the Virgin Mary that used to be in this church has been stolen.

Iona

Getting There

The passenger ferry from Fionnphort, on Mull, to Iona, takes five minutes. There is also a Sacred Isles Cruise, on certain days in the summer, sailing from Oban, via Staffa, to Iona. They allow two and a half hours on Iona before the return journey.

No one can visit Mull without making a pilgrimage to the 'cradle of Christianity', though, in fact, St Ninian was spreading the word for nearly 150 years before St Columba founded his church on Iona in 563. The island is beautiful; white cockle-shell sand and vivid green slopes, slashed with rust-red granite and painted with wild flowers.

The powerful Irish saint, of royal descent, outlawed from his own land, came here with a few followers and set about converting the heathen Picts of Scotland to the Celtic Christianity of his homeland. Many Scots, Irish and Norse kings were buried on Iona including Macbeth and Duncan.

In 1938, George Macleod, a saintly Presbyterian Socialist, who renounced an inherited title but accepted one bestowed by the State, settled a new community on the island. Its purpose was to restore the ancient stones and create the present abbey and its domestic building. When Johnson and Boswell came here in 1773, the abbey was a complete ruin. Johnson was deeply moved by the atmosphere: 'That man is little to be envied . . . whose piety would not grow warmer among the ruins of Iona.' Today he may not have been so impressed. Opinions differ about this historic abbey: for some, the sanctity of the stark, unadorned interior has been erased by stalls selling postcards, souvenirs and booklets. They complain that the sightseers, slung about with cameras, are seldom inspired to kneel and say a prayer, and unfriendly ferrymen have been known to ram visiting boats which innocently trespass on ferry berths. But even if it does not, at first sight, feel like the house of God, Iona is special because St Columba was here, all those years ago. If you scratch below the rather worldly exterior, you will find informal services, taken by the warden and his wife, at which visitors are welcomed to share in the community worship. Visiting preachers and members of the community take part and everyone is encouraged to meet up afterwards for tea and coffee. There is a well-stocked bookshop.

Anyone feeling a tug of disappointment at the museum-like feeling of this sacred spot should climb the small hill, **Dun I**, to the north of the abbey. Look down on the buildings, the boats around the pier, the trails of people in bright anoraks and strap-hung impedimenta chattering, munching and scattering litter. Stay very quiet and listen: you may catch a faint echo of ironic laughter, and feel a gentle Celtic presence beside you. St Columba was known to have a well-developed sense of humour.

Look out for **Iona Scottish Crafts** by the nunnery where they sell everything from jewellery and pottery to knitwear—very reasonable.

Where to Stay

expensive

Druimnacroish Country House Hotel, Dervaig, © 06884 274/212, has what its name implies: a country-house atmosphere and excellent service; *céilidhs* often erupt when locals visit the bar. In conjunction with the Mull Little Theatre, they serve excellent dinners, by arrangement, before the plays begin. **Tiroran House**, © 06815 232, is another place specializing in a small country-house atmosphere with candlelit dinners. The food is renowned.

moderate

Western Isles Hotel, Tobermory, © 0688 2012, stands high above the harbour, open March to October. It is an old-fashioned, comfortable hotel. **Ardfenaig House**, Bunessan, © 06817 210, is a small, country-house hotel, peaceful and remote, open May to September, with good food. **Isle of Mull Hotel**, Craignure, © 06802 351, is a Benidorm-style monstrosity with 60 bedrooms.

inexpensive

Tobermory Hotel, © 0688 2091, is right on the waterfront, and full of character. **Craignure Inn**, © 06802 305, is the original drovers' inn, once scene of pungent activity, now more genteel with cars rather than beasts parked outside. It has four bedrooms and one public bathroom—which was more than the drovers got. **Quinish House** is a guesthouse in Dervaig, © 06884 223, family run and comfortable. **Glenforsa Hotel** near the airport at Salen, © 06803 377, is a log-cabin hotel with an easy, relaxed atmosphere.

Artists should head for **Inniemore**, at Pennyghael, © 06814 201, a guesthouse-painting-school for promising amateurs, with first-class tuition. Prices on application.

On Iona, The Abbey, © 06817 404, offers full board from March to December: visitors are expected to take part in the day to day activities of the community. There are also week-long courses: details from the joint wardens, Philip and Alison Newall. It's very cheap and pretty spartan, with 23 rooms, four bathrooms and monkish food (no licence). **Argyll Hote**l, © 06817 334, on the shore looking back towards Mull, is open April to October. **St Columba Hotel**, © 06817 304, is a modern, rather utilitarian place with 27 bedrooms and not much soul.

Eating Out

For an evening out, try **The Puffer Aground**, in Salen, © Aros 389. The food is good and you should book.

Coll and Tiree

Coll and Tiree, less than 11 miles (17.5km) off the northwest tip of Mull, are low islands which look barren from the sea but are charming, with green fields surrounded by an almost continuous string of deserted white beaches, where you may see many sea birds, seals and even otters. Sturdy cottages have rounded, thatched or tar-felted roofs to withstand the winter gales.

Getting Around

You can hire cars which meet you at the ferry, very reasonably.

Coll

Coll is fish-shaped, about 13 miles long and 3 miles ((5km) wide. Sandy beaches, azure water, rocky coves, backed by machair strewn with wild flowers in spring, make this another away-from-it-all paradise. The record of sunshine is good (usually tempered by a persistent wind).

Two standing stones at Totronald, called *Na Sgeulachan* (the Tellers of Tales), are thought to be part of a pagan temple, and traces of prehistoric forts and duns scatter the island. Adamnan, Saint Columba's biographer, mentions it in his *Vita Sancti Columbae*. During the Norse occupation of the islands, Coll was the headquarters of Earl Gilli, brother-in-law of Sigurd, Ruler of the Orkneys and Hebrides in 1000. By the end of 13th century it belonged to the MacDougalls of Lorne, from whom it was taken by Robert the Bruce because they opposed him. It passed to a second son of the Macleans of Duart in the early 1400s and remained in their keeping until 1856, when Hugh Maclean, last laird of Coll, was forced to sell his estates to pay for his extravagant life style. John Stewart of Glenbuckie, factor to the Duke of Argyll, bought it and his ruthlessly efficient farming methods resulted in mass emigration to Canada and Australia by the unfortunate crofters who could no longer afford his inflated rents (see 'Topics: Highland Clearances'). Traces of their abandoned croft houses can be seen at the northern end of the island. The resident population is now about 130, with quite a few incomers and holiday-home owners. Coll has attracted a number of *literati* and features now and then in glossy magazines. The island is known for its trout-filled lochs. Sea fishing is also good and local fishermen will take visitors out in their boats. Walking, bicycling, swimming, birdwatching, botany and relaxation are the chief occupations for visitors. There is a nine-hole golf course at **Arinagour**. This village has the main concentration of population, a trim place which lies round the western shore of Loch Eatharna, with twee cottages and gardens.

The economy depends mainly on farming, commercial fishing and tourism. A recent innovation is a small factory in Arinagour where a range of herbal skin-care products is made.

Breachacha Castle, recently restored and private, dates from the 15th-century, © 08793 444/353.

Getting There

Boats run from Oban, four times a week in summer and three times in winter, and take three hours. Boats also run from Tobermory, taking two hours. For details, contact Caledonian MacBrayne, © 0631 62285.

Tourist Information

Tourist Information Centre, **Oban**, © 0631 63122.

Where to Stay

inexpensive

Isle of Coll Hotel, © 08793 334, at the head of Arinagour Bay overlooking the Treshnish Islands, has six bedrooms and a Hebridean atmosphere. Also in Arinagour, with a restricted drink licence, **Tigh-na-Mara Guest House**, © 08793 354, is a modern house overlooking the bay with eight bedrooms. Self-catering places include: one chalet and three flats in Arinagour, c/o Janet Driver, Arinagour, Isle of Coll, © 08793 373; and a house, a bungalow and a bothy, c/o Mrs Stewart, Estate Office, Isle of Coll, © 08793 339.

Tiree

Tiree, southwest of Coll, is about 12 miles (19km) long, 7 (11km) at its widest, dwindling to less than 1 mile (1.5km) at its narrowest. Its name comes from *Tir Eth* (Land of Corn), dating from the days when it supplied corn to Iona. It is so low and flat that it has the Gaelic nickname *Tir fo Thuinn* (Land Below the Waves). It used to be famous for its snipe before much of the ground was drained. The highest hill, **Ben Hynish**, is a 480-foot (148m) pimple. It shares with Coll a reputation for glorious beaches, abundant wild flowers and birds, as well as a high average of sunshine. This, with its magnificent Atlantic rollers, has earned it the title 'Hawaii of the North'. Windsurfers come from all over Britain to compete in Tiree where conditions are first rate. During championship weeks, world-class windsurfing can be watched. Tiree also has a phenomenal population of hares.

A standing stone near **Balinoe** is thought to have been part of a Druid temple. Many of the island names are Norse in origin, dating from the 400 years of Norse occupation from about 890 to 1266. Among the many ancient remains scattered over Tiree is **Dun Mor Broch** on **Vaul Bay** on the north coast. A well-preserved ruin, it is one of the tall, hollow towers probably built for refuge from Norse and other invaders. It is 30 feet (9m) in diameter, its walls as much as 13 feet (4m) thick.

Gott Bay is a 3½-mile (5.5km) crescent of sand, backed by rich machair carpeted with wild flowers. **Hynish** has a small dry dock, flooded by an elaborate system of fresh water from springs. **Skerryvore Museum**, in the old signal tower at Hynish, tells the story of the construction of the Skerryvore Lighthouse, visible at the end of a telescope, built by the father of Robert Louis Stevenson. There is a young people's outdoor training centre based in the lighthouse cottages. On the north shore of **Balephetrish**, another good beach, *Clac á Choire* (Stone of the Corrie) is a large granite boulder perched on a rocky base, a relic from the Ice Age. Decorated with intriguing prehistoric carvings, it is known locally as the Ringing Stone because of the metallic note it produces when struck. It is said that when *Clac á Choire* shatters, Tiree will sink below the waves.

Views are marvellous all round the coast, especially those to the Treshnish Islands to the east with the aircraft-carrier-shaped *Bac Mor* (The Dutchman's Cap). One of the best places to see the birdlife is under the sheer cliffs below Carnan Mor in the south. Look for the distinctive 'greenstone' on the beaches, found also in Iona. Tiree has a nine-hole golf course.

Getting There

Loganair fly twice daily from Glasgow to Tiree, ✆ 041 889 3181.

The car ferry from Oban to Tiree usually calls at Coll on the way, a four-hour journey in all. Boats also run from Tobermory. Further information: Caledonian MacBrayne, ✆ 0631 62285.

Tourist Information

Tourist Information Centre, **Oban**, ✆ 0631 63122.

inexpensive

Scarinish Hotel, ✆ 08792 308, stands on the sea, with 11 rooms, one with private bathroom and two public bathrooms between the other 10. Good Highland hospitality.

Tiree Lodge Hotel, ✆ 08792 353/368, also overlooking the sea, has 12 bedrooms, seven with private bathrooms plus two public ones, and the same easy atmosphere.

Balephetrish Guest House, ✆ 08792 549, is a pebble-dash croft house, overlooking Balephetrish Bay, with four bedrooms and one bathroom.

The Glassery Guest House, with a restaurant, is at Sandaig on the west coast, ✆ 08792 684.

Central and Tayside

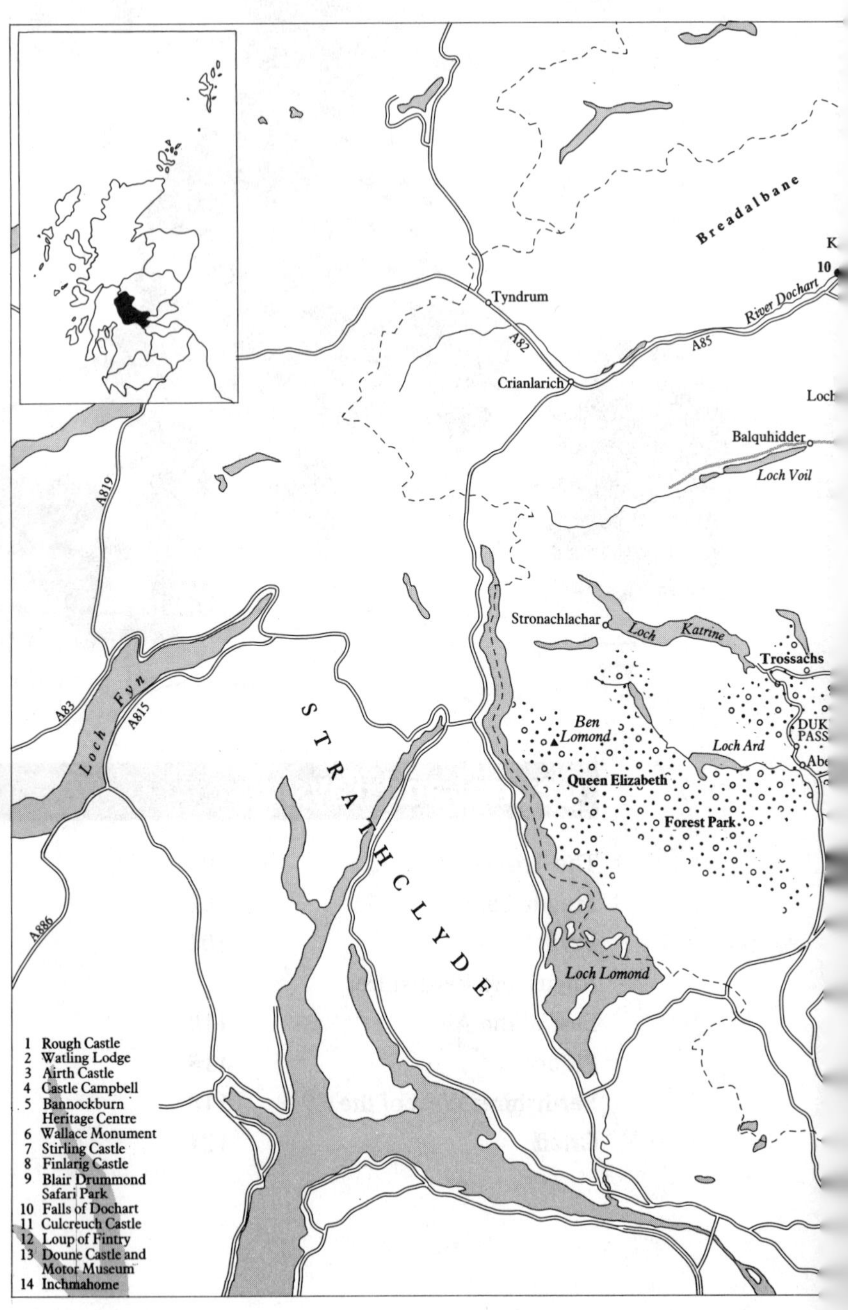
Breadalbane
Tyndrum
A82
River Dochart
A85
Crianlarich
Loch
Balquhidder
Loch Voil
A819
Stronachlachar
Loch Katrine
Trossachs
A83
Loch Fyn
A815
STRATHCLYDE
Ben Lomond
Loch Ard
Queen Elizabeth
Forest Park
A886
Loch Lomond
10
1 Rough Castle
2 Watling Lodge
3 Airth Castle
4 Castle Campbell
5 Bannockburn Heritage Centre
6 Wallace Monument
7 Stirling Castle
8 Finlarig Castle
9 Blair Drummond Safari Park
10 Falls of Dochart
11 Culcreuch Castle
12 Loup of Fintry
13 Doune Castle and Motor Museum
14 Inchmahome

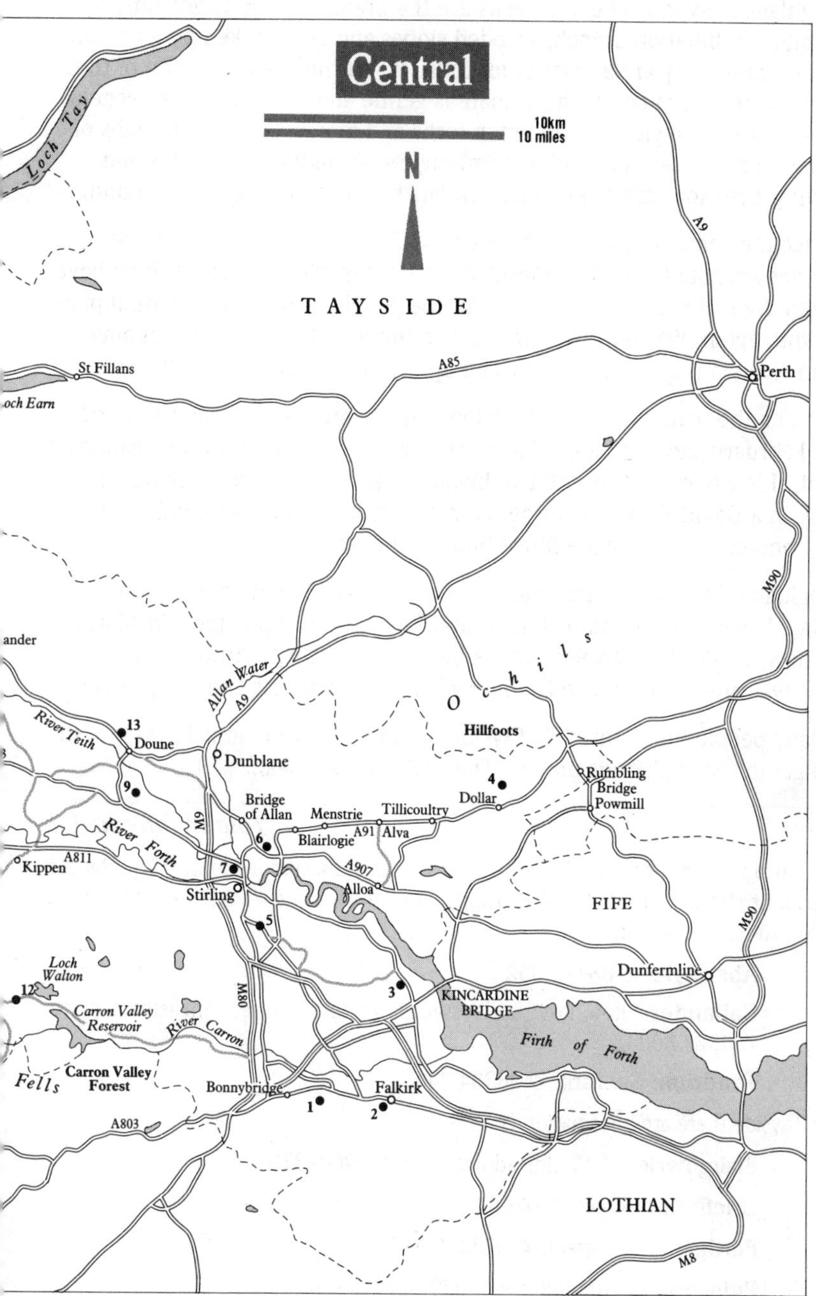
Central
10km
10 miles
N
TAYSIDE
Loch Tay
St Fillans
Loch Earn
A85
Perth
A9
M90
Ochils
Allan Water
A9
River Teith
13
Doune
Dunblane
Hillfoots
4
Rumbling Bridge
Powmill
9
Bridge of Allan
Menstrie
Tillicoultry
Dollar
M9
River Forth
6
Blairlogie
A91
Alva
Kippen
A811
7
A907
Stirling
Alloa
5
FIFE
M90
Loch Walton
12
M80
3
Dunfermline
KINCARDINE BRIDGE
Carron Valley Reservoir
River Carron
Firth of Forth
Fells
Carron Valley Forest
Bonnybridge
1
2
Falkirk
A803
LOTHIAN
M8

Central lies at the heart of Scotland. The long view, as you enter Central region from the south, is of hills on the horizon and the promise of Highlands beyond. The Trossachs are the prelude to the Highlands. A subtle combination of loch, wooded slopes and crag backed by green and russet hills, they are a magnet for tourists. Within the protection of these hills, with no sea coast, the climate is gentle and often hot. Lush vegetation carpets the glens, vivid green ferns and mosses, with great slabs of forest, hardwood and conifer, climbing the shoulders of the hills and giving a glorious display in autumn. Further north is rugged moorland.

Once the centre of the Pictish kingdom, Tayside's hill forts and stone circles are haunted by the ghosts of the Picts. Agriculture and fishing have been the main sources of income for the people who live in the rural parts of the region. Whisky distilling plays an important part in the economy and tourism is growing fast, backed up by the revival of old crafts.

Among the many local events to look out for are the Bull Sales in Perth, in February and October. Whether you are interested in cattle farming or not, this wonderful assembly of bucolics has faces as rich in character as any in a David Wilkie painting. Farmers come from far and wide and pay astronomic prices for the finest bulls in the land.

Highland Games are held in a number of places, including Blair Atholl in May, Perth and Birnam in August and Pitlochry in September. In May, the renowned Perth Festival of Arts is held and Pitlochry's Annual Summer Festival runs from May to October with plays, concerts and Fringe events.

Many people hurry through Tayside, blind to its attractions in their rush to get to the Highlands proper. They miss a great deal.

Tourist Information

The head office for Central Region is at Tourist Information Centre, Dumbarton Road, **Stirling**, ✆ 0786 475019, open all year round. The smaller centres, usually open April–Oct, are at:

Aberfoyle: ✆ 08772 352

Callander: Rob Roy & Trossachs Visitor Centre, Ancaster Square, ✆ 0877 30342

Tyndrum: Car Park, ✆ 08384 246

In Tayside there are information centres at:

Blairgowrie: 26 Wellmeadow, ✆ 0250 2960/3701

Crieff: High Street, ✆ 0764 2578

Perth: 45 High Street, ✆ 0738 38353

Pitlochry: 27 Atholl Road, ✆ 0796 2215/2751

Central

The Trossachs

Callander

It is here that you begin to feel the lure of the Highlands. Callander, 13 miles (21km) from Stirling and 34 miles (54km) from Crieff, is a good holiday centre for this area and a convenient centre for exploring the Highland parts of both Central and the western half of Tayside. It is a sturdy town to the east of the Trossachs, overshadowed by Ben Ledi. The town was rebuilt to its present wide design by military architects in the wake of Prince Charles, perhaps because it is easier for rebels to hold a town if the streets are narrow and houses close together. Television addicts might experience a sense of *déjà vu* here, for this was Dr Finlay's *Tannochbrae.* It also features in *The Country Diary of an Edwardian Lady.* From here you are within easy reach of the Trossachs and invigorating walks up through wooded glens onto the moors, with streams and rivers rushing down to fill Loch Lubnaig and the River Teith. Walk up to the Bracklinn Falls and remind yourself that Sir Walter Scott once rode his horse across here for a bet: or to the Falls of Leny and watch out for the water sprites, dancing in the spray-mist. In the summer, Callander is the stage for a variety of entertainments such as organized *céilidhs*, open-air pipe-band concerts and Highland dancing, as well as wildlife slide shows. Callander International Highland Games are in August.

Rob Roy & Trossachs Visitor Centre, in Ancaster Square (open daily, March–Dec), tells the life of the Highland folk hero. There's traditional entertainment on summer evenings.

There is no one particular thing to see in and around the Trossachs. The scenery is attractive if you have not already been spoiled by the Highlands. Because it is easily accessible from the densely populated industrial towns to the south, it has become popular and perhaps over-rated. Preferably explored outside the tourist season, this area is best appreciated on foot. Even in the high season, most sightseers prefer to stay within sight of their cars and few are on the prowl before ten o'clock in the morning. Avoid weekends. You have only to make an early start and get away from the roads to shake off the feeling of claustrophobia that can attack when there are too many people. Autumn and early spring are the best time in this land of forested ravines and gullies.

Although people tend to refer to the whole of the area between Callander and Lochearnhead on the east, and Loch Lomond on the west, as the Trossachs, in fact the Trossachs proper is only the gorge that runs from Loch Achray to Loch Katrine, a rugged pass barely a mile (1.5km) long. Locals will give you two meanings for this strange name: 'bristly country' or 'the crossing place'; no one is sure which is correct. Thick woods often obscure the view, but now and then you get a hint of the magic that enchanted Sir Walter Scott. The road twists and climbs through gorse and bracken and very green moor, past rhododendrons, with plenty of footpaths leading off.

Loch Katrine

Loch Katrine, 9 miles (14.5km) west of Callander, is the setting for Walter Scott's 'Lady of the Lake'. Ellen's Isle is named after the heroine of the poem. From 1 May to 28 September you can take a 45-minute trip in the Victorian steamer *Sir Walter Scott* and cruise along the length of the loch from Trossachs Pier to Stronachlachar. As you watch the passing shore, picture fair Ellen being wooed by the mysterious James FitzJames, who bore a remarkable resemblance to King James V, the monarch who enjoyed roaming the countryside disguised as the Goodman of Ballengiech. A prosaic guide will tell you that this loch is also Glasgow's water supply. Because of this, there is a large notice at the pier forbidding you to swim, paddle, picnic, fish, camp, light fires, or throw coins in the loch: though why anyone should feel the urge to throw their money into a loch is a mystery. There is a café at the pier and souvenir shops.

Aberfoyle

Aberfoyle guards the southern approach to the Trossachs and is a lively holiday centre. The road north, 'Duke's Pass', is too densely wooded to give more than a glimpse of the lochs below. Walter Scott made his first notes for *Rob Roy* in the dining-room of the village manse.

The Scottish Wool Centre (open daily: adm), in Aberfoyle, displays the history of sheep in Scotland over 2000 years and the story of wool, with films, sheepdog demonstrations, spinning and weaving, a children's farm, shop and restaurant.

Queen Elizabeth Forest Park Visitor Centre is a modern stone building just before you come down into Aberfoyle, with an ornamental lake and walks. In the lodge, displays illustrate the wild-life and vegetation of the park and there is a shop and café. You can walk right through the park to the eastern side of Loch Lomond. A single track road runs south from Rowardennan and you can climb Ben Lomond from here (3192 feet—982m), for a bird's-eye view. For those who like organized sightseeing, the 45,000-acre park includes a forest car trail, and a cycle-way.

Inchmahome Priory

Before going on north from Callander, take the A81 6 miles (9.5km) southwest to Lake of Menteith and take the ferry to Inchmahome Priory, a semi-roofed ruin on the largest island of three on the lake. (The weather dictates the running of the ferry, for which you pay, and the priory is open daily April–Sept: free.) Founded for Augustinians in 1238, the priory was a refuge for Mary, Queen of Scots for a short while before she was sent off to France to grow up out of range of Henry VIII's 'Rough Wooing'.

A surprising number of pilgrims come here to see the grave of Robert Cunninghame Graham, the 'rebel laird' of the estate, who died in Buenos Aires in 1936 aged 84. This flamboyant character travelled extensively in South America, Spain and Morocco; married a Chilean poetess; was imprisoned for 'illegal assembly' in 1887 (a Socialist demo in Trafalgar Square); was elected first president of the Scottish Labour Party in 1888 and wrote many travel books, essays and short stories. He was a close friend of both Joseph Conrad and W. H. Hudson.

The Farmlife Centre (open daily, May–Oct: adm) at Dunaverig Farm, 2 miles (3km) west of Thornhill, has traditional farm buildings with old farm implements, machinery and memorabilia, farm animals, an adventure playground, nature trails, a craft shop and tearoom.

Balquhidder

A famous man is Robin Hood,
The English ballad-singer's joy!
And Scotland has a thief as good,
An outlaw of as daring mood;
She has her brave Rob Roy . . .

from 'Rob Roy's Grave', by William Wordsworth

Another popular literary association in this area is at Balquhidder, on Loch Voil, north of the Trossachs, 10 miles (16km) or so north of Callander, and just west of the A84. This is where **Rob Roy** lived, died and is buried. This colourful, Robin Hood-like character, much romanticized by Scott, lived between 1671 and 1734, son of Macgregor of Glengyle. Rob Roy started life peacefully enough as a herdsman. But the Macgregors had been outlawed for their bloodthirsty habits and life was hard. He took to cattle rustling and smuggling, robbing the rich to pay the poor, and legends of his daring escapades and narrow escapes around Loch Katrine make good reading, even if, in reality, he was no doubt a rogue and a menace to his neighbours. He died uncharacteristically in his bed and was buried in Balquhidder churchyard. You can't miss the grave: the Clan Gregor have been unable to resist the temptation to 'do it up'.

Stronvar House (*see* Where to Stay, *below*) has a Bygones Museum and Balquhidder Visitor Centre (open daily March-Oct: adm) with a collection of memorabilia.

Lochearnhead

Fourteen miles (22.5km) north of Callander on the A84, you come to Lochearnhead, on the western corner of Loch Earn. There are several good hotels here and a boating and water-skiing centre. The loch runs 7 miles (11km) east to St Fillans, a ribbon of water sheltered by hills and an ideal place for a holiday. You may, if you wish, follow the A85 to Crieff (page121), 20 miles (32km) from Lochearnhead.

Where to Stay

expensive

Probably your best bet is **Roman Camp Hotel** in Callander, © 0877 30003. In 20 acres of garden beside the River Teith, on which you can fish, this hotel dates from 1625 and was a hunting lodge of the Dukes of Perth. It's only open from mid-March to mid-November. It's comfortable and the food is good.

moderate

The Lake Hotel, Port of Menteith, © 08775 258, stands right on Scotland's only lake, looking across to Inchmahome. They've retained much of the art deco furniture and decor and provide good food. The **Stronvar Country Hotel** in Balquhidder, © 08774 688, has four-poster beds in a laird's mansion with crow-stepped gables overlooking Loch Voil. With only five bedrooms, this hotel is peaceful. There is a Bygones Museum and Visitor Centre in the house.

Bridgend House Hotel, in Bridge Street, Callander, © 0877 30130, faces the road with a mock-Tudor face and has good views, four-poster beds and tries hard with its garden.

Forest Hills Hotel in Kinlochard, near Aberfoyle, © 08777 277, is a big country-house hotel with a multi-million-pound leisure centre, including a swimming pool, set in 20 acres of informal gardens overlooking Loch Ard. It also has luxury self-catering apartments.

inexpensive

Victorian **Brook Linn**, in Callander, © 0877 30103, has spectacular views from a two-acre garden. It is only open from March to November and the food isn't bad.

In Lochearnhead, **Clachan Cottage Hotel**, © 05673 229, is a charming old white cottagey building overlooking Loch Earn, with lovely views. What it may lack in sophistication is made up for in atmosphere.

For an exceptional bed and breakfast, in a charming house with a warm, friendly welcome, try Mrs Duke, Norrieston, Thornhill, © 0786 85 234.

Breadalbane

Called after the Earls of Breadalbane (emphasis on the middle syllable) who used to own most of it, the land north of the Trossachs is your overture to the Highlands. In the days before the clan system was abolished, many bitter battles were fought for supremacy over these hills and moors. Campbells, MacNabs, Macgregors and MacLarens contested every inch, committing ghastly atrocities to wreak revenge on each other. You are likely to find a different sort of tourist here: more energetic, striding out with knapsack and climbing boots. It is rugged territory, where you may see roe deer and golden eagles, tumbling rivers, spectacular falls, and dark lochs. For botanists there are masses of wild flowers and unusual plants. Cut by the glens of the rivers Dochart and Lochay, and veined by the network of burns that pour out of the hills to feed them, this is walking and climbing country, backed by the massive hills of Strathclyde to the northwest.

Killin

Killin is about 7 miles (11km) north of Lochearnhead, a couple of miles off the A85, on the A827. This attractive village with hotels, shops and eating places has an almost alpine feel to it, especially when there is snow on the hills. It sits astride an old bridge, under which the Falls of Dochart carry the River Dochart in a tumble of falls and rapids, swirling down through the village into Loch Tay, long and deep between two ranges of hills (*see* p.120 for the Ben Lawers Visitor Centre, on the north side of Loch Tay). Aberfeldy is 25 miles (40km) from Killin along the AA827 (page 119).

On **Inchbuie**, the lower of two islets below the old bridge in Killin, is the burial ground of the MacNabs, an aggressive clan who ruled the district until they emigrated to Canada in the 19th century, forever at loggerheads with the neighbouring clans of Neish and Gregor. The tourist information centre has the key to the burial ground.

Finlarig Castle, hidden among trees on a primrose-carpeted mound, half a mile (1km) north of Killin past the cemetery, is a dangerous ruin now. It was the seat of the sinister sounding Black Duncan of the Cowl, a fierce Campbell chief. All that remains is a stark keep and a separate building with a coat of arms on it, possible a chapel. Close to the tower, you can still see a gruesome 'beheading-pit'. It is said that it was the privilege of the gentry to be beheaded, while the common people were hanged from a tree. Beyond the ruin are two 20th-century graves with simple Celtic crosses: Sir Gavin Campbell, Marquess of Breadalbane, and his wife of 50 years, Lady Alma.

Crianlarich

From Killin the A85 goes about 11 miles (17.5km) west to Crianlarich, tucked in among the moors, about 13 miles (21km) southwest of Killin. Isolated but by no means deserted, it has the somewhat incongruously urban-sounding title of 'railway-junction'. This is where the railway lines from Oban and Fort William join up on their progress south. (The West Highland Line, from Glasgow to Mallaig, takes you through such glorious scenery that it is worth travelling on it for the journey itself.) There are usually a number of people striding around Crianlarich in climbing boots and knapsacks: the 90-mile (144km) West Highland Way passes by on its way from Milngavie (pronounced Mull-guy) to Fort William and this is a favourite staging post.

Three road-routes also meet in Crianlarich: south to Loch Lomond, northwest to Oban and Fort William, or northeast to Pitlochry.

Tyndrum

Five miles (8km) north, on the A82, brings you to Tyndrum, nestling in a glacial valley, gateway to the Highlands. This is another junction of three roads: south, north and west, where the cattle drovers used to meet up on their way to markets at Falkirk and Crieff. Some years ago Tyndrum gained a 'gold rush' status: extensive gold mining in the area led to the speculation that this was about to become an important gold centre in Britain and some rather hideous hotels were built. The gold fever seems to have died down now, but the hotels remain. Tyndrum is now a place to stop off *en route* to the western Highlands and for walkers and climbers. There are walks in all directions and several hills rising to heights above 3000 feet (923m).

moderate

Ardeonaig Hotel, near Killin, © 05672 400, is a drovers' inn, dating from 1680, on the south side of Loch Tay. Its standards have improved since the drovers used to come here. **Morenish Lodge Hotel,** also near Killin, © 05672 258, is a former shooting lodge with panoramic views over Loch Tay, and private fishing rights. Open from April to October, this is a friendly, cosy place.

inexpensive

Clachaig Hotel, Killin, © 05672 270, overlooking the bridge, is good value. The bedrooms are all en-suite, and there's a cosy bar-restaurant, the Salmon Lie, in a converted smithy, with stone walls, a big log stove and reasonable food.

In Crianlarich, try **Portnellan House**, © 08383 284, a 19th-century shooting lodge overlooking Loch Dochart, with clay-pigeon shooting and free fishing. As well as the hotel, which only has three bedrooms, there are also 17 rooms in chalets on the surrounding hillside. **Invervey Hotel**, Tyndrum, © 08384 219, is a friendly, family-run hotel.

Tayside

Perth

Anyone visiting Perth for the first time should have Walter Scott's *The Fair Maid of Perth* as a companion. The city is 17 miles (27km) north of Kinross and as you come down into it from the motorway, you get a fine view of the town, spread out below, round the Tay. This view, 'new' since the building of the motorway, is in fact the old one, extolled by Scott in the first few pages of introduction to *The Fair Maid.* Two wide green parks, North and South Inch, unfold on either side, with a collage of spires reaching for the sky.

Perth was the first place where it was easy to bridge the river. It was a thriving port in the old days and is now an important livestock market at the centre of a productive agricultural area. Its fine setting earned Perth the title 'The Fair City' in the past, and a recent transformation has done much to restore it to that status. In the days before conservation became fashionable, many of its old buildings were replaced by utilitarian monsters that are little short of architectural vandalism, but now, with traffic-free shopping streets and award-winning floral displays, Perth is once again an attractive town. If you poke around you will find traces of the past and there are some very fine late-Georgian terraces, especially round the Inches, and nice vistas of the river. When a new Marks and Spencer store was being built in the High Street some time ago, the remains of a medieval market were unearthed, resulting in a valuable stay of execution. A new by-pass has considerably eased traffic congestion in the town centre.

Traces of an old city wall indicate that there was a Roman camp here, although Perth doesn't appear in the records until the 12th century. A devastating flood destroyed Old Perth in 1210 and William the Lion granted a Royal Charter to the town that was built in its place the same year. It was the capital of Scotland for a while, until the middle of the 15th century.

The Battle of the Clans

Among the city's more colourful events was the Battle of the Clans, so graphically woven by Scott into the convoluted plot of *The Fair Maid*. This was a contest between the Clans Chattan and Quhele (pronounced Kay), to establish who should take precedence in battle—a hotly disputed honour in those swashbuckling days. Thirty men from each side were to fight in a tournament on the North Inch, watched by King Robert III, his wife and court. One of the Clan Chattan lost his nerve at the last moment and fled. The rule was that the two sides must be matched man-for-man, so a blacksmith, small and bandylegged, offered to stand in for the price of half a French crown. All but one of the Quhele Clan were slaughtered. Among the survivors of the Chattans was the blacksmith, who had done more than anyone else to secure victory.

The highly dubious drama of the Gowrie Conspiracy took place in 1600, in the now demolished Gowrie House. According to James VI, the Earl of Gowrie and his brother, Alexander Ruthven, lured him to an upstairs room in the house and tried to tie him up. He shouted for his lords through an open window and was rescued, while Gowrie and Ruthven were killed in the flurry. The whole affair was shrouded in mystery and speculation, with hints of homosexual motives mingled with hints that the king set the thing up in order to get rid of the brothers, whose ruthless political ambition was notorious.

Perth Art Gallery and Museum (open daily except Sundays: free), in George Street, has local history displays and an exhibition showing the growth of the whisky industry which plays an important part in the economy of the area.

St John's Church (open daily) was restored in 1923, with a War Memorial Chapel designed by Robert Lorimer. It dates from the 15th century and is on the site of a church built in the 12th century. Edward III is said to have killed his brother, the Earl of Cornwall, in that earlier church in 1335. John Knox preached one of his iconoclastic sermons in St John's in 1559, urging his followers to purge the churches of idolatry; this sermon led to the destruction of many of the churches and monasteries in the area and helped to fuel the Reformation. This church alone had at least 40 richly decorated altars, dedicated to saints. A few of the treasures rescued from the purgers include the 16th-century German Cellini Cup, given to Mary of Guise-Lorraine by the Pope, 17th-century chalices and a 16th-century baptismal basin.

The Fair Maid's House (open daily except Sun: free, gallery shut in Jan) is behind Charlotte Street, in North Port, and was the home of virtuous Catharine Glover, The Fair Maid of Perth. One of the oldest buildings in the town, it holds a series of month-long

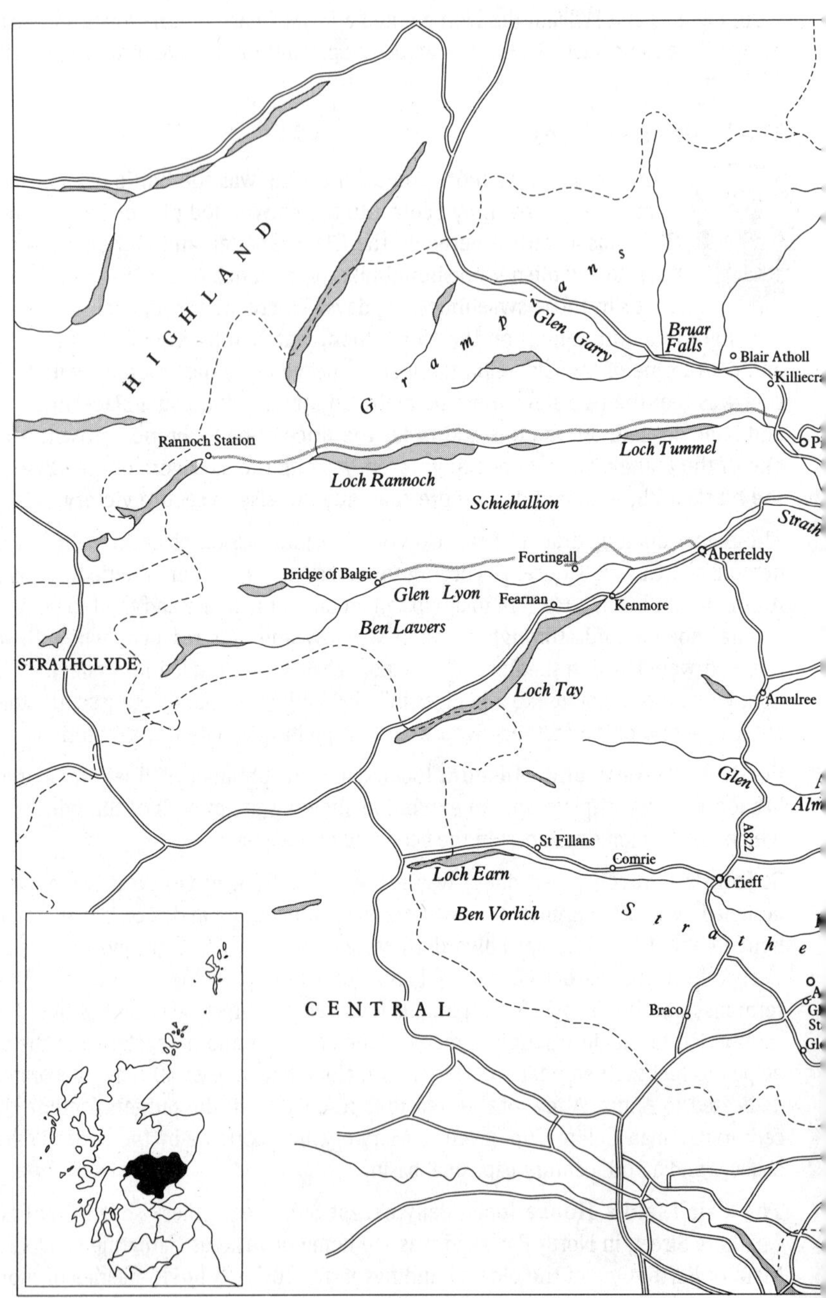
HIGHLAND
Grampians
Glen Garry
Bruar Falls
Blair Atholl
Rannoch Station
Loch Tummel
Loch Rannoch
Schiehallion
Fortingall
Aberfeldy
Bridge of Balgie
Glen Lyon
Fearnan
Kenmore
Ben Lawers
STRATHCLYDE
Loch Tay
Amulree
Glen
A822
St Fillans
Comrie
Loch Earn
Crieff
Ben Vorlich
Strathe
CENTRAL
Braco

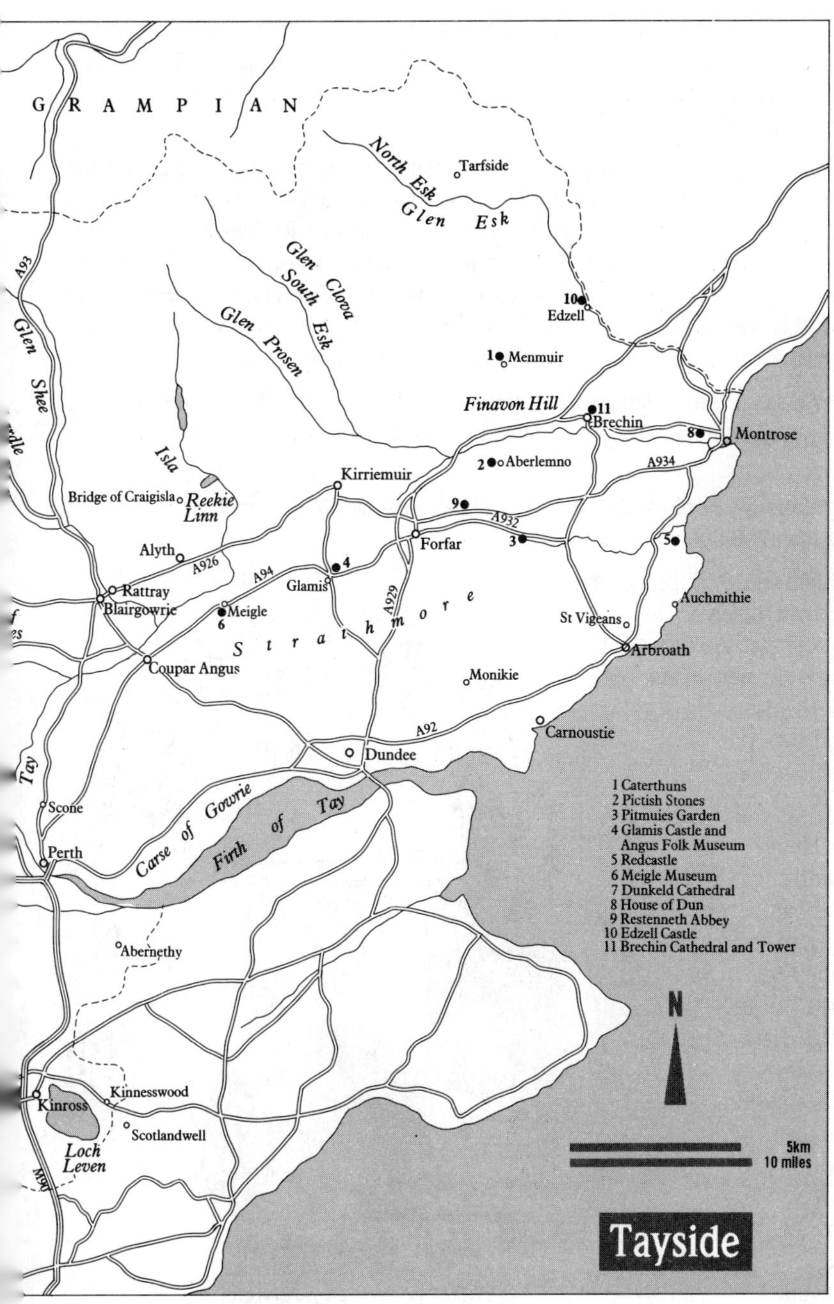
GRAMPIAN
North Esk
Tarfside
Glen Esk
Glen Clova
South Esk
Glen Prosen
Glen Shee
Isla
10
Edzell
1 Menmuir
Finavon Hill
11
Brechin
8
Montrose
2 Aberlemno
A934
Kirriemuir
Bridge of Craigisla
Reekie Linn
9
A932
Forfar
3
5
Alyth
A926
A94
4
Glamis
Rattray
Blairgowrie
Meigle
6
Strathmore
A929
Auchmithie
St Vigeans
Arbroath
Coupar Angus
Monikie
Carnoustie
A92
Dundee
Tay
Scone
Carse of Gowrie
Firth of Tay
Perth
Abernethy
Kinross
Kinnesswood
Scotlandwell
Loch Leven
M90
1 Caterthuns
2 Pictish Stones
3 Pitmuies Garden
4 Glamis Castle and Angus Folk Museum
5 Redcastle
6 Meigle Museum
7 Dunkeld Cathedral
8 House of Dun
9 Restenneth Abbey
10 Edzell Castle
11 Brechin Cathedral and Tower
N
5km
10 miles
Tayside

exhibitions of contemporary Scottish crafts and paintings. Perhaps a little over-restored, it is nevertheless an intriguing place. There is a craft shop.

Blackfriars Street, nearby, was the site of the now long-vanished Blackfriars Monastery, where James I was murdered in 1437. The story of Catherine Douglas, Catherine 'Bar-Lass', who supposedly tried to bar the door to the murderers by using her arm as a bolt, is a 16th-century invention.

Balhousie Castle, a 15th-century Scottish Baronial castle beyond Rose Terrace on the west side of North Inch, has been restored. Former home of the Earls of Kinnoull, it is the Regimental Headquarters of the Black Watch and contains its **Regimental Museum** (open weekdays, and Sun in summer: free). The Black Watch was raised in 1739 to help the government pacify the rebellious Highlanders. There is a comprehensive display of the history of this famous regiment, with uniforms, weapons, pictures, documents, photographs and trophies, all recording its many honours and triumphs.

Dewars Whisky Plant dominates the western suburbs of Perth. Free conducted tours during the week demonstrate how Scotland's most popular export finds its way into bottles.

The Perth Leisure Pool has the reputation of being the best in Scotland, with more than 700,000 visitors a year.

Kinnoull Hill rises 729 feet (224m) above the town, barely a mile (1.5km) to the east. An easy climb gives a bird's eye view of the geological 'Highland Line' that divides the Highlands from the Lowlands.

Fairways Heavy Horse Centre is at Kinfauns, about 2 miles (3km) east of Perth on the A85, between the Tay and Kinnoull Hill. Here, you can see great Clydesdales and shire horses and their foals, ride in waggons, or watch video shows of horses and farriers at work.

Replica of the Stone of Scone

Elcho Castle (always accessible) is a ruin 4 miles (6.5km) east of Perth. This is one of the more interesting of the later Scottish castles, having been both defensive and incorporating palace-like comforts. The square tower with a crow-stepped gable dates from the 15th century. The huge kitchen has a fireplace as big as a small room and there are traces of fine plasterwork in the hall on the first floor.The bedrooms above had en-suite garderobes. James III granted the lands of Elcho to John de Wemyss in 1468. A subsequent Sir John de Wemyss became the first Earl of Wemyss under Charles I but sided with the Parliamentarians in the Civil War.

Scone Palace

Scone Palace (open daily, Easter–Oct, or by arrangement, © 0738 52300: adm) is 2 miles (3km) north of Perth on the A93. Pronounced 'Scoon', the palace is a 19th-century restoration of 16th-century and earlier buildings, with battlements, a toy fort façade and the original gateway. In 1297, Edward I stole the Stone of Scone and took it to London. (*See* 'History', p.33.)

The abbey and palace that stood here in the 16th century were destroyed by John Knox's followers, after he had denounced 'idolatry' in his sermon from St John's in 1559.

The palace contains French furniture, including Marie Antoinette's writing desk; 16th-century needlework, including bed hangings embroidered by Mary, Queen of Scots; porcelain; 17th- and 18th-century ivories; 18th-century clocks. The walls are lined with Lyons silk. There is a coffee shop serving home-baked food, a gift shop and gardens with a playground and pinetum.

Where to Stay

expensive

If luxury is what you seek, particularly if you are a golfer, **The Murrayshall Hotel** at Scone, © 0738 51171, will suit you. This country-house hotel stands in 300 acres of parkland with an 18-hole golf course. It has an award-winning chef, and provides tennis, croquet and bowls, and, if you book ahead, shooting, fishing and riding.

moderate

Ballathie House Hotel at Kinclaven, 10 miles (16km) north of Perth, © 025 083 268, is an overgrown shooting lodge in its own estate overlooking the Tay; open from early March to mid-January. It has four-poster or canopied beds, ancestral furniture and paintings, *haute cuisine*, croquet, tennis, putting, trout and salmon fishing, shooting and all mod cons. (The shooting and fishing must be booked ahead.) It even has its own helipad for tycoons. Prices vary seasonally and can be expensive.

The Royal George, Tay Street, Perth, © 0738 24455, got its Royal appendage from a visit paid by Queen Victoria in 1848. It is a Trust House of the good old-fashioned style, in the moderate to expensive price bracket, right on the river.

The Station Hotel, Leonard Street, © 0738 24141, is one of Perth's dowagers—comfortable and reasonably priced with four crowns. Modern **Isle of Skye Hotel**, Dundee Road, © 0738 24471, is popular.

inexpensive

Salutation Hotel, 34 South Street, Perth, © 0738 30066, was established in 1699 and was Prince Charles's headquarters for a while. Considerably more comfortable today, the hotel has the largest Adam-style window in Scotland in its dining room. Modernization has obliterated all trace of the past, but you can see the Prince's ops room, now a meeting room.

If you are an outward-bounder and like a cheap, organized holiday, try **Kinfauns Castle,** a couple of miles east of Perth on the A85, © 0738 20777, but don't expect to be pampered. Another baronial pile with battlements, in 40 acres of woodland, Kinfauns is owned by the Countrywide Holiday Association. They lay on walking and outdoor holidays, with group-leaders and a host and hostess who arrange your evening entertainment.

Eating Out

Timothy's, 24 St John's Street, Perth, © 0738 26641, is a cheap, informal restaurant, half-Scottish and half-Danish, where you'll eat well.

Angus and Perthshire: East of the A9

Angus covers most of that part of Tayside that lies to the east of the A9, north of the Firth of Tay. The coastal plain consists of gently rolling farmland in the Carse of Gowrie, running back up into the Sidlaw Hills where winter can linger into spring, and from whose southern slopes you can get magnificent views across the firth of Tay to northern Fife. The coast is rugged red sandstone with sandy bays. The rest of the land east of the A9 is Perthshire, and here you are in the Highlands with all the wonderful range of scenery they contain. Perth is the hub from which all the following routes lead.

Perth to Forfar via Glamis

Coupar Angus

Coupar Angus, about 12 miles (19km) southwest of Meigle, is in the Tay valley and is a good centre from which to tour this area. It is a market town, very typical of the area and so called to distinguish it from Cupar Fife. Only the gatehouse remains of a once-flourishing Cistercian abbey, beside the Dundee Road. It was built about 1164 by Malcolm IV and destroyed in 1559. The parish church stands on the site of the old monks' chapel and you can still see the remains of the original piers from the nave.

Meigle

Meigle, nearly 4 miles (6km) northeast of Coupar Angus, is the legendary burial place for King Arthur's poor faithless Guinevere. It also has a remarkable collection of early Christian Pictish stones. **Meigle Museum** (open daily except Sun: adm), in the old school, contains about 30 stones, from the 6th to the 10th centuries, almost all found in or near the old churchyard. The carvings disprove any idea that the Picts were half-naked savages. Instead, they show elaborate clothing, weapons and equipment and an unquestionably civilized culture. The large stone in the centre is thought to be Queen Guinevere's gravestone and portrays *Daniel in the Lion's Den*, possibly symbolizing Guinevere being torn apart by wild beasts. Beautifully displayed, with a descriptive leaflet, these stones stir the imagination.

Glamis

The A9 takes you next to Glamis (pronounced *Glahms*), about 7 miles (11km) northeast, a hamlet in a wooded hollow just off the main road.

Glamis Castle (open daily, April–Oct or by appointment, © 030784 242: adm) is approached down a wide tree-lined avenue and is so familiar from photographs that the reality is almost an anti-climax. From the top of the avenue the pink-grey castle stands out against the distant hills, all angles, towers, wings, turrets and heraldic embellishments. It is grand rather than beautiful.

The land was granted to the Lyon family, Earls of Strathmore, by King Robert II in 1372, and it was their descendants who became Earls of Glamis, Kinghorne and Strathmore. Glamis has the reputation for being the most haunted castle in Scotland and many are the spine-chilling tales that have been born from its stones. No one dares to enter the sealed crypt where huge red-bearded Beardie Crawford played cards with the Devil on the Sabbath; no one can account for the window that looks out from a chamber that does not exist on an upper floor.

The present castle dates mostly from the 17th century with bits of the older building incorporated, including King Malcolm's room where Malcolm II is said to have died. The oldest part is Duncan's Hall, traditionally the setting for Shakespeare's Macbeth.

There are formal 19th-century Italian gardens and extensive parkland. A licensed restaurant sells light lunches and teas and there is a gift shop, a gallery shop selling paintings by Scottish artists, a garden shop and a playground.

The Angus Folk Museum (open Easter weekend; daily, 1 May–30 Sept: adm) is in Kirkwynd in the village beyond the castle, past the Strathmore Arms and a thatched cottage that is a rare sight among the pantiles and slates in this area. In the care of the National Trust for Scotland, the museum is in a terrace of picturesque early 19th-century cottages, meticulously restored in 1957, with stone-slabbed roofs and flagged floors. There are over 1000 things to see, including a kitchen from 1807 with all the original fittings and furnishings, and a collection of agricultural tools and equipment. The museum gives a picture of how country people lived, up to 200 years ago. There is even a Victorian manse parlour.

The Glamis Stone is in the garden of today's manse, opposite the museum, visible from the road. This 9-foot (3m) high stone has intricate Pictish carvings. It is also called King Malcolm's Stone, from the belief that Malcolm II was buried here in 1034, having died in the castle. In fact, the stone is of an earlier date, possibly 9th century.

If ancient stones are what you enjoy, you will find plenty more nearby including **St Orland's**, or the **Crossans Stone**, standing 7 feet (2m) tall in a field by the railway 2 miles (3km) to the north. This slender, repaired stone has carvings showing men in a boat.

Forfar

Twenty-seven miles (43km) northwest of Perth, along the A94, the busy town of Forfar has little left to see of its history. Once a thriving jute and linen milling centre, it now produces synthetic textiles, as well as tartans and tweeds. The **town and county hall** is early 19th century, designed by William Playfair, with a splendid council chamber in which you can see paintings by Raeburn, Romney, Hoppner and Opie. The town centre is attractive, with cobbled streets and warm sandstone buildings swirling round an island on which the town hall stands. Just round the corner in West High Street is the **Meffan Institute** (open daily except Sun: free) which houses, as well as the library, a small museum of local interest, in which you can see the dreadful **Forfar Bridle**. This is a metal collar, hinged to clip round the neck, with a prong in front to gag the unfortunate women who wore it while being burned at the stake as witches in the 17th century. Forfar Loch, west of the town, is a so-called pleasure park, with picnic areas around an uninspiring small stretch of water.

From Forfar, you can return to Perth via Blairgowrie.

Forfar to Perth via Blairgowrie

Kirriemuir

If you take the northern route back to Perth from Forfar on the A926, Kirriemuir is 6 miles (9.5km) to the west, on a hillside with a straggle of narrow streets lined by picturesque houses. This jute manufacturing town is where J. M. Barrie was born. He renamed it 'Thrums' in the series of novels he wrote based on small-town life in Scotland. The house where Barrie was born, 9 Brechin Road, is maintained by the National Trust for Scotland as a museum called **Barrie's Birthplace** (open Easter weekend; daily, 1 May–30 Sept: adm). It contains a nostalgic collection of manuscripts, letters, personal possessions and mementoes of the writer who belonged to that group known as 'The Kailyard School' at the end of the 19th century. These Kailyard writers exploited a sentimental, romantic image of life in Scotland that brought them a certain amount of contempt from their critics. Their naivety was blown by George Douglas, in *The House with Green Shutters* which, according to J.B. Priestley, 'let the east wind into this cosy chamber of fiction'. However much people may despise whimsicality, no one can deny the talent of the man who created Peter Pan, Mary Rose, Dear Brutus and the Admirable Crichton. James Barrie was made a Freeman of Kirriemuir and was buried in the churchyard in 1937.

A **Camera Obscura** in the Barrie Pavilion above the town gives a panoramic view of Strathmore by an ingenious method of reflection.

You should make time to go north from Kirriemuir to explore some of the glens that stretch back into the Grampians—Glen Clova, Glen Prosen, Glen Isla; each with a mass of tributary glens like the veins of a feather, with tumbling rivers and tranquil lochs, hidden away among the hills.

Reekie Linn

It is worth making a detour from Kirriemuir to see Reekie Linn. It is about 9 miles (14.5km) due west and if you've got a good map, the back roads are very attractive. Park at the Bridge of Craigisla and take the footpath through the wood. Reekie Linn is a dramatic waterfall haunted by water sprites and kelpies. The River Isla, constricted by narrow rock cliffs, pours into a deep gorge in a single cascade, the spray rising like smoke, stirring the dark waters of the river into tumult. The path takes you to a spur jutting out level with the top of the falls. If you suffer from vertigo you should go along to the right and see them from further off.

Barry Hill is beside the road about 3 miles (4.5km) south of the falls, just short of Alyth. It is a short, steep climb through whins and bracken, over turf honeycombed by rabbits. On top are the ruins of a large Pictish fort in a shallow depression. The oblong shape is very clear with round turrets and ramparts. Romance clings to these stones. If you believe the Scottish versions of the Arthurian legends, Queen Guinevere was imprisoned in this fort by King Arthur because of her love affair with a Pictish prince. If this was true, the captive queen had glorious views to comfort her.

Alyth, below the hill, is a pleasant little milling town bisected by the Alyth Burn.

Blairgowrie

Blairgowrie, 5 miles (8km) southwest of Alyth, beside fast-flowing Ericht Water, is a popular tourist centre all the year round, much favoured by golfers. Old mills still stand along the river, some derelict, some converted into dwellings and at least one open to the public. In summer there are the Highlands to explore and in winter you can ski at Glenshee. The fertile soil produces abundant raspberry crops. This is magic walking country: fast-flowing rivers slice through steep mountain glens, with sudden glimpses of snow-capped peaks, massing on the horizon.

Glenshee

Glenshee runs north from Blairgowrie into the Grampian region and is one of Scotland's main skiing centres. Its challenging pistes are often icy and demanding. Weather conditions can be extreme, roads sometimes becoming impassable in snow. For skiing information, ring the Glenshee Information Officer, Blairgowrie, © 0250 5509.

From spring to autumn, the A93 to Braemar—Britain's highest main road—is a spectacular route and in the summer you can take the chairlift up to the top of Cairnwell mountain for panoramic views and invigorating walks. **Strathardle** forks off west of Glenshee from the **Bridge of Cally** where the River Ardle and Black Water converge: another good launching pad for climbers and walkers.

From Blairgowrie, it is about 16 miles (26km) back to Perth on the A93.

Birnam

Be lion-mettled, proud, and take no care
Who chafes, who frets, or where conspirers are:
Macbeth shall never vanquish'd be until
Great Birnam wood to high Dunsinane Hill
Shall come against him.

William Shakespeare, *Macbeth*, Act 4, scene 1.

Birnam, about 14 miles (22km) north of Perth, bypassed by the A9, is a village familiar to all lovers of Shakespeare. From Birnam Hill you can see Dunsinnan, or Dunsinane, 12 miles (19km) to the southeast—opinions and tastes dictate the spelling. Macbeth, in his castle on 'Dunsinane Hill', confidently believed the witches' prophecy that he was immortal until 'Birnam Forest come to Dunsinane'. Meanwhile, Malcolm was busy instructing his soldiers to camouflage themselves with branches from the trees in Birnam Wood and march on Dunsinane. There are remains of a fort on Dunsinnan Hill, thought to be Macbeth's. Some of the trees in Birnam Wood are thought to date from the original forest.

Dunkeld

Fifteen miles (24km) north of Perth, just off the A9 route, Dunkeld is an old cathedral town on the banks of the Tay, sheltered by wooded hills and much favoured by fishermen. Its history goes back to when it was a refuge for Pictish kings. Being close to the ancient capital of Scone, Dunkeld became a stronghold of Columban monks who founded an abbey here in 729, having been driven from Iona by Norsemen. They enshrined holy relics of St Columba in their abbey. The saint himself is believed to have come to Dunkeld in the 6th century and to have founded some sort of religious establishment with the help of St Mungo. There is a St Colms Well nearby.

Dunkeld suffered badly during the Covenanting Wars and it was here that the Cameronians, extreme Covenanters, held the town against a troop of Highlanders in 1689. Triumphant after Killiecrankie, the Highlanders stormed the town, whereupon the Cameronians set fire to most of its buildings, driving the Highlanders out and securing eventual supremacy for William and Mary.

Dunkeld Cathedral (open daily: free) is a substantial ruin beside the River Tay. The choir has been restored and is the parish church. The nave and great northwest tower date from the 15th century. The original medieval cathedral, which took two centuries to build, was only entire for about 60 years before the Reformers reduced it to a roofless ruin. Ironically, it contains the rather splendid tomb and effigy of the Wolf of Badenoch, who was a keen destroyer of churches, including Elgin Cathedral.

The Little Houses, lining Cathedral Street, were built after the destruction of the town in 1689 and were saved from demolition by the National Trust for Scotland in 1950. Well restored and privately occupied, they form a delightful approach to the cathedral and give the old part of the town a unique character.

The Dunkeld Smokehouse at Springfields sells excellent smoked products and will also smoke any of the fish you may have been lucky enough to catch.

Loch of the Lowes

A couple of miles northeast of Dunkeld, Loch of the Lowes is a nature reserve, where you can watch ospreys from a hide. These large brown and white sea-eagles, cousins to the falcon, are common in America, where they nest on every navigation mark in the estuaries. Here, they are a rare, protected species, though their numbers are increasing slightly now that their nesting sites are so fiercely protected.

Pitlochry

Pitlochry, 13 miles (21km) north of Dunkeld on the A9, is in the middle of Scotland, cradled by hills, with Ben Vrackie (2759 feet—849m) looming to the north. With above-average hours of sunshine and below-average rainfall, this has been a popular holiday town since Queen Victoria, staying at Blair Atholl, declared it to be one of the finest resorts in Europe. This royal stamp of approval resulted in many fine houses and mansions being built in the area, with spas that are now hotels. Today, it is hard to believe it was once a remote hamlet. There were no roads north of Dunkeld until General Wade built his network of military roads after the Jacobite uprisings, linking the trouble-spots in the Highlands. In spite of its popularity—it gets very crowded in the summer and caters well for its tourists—it manages to retain a leisurely, strolling atmosphere, a perfect centre from which to explore the Highlands. The rivers Tummel and Garry converge from their valleys into Loch Faskally, 2 miles (3km) to the north, and hurry through the town to join the Tay at Ballinluig to the south. The main street is cheerful with its bright façades, hotels and shops, distilleries and, not far off the road, hydroelectric development. Pitlochry runs a summer school in July with a host of activities ranging from pottery to clay pigeon shooting. There is also a Gala Day in July.

The Pitlochry Festival Theatre was founded in 1951. Its lively summer programme includes drama, concerts and foyer events and you can also see exhibitions of Scottish art.

The Hydroelectric Dam and Fish Ladder, open all year, has an observation chamber from which to see the ingenious method of ensuring the salmon cycle is not broken. Thousands of salmon are 'lifted' annually and you can watch them through glass walls. Sometimes you can see sealice clinging to the fish, showing that they have come fresh from the sea. There is also a **Visitor Centre and Exhibition**, with a description of all the activities throughout the country and in the Loch Tummel group in particular. Few can deny that the hydroelectric schemes often enhance rather than spoil the Highland scenery.

Blair Atholl Distillery, on the southern edge of Pitlochry, has a visitor centre (open daily, Easter–Oct; daily except Sun for the rest of the year: free). There are conducted tours with a free dram, audio-visual shows, a coffee shop, a bar with snacks and a shop selling whisky.

Edradour Distillery (open daily, Easter–31 Oct: free) is the smallest in Scotland, hidden in the hills, less than 3 miles (4.5km) east of Pitlochry. It was founded in 1825 by local farmers, a small complex of white-washed buildings under neat grey slate roofs, tucked into a hollow beside the Edradour Burn. After a conducted tour of the distillery, virtually unchanged since Victorian times, you get your free dram in a cosy barn before a peat and log fire.

Walking in this area is endlessly rewarding; every path you choose reveals fresh beauty and unexpected views. There are waterfalls and gorges, festooned with lush ferns; woods and hills; rivers running fast over shallow rocky beds.

Pass of Killiecrankie

Six thousand Veterans practised in War's game,
Tried Men, at Killicranky were arrayed
Against an equal Host that wore the Plaid,
Shepherds and Herdsmen.—Like a whirlwind came
The Highlanders, the slaughter spread like flame

from a sonnet by William Wordsworth

The road north from Pitlochry climbs along the upper slope of the Pass of Killiecrankie, a recently opened section of road that cost a great deal of money and took considerable skill to engineer. It clings precariously to the densely wooded gorge where, far below, the River Garry cuts its way through to join up with the Tummel. At the far end of the pass about 3 miles (4.5km) from Pitlochry, there is a National Trust for Scotland **Visitor Centre** (open daily from 1 May to 31 Oct: free) with a pictorial description of the history of the Battle of Killiecrankie. Graham of Claverhouse, 'Bonnie Dundee' and his brave Jacobite Highlanders charged the British Army under General Mackay in 1689, in an attempt to depose William of Orange and restore James VII/II to the throne. The British were almost annihilated by the Highlanders, but Claverhouse was mortally wounded and his death, leaving his army leaderless, ensured the subsequent victory of the government troops three weeks later at Dunkeld.

You can walk down to the river from the visitor centre, past the terrifying **Soldier's Leap**, an 18-foot (5.5m) jump across the gorge, said to have been made by one of Mackay's soldiers, escaping from the Highlanders. Queen Victoria walked along this path and noted its great beauty in her diary in 1844.

Blair Atholl

Three miles (4.5km) north of Killiecrankie, the new road bypasses the village of Blair Atholl giving a good view of **Blair Castle** from across the river. This white, turreted baronial castle (open daily, Easter–mid-Oct: adm) is the home of the Duke of Atholl, dating from 1269 though much Victorianized. It has seen many royal visitors: Mary, Queen of Scots stayed here; Prince Charles accepted hospitality here on his march south in 1745; Cumberland garrisoned his troops here the following year, during which time the Duke of Atholl's brother, Lord George Murray, inflicted severe damage on the castle in his attempts to win it back; Claverhouse stayed here before the Battle of Killiecrankie and it was here that his body lay after the battle.

Queen Victoria visited the castle in 1844 and granted the Duke of Atholl the privilege of being the only British subject allowed to retain a private army, the Atholl Highlanders.

The interior gives a good idea of what castle life was like in the old days. The rooms are numbered and there is a guide book. Look for the Tapestry Room, hung with rich tapestries and containing a sumptuous four-poster bed topped by two vases of ostrich feathers. The Old Scots Room is furnished in the style of a simple cottage living room, complete with box bed, cradle and spinning wheel. There is much to see, from arms and armour, to Jacobite relics, china, toys, furniture, lace, paintings (including portraits by Lely, Ramsay and Raeburn) and even a natural history museum. There is a licensed self-service restaurant and, if you want to impress your friends, there is a separate dining room for private parties of up to 50 people. If you really want to splash out, you can also use the ballroom for up to 200 people, a truly noble setting for a knees-up, its panelled walls hung with a forest of antlers under a timber-ribbed roof with plenty of ancestral portraits to add distinction. In the grounds there is a large caravan park.

Beyond Blair Atholl is good walking and climbing country, over moor and scree, with lovely views. A nice walk is that to **The Bruar Falls**, well signed about 3 miles (4.5km) to the west: you can park by the road. A short walk takes you up to the falls, where the River Bruar cascades down through rocky chasms and over great gleaming slabs of granite. Robert Burns came up here when he was a guest of the Duke of Atholl. He was so disgusted by the treeless moorland that then surrounded the falls that he dashed off a poem: 'The Humble Petition of Bruar Water', and dispatched it to the Duke.

Would then my noble master please,
To grant my highest wishes,
He'll shade the bank wi' towering trees,
And bonie spreading bushes.

This plea, as you can see, found its mark and inspired the fourth Duke of Atholl to plant the trees now growing there. Walk on beyond the falls up the path for another mile or so, through birches and rhododendrons. A bridge then takes you over the stream and down the other side, making a round trip of about 2½ miles (4km). You can get a good pub lunch in the hotel down by the car park.

Where to Stay and Eating Out

expensive

If you want modern comfort, **Stakis Dunkeld House**, ✆ 03502 771, won't let you down.The hotel stands in 280 acres on the Tay at Dunkeld and provides just about everything you could ask for, except simplicity. There is a swimming pool, sauna, spa bath, steam room, solarium and multi-gym. If you've any energy left, there are tennis courts, croquet, salmon and trout fishing and mixed game shooting.

moderate

Kinloch House Hotel, near Blairgowrie, © 025084 237, is highly recommended with four crowns. It is a typical Scottish country house with oak-panelled hall, gallery, antique furniture and paintings, in 20 acres of wooded grounds. The food is first class and has won an award. Moderate to expensive, its rates vary seasonally. Shooting, fishing and golf can be arranged.

Altamount House, Coupar Angus Road, Blairgowrie, © 0250 3512, is a Georgian manor house with four crowns in 6 acres of ground. It shuts from early January to mid-February. **Castleton House Hotel** by Glamis, © 030 784 340, in 11 acres of garden and woodland, was built in 1902 within a 13th-century moat.

Pitlochry Hydro, © 0796 2666, is a great stone building above the town overlooking the Tummel Valley. Moderate to expensive, it has an indoor swimming pool, jacuzzi, sauna, solarium and gymnasium. **Fisher's Hotel**, Atholl Road, Pitlochry, © 0796 472000, is large and comfortable. **Killiecrankie Hotel and Restaurant**, © 0796 3220, once a dower house, is attractive in pleasant grounds close to the Soldier's Leap. The staff tend to wear kilts and the food is excellent. It's only open from February to November.

Dalmunzie House Hotel, Glenshee, © 025 085 224, is known as 'the Hotel in the Hills'. It is a vast Highland mansion in 6000 acres with a nine-hole golf course, tennis courts and fishing. Shooting and stalking can be arranged. Comfortable, with log fires and good Scottish cooking, it is only 5 miles (8km) from the ski slopes.

inexpensive

Bridge of Cally Hotel, © 0250 886231, has three crowns.

Perthshire: West of the A9

Lochs Tummel and Rannoch

If you take the B8019 west from Pitlochry, you should start humming Harry Lauder's famous song 'The Road to the Isles': 'by Tummel and Loch Rannoch and Lochaber I will go . . .' The drive out to Rannoch Station, on the northern side of lochs Tummel and Rannoch, to where the road ends and back along the south side, is a round trip of about 65 miles (104km). The scenery is beautiful, dominated by the great cone of **Schiehallion** in the south, with a kaleidoscope of vistas through the trees and the wasteland of Rannoch Moor stretching away to the west. Loch Tummel is less dramatic than Loch Rannoch, its gentler scenery reshaped by the hydroelectric development.

Queen's View, 2 miles (3km) up from the dam, was so called before Queen Victoria visited it in 1866. Perhaps Mary, Queen of Scots also stood on the promontory and looked down to the water, glinting in the sunlight, far below.

The **Loch Tummel Forest Centre** (open daily April–Sept: donation box) is at the south-east corner of the loch. Here you can learn about the geography and ecology of the area and how to find the Black Wood, south of Loch Rannoch, with part of the remains of the old Caledonian Forest. Harry Lauder must have taken to the moors when he was 'walking with his crummock to the isles' because the road ends at Rannoch Station. Five miles (8km) south of Pitlochry, the A827 takes you 10 miles (16km) west to Aberfeldy, and then out through Strath Tay to Loch Tay, a memorable drive especially in late summer, winding through small villages, with the river shaded by overhanging trees, backed by the hills beyond.

Aberfeldy

Let Fortune's gifts at random flee,
They ne'er shall draw a wish frae me,
Supremely blest wi' love and thee
In the birks of Aberfeldy.

'The Birks of Aberfeldie', by Robert Burns

Aberfeldy is a pleasant little town on the Urlar Burn at its confluence with the River Tay. Robert Burns' poem refers to the silver birches beside the burn. The bridge over the Tay was built by General Wade in 1733 and is said to be the best of the many he was responsible for during his arduous task of trying to link up all the remote trouble-spots in the Highlands during the Jacobite uprisings. The dramatic **Falls of Moness** are just a short stroll south of the town.

The **Black Watch Monument**, a kilted soldier, is at the south end of the bridge, erected in 1887 to commemorate the raising of the Black Watch by General Wade in 1739.

The Oatmeal Mill (open Mon–Fri: adm) in Mill Street shows the process of milling raw grain into oatmeal, and you can buy the finished products. **Aberfeldy Distillery** runs free tours and tastings from April to October.

Castle Menzies (pronounced Mingies) (open daily, 1 April–30 Sept: adm), a mile (1.5km) west of Aberfeldy, is a 16th-century, Z-plan fortified tower house, with carved gables over its dormers. In the process of restoration after centuries of neglect, it belongs to the Clan Menzies Society and houses their Clan Museum.

Monument to the Black Watch at Aberfeldy

Loch Tay, 5 miles (8km) west of Aberfeldy, is a long, dark snake of water under the brooding hulk of Ben Lawers, Perthshire's highest hill, 3984 feet (1226m) high. All types of water sports take place on the loch, though keen fishermen might wish otherwise.

Ben Lawers is well worth climbing on a clear day if you are fit—allow about 3 hours. At the top you can see from the Atlantic to the North Sea. There are masses of mountain flowers and birds. Look out for the great brown buzzard, sailing lazily on broad wings, or the kestrel, hovering on pointed wings, long tail fanned out. Listen for the distinctive whirring of red grouse, and their 'go-bak, go-bak-bak-bak-bak', the mournful, liquid song of the golden plover, the lonely cry of the curlew and the silly cuckoo call. Needless to say, there is a visitor centre, for those who like their wildlife in consumer packages, off the A827 six miles (9.5km) northeast of Killin. Run by the National Trust for Scotland, who care for the southern slopes of the hill, it is a particularly dismal place where they dish up the inevitable booklets, information sheets and audio-visual programmes together with instructions about what to wear and take if you climb the hill. (For which they can be forgiven: the Mountain Rescue people are frequently called out to risk their lives rescuing idiots who would do better to confine their outdoor activities to their gardens.)

Kenmore, at the head of the loch, was built for estate workers of Taymouth Castle in 1760 by the fourth Earl of Breadalbane and is now a conservation village. The gigantic castle is empty, in a magnificent designed landscape, and has a golf course in its grounds. You can hire boats here for fishing on the loch.

If you can't climb Ben Lawers, you can drive round it—about 25 miles (40km) in all. Leave the A827 at Fearnan on Loch Tay and take the back road along Glen Lyon, Scotland's longest glen, to **Bridge of Balgie**, and then drive south through the hills, back to the loch past the NTS visitor centre. You can complete the circle on the main road along the loch back to Fearnan, but the nicest way to see Loch Tay by car is on the minor road that hugs the southern shore.

At **Fortingall**, 2 miles (3km) to the northwest as the crow flies, the yew tree in the churchyard is said to be over 3000 years old—Europe's oldest living object. This delightful little village has a single street of cottages, some thatched and rather English in character, and an intriguing legend. Some say that Pontius Pilate was born here, son of a Roman officer who had been sent on a peace mission to the Picts in Dun Geal, a fort on the steep, rocky hill behind the village. True or not, it adds romance to an already enchanted spot. You should try to abandon your car in this area: it is marvellous walking and climbing territory.

From Kenmore, take the narrow back road through **Glen Quaich** to **Amulree**, 9 miles (14.5km) south of Aberfeldy. This was an important junction of the old drove roads, where drovers broke their lonely journeys to exchange news and banter.

The Sma' Glen

The Sma' Glen is the moorland valley through which the A822 descends from Amulree to Crieff. It follows the River Almond as it thunders down over rapids and falls, with hills rising steeply to about 2000 feet (615m) on either side. You can see salmon leaping in September and October; the best place for this is the Buchanty Spout, in Glenalmond on the B8063, just off the A822.

After Newton, look out on the left of the road for **Ossian's Stone**, which is said to mark the grave of Ossian, the legendary Gaelic hero and bard who spent many years in fairyland until he was baptized by St Patrick. The stone was in fact moved to its present position by General Wade's road-builders, when it blocked the path of one of their roads. Traces of a prehistoric burial, found when they lifted the stone, were given a reburial in a secret place by local Highlanders who were convinced that they were indeed the remains of the poet. Wordsworth thought so too:

In this still place, remote from men,
Sleeps Ossian, in the narrow glen.

Crieff

Crieff, about 12 miles (19km) south of Amulree, is a Highland holiday town, built on a steep hill facing south over the valley of the River Earn. The town is dominated by the Knock of Crieff, 911 feet (280m) high in the north, a woodland area with footpaths and good views from the top. Nothing much is old in the town today. It was sacked and destroyed by Highlanders during the Jacobite rebellion. Later, a bleaching and tanning industry brought prosperity to its people. It became a spa town in the 19th century and you get echoes of Victorian splendour as you look at the Crieff Hydro Hotel, above the town, with its glass domes and pavilions.

Glenturret Distillery (open daily, March–Dec; weekdays, Jan–Feb: adm) is the oldest in Scotland. Conducted tours show all stages of whisky distilling. The tour includes a taste, and a visit to the award-winning **Visitors' Heritage Centre** with an audio-visual show, exhibitions, a whisky museum and retail shop.

Stuart Crystal (open daily: free), in Muthill Road, is a crystal factory where you can see glass being engraved. There is an audio-visual show, shop and café.

Crieff Visitor Centre (open daily) has factory tours showing Thistle pottery and Perthshire paperweights being made. There is a video presentation, showroom and restaurant.

Bookworms should slip off to **Innerpeffray Library**, 4 miles (6.5km) southeast of the town (closed Thurs: adm). This is the oldest public library in Scotland, founded in 1690 by Archbishop Hay Drummond, in the attic of the chapel next door, and moved here in the middle of the 18th century. Among the collection of old and antiquarian books, mostly religious or classical, is the Bible printed in 1508 and carried by Montrose when he was finally defeated at the Battle of Carbisdale in 1650. If you are good on scripture, look out for the *Treacle Bible*, so called because 'Is there no balm in Gilead?' is translated as 'Is there no treacle ..?'.

Comrie

Comrie, 6 miles (9.5km) west of Crieff along the River Earn, is an attractive conservation village. At midnight on Hogmanay, the unique Flambeaux Procession takes place, with villagers parading round in a torchlit procession, followed by much revelry. This custom has its roots in the ancient pagan fire-festivals, held to drive off evil spirits for the coming year.

Because it lies on the Highland Line—the geological fault that divides Highland and Lowland Scotland—more seismological tremors have been recorded here than anywhere else in Britain. Shocks were especially common during the 19th century: in recent years tremors have never done more than rattle the village teacups. **Earthquake House** was built in 1874 to house one of the earliest seismometers in the world. They have a model of the original instrument as well as a modern one, in use, and a chart recorder.

The Tartans Museum (open daily: adm, but check, ✆ 0764 670779) is the world headquarters of the Scottish Tartans Society, the leading authority on tartan and Highland dress. They have over 1300 tartans on display as well as comprehensive information, a library, weaving demonstrations and a garden that shows which plants produce what dyes. You can look up your own name and discover which tartan you are entitled to wear.

Drummond Fish Farm (open daily: adm) is a working fish farm where you can catch your own supper.

Just north of Comrie, and a pleasant walk, **Deil's Cauldron** is an impressive waterfall carrying the River Lednock down to meet the River Earn.

Fowlis Wester is a hamlet, 5 miles (8km) east of Crieff. Here, 13th-century St Beans Church has a leper squint, an 8th-century Pictish stone and a fine lychgate—the roofed gateway to the churchyard where coffins could await the arrival of the priest, sheltered from the elements.

St Fillans, on Loch Earn 6 miles (9.5km) further west, is a popular holiday resort for anyone who enjoys sailing, waterskiing and windsurfing. It is also a good centre for walking and climbing.

Drummond Castle Gardens

Two miles (3km) south of Crieff, Drummond Castle Gardens (open every afternoon, May–Sept: adm) are approached down a mile-long avenue. The sundial is dated 1630 and there are flowers and shrubs in a formal Italian setting, against the backdrop of the castle. Founded in 1491, this was the setting for a terrible murder in 1502. Margaret Drummond and her sisters were poisoned, to prevent James IV from making Margaret his queen. Cromwell did his best to destroy the castle and it was deliberately damaged in 1745 by its owner, the Duchess of Perth, to prevent Hanoverian troops from capturing it.

Muthill

Muthill is a conservation village 3 miles (4.5km) south of Crieff, with late 18th- and early 19th-century houses delightfully unspoiled. Muthill (pronounced Mew-thill) is derived from

Moot-Hill (hill of meeting). **Muthill Folk Museum** (open April–Sept: adm) has exhibits illustrating past domestic life in the village. Also in Muthill are the ruins of a once-important 15th-century church with its 12th-century Norman tower.

A couple of miles to the east of Muthill, **Tullibardine Chapel** is one of the very few of its kind that has not been altered. Cruciform, built of red sandstone, it was founded as a collegiate church in 1445 by Sir David Murray, whose arms and those of his wife can be seen on the inside west wall. Since the Reformation it has been used as a burial vault for the Drummond Earls of Perth.

Gleneagles Hotel

About 6 miles (9.5km) south of Muthill and a mile (1.5km) or so west of the village and station, Gleneagles Hotel is Scotland's premier golfing mecca, whose internationally famous courses lie along the edge of the Muir of Ochill, looking towards the Ochil Hills and Glen Devon—*see below*.

Braco

Ardoch Roman Camp is at Braco, about 4 miles (6.5km) west of Gleneagles Hotel. Grass-covered earthworks are all that remain of a Roman fort, dating from the 2nd century. It was once big enough to house as many as 40,000 men. You can still see the shape of it—a great rectangle with ditches and ramparts. Here, in wooden dwellings, the Romans tried to subdue the barbaric tribes who swooped down on them from the hills and glens and forests. The old Roman road runs north of Muthill and then east towards Perth, and an overgrown arch beside the bridge over the River Knaik is all that remains of the Roman bridge.

Auchterarder is 8 to 10 miles (13 to 16km) southeast of Crieff depending on which road you take, tucked in under the northern slopes of the Ochil Hills. This is another holiday centre, with a golf course, good fishing and walks.

Where to Stay

expensive

Gleneagles Hotel, Auchterarder, © 076 46 2231, is Scotland's only 5-star hotel. Prices and details on application (comfort doesn't come cheap). If you get fed up with the sauna, the solarium, the jacuzzi, the gymnasium, the shooting, the fishing, the snooker, the swimming, the squash, the bowling, the croquet and the tennis, you can always fall back on a round of golf. The 5-star rating embraces the chef as well as everything else. Don't look at the right-hand side of the menu: who wants to toy with an omelette in a place like this?

Farleyer House Hotel, near Aberfeldy, © 0887 820332, is very much a country house hotel on the esatate of the old Castle Menzies where Bonnie Prince Charlie took refuge. The food is excellent. No dogs in the hotel and no smoking in the dining room.

moderate

Drummond Arms Hotel, on Loch Earn in St Fillans, © 0764 685212, is quiet and unspoiled, with a friendly staff and relaxed atmosphere. **Four Seasons Hotel**, St Fillans, © 076485 333, is more expensive and has an excellent reputation for food. **Kenmore Hotel**, © 08873 205, is Scotland's oldest inn, established in 1572, with its own salmon fishing and rights over all Loch Tay. It has a good atmosphere and a golf course on the estate. **Loch Rannoch Hotel**, © 088 22 201, in 250 acres beside the loch, has pretty well every sort of facility to offer: indoor pool, jacuzzi, sauna, solarium, steam bath, squash, tennis, sailing, windsurfing, canoeing, dry-ski slope, snooker, bicycles, fishing plus live entertainment and Highland Evenings.

Crieff Hydro, © 0764 655555, beams down on the town from the hill like a very respectable dowager, with its splendid glass pavilion in front. It provides an indoor swimming pool, riding, tennis, free golf, sailing, windsurfing and waterskiing. In the evenings activities include dancing, films, discos and competitions, if you are the sort of person who likes to be organized.

inexpensive

Achray House Hotel in peaceful St Fillans, © 0764 685231, is cosy, right on Loch Earn, with excellent food. Their high reputation is endorsed by the fact that people go back.

Ailean Chreggan, Weem by Aberfeldy, © 0887 20346, is a small and friendly, family-run hotel facing south over the River Tay to the hills beyond. The food is prepared to a high quality using local ingredients.

Grampian

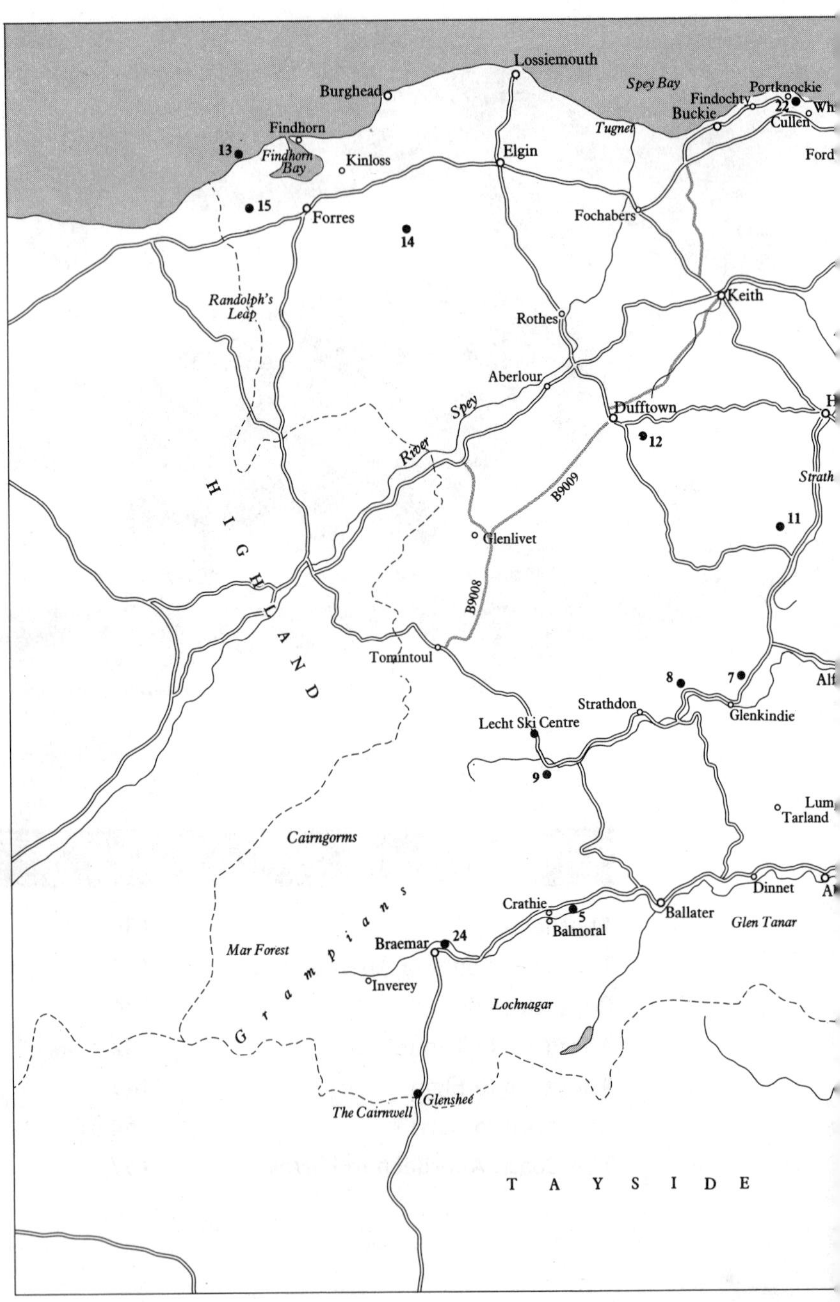
Lossiemouth
Burghead
Spey Bay
Portknockie
Findochty
22
Buckie
Cullen
Findhorn
Tugnet
13
Findhorn Bay
Kinloss
Elgin
15
Forres
14
Fochabers
Randolph's Leap
Keith
Rothes
Aberlour
Spey
Dufftown
River
12
HIGHLAND
B9009
Strath
11
Glenlivet
B9008
Tomintoul
8
7
Strathdon
Glenkindie
Lecht Ski Centre
9
Tarland
Cairngorms
Dinnet
Crathie
5
Ballater
Glen Tanar
Balmoral
Braemar
24
Mar Forest
Grampians
Inverey
Lochnagar
Glenshee
The Cairnwell
TAYSIDE

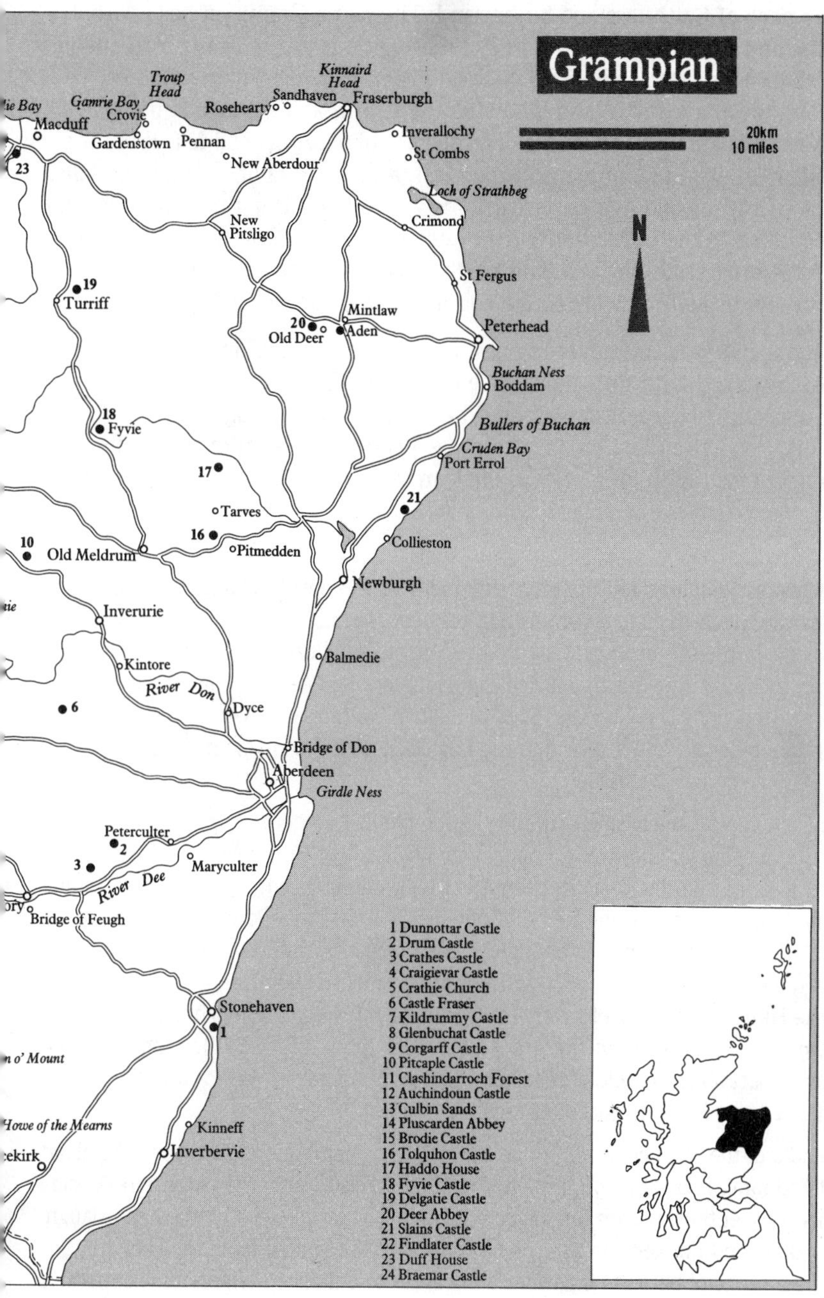
Grampian
20km
10 miles
N
Troup Head
Kinnaird Head
Gamrie Bay
Crovie
Macduff
Gardenstown
Pennan
Rosehearty
Sandhaven
Fraserburgh
Inverallochy
St Combs
New Aberdour
Loch of Strathbeg
Crimond
New Pitsligo
St Fergus
Turriff
Mintlaw
Old Deer
Aden
Peterhead
Buchan Ness
Boddam
Fyvie
Bullers of Buchan
Cruden Bay
Port Errol
Tarves
Old Meldrum
Pitmedden
Collieston
Newburgh
Inverurie
Balmedie
Kintore
River Don
Dyce
Bridge of Don
Aberdeen
Girdle Ness
Peterculter
Maryculter
River Dee
Bridge of Feugh
Stonehaven
Howe of the Mearns
Kinneff
Inverbervie
1 Dunnottar Castle
2 Drum Castle
3 Crathes Castle
4 Craigievar Castle
5 Crathie Church
6 Castle Fraser
7 Kildrummy Castle
8 Glenbuchat Castle
9 Corgarff Castle
10 Pitcaple Castle
11 Clashindarroch Forest
12 Auchindoun Castle
13 Culbin Sands
14 Pluscarden Abbey
15 Brodie Castle
16 Tolquhon Castle
17 Haddo House
18 Fyvie Castle
19 Delgatie Castle
20 Deer Abbey
21 Slains Castle
22 Findlater Castle
23 Duff House
24 Braemar Castle

Grampian, better known as the shires of Kincardine, Aberdeen, Banff and Moray, is that shoulder of Scotland that juts out into the North Sea below the neck of Caithness and Sutherland. The name Grampian has a forbidding and stark ring to it, but in fact the region is lovely. It is a fertile land veined with rivers, half-girt by sea and backed by mountains. Routes, along the coast and inland following the straths and glens of famous rivers, radiate from Aberdeen like the ribs of an outspread fan. From the Cairngorms and Grampians in the west, a series of ravines and waterfalls, wooded glens and heathery straths carry the River Dee through forest and moorland to the east coast. Further north the River Don makes more gentle progress to the sea, and north again, the Spey completes its journey through very attractive country to join the sea at Tugnet.

Moors give way to undulating farmland that forms a wide coastal plain, patchworked with neat fields. The coast road links a chain of fishing towns and villages with sheltered harbours offering refuge from the wild North Sea. The coastline is both rugged and gentle—gaunt rock cliffs interspersed with long sweeps of clean sand.

History

Many prehistoric remains tell of early settlement on the fertile plains, but the region doesn't feature much in history books until Kenneth Macalpine united its Picts with the Dalriada Scots in the 9th century. One of the Comyns, who came over with William the Conqueror, made his way north, married the daughter of a local chief and rapidly gained supremacy in the area. The Comyns, Earls of Buchan, were as much of a threat to Robert the Bruce's ambition to rule Scotland as the English. In 1307 he came north and crushed them in a couple of decisive battles.

With the Comyns effectively subdued, the Gordon family clambered to power. They ruled the land like despots for about 250 years, becoming Earls of Huntly and too big for their boots. Being so far from the seat of government their dominance didn't seem threatening until Mary, Queen of Scots came to the throne in 1561. Sir John Gordon, third son of the 4th Earl of Huntly, was then rash enough to boast of his aspirations to be consort to the widowed queen. Mary raged north with an army to curb such impertinence. Having hanged the Huntly Governor of Inverness Castle for refusing to admit her, she stormed into Aberdeen and disposed of the 4th Earl and Sir John (*see* p.130). From then on, except for an occasional rumble of rebellion, the city of Aberdeen was loyal to the Crown and disinclined to rally to the Jacobite standard.

In the middle of the 19th century, Prince Albert and Queen Victoria discovered Scotland and built Balmoral. From then on, a stampede of tartan-clad southerners over-ran Deeside and its environs, enthusing over the scenic splendours. They tiptoed after the deer, slaughtered the game and hooked the fish, integrating with the landed families. They built or refurbished a series of baronial mansions and castles to enhance their status. Balmoral is still the holiday home of the British Royal Family and even today the struggle for royal recognition goes on.

The oil boom of the 1970s brought great prosperity to Grampian, whose wealth had relied previously on farming, fishing, granite, textiles and paper. Land prices soared; property speculators thrived. But now that the oil in the established offshore oilfields is past its peak, many of the jobs that went with its exploitation will suffer. A number of upwardly mobile incomers have taken advantage of plummeting land prices and Grampian is gradually changing hands, though a number of the old landed families remain. To wring a living from vast estates, some are forced to supplement farming revenues by opening their castles and stately homes to the public and also by squeezing fortunes out of trigger-happy sportsmen and fishermen.

Grampian is the home of the Gordon Highlanders, raised in 1794 by the Duke of Gordon to fight the Napoleonic Wars. They wear the Gordon tartan and it is said that the Duchess of Gordon helped in a recruiting drive by giving a kiss and a silver shilling to each volunteer. (She was well over 40 and described as 'well run'.) The Gordons are fiercely resisting plans to amalgamate them with the Queen's Own Highlanders.

From June to September the tartan-tinged air vibrates with the skirl of pipes and the thud of the caber, as towns stage exuberant Highland Games. These unique Scottish gatherings, dating from the 11th century when Malcolm Canmore held contests to find the best soldiers for his struggles against the Normans, are usually well supplied with beer tents and sideshows. The most popular is probably the Braemar Highland Gathering in September because of the presence of the Royal Family: others include Aberdeen, Drumtochty, Grange, and Burghead in June; Forres, Elgin, Dufftown, Tomintoul, Stonehaven and Strathavon in July; Aboyne, Aberlour, Strathspey, Ballater and the Lonach, in August. A large number of other entertainments take place throughout the region during the summer months.

One of Grampian's attractions is the 70-mile (112km) Malt Whisky Trail that takes in conducted tours of eight distilleries where some of the best-known malts are produced. It would be churlish to say 'if you've seen one, you've seen the lot': it is an attractive drive and you don't have to go over them all. (But each one beckons with a free dram.) There is also a Castle Trail, a Victorian Heritage Trail and a Coastal Trail, all excellent.

Tourist Information

There are a number of tourist information centres throughout Grampian. The following are open all year:

Aberdeen: St Nicholas House, © 0224 632727
Banchory: Bridge Street, © 03302 2000
Banff: Collie Lodge, © 0261 812789/812319
Braemar: The Mews, © 03397 41600
Elgin: 17 High Street, © 0343 542666/543388.

Aberdeen

Aberdeen is the obvious place from which to begin to explore the Grampian Region. It is an ever-changing city, the third largest in Scotland, hiding its true nature under a brittle, cosmopolitan exterior.

Always a great port as well as a fish and cattle market, exporting granite, textiles and paper, Aberdeen suddenly found itself in the centre of an oil boom in the 1970s. Property prices soared: entrepreneurs flourished.

Somehow, through all this, Aberdeen managed to retain its character. The Granite City, they call it, and no oil boom could change the silvery-granite splendour of the Georgian part of the city, with gracious terraces, squares and crescents; nor the solid Victorian buildings that accompanied the 19th-century prosperity brought to the city by astute merchants; nor the long, wide sweep of Union Street; nor even, for all the smart new buildings, the waterfront. Expensive oil-rig supply vessels can never spoil the character of the harbour—a salty old reprobate smelling of fish.

History

Aberdeen was granted a Royal Charter by William the Lion in 1179, now preserved in the Town House in Union Street, endorsing an earlier one granted by David I. William Wallace is said to have burned 100 ships in the harbour in the 13th century. Robert Bruce held a council here in 1308. As a reward for the loyal support of the citizens, who forced the English to surrender their hold on the castle, he gave the city its coat of arms and the motto *Bon Accord.* Edward III burned down Aberdeen in 1336.

The Gordon clan, incomers from Berwickshire and Lothian, who had dominated this northeastern corner for 250 years, over-reached themselves in their ambition for power and began to eye the throne. Mary, Queen of Scots was forced by her Protestant half-brother, Moray, to come north in an attempt to quell them. The Countess of Huntly, however, had been promised by a local witch that the Earl would be in the Tolbooth in Aberdeen, entirely unwounded after any battle he cared to fight. She begged her husband to stand up to Mary so he summoned his army and fought. He was defeated and he and his son were captured. The shock brought on a massive heart attack which killed him. His unwounded body was taken to the Tolbooth. Mary executed Sir John Gordon and ordered the posthumous trial of the embalmed body of his father for treason.

Montrose sacked the city in 1644, fighting for the cause of Charles I. General Monk occupied it during in the mid-17th century when he was Governor of Scotland for Cromwell. Although nominally Jacobite, the citizens of Aberdeen were not enthusiastic supporters of the cause.

Old Aberdeen

This area, north of the city centre, is best explored on foot. Start at the little **Brig o' Balgownie**, a Gothic bridge spanning the River Don near its mouth. This is the oldest medieval bridge in Scotland, built by Richard the Mason, affectionately known as Dick the Cement, on the orders of Robert the Bruce. On the north side of the bridge you can see a terrace of old stone cottages with colourful gardens: the one nearest to the bridge was once an ale-house on the drove road.

Stroll through **Seaton Park**, Old Aberdeen, to twin-spired, fortified **St Machar's Cathedral** (open daily: free) in the Chanonry. It is the oldest granite building in Aberdeen and the only granite cathedral in the world. Founded in 1157, St Machar's stands on a promontory overlooking the Don, taking its name from the saint who founded a Celtic church here in the 6th century. A 14th-century red sandstone arch is all that remains of an older building, in contrast to the simple dignity of the later granite. Look for the oak heraldic ceiling, added in 1520, with 48 heraldic shields.

Old Aberdeen grew up round the cathedral, an independent burgh with its own council and charter. Today, cobbled streets and charming old houses, some of which date back to 1500, give an air of tranquillity undisturbed by the roar of the modern city beyond. Near the cathedral, **Cruickshank Botanic Gardens** (open daily May–Sept; weekdays in winter: free) belong to the university, with extensive collections of shrubs, herbaceous and Alpine plants, and a rock and water garden.

King's College, in the High Street (open daily except Sun: free), stands on a green sward with a distinctive 'crowned' tower and buttressed walls. This was Aberdeen's first university, founded in 1495, in the reign of James IV. Its chapel, first Catholic, then Protestant, is now interdenominational. The tomb of its founder, Bishop William Elphinstone, is a magnificent sarcophagus outside the chapel, supported by figures of the Seven Virtues. **King's College Visitor Centre** (open daily except Sun in winter: adm), in the former University Library, tells the story of 500 years of the university and its students.

Marischal College (pronounced Marshal), Broad Street, in the city centre, was founded in 1593 as a Protestant rival to King's, the two colleges being united to form Aberdeen University in 1860. The present building has its roots in the 19th century with some of the older parts incorporated. The granite façade was added in 1906.

Provost Skene's House (open daily except Sun: free) is opposite the college. Now a museum, this well-restored building dates from 1545. It was named after one of its owners, Sir George Skene, who was Provost of Aberdeen in 1676 and responsible for extensive renovation of the house. The Painted Gallery, known as the Chapel, on the second floor of the west wing, revealed traces of religious paintings in 17th-century style, showing that medieval ideas and imagery persisted in this northeastern corner of Scotland far into the Reformation period. On the top floor, exhibits illustrate the history and domestic life of Aberdeen over the ages. There is a coffee shop in the original kitchen.

The Tolbooth, on the corner of Broad Street and Castle Street, was built in 1627. Its ancient town jail with original cells was the stage for the death of the 4th Earl of Huntly after his wife's witch had misleadingly promised him immunity from battle scars.

From the Tolbooth, go up Union Street to **Kirk of St Nicholas**, beyond the shopping precinct a few blocks along on the right. The old parish church (open daily) stands among trees in a peaceful churchyard, bordered by Upperkirkgate and Back Wynd. Its 48-bell carillon rings out across the roar of the city. Founded in the 12th century and split into two at the Reformation, the present building dates from 1752. In the east part of the church, the little stone-vaulted crypt-chapel, St Mary's, dates from the 14th century. Witches were imprisoned down here in the 17th century, and you can see the rings to which they were chained. The **Oil Industry Chapel** is in the church.

Aberdeen Art Gallery and Museum (open daily: free) is also in Schoolhill. Among the many things to see here are 20th-century British paintings and sculptures, Raeburn portraits, works by Zoffany, Romney, Reynolds, Augustus John and Ben Nicholson, and an important collection of Scottish domestic silver and glass. There is also a reference library, gallery shop, print room and café.

The Maritime Museum (open daily except Sun: free) is in Provost Ross's House, Shiprow, north of Trinity Quay and the Upper Dock. Overlooking the harbour, it is one of the oldest houses in the town and a fine example of early Scottish domestic architecture. Displays include Aberdeen's maritime heritage of fishing, shipbuilding and trade and models of offshore oil installations.

Aberdeen Harbour is a conglomeration of seafaring life: fine old buildings line the waterfront where fishing boats are packed into the inner basins. If you want to see another face of Aberdeen, get up early one weekday morning and visit the **fish market** before the sales start at 7.30am. The action starts at around 4.30am and the earlier you go, the more impressive it is.

Satrosphere (open daily except Tue: adm) is a marvellous science and technology centre where you can find out about such subjects as prisms, light, lasers etc., and you are encouraged to take part in do-it-yourself experiments. This is a discovery place for all ages, whether science is your thing or not.

The Gordon Highlanders Regimental Museum (open Tues and Thurs and one Sun a month: free) in Viewfield Road, southwest of the city centre, displays the uniforms, pictures, medals, letters and documents, weapons and memorabilia of this famous, locally recruited regiment. The Gordons fought with distinction all over the world and are now fighting amalgamation with the Queen's Own Highlanders.

Duthie Park Winter Gardens, south of the city on the banks of the Dee, were recently hailed as Scotland's top tourist attraction. The glasshouse extension makes them the largest glassed gardens in Europe. They include a Japanese Garden, the biggest collection of cacti in Britain, birds, fish, and turtles. Sit under a palm tree in mid-winter and picture yourself in some tropical paradise.

Footde, known locally in the inimitable Aberdonian accent as 'Fittie', is a fishing village at the mouth of the Dee. The early 19th-century houses were designed by the fisherfolk themselves. Come here in an easterly gale and watch the sea breaking high over the harbour walls.

Festivals

Regular festivals include: Scottish Connection, a festival celebrating all things Scottish, in March/April; Scottish Fiddle Orchestra Concert and Granite City Car Rally in April; a Marathon Road Race in May; Aberdeen Highland Games and the Bon Accord Carnival Parade and Aberdeen Festival in June; an International Football Festival in July; Clydesdale Horse Show, Summer Flower Show, and the International Youth Festival in August; Aberdeen Alternative Music Festival in October; Christmas Shopping Festival in November/December and finally, St Nicholas Festival in December.

Where to Stay

expensive

Altens Skean Dhu Hotel, Souter Head Road, ✆ 0224 877000, is comfortable and has a heated outdoor swimming pool. **Copthorne Hotel**, Huntly Street, ✆ 0224 630404, is a city-centre hotel off Union Street and near the Catholic Cathedral. The decor is fanciful, with fluted columns and dribbling fountains, and it has a good restaurant called **Poachers**.

Ardoe House, South Deeside Road, Blairs, ✆ 0224 867355, on the outskirts of Aberdeen, is a baronial-style mansion overlooking the Dee Valley. It's expensive, elegant and comfortable and the food is excellent.

moderate

Atholl Hotel in Kings Gate, ✆ 0224 323505, is a typical Aberdeen granite town house in the west end; no frills but respectable. Golfing, fishing and shooting can be arranged, and also distillery tours. You can even have secretarial services.

Caledonian Thistle Hotel, overlooking Union Terrace Gardens in the city centre, ✆ 0224 640233, is moderate to expensive, with modern fittings, good food and not much character. There are in-house movies, tea/coffee-making facilities in the bedrooms, sun-beds and a sauna room. **Imperial Hotel**, Stirling Street, ✆ 0224 589101, is also central and has an imposing frontage that makes you think of top hats and carriages. They give good service and the food's not bad. **Stakis Tree Tops Hotel** in Springfield Road, ✆ 0224 313377, is in wooded landscaped grounds, 10 minutes from the city centre; it's moderate to expensive depending on what sort of room you take. The hotel has all the Stakis extras, like a swimming pool and leisure complex, and excellent food in a split-level Regency-style restaurant.

If you want something less overpowering, **Palm Court Hotel**, 81 Seafield Road, ✆ 0224 310351, is cosy and friendly in a quiet residential area.

Try **Mr G's**, 74 Chapel Street, © 0224 242112. This is a wine bar and restaurant where the food is excellent and there is a friendly atmosphere. **Gerards**, 50 Chapel Street, © 0224 639500, has an outstanding chef: you eat in a garden room with a glass roof. **Atlantis Seafood**, 16 Bon Accord Crescent, © 0224 591403, do good, fresh sea-food and **Poldinos**, 7 Little Belmont Street, © 0224 647777, do excellent pizzas. Otherwise, ask around for the current 'in' eating place: fashions change fast.

The Coast South of Aberdeen

The A92 south from Aberdeen takes you along the coast with the North Sea stretching away to the horizon, always busy with shipping. When the wind is in the east, big seas pound the beaches and cliffs, sending up great plumes of spray.

Stonehaven

Stonehaven is a holiday resort town, as sturdy as its name implies, 14 miles (22km) south of Aberdeen, crouched around a bay below red sandstone cliffs. The sheltered harbour is used mainly by pleasure boats now. Stonehaven has a heated open-air swimming pool, a golf course, boating and windsurfing, fishing and sea-angling, and an indoor leisure centre with swimming pool.

Tolbooth Museum (open daily except Tues, June–Sept: free) is a 16th-century building on the quay by the north pier, displaying local history and archaeology, with a special emphasis on fishing. The building was a storehouse of the Earls Marischal, later used as a prison. In 1748–9, three Episcopal priests were imprisoned here, for their insistence in following the old religion. During their incarceration, women came from all over the county, smuggling babies in creels on their backs, to hold them up to the barred windows so that the priests could baptize them.

Every New Year's Eve the town celebrates a 'Swinging the Fireballs' ceremony, going back to pagan times when fireballs were swung through the streets to ward off evil spirits.

Dunnottar Castle (open daily except closed weekends in winter: adm) is about 2 miles (3km) south of Stonehaven, just off the A92. This spectacular ruined fortress stands high on a rocky promontory towering 160 feet (49m) above the boiling sea, protected to landward by a deep natural cleft. It has been written: 'Dunnottar speaks with an audible voice; every cave has a record, every turret a tongue.' A Pictish fort stood here in the Dark Ages, and one of the earliest Christian chapels. The fort was replaced by a primitive castle in the 13th century. William Wallace stormed the English garrison in 1297, burning down the church where they had taken refuge, but failing to take the castle. Dunnottar was a stronghold of the Earls Marischal of Scotland from the 14th century. The extensive ruins include a great square tower and the chapel, built by Sir William Keith in 1392, and a gatehouse, built in 1575, said to be the strongest in Scotland. In 1645, the 7th Earl Marischal, a stubborn Covenanter, withstood a siege by Montrose, who took his revenge by laying waste to Stonehaven and the surrounding lands. His actions are recorded by a chronicler as having left the country 'utterlie spoilzeit plunderit and undone'.

During the Civil War, the Scottish Regalia were brought to Dunnottar for safety. The castle was besieged in 1652, but the governor refused to surrender until the Regalia had been smuggled out in the apron of the local minister's wife, Mrs Grainger, and in a bundle of flax carried by her servant. They were hidden in the kirk at Kinneff and kept safe until the Restoration of the Monarchy.

In 1685, 167 Covenanters were imprisoned at Dunnottar in the 'Whigs Vault'. They were confined: 'ankle deep in mire, with one window to the sea, they had not the least accommodation for sitting, leaning or lying and were perfectly stifled for want of air and no access to ease nature'. Some tried to escape through the window that overlooks the sea, but were recaptured and cruelly tortured. The castle was used as the setting for Zeffirelli's film *Hamlet.*

Dunnottar's history is further commemorated in the 18th-century kirk at **Kinneff** (usually open). Kinneff is 7 miles (11km) to the south, just off the A92. Parts of the old kirk are incorporated into the current building and include those parts in which the Scottish Regalia were hidden for nine years by the Rev. James Grainger. The hiding place was under the flagstone below the pulpit. You can see memorials to Grainger, his wife, and to Sir George Ogilvy, Governor of Dunnottar Castle at the time.

Fowlsheugh is an RSPB reserve, signed off the A92, 3 miles (4.5km) south of Stonehaven. Always open but best in spring and summer, this is home to one of the largest seabird colonies in Scotland.

Inverbervie

Inverbervie is a milling town just to the south on the banks of Bervie Water. Here, at Craig David on the north shore, David II and his wife, Johanna, were driven ashore by a storm while returning from nine years' exile in France in 1341. King's Step is the rock where David is said to have stepped ashore. He granted the town a Royal Charter the following year. There is also a memorial to Hercules Linton, the man who designed the famous clipper *Cutty Sark.* Today, this wild, rugged coastline offers little refuge from the ferocious storms that often rage in from the North Sea. The villagers take what shelter they can from harbours built into the cliffs.

Arbuthnott House and Gardens are 3 miles (4.5km) inland from Inverbervie (open by arrangement, © Inverbervie 361226: adm). The house has a 17th-century Renaissance façade, with 18th-century additions, and there is an extensive 17th-century formal garden, attractively terraced with a pretty 18th-century stone bridge. A tower on the site of the house was the home of the Arbuthnott family in 1206. The chancel of the village church dates from 1242.

The Grassic Gibbon Centre at Arbuthnott (open daily, April–Oct: adm) is a memorial to Lewis Grassic Gibbon (James Leslie Mitchell), the writer whose powerful Scottish prose in his trilogy *A Scots Quair* brings to life the Mearns at the beginning of the century. He spent his childhood here and used recognizable local settings in his books.

From here you can make a quick detour inland through Laurencekirk to Fettercairn where you can tour the Fettercairn Distillery. Go on to Fasque almost on the border with Tayside, often missed by tourists hurrying north on the main road.

Fasque

Just to the north of **Fettercairn**, with its turreted arch into the village commemorating a visit by Queen Victoria and Prince Albert in 1861, Fasque is down a side road to the left. This delightful, rambling mansion is for Victoriana addicts. (Open every afternoon except Fri, May–Sept: adm.) The house, built in 1809, was the home of the Gladstones, including one of Britain's best-known prime ministers, W. E. Gladstone. Fasque, still owned by the family, has managed to preserve all the marvellous relics of Victorian times without becoming like a museum. Nothing seems to have changed for a hundred years. The kitchens are a joy and you can see portraits of all the family servants. A slightly ramshackle air hangs over the whole fascinating place and there is a splendid deer park.

Where to Stay

moderate

You shouldn't go far wrong at **Heugh Hotel**, Westfield Road, Stonehaven, © 0569 62379. A turreted granite baronial mansion, with lots of oak panelling and nice grounds, it won't raise your blood pressure with excitement but you'll eat well and be comfortable.

inexpensive

The best thing about the **Marine Hotel**, Shorehead, Stonehaven, © 0569 62155, is that it is right on the waterfront in the harbour. The staff are friendly and they cater for children.

If you want something a bit different but aren't much good at planning, try **Hiking and Biking Scotland**, Bogfur, Inverurie, © 0467 21312. From April to November, they lay on walking and cycling holidays, guided or independent, using guest-house accommodation or country hotels, with comprehensive information packs. Their routes take in the Castle Trail and the Whisky Trail, as well as mountain and island tours.

Royal Deeside

The River Dee is born high in the Cairngorms, to the west. It boils down through steep-sided ravines, thunders over precipices gathering myriad tributaries from corries in the surrounding hills, foams through the deer forests of Mar, ripples at a suitably majestic pace past Balmoral Castle and finally meets the North Sea in Aberdeen.

You can enjoy Deeside all through the year: perhaps it is best of all in autumn when the rich blaze of colour is unforgettable. In winter the landscape becomes a dramatic sweep of snow-covered hills and torrents of ice: a skier's delight, with the Glenshee and Lecht Ski Centres. In summer, with a good map and sensible equipment, you could spend a whole holiday exploring the hills and valleys of the Cairngorms and Grampians.

Peterculter and Maryculter

Leaving Aberdeen on the A93, to follow the Dee west, you pass Peterculter and Maryculter (pronounced kooter), 7 miles (11km) from the city and once a Roman camp. William the Lion granted the lands to the Knights Templar—the powerful soldier-monks of the Crusades—who built a chapel to St Mary, in the late 12th century. Its ruins can still be seen in Templars' Park on the south bank of the river. The highly coloured statue of Rob Roy standing above the Leuchar's Burn has no historic significance. It was originally a ship's figurehead and has been replaced twice since it was erected.

Drum Castle (open daily 1 May–30 Sept; weekends in April and Oct; grounds open all year: adm) is about 3 miles (4.5km) to the west, signposted off the A93, and is one of the three oldest tower houses in Scotland. A massive granite tower, built towards the end of the 13th century, adjoins a mansion built in 1619. Robert the Bruce gave Drum to his standard bearer, William de Irwin, in 1324, and it remained in the possession of the family until the late Mr H. Q. Forbes Irvine left it to the National Trust for Scotland in 1975. It contains antique furniture, silver, portraits, family treasures and relics. The grounds are lovely, with an oak wood, rare trees and shrubs, sweeping lawns, woodland nature trails, and a café.

Crathes Castle and Gardens

Crathes is 5 miles (8km) beyond Drum, signposted off the A93. (The castle, visitor centre, shop and restaurant are open at Easter, at weekends in April and Oct, and daily 1 May–30 Sept; the grounds are open all year: adm.) Although Crathes is familiar to many people from picture books, postcards, calendars and chocolate boxes, it is still a pleasant surprise when seen in reality. The Burnett family had been granted lands north of the Dee by Robert Bruce early in the 14th century, and it was Alexander Burnett who, in 1552, decided to move from his stronghold on an island in the Loch of Leys nearby, and build a modern house, in keeping with his status as laird. The castle took many years to complete and is one of the best examples of Scottish domestic architecture as it developed from the previously necessary fortified dwellings—a style that was to die out within 60 years. When a Victorian extension, overlooking the upper garden, was burnt down in 1966, it was agreed to restore the castle to its present, original proportions. The interior is just as it was, with painted decorations on the beams and woodwork, allegorical designs, proverbs and biblical texts. You can also see some of the original furnishings, among some of the many treasures that are on show. The little ivory hunting horn in the main hall symbolizes the Burnetts' right of tenure over part of the Royal Forest, given them by Robert the Bruce.

The Green Lady

Crathes has its ghosts, notably the Green Lady, who, dressed in green and carrying a baby in her arms, haunts certain rooms. A baby's skeleton was unearthed under the hearthstone in the Green Lady's room during the 19th century, and the story is told of a young girl, under the laird's protection, giving birth to a baby, fathered by one of the servants. Mother and infant died, under mysterious circumstances.

The gardens are a delight in every season of the year and you could happily pass days enjoying them. They consist of a series of small, interlinked gardens, each with its own motif and character, a profusion of colours, scents and blended textures. There are also nature trails in the grounds.

Banchory

Banchory, about 3 miles (4.5km) beyond Crathes, is a pleasant, sheltered town on the Dee. It rises in layers of terraced streets, backed by the **Hill o' Fare**, 1545 feet (475m), to the north, and rolling hills to the south. You catch an air of genteel respectability as you stroll among its antique shops and high-class boutiques.

The brand-new **Banchory Museum** in Bridge Street (open daily, April–Oct: free) tells the history of the area. In the 5th century, St Ternan, a local man and follower of St Ninian, established a monastery where the churchyard now is, and you can still see traces of its medieval successor. Incorporated into the walls of the manse, carved wheel-crosses date from this early Christian period. Palaeolithic flints, excavated nearby, suggest a very early settlement. There is a golf course by the river and the salmon fishing is renowned.Walk to the south of the town, where the Dee is joined by the Feugh, at **Bridge of Feugh**. The footbridge above the rapids is a good place from which to watch the salmon leaping up the ledges to get to their spawning grounds. There are forest and riverside walks as well as energetic hill climbs.

Aboyne

Aboyne, 13 miles (21km) to the west, is famous for its annual Highland Games. They take place every August on the large green, with all the traditional activities such as tossing the caber, putting the weight, piping and dancing. Aboyne is a good base from which to explore this part of Deeside and there are some excellent walks in the area. Follow the Water of Tanar, southwest of the town, through Glen Tanar, in whose woods you can see remnants of the old Caledonian Forest. Tanar oak was much used in the building of ships, being floated down the Dee to Aberdeen, in the 19th century. **The Braeloine Visitor Centre** (open daily April–Sept: donation box) is 5 miles (8km) up the glen, with all the usual educational information on local wildlife, farming, and forestry, as well as advice on where to walk. There are several tracks leading south, over the hills, one of which, Fir Mounth, is thought to be the route taken by Macbeth as he fled from the castle at Dunsinane to his death at Lumphanan.

Lumphanan is 5 miles (8km) northeast of Aboyne. The **Peel Ring** is a medieval motte with wall, earthworks and ditches and is believed to be where Macbeth fought his final battle against Malcolm Canmore in 1057. Macbeth's Cairn, in a circle of trees on the hill-side, marks the spot where he is said to have died, crying: 'Lay on Macduff; and damn'd be him that first cries "Hold enough!" ' (Shakespeare sets the death scene at Dunsinane.)

Tarland

Tarland, less than 5 miles (8km) northwest of Aboyne, is an old-world village set round a square and is the centre of the MacRobert Trust—a huge complex of farming and charitable foundations. Walk a short way to the east, beyond the golf course to the well-preserved souterrain, **Culsh Earth House** (open daily: free), by Culsh Farmhouse. Its roofing slabs are intact over a large chamber. Another prehistoric feature is **Tomnaverie Stone Circle**, on a rocky hillock a mile (1.5km) to the southeast, unexcavated and recumbent, probably dating from 1800 BC.

Ballater

Ballater, 11 miles (17.5km) west of Aboyne on the A93, used to be the end of the line for the Royal Train, before the railway was closed. It's a popular holiday centre in the summer, in wooded moorland where you can roam for miles, discovering fresh enchantment at every turn.

The town developed in the late 18th century after an old woman discovered the healing powers of the spring water at the foot of Pannanich Hill. Her discovery was exploited by an ex-Jacobite, Francis Farquharson of Monaltrie, 20 years after his exile and near-execution, following Culloden. This enterprising entrepreneur built an inn at the hamlet of Cobbletown of Dalmuchie and developed it into a spa, which quickly became fashionable. After Queen Victoria fell in love with Scotland and came to Balmoral, the whole area developed into the prosperous place it is today.

The views from **Ballater Golf Course**, sweeping away to the hills, must be distracting enough to kill concentration on the game. Ballater Highland Games are in August in Monaltrie Park, with all the traditional events, both athletic and musical, and a Hill Race to Craig Cailleach, south of the bridge. Victoria Week is in August.

Balmoral

Balmoral (grounds and paintings in ballroom open daily except Sun, in May, June and July: adm), 7 miles (11km) west, is another of those places so familiar from photographs that its reality is almost an anti-climax. Queen Victoria lost her heart to 'this dear Paradise', and she and Prince Albert bought the estate and the old castle in 1852, for £31,000. The old building, however, was too small for the royal household, and Prince Albert commissioned the building of the present granite mansion in 1853, a Scottish baronial edifice designed by William Smith of Aberdeen. It is still the Royal Family's holiday home.

Crathie Church, just north of the castle, was built in 1895 to replace a series of previous churches whose origins went back to the 9th century. It is attended by members of the Royal Family when they are on holiday.

Lochnagar towers over the Balmoral area, among 11 peaks over 3000 feet (923m) high: massive sentinels, reflected in the waters of Loch Muick to the south. This scenery inspired Byron to write:

England! thy beauties are tame and domestic
To one who has roved o'er the mountains afar:
Oh, for the crags that are wild and majestic!
The steep frowning glories of dark Lochnagar.

Royal Lochnagar Distillery (open daily, Easter–Oct: free) was founded in 1845.

A good 8-mile (13km) walk starts at **Spittal of Glenmuick** north-east of Loch Muick and goes round the loch anti-clockwise to the southwest corner and then across to the Dubh (black) Loch, deep in a corrie among brooding cliffs. You are about 2000 feet (615m) up here, and ice lingers on the water well into summer. Watch out for golden eagles, soaring overhead on long, splay-tipped wings. Less rare than they used to be, they are still a protected species, hated by sheep farmers. Another bird of prey you might see up here, also protected, is the peregrine falcon, plummeting to earth, its long pointed wings and tail streamlined, diving on its prey at speeds of 112 miles per hour (180km/h). In autumn you might hear the roaring of rutting stags.

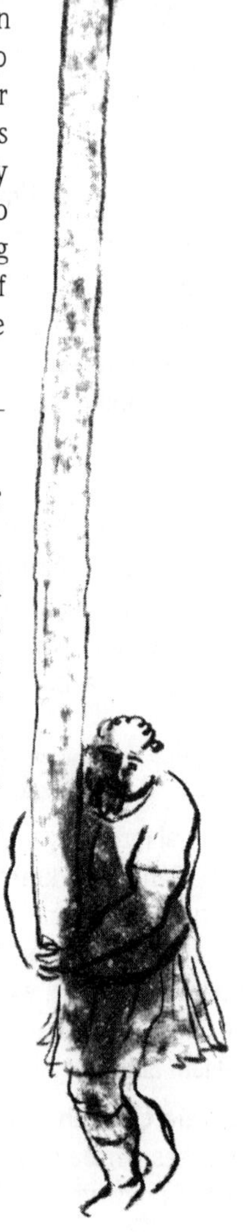

Braemar

Braemar, 9 miles (14.5km) southwest of Balmoral, is a very popular holiday centre surrounded by beautiful scenery.

Braemar Castle (open daily except Fri, May–mid Oct: adm) is a massive turreted fortress, built by the Earl of Mar in 1628. It was burnt by the Farquharsons in 1689 and garrisoned by the English after the Jacobite risings in 1715 and 1745 to protect the military road from Perth. The castle has barrel-vaulted ceilings, a sinister pit prison, spiral stairways and gun loops. Look for the carved graffiti on the internal woodwork, left by off-duty soldiers in the 18th century.

The Invercauld Arms stands on the spot where the Earl of Mar raised the Jacobite standard in 1715 and a plaque in the hotel commemorates the occasion.

Braemar Royal Highland Gathering is held every year on the first Saturday in September, drawing upwards of 20,000 people. It includes all the traditional events, both athletic and musical, together with plenty of stalls and sideshows. The Royal Family attend the games, which might be why it is one of the biggest events of its kind in Scotland. The origins of these Highland Games are said to date from the 11th century, when Malcolm Canmore held contests to find the best soldiers for his struggles against the Normans.

Linn of Dee

A tour of about 12 miles (19km) takes you west from Braemar through the wooded Dee Valley to the Linn of Dee. It is an attractive drive, which means it is also popular. The traffic can be tedious as the narrow road winds up through birches, with splendid views to the Cairngorms. Park at **Inverey** and walk the couple of miles on to the Linn of Dee. The narrow, rocky gorge is about 150 yards (138m) long and the river boils through this bottleneck in a tumultuous frenzy, filling the air with noise and a haze of spray. This lovely place is best appreciated early or late in the day.

Experienced walkers should try the famous **Lairig Ghru**, a testing walk from Linn of Dee over the Cairngorms to Aviemore.

Another walk from Inverey is south up the Ey Burn to **The Colonel's Bed**. The Colonel was John Farquharson of Inverey, a legendary character known as the Black Colonel, who used to ride his horse up sheer rock slopes and summon his servants by firing at a shield on the wall which rang like a bell when hit by a bullet. The Colonel's Bed is a ledge of rock in a gorge through which the Ey runs, where the Black Colonel hid after his castle had been burnt down by government troops following the Battle of Killiecrankie in 1689.

Where to Stay

expensive

Invery House, Banchory, © 03302 4782, is a luxury country-house mansion by the River Feugh, where you could be forgiven for trying to remember who has invited you so you can thank them for having you to stay—until you get the bill. They'll arrange golf and salmon fishing for you and you'll eat like a king. **Raemoir House Hotel**, at Raemoir, near Banchory, © 03302 4884, is an 18th-century mansion, converted from a private house in 1943. A number of the rooms have tapestried walls and antique furniture as well as all mod cons. They will arrange shooting, game fishing and stalking in season, and there is a tennis court and a mini nine-hole golf course in the grounds. There are also four self-catering apartments in the coachhouse. The food is first class.

Craigendarroch Hotel and Country Club, Ballater, © 03397 55858, prides itself on its leisure facilities. It is comfortable, if a little soulless, and stands in 29 acres of wooded hillside overlooking the River Dee and Lochnagar. Facilities include a 55-foot (17m) indoor swimming pool, whirlpool bath, two saunas, two squash courts, snooker table, games room, gymnasium, health and beauty treatments rooms, and a dry ski slope. When you've worked up an appetite, there are three restaurants to choose from.

moderate

Banchory Lodge Hotel, Banchory, © 03302 2545, is a Georgian house where the Water of Feugh flows into the Dee. Nice old-world hospitality and decent food makes this popular with the fishing fraternity. Closed in January. **Darroch Learg Hotel**, Ballater, © 03397 55443, is worth a visit for the views alone. This granite country house is in five acres of garden with views across the golf course to Lochnagar. Closed in January.

inexpensive

Invercauld Arms Hotel, Ballater, © 03397 55417, is a Victorian pile overlooking the Dee. It stands on the spot where the Earl of Mar raised the Jacobite standard in 1715 and displays a plaque commemorating the event. Some rooms overlook the river. The food isn't bad. Further down the scale, **Hazelhurst Lodge,** Aboyne, © 03398 86921, is a really friendly little place, with only four bedrooms and excellent candlelit dinners.

For really good value, try **Netherley Guest House**, Ballater, © 03397 55792. This pretty little house overlooks the green in the centre of the town

Aberdeen to Tomintoul

The A944 takes you west from Aberdeen through farm and moorland towards the hills. Less spectacular than Deeside, it is nevertheless attractive country with several prosperous private estates.

Castle Fraser

Castle Fraser (open every afternoon 1 May–30 Sept: adm; gardens and grounds open daily all year: donation) is about 15 miles (24km) from Aberdeen, to the north of the road. It is one of the most spectacular of the Castles of Mar, Z-plan, dating from the 16th century and incorporating an earlier castle. The Great Hall conjures dreams of feudal lairds: look for the eavesdropping device known as the 'Laird's Lug'. If you look closely at the great heraldic panel on the north side, you can see the inscription 'I Bel', left by one of the Bel family, who were important master masons, very active in Aberdeenshire. They may also have helped to build both Crathes and Craigievar. An exhibition, off the courtyard, tells the story of the Castles of Mar.

Alford

Montrose fought one of his victorious battles against the Covenanters in 1645 near Alford (pronounced Arford), 10 miles (16km) further west, on the ground between the village and the bridge over the Don. A sad story hangs over **Terpersie Castle**, recently rebuilt and lived in by its restorer, 4 miles (6.5km) northwest of Alford, and dating from 1561. The last owner, George Gordon, fought for Prince Charles at Culloden. He fled to the castle after the battle, to lie low until the worst of the reprisals were over. His young children, unaware of the threat, revealed that 'papa was at home' to his pursuers. He was captured in the castle and later executed.

Alford is on the Castle Trail and has a heritage centre in the old cattle mart (open daily, April–Sept: free). Also in the village is the **Grampian Transport Museum** (open daily April–Oct: adm); **Alford Valley Railway**, a narrow-gauge passenger railway which runs half-hour trips; and **Montgarrie Oatmeal Mill** (open Tues and Thurs, April–Oct: adm), a traditional, water-powered mill.

Kildrummy Castle

Kildrummy (open daily, April–Sept: adm) is a ruined courtyard castle 10 miles (16km) west of Alford, on the A97. Founded in the early 13th century, it is one of the most impressive and historic of the castles in this area. Edward I captured it and altered its design. Robert the Bruce sent his wife and children here when he went into exile on Rathlin Island in 1306. The story is told of a treacherous blacksmith who betrayed the fugitives to the English in return for their promise of 'as much gold as he could carry'. He set fire to the castle, whose inhabitants surrendered, receiving as his reward the molten gold, poured down his throat. The English executed Nigel Bruce, Robert's brother; the garrison was 'hangyt and drawyn' but Robert's intrepid wife, Elizabeth, escaped with her children and fled north to Tain. In 1404, Alexander Stewart, son of the Wolf of Badenoch, kidnapped the Countess of Mar, having killed her husband in order to widow her, and forcibly married her, to gain the title of Mar. The castle was destroyed because of the part it played in the 1715 rebellion.

Two miles (3km) to the south, at **Glenkindie**, you can see a well-preserved earth house in a clump of trees, its short entrance passage leading to two chambers, under massive roof slabs. You need a torch for the inner chamber.

From Glenkindie, follow the course of the Don through the valley of Strathdon and up into the hills to the west for less than 3 miles (4.5km). **Glenbuchat Castle** stands by the road at Bridge of Buchat, and dates from the 16th-century. It was the seat of 'Old Glenbucket' (sic), a staunch Jacobite, who died in exile in France after Culloden.

Big Foot, at Heughhead, is an adventure holiday establishment, with climbing, canoeing, etc: © 09756 51312.

Corgarff Castle

About a mile (1.5km) south, go right on the B973 for 8 miles (13km), through Strathdon to the A939: turn left to **Corgarff Castle** (open daily, April–Sept: adm; contact key keeper in winter, © 097 54 206). It is a stark, 16th-century tower house, within a star-shaped wall with gun loops. One terrible day in 1571, the family of the laird, Alexander Forbes, was besieged here by supporters of the deposed Mary, Queen of Scots. In her husband's absence, Forbes' wife refused to surrender. Edom o' Gordon ordered that the castle be burned, and she died in the flames, with her entire family and household, 24 in all. Corgarff was used by Jacobites in both 1715 and 1745. In 1748, in the aftermath of

Culloden, the Hanoverians converted it into a garrison post and barracks to guard the military road from Perth to Fort George. In the 19th century the castle was used by the Redcoats in their unpopular campaign against whisky smuggling. Recently reconstructed rooms are excellent.

This is skiing country, for hardy skiers who don't need too many sophisticated lifts and resorts. **The Lecht Road**, from Corgarff to Tomintoul, is part of the military road built by the Hanoverians after Culloden. It rises steeply from 1330 feet (409m) to 2100 feet (646m) within a distance of about 3 miles (4.5km). The wild moorland is frequently cut off by snow in winter, when fierce winds cause high drifts: remote farms and communities can be isolated for days.

Lecht Ski Centre is at the summit of the road, with several ski tows, a dry ski slope, ski school, ski hire and a café and crêche. A little further on is the **Glenmulliach Nordic Ski Centre** for cross-country skiers, with ski hire and tuition and miles of trails.

Lecht Mine, in the hills north of the Lecht Road near Well of Lecht, is where lead was mined between 1730 and 1737. The ore was taken on pack horses over the hills to Nethy Bridge where there was timber for smelting. Later it became a manganese ore mine but fell into disrepair when the price of ore fell.

Tomintoul

Tomintoul, 8 miles (13km) northwest of Corgarff, is second only to Dalwhinnie as the highest village in the Highlands, at 1150 feet (354m). Pronounced 'Tommin-towl', the name comes from the Gaelic *Tom-an-t-sabhal*, meaning 'hill of the barn'. The village lies along a gentle ridge flanked on one side by the River Avon (pronounced 'Arn'), famous for the clarity of its water, and on the other by Conglass Water. It is easy to drive through in a hurry and miss the attractions of this lofty, wild territory. Walkers will discover glens hidden in folds of the hills, with tumbling burns and tiny lochans, rich in bird, animal and plant life. The Tomintoul and Strathavon Highland Games are held on the third Saturday of July every year.

Tomintoul Museum (open daily from Easter to the end of Oct: free) is in an old baker's shop in the square and incorporates a tourist information centre. Displays include a reconstructed farm kitchen with all the old implements, a blacksmith's shop, a peat-cutting exhibition and information on wildlife, climate, landscape and geology.

Glenlivet, running north to the Spey, is not only at the heart of malt whisky country but also a settled farming area. In 1594, 1500 local men routed 10,000 Highlanders at the Battle of Glenlivet, and after the 1745 Rising army units were garrisoned in Glenlivet to maintain order and to try to stamp out the illicit distilling of whisky. Catholicism has remained strong here, especially in the secluded Braes of Glenlivet where, in the 18th century, the Seminary of Scalan was the only place in Scotland for young men to train for the priesthood. The college survived several attacks by Hanoverian soldiers and was finally moved to become Blairs College, near Aberdeen. The building at Scalen is being restored as a museum—a beautiful remote spot.

Tamnavulin Distillery (open daily except Sun, mid-March–end Oct: free) is about 5 miles (8km) north of Tomintoul on the B9008 and is one of the eight on the Malt Whisky Trail. It gives the usual tour, audio-visual show and free dram, and claims to be the most attractive and friendliest of them all. Opinions may differ on this, depending on how many free drams have already been tucked away, if you are doing the whole trail.

The Glenlivet Distillery Visitor Centre (open daily except Sun, Easter–end Oct: free) is a couple of miles north and also on the trail. It was founded as an illicit still in 1746 by a fugitive Jacobite after Culloden. (He changed his name from Gow to Smith because Gow, being the anglicized spelling of the Gaelic equivalent to Smith, was liable to arouse suspicion.) The distillery was subsequently made legal by his grandson. It offers the usual tours and a 10-minute audio-visual show called 'The Ballad of The Glenlivet'. There is a coffee shop and salad bar and a souvenir shop. Adults get their free dram but children under eight aren't allowed on the tours: either for safety or perhaps to protect them from the evils of the demon drink.

Where to Stay

moderate

If you like a touch of class, **Kildrummy Castle Hotel**, by Alford, ✆ 09756 71288, will suit you well. With all the style of a country mansion and the comforts of a modern first-class hotel, it stands in gardens and woods overlooking the castle from which it takes its name. It has a good restaurant and offers skiing, fishing and shooting packages.

The Glenavon Hotel, Tomintoul, ✆ 0807 580218, is comfortable and has good food.

inexpensive

For impoverished skiers, **Allargue Arms Hotel**, Corgarff, by Strathdon, ✆ 09754 210, is close to the Lecht slopes in gorgeous scenery. It is very friendly and relaxed. **Minmore House Hotel**, Tomintoul, ✆ 0807 590378 is also good value and friendly.

If you want something different, try **Glenavon Hotel**, Tomintoul, ✆ 0807 580218. They do adventure activity holidays, including hill-walking, rock-climbing, abseiling, canoeing, pony-trekking, gorge-walking and mountain-biking, all with instruction. Prices vary and they will tailor-make courses for you if you prefer.

Aberdeen to Elgin

The A96 is the main road from Aberdeen to Inverness, flanked by rich farmland and studded with ancient castles. Along the minor roads lie farming communities in pleasant, undulating scenery.

Kintore

About 10 miles (16km) from Aberdeen is the village of Kintore, a Royal Burgh since 1506. Its town hall, with outside stairs, was built in 1737. The church has a 16th-century tabernacle decorated with painted angels on a panel. A Pictish stone in the graveyard has both Christian and Pictish carvings—a good example of how careful those early Christians were not to offend any pagan gods that just might exist in spite of what the missionaries said. (The more prosaic explanation is that the converted Picts recycled the old stones after their conversion.)

Inverurie

Inverurie, 16 miles (25.5km) from Aberdeen, is surrounded by Pictish remains. The **Museum** (open daily except Wed and Sun: free) has an interesting permanent archaeological exhibition. It also stages three 'thematic' exhibitions each year. The **Bass** is a 60-foot-high (18.5m) motte, just outside the town, the site of a 12th-century castle. Mary, Queen of Scots visited a castle on this site in 1562. Pictish stones in the cemetery have clear carvings on them. There is a tourist information centre in the town hall in the Market Place, open from May to September.

Brandsbutt Stone is 2 miles (3km) north of Inverurie, with clear Pictish symbols and Ogham inscriptions, dating from the 8th century. The **Harlaw Monument**, on the B9001 less than 5 miles (8km) north of Inverurie, is a red granite obelisk marking the site of a particularly bloody clan battle in 1411. The cause of this carnage was the Countess of Ross. She renounced her inheritance to become a nun, leaving two uncles to fight for it: Donald, Lord of the Isles and Buchan, son of Regent Albany. Donald was beaten, lost his claim to the title, and was forced to swear allegiance to the Crown at a time when the Lords of the Isles considered themselves to be kings. Not much further along the road, the **Loanhead Stone Circle** is a burial cairn marked by a ring of standing stones surrounding a mass of smaller ones.

Pitcaple Castle

Pitcaple Castle (open if convenient: © 04676 204) is on the A96, south of Loanhead, a 15th- to 16th-century Z-plan tower house with 19th-century additions including two round towers. It is still a family home. Mary, Queen of Scots came here in 1562 and danced on the lawn, as did her great-grandson, Charles II, in 1650. The tree under which these two monarchs danced was replaced with a red maple by Queen Mary in 1923. Also in 1650, Montrose was brought here, a prisoner, renounced by the king for whom he had fought, on his way to execution in Edinburgh.

A mile (1.5km) south of Pitcaple, the 9th-century **Maiden Stone** is thought to be one of the finest early Christian monuments. It is 10 feet (3m) high and has a Celtic cross and Pictish symbols.

Bennachie is the long, wooded ridge rising to 1733 feet (533m) to the south, with an Iron Age hill fort on **Mither Tap**, one of the peaks. From all around this part of

Aberdeenshire, Bennachie dominates the skyline with its distinctively shaped top. Many claim it to be the site of the Battle of Mons Graupius, where Agricola penetrated the northeast and defeated the tribes in AD 83. Forestry Enterprise has developed signposted walks in this area for those who like to be guided.

The Picardy Stone, dating from the 7th or 8th century, is about 13 miles (21km) north-west of Inverurie on the B9002. Its Pictish symbols include a serpent, mirror and the mysterious 'spectacles' that are featured so often in those ancient carvings.

Leith Hall

Leith Hall (open every afternoon 1 May–30 Sept: adm; garden and grounds open all year: donation) is 4 miles (6.5km) west of the Picardy Stone, down an avenue. The earliest part of the house dates from 1650, a tower house with turrets and gables, with further wings added during the 18th and 19th centuries, around a central courtyard. In the exhibition room, you can see a writing case presented to Andrew Hay, the laird, by Prince Charles on the eve of Culloden, and the official pardon given to him after he had fought for the prince. Andrew Hay, known as 'The Gentle Jacobite', was a philanthropic man, 7ft 2in (2.2m) tall. The grounds include a zigzag herbaceous border, a rock garden, a pond walk with observation hide, a picnic area and a flock of Soay sheep. There are 18th-century stables and an ice house.

Eight miles (13km) north of Leith Hall, you pass through **Strath Bogie**, with **Clashindarroch Forest** to the west, cut by picturesque valleys.

Huntly

Huntly, 38 miles (61km) northwest of Aberdeen, is an 18th-century town on the plain, surrounded by hills, lapped by the rivers Deveron and Bogie.

Huntly Castle, once Strathbogie Castle (open daily: adm), is the ruin of a stately 17th-century palace in a wooded park above Deveron Water. It was the seat of the Marquesses of Huntly (the Gay Gordons), the most powerful family in this part of Scotland until the middle of the 16th century. The 12th-century fortress on the motte was owned by the Earl of Fife, a Gaelic Norman. Robert the Bruce convalesced here in 1307 after an illness. Just before the Battle of Bannockburn, the laird turned against Bruce. After the battle, his lands were forfeited and given to Sir Adam Gordon of Huntly, who had supported Bruce.

In those days the fortress was made of wood, which was gradually replaced by stone. It was finally destroyed during the Civil War of 1452, in the reign of James II. James IV was a frequent visitor, during an era when the Gordon Earls of Huntly were at the zenith of their power, and it was here that he witnessed the marriage between Catherine Gordon and Perkin Warbeck in 1496. Warbeck was a Flemish impostor, Pretender to the English throne, claiming to be Richard, Duke of York, the younger of the two 'princes in the tower'. It suited the Scottish king to encourage his claims, but Warbeck met his come-uppance in the Tower of London and was executed in 1499.

The rise and fall of the Gordons was reflected in the rise and fall of Huntly Castle, until the second Marquis of Huntly lost his head for supporting Charles I, having first been imprisoned in the castle. Don't miss the awful dungeons and the basement passage walls marked by the graffiti of the dungeon guards. The carved fireplaces and heraldic doorway are splendid.

Huntly Museum (open Tues–Sat: free), in the library in Main Square, gives a good grounding in local history, with temporary 'thematic' exhibitions throughout the year. **Glendronach Distillery** is open on weekdays for tours. **North East Falconry Centre**, at nearby Cairnie, flies eagles, owls and falcons daily (open April–Oct: free).

Dufftown

Dufftown, 10 miles (16km) west of Huntly, was founded in 1817 by James Duff, 4th Earl of Fife, to give employment after the Napoleonic Wars.

The Clock that Hanged MacPherson

The clock on the battlemented tower at the junction of the four main streets is known as 'the clock that hanged MacPherson'. MacPherson was an infamous freebooter who was condemned to death in Banff, to the north, in 1700 for robbing the rich and giving to the poor. A local petition for his reprieve was successful, but Lord Braco, the Sheriff of Banff, who loathed MacPherson, advanced the clock by an hour and hanged him before the reprieve arrived. The clock was subsequently removed from Banff and installed in this tower.

Dufftown is known as the capital of Scotland's malt whisky distilling, giving rise to an old couplet:

Rome was built on seven hills
Dufftown stands on seven stills.

Good barley, peat and the right sort of water are the three essential ingredients for whisky making and this area has them all. Whisky is more than just an industry in Scotland, it is part of its social history, with romantic tales of smugglers and illicit stills. The **Glenfiddich Distillery** is part of the Malt Whisky Trail (open weekdays all year and also at weekends May–mid-Oct; closed from Sat before Christmas to Sunday after New Year: free). It was founded by William Grant who bought second-hand equipment at a knock-down price in Cardhu, and produced the first bottling on Christmas Day, 1887. This is one of only two distilleries to have its own bottling plant. The audio-visual show is in six languages and you get your free dram at the end.

Dufftown Museum in the Clock Tower (open daily except Sun, May–Sept, and including Sun in July and Aug: free) has a collection of local photographs and information about Lord Mount Stephen who founded the Canadian Pacific Railway. The tourist information centre is here too.

Auchindoun Castle (plainly visible on a steep hill above the River Fiddich but unsafe and not open to the public), 2 miles (3km) southeast of Dufftown, is a massive three-storey keep, enclosed by prehistoric earthworks. It was built by Robert Cochran, who was one of the favourites of James III and was hanged by enraged barons in 1482. In 1689, a party of Jacobites gathered within these walls to hold a council of war after the death of their gallant leader, Graham of Claverhouse (Bonnie Dundee) at Killiecrankie.

Balvenie Castle

Some of the stones from Auchindoun were removed and used in the building of Balvenie Castle (open daily April–Sept: adm), a mile (1.5km) north of Dufftown, next to the Glenfiddich Distillery. Now a ruin, this was a 14th-century stronghold owned by the Comyns. Edward I was a visitor in 1304; Mary, Queen of Scots spent two nights here in 1562 while campaigning against the powerful Gordons; Montrose took refuge here in 1644; victorious Jacobites occupied the castle in 1689 after Killiecrankie, and Cumberland's troops occupied it in 1746.

Mortlach Parish Church (check opening times, © 0340 20380), on the southern edge of the town, is one of the oldest places of Christian worship in Scotland, believed to have been founded in 566 by St Moluag, a contemporary of Columba. There are monsters, beasts and a horseman carved on the weathered Pictish cross in the graveyard and an earlier Pictish stone in the porch. Substantially reconstructed in 1876 and again in 1931, it still has traces of an earlier building. There is a leper squint in the north wall and the lancet windows date from the 13th century. The watchtower in the graveyard, now used as a power house, was originally used to keep watch for body-snatchers.

Speyside Cooperage Visitor Centre at Craigellachie, 4 miles (6.5km) north of Dufftown (open weekdays all year, and Sat from Easter to mid-Oct), displays the cooper's craft over thousands of years and you can watch coopers at work.

A slight detour takes in three more distilleries on the Malt Whisky Trail: **Cardhu** (open weekdays all year and Sat from May to Sept: free), at Knockando, about 6 miles (9.5km) west of Craigellachie; **Tamdhu** (open weekdays, April–Oct and Sat from June to Sept: free), also at Knockando and **Glenfarclas** (open weekdays all year and Sat from June to Sept: free) at Ballindalloch, on the A95.

Ballindalloch Castle (open daily, Easter–Sept: adm), close to the distillery, is one of the few castles to be lived in continuously by its original family, the Macpherson-Grants, since 1546. The fortified 16th-century tower house is flanked by later additions down to Victorian times and some of the interior is impressive. Nice grounds, too.

The eighth distillery on the Malt Whisky Trail is **Glen Grant**, at Rothes, about 3 miles (4.5km) north of Craigellachie, (open weekdays Easter–Sept and Sat in July and August: free).

Keith

Keith is 11 miles (17.5km) northwest of Huntly, on the Isla, the hub of an area of rich farmland. The present town was developed in the late 18th and early 19th centuries but its history goes back to at least 700 when St Maelrubha of Applecross converted the inhabitants to Christianity. Scotland's post-Reformation saint St John Ogilvie was born in 1580 at Drumnakeith. He studied in Europe and returned to preach to his own people. He was hanged in 1615 for refusing to take the anti-Catholic oath of loyalty to the Crown. Beatified in 1929, he was canonized in 1976. There is a statue of him in the Roman Doric-style Catholic church. This building, partly copied from Santa Maria degli Angeli in Rome, comes as a surprise in an area that is not given to ornamentation of churches. It was built in 1830, helped by a donation from King Charles X of France, who took refuge in Scotland after he was exiled. He also gave the picture over the altar, *The Incredulity of St Thomas* by François Dubois. The stained-glass windows are by Father Ninian Sloane of Pluscarden Abbey. The imposing copper dome was added in 1915.

Keith has a Festival of Traditional Music and Song, the second weekend in June, and a major agricultural show in August.

Strathisla Distillery (open on weekdays, mid-May–mid-Sept: free) is nearby, on the Malt Whisky Trail, giving you another chance to watch the processes that produce Scotland's most popular export and to sample the result.

Fochabers

Fochabers, 8 miles (13km) northwest of Keith, on the Spey, is a good base from which to explore this area with riverside walks, excellent fishing and proximity to the Malt Whisky Trail. The village grew in the shadow of the walls of Gordon Castle, which provided employment for most of the people in the old days. It was moved to its present site in the 18th century to make room for extension of the castle. Part of the High Street is conserved and the buildings are much as they were when first built.

The Spey, with only 4 miles (6.5km) left in its race to the sea, runs slower now through shingle banks that threaten to close the mouth which has had to be dredged four times in this century, the most recent being in 1989. Salmon netting has been carried out for centuries from the spit at Tugnet, just down the river at Spey Bay, and this estuary region is rich in birds: kittiwakes, fulmars, cormorants, sandpipers swooping low over the water, curlews with their long curved beaks, tan-headed teal, black-collared ringed plovers, gannets, terns, shelduck, heron and osprey, to name but a few.

The northern section of the **Speyside Way** goes south from Spey Bay for 30 miles (48km) to Ballindalloch; from there, if you are still feeling energetic, it's only another 15 miles (24km) to Tomintoul. The walk begins at **Tugnet Ice House**, built in 1830 to store ice for packing the netted salmon and now a visitor centre with an exhibition on the salmon fishing industry, as well as information about local wildlife (open daily, June–Sept: free).

Fochabers Folk Museum in the High Street (open daily: adm) has the largest collection of horse-drawn vehicles in the north of Scotland and a mass of memorabilia from the days of service to the castle. There is a reconstructed village shop from the turn of the century, before the days of plastic wrappings and prepacked food.

Baxters Visitor Centre, a mile (1.5km) west of Fochabers, is well worth a visit (open weekdays, Jan–Dec; weekends during summer; check for tour days, © 0343 820393:

free). George Baxter was a gardener at Gordon Castle 120 years ago. He opened a grocery shop in Fochabers and sold jam made by his wife, Margaret. From this simple beginning evolved a business that has been handed down through the family to the present, producing a wide range of food that can be bought all over the world. The Duke of Richmond and Gordon, Baxter's old boss, took a keen interest and personally measured out the site for the factory one Sunday on his way home from church. You can see a Victorian kitchen similar to the one where the first Mrs Baxter tried out new recipes, and the modern kitchen where they are still experimenting to create new products. There are guided tours, an audio-visual show, shops, and a restaurant. Outside there are landscaped gardens by the river.

Elgin

Elgin, 9 miles (14.5km) west of Fochabers on the banks of the River Lossie, is the administrative and commercial capital of Moray, a busy market for the prosperous farms of the region and a popular holiday centre. The ruined cathedral is one of Scotland's jewels. The town, at first sight sturdy and austerely granite, invites closer inspection. Wander through it and you will discover a number of fine old buildings, excellently proportioned with delightful embellishments, and intriguing glimpses into wynds and closes. Elgin is drenched in history and is an excellent centre for exploring the northwest corner of Grampian.

First mentioned in history books in 1190, Elgin was the northern limit of English King Edward I's progress through the country. The town was partly burned by the Wolf of Badenoch in 1390, and again in a struggle for power between the Douglases and Huntlys in 1452. James II of Scotland used Elgin as a royal residence in the 15th century and Prince Charles lodged at Thunderton House for 11 days before the Battle of Culloden.

The town's Highland Games are held in July and there is a Fiddlers' Rally in September.

Elgin Cathedral (open daily: adm) stands on grass beside the river, a soaring symphony of arches, towers and windows, fretted against the sky. It was founded in 1224 and damaged by fire in 1270. In 1390, the Wolf of Badenoch, the wild and vicious natural son of Robert II, having been excommunicated by the bishop, burned down both town and cathedral, which contained treasures and valuable documents and manuscripts, with his 'wyld, wykked Helandmen'. After many ups and downs, the cathedral was stripped of its lead in 1567, by order of the Privy Council, in order to raise funds for defence. This act of authorized sacrilege was rewarded by the sinking of the ship that carried the lead. In 1650, Cromwell's troops did their worst to what remained, tearing down a beautiful rood screen and smashing the tracery of the west window. In spite of all this, peace and sanctity cling to this mellow ruin.

Bishop's House is just northwest of the cathedral. Here you can see a wing of the Precentor's Manse, with a 16th-century coat of arms on the wall.

Elgin Museum (open Tues–Sat, June–Sept and by appointment in winter: adm) is in an Italian-style building in the High Street, and won the 1990 Scottish Museum of the Year award. There is a collection of old red sandstone, Permian and Triassic fossils. Other exhibits include Bronze Age relics and natural history displays.

Little Cross in the High Street, dating from 1733, replaced an earlier one erected in 1402. In the old days, this was the place of public punishment, with stocks and jougs.

Lady Hill, opposite the post office in the High Street, bears only scant remains of the castle which once stood here, occupied by Edward I in 1296. The column, 1839, and statue, 1855, were put up in memory of the 5th and last Duke of Gordon.

Moray Motor Museum (open daily, April–Oct: adm) is in an old converted mill in Bridge Street. The small collection of vintage cars and motorbikes includes a stately 1929 Rolls Royce Phantom I, a 1913 Douglas motorbike and a macho 1939 SS100, gleaming red.

Old Mills (open daily except Mon, May–Sept: adm), west of the town on the Lossie, is a working meal mill dating from 1793. You can watch the milling in progress and learn what it's all about in the Old Mills Visitor Centre.

Johnstons Cashmere Visitors Centre at Newmill, to the east of the town (open daily except Sun: free), has exhibitions, production demonstrations, a coffee shop and a mill shop.

The ruins of **Spynie Palace** are a couple of miles (3km) north of Elgin—there is access to a small car park from the Elgin–Lossiemouth Road. This was the castle of the Bishops of Moray in the 13th to 17th centuries. At one time the sea reached as far as the hillock on which the palace stands, with a good harbour and town. The sea then threw up a bar of sand and shingle across the mouth of the estuary, cutting off Spynie and turning the area into a loch surrounded by marshland. A canal was built by Thomas Telford in 1808, to drain the loch into the sea 5 miles (8km) north at Lossiemouth. Great floods in 1829 destroyed all the works and the loch grew again until the 1860s. The old palace saw much history. Mary, Queen of Scots stayed there in 1562 during her tour of the north, and it became a refuge for Covenanters in 1654, during Montrose's campaigns. James Ramsay MacDonald, Britain's first Labour Prime Minister, was buried in Spynie churchyard in 1937. (The church was moved to New Spynie, 4 miles (6.5km) to the west.)

Pluscarden Abbey

Pluscarden Abbey (always open: free) is signposted off the A96, about 5 miles (8km) southwest of Elgin, and is one of Grampian's jewels. Lying in a sheltered valley below a ridge of wooded hills, Pluscarden represents an act of faith that must be an inspiration to believer and non-believer alike and is spiritually uplifting. The original abbey was founded by Alexander II in 1230, for an order of white-habited monks, the Valliscaulians, whose mother house was in France. It suffered damage at the hands of Edward I of England in 1303, and far worse damage from the Wolf of Badenoch, during his revenge on the Bishop of Elgin in 1390. In 1454 it took in Benedictines from Urquhart Priory, probably for economic as well as political reasons. Just before the Reformation took off, a greedy, scheming prior, Alexander Dunbar, anticipating what was to come, managed to 'redistribute' priory funds and lands in favour of his family. He died in 1560 and by the end of that century the priory had passed into the authority of a lay commendator. The estate passed through various hands, gradually falling into disrepair and ruin.

In 1943 the Pluscarden lands were given to the Benedictine community of Prinknash Abbey, near Gloucester, a breakaway community from an Anglican order, whose proposals of doctrinal reform had caused some of its monks to rebel and become Roman Catholic. This order of converted Benedictines started rebuilding Pluscarden in 1948 and today you can see what they have achieved: a truly remarkable feat. Monks, dressed in coarse white habits, busy about their work on the land, add a medieval touch.

The choir and transepts are entire, as are the domestic buildings. The interior is a haven of timeless tranquillity, lit by a rich glow of colour from the modern stained-glass windows and overlaid by a lingering smell of incense. If you are lucky, you may hear, filtering through the walls from the Lady Chapel, the sound of the monks singing their daily office. You can go into the transept aisles, now a public chapel, and kneel at the south end to look through a wide squint into the Lady Chapel.

Coastal towns and villages beyond Elgin are mentioned in the final section of this chapter.

Where to Stay

expensive

The pick of the bunch on this route has to be **Leslie Castle** near Insch, © 0464 20869, especially if you fancy a touch of class and don't mind paying for it. This nicely restored 17th-century castle, with corner turrets and a truly ancestral feeling, will fill you with illusions of grandeur and you'll eat well. **Pittodrie House Hotel**, at Pitcaple, is a 15th-century pile overlooking farmland, furnished with antiques, tapestries and fine paintings. The food is cordon bleu and they have two squash courts, tennis court, billiards, croquet and clay pigeon shooting.

moderate

Delnashaugh Inn, Ballindalloch, © 0807 500255, is excellent value. **Rothes Glen Hotel**, Rothes, © 03403 254, is a castle-style Victorian mansion designed by William Smith who designed Balmoral, in 40 acres of attractive parkland grazed by Highland cattle. The food is good, especially the local beef and fish. **Thainstone House Hotel** in Inverurie, © 0467 21643, is a country house surrounded by meadows and woods, with a comfortable, easy-going atmosphere. There are only eight bedrooms and the food isn't at all bad.

Gordon Arms Hotel, in Fochabers High Street, © 0343 820508/9, is an old coaching inn on the A96 to Inverness, full of old-world atmosphere and an ideal stopping-off place for excellent food. **Mansion House Hotel**, The Haugh, Elgin, © 0343 48811, is a comfortable mock castle by the river where you will eat and sleep well and not feel cheated.

The Old Manse at Bridge of Marnoch, near Huntly, © 04665 873, is an attractive Georgian country guest-house in peaceful surroundings in the Deveron Valley. **Ugie House Hotel** in Church Road, Keith, © 05422 7671, is an unpretentious and dependable establishment.

Aberdeen to Turriff

The northeast shoulder of Grampian, well clear of the dramatic hills and spectacular glens further west, is mainly flattish farmland, studded with clumps of trees and a maze of burns and small rivers.

Pitmedden Garden and Museum

Pitmedden is best reached along the rural lanes to the east of the A947, 14 miles (22km) north of Aberdeen off the B999. The garden (open all year, daily: adm) was created by Sir Alexander Seton who inherited Pitmedden in 1667: it was restored by the National Trust for Scotland in 1952. July and August are the best months to see this re-creation of a formal 17th-century garden, split-level with an upper garden and terraces overlooking the Great Garden. Sir Alexander modelled three out of the four symmetrical parterres, bordered by box hedges, on floral designs first used in Holyrood in 1647, in honour of Charles I. The fourth depicts the Seton coat of arms. Pillared gates lead into the Great Garden, down a graceful twin stairway, with two ogee-roofed pavilions. There is a fountain in each garden and no less than 27 sundials, none of which is more than ten minutes off true time. Whether you admire formal gardens or not, you cannot fail to appreciate the splendour of this one. You can see Sir Alexander's bathhouse, in one of the two-storied pavilions, and a key to all the flowers in the garden. (The two 'thunder houses' are rare in Scotland.) In the other pavilion is an exhibition on the evolution of formal gardens.

The Museum of Farming Life (open daily 1 May–30 Sept: adm) has a collection of agricultural and domestic implements. You can walk around the 100-acre estate, through attractive woods and farmland, and there is the usual adventure playground, picnic area and visitor centre.

Tolquhon Castle

Tolquhon Castle (open daily: adm) is a roofless ruin, a mile (1.5km) northwest of Pitmedden. Once the seat of the Forbes family, a 16th-century quadrangular mansion was built on to an early 15th-century rectangular tower. The forbidding fortress exterior hides a domestic residential inner court. You can still see the kitchen, cellars and stairways, with the hall and laird's room (which has a private stair to the kitchen) on the first floor. An inscription on the gatehouse is an endearing trumpet blast from the laird who did so much to enlarge the original castle: 'Al this wark, excep the auld tour, was begun be William Forbes 15 Aprile 1584, and endit be him 20 October 1589'.

William Forbes' master mason was Thomas Leiper, of a renowned family of masons, and it was he who designed the elaborate Gothic tomb of William and his wife, Elizabeth Gordon, in the church at **Tarves** a couple of miles north. It is rich in Renaissance detail, with statuettes of the couple standing on either side.

Haddo House

Haddo (open daily 1 May–30 Sept: adm) is less than 4 miles (6.5km) north of Tarves. This fine Georgian mansion was built in 1732 by William Adam on the site of a former house, House of Kellie, home of the Gordons of Haddo, Lords of Aberdeen, for over 500 years and burned down by Covenanters. The present house stands in a park surrounded by lovely gardens, showing all William Adam's mastery of symmetrical design. It contains antique furniture, pictures and treasures in its elegant rooms. The stained-glass window in the chapel is by Burne-Jones.

Haddo has developed its own choral society, with a theatre, beside the house. This is one of Scotland's leading musical bodies with productions of opera and concerts starring international artists. (If you are interested, write to the Choral Secretary, Haddo House, Grampian. Seating is limited.)

Fyvie Castle

Fyvie is about 6 miles (9.5km) northwest of Haddo, and is off the A947 (open daily 1 May–30 Sept: adm). Dating from the 13th century, the castle has been described as the 'crowning glory of Scottish baronial architecture'. It stands on a mound above a bend in the River Ythan, approached up a long drive that skirts the lake among trees and rhododendrons. In the days when kings moved from house to house, William the Lion used to visit Fyvie. It passed through many hands over the centuries and its five towers represent its five dynasties of lairds: Prestons, Meldrums, Setons, Gordons and Leiths. The National Trust for Scotland acquired it from Sir Andrew Forbes-Leith in 1984. The splendid structure incorporates substantial remains of the medieval Fyvie. The square and round towers soar to a mass of corner turrets, conical roofs and corbels and inside there is an impressive wheel stair.

Alexander Forbes-Leith bought the estate in 1889. He used the fortune that he had made in the American steel industry to restore the castle, sweeping away much of the ugly additions that had been added over the years, and filling it with treasures that can still be seen there today. The paintings include some of the finest portraits you could ever hope to see, by Gainsborough, Romney, Opie, and Raeburn. The *pièce de résistance*, perhaps, is the 18th-century portrait of Colonel William Gordon, by Pompeo Batoni—a deliciously romantic study of a patrician colonel, standing in rich silken tartan, gazing somewhat disdainfully at a statue of Roma. Fyvie is a stately home not to be missed.

Gight Castle is a scant ivy-clad ruin to the east of Fyvie, by the River Ythan, reached by a footpath off the B9005. There isn't a signpost, but look for a turning by the scrapyard near Cottown. It dates from about 1560 and is associated with a particularly wild branch of the Gordon family, infamous for murders and suspiciously sudden deaths. Watch out for the Hagberry Pot, close to the castle—a bottomless pit reputed to be a direct route to Hell.

The 13th Laird of Gight was Catherine Gordon who married 'Mad' Jack Byron. Their son was George Gordon, Lord Byron. Mad Jack, alas, was a compulsive gambler and gambled the castle away long before the birth of his talented son.

Towie Barclay Castle (open by appointment, © 088 84 347), 3 miles (4.5km) north of Fyvie, is an ancient stronghold of the Barclays dating from 1136, recently restored and the winner of a number of major European restoration awards. There is a formal walled garden in the grounds.

Turriff

Turriff, 8 miles (13km) north of Fyvie on the A947, stands at the confluence of the River Deveron and the Water of Idoch. It is a red sandstone town, first mentioned in the 6th century when the Gaelic poet Ossian described it as the capital of a Pictish prince, Lathmon. It is believed that St Congan founded a monastery near the village in the 8th century. The old church, now a ruin, at the end of Castle Street existed in the 11th century, and in 1179 Knights Templar—soldier monks of the crusades—were given land in Turriff to found their second Scottish base. The 20-foot (6m) mercat cross in Castle Street is 16th-century. The town is still remembered for 'The Trot of Turriff', when a party of Royalists defeated the Covenanters in the first skirmish of the Civil War, in 1639.

The two-day annual Turriff Show in August is one of the largest agricultural events in Europe, attracting over 50,000 people each year.

Delgatie Castle (open by appointment only, © 0888 63479: adm) is 2 miles (3km) east of Turriff. This L-plan tower house, home of the Clan Hay, dates back to the 12th century, with later additions. Inside there are pictures, weapons, the widest turnpike stair in Scotland and 16th-century painted ceilings which are believed to caricature people who lived in the castle at the time. Mary, Queen of Scots stayed here for three days in 1562 and there is a portrait of her in the room she used. Part of the castle and stables have been converted into self-catering holiday flats.

Eden Castle, 7 miles (11km) north of Turriff, not open to the public but visible from the outside, is a ruin with a grisly legend attached to its 17th-century stones. The wife of a tenant on the estate asked the laird to control her wild son. He did so, by drowning the boy in the river, and the mother's subsequent curse caused the castle to fall down. All that remains now is the tower, inhabited by animals from a nearby farm.

Where to Stay

Fife Arms Hotel, Turrif, © 0888 63468, is very reasonable and comfortable. Otherwise, the hotels mentioned in the previous section, Aberdeen to Elgin, and those in the following, coastal route section, are the best ones to go for, unless you want to sample one of the self-catering flats mentioned under Delgatie Castle, above. The prices vary: © 0888 63479 for details.

The Coast: Aberdeen to Forres

Going north from Aberdeen on the coast road, you see another face of Grampian: miles of sandy beaches interspersed with rock cliffs, bordering an endless stretch of ocean to the east and north. Fishing towns and villages are strung out along the way, each with its legends of seafaring adventures and smuggling. Inland lie prosperous farms and good fishing rivers.

Leaving Aberdeen on the A92, you go through **Bridge of Don**, past the barracks that were once the home of the Gordon Highlanders. Long, dune-backed beaches fringed by brambly golf courses, and an army firing range, stretch north for 6 miles (9.5km) to **Balmedie Country Park**. Further up, **Ythan Estuary** cuts into the dunes at **Newburgh** and from here to **Collieston** a vast nature reserve comprises heath, dunes, pasture and cliff: a haven for both ornithologist and botanist. Collieston is a picturesque village with a harbour, very similar to the villages in the East Neuk of Fife. T. E. Lawrence wrote much of *The Seven Pillars of Wisdom* here.

The sandy sweep of **Cruden Bay**, about 5 miles (8km) north of Collieston, is where the pipeline comes in from the Forties Oil Field, over 100 miles (160km) out in the North Sea. The name Cruden comes from *croju-dane*, meaning slaughter of the Danes. This refers to a bloody battle between Malcolm II and the Danes in 1012, led by Canute, later King of England. The Scots won and the Danes withdrew, undertaking to leave Scotland alone. Canute then turned his attention to England which he conquered four years later.

Whinnyfold, the cliff-top village at the south of Cruden Bay, once had 24 fishing boats, despite not having a harbour. The boats were drawn up on the shingle beach and the fish laid out on the stones to dry. The jagged rocks off here—the Scours of Cruden—have claimed many wrecks. It is said that at a certain time of year the bodies of those who have perished during the previous 12 months come out of the sea to join their spirits in heaven or hell. (This legend inspired Bram Stoker to write *Mystery of the Sea*. It is said that Stoker was inspired by Slains when he wrote *Dracula*. He used to holiday in the area and finally retired to Whinnyfold.)

New Slains Castle

Walk north from Cruden Bay, a couple of miles (3km) along the cliffs, till you get to New Slains Castle (always accessible: free). This extensive ruin stands high above the sea, which rages at its feet in rough weather. It was built by the 9th Earl of Errol in 1598 to replace Old Slains Castle, further south, of which only a fragment remains. Old Slains was destroyed by James VI to punish Erroll for taking part in a revolt of Catholic nobles. 'New' Slains is a splendid, awe-inspiring ruin and its extremely dangerous situation makes it unsuitable for children to visit unaccompanied. It is amusing to walk among its massive, rather gloomy walls and recall Johnson and Boswell's visit in 1773. Johnson was most impressed by its position, writing: 'when the winds beat with violence it must enjoy all the terrifick grandeur of the the tempestuous ocean . . . the walls of one of the towers seem only a continuation of the perpendicular rock, the foot of which is beaten by the waves.'

Boswell, always fastidious about his comforts, wrote: 'I had a most elegant room: but there was a fire in it which blazed; and the sea, to which my windows looked, roared; and the pillows were made of the feathers of some sea-fowl which had to me a disagreeable smell: so that by all these causes I was kept awake a good while.' Slains reached its zenith at the turn of the century when the 19th Earl, a philanthropic man, created what has been described as a mini welfare state in the district and played host to many writers, actors, musicians and singers of the day. As a result of crippling death duties, taxation and the 19th Earl's generosity, his heir was forced to sell the castle to an absentee landlord who allowed it to fall into disrepair.

Johnson and Boswell also visited the **Bullers of Buchan**, just north of Slains Castle. Here the sea has eroded a sheer 200-foot (60m) rock chasm, into which the water pounds through a natural archway. Bullers means 'boilers'. Johnson wrote of this: 'which no man can see with indifference, who has either sense of danger or delight in rarity'. Much to the horror of Boswell, Johnson insisted on exploring the cavern by boat, writing later: 'If I had any malice against a walking spirit, instead of laying him in the Red Sea, I would condemn him to reside in the Buller of Buchan'.

Buchan means 'the land at the bend in the ocean' and was the name of Scotland's most northeasterly corner where the North Sea meets the Moray Firth. **Boddam**, about 3 miles (4.5km) north of Slains, is an old fishing village on Buchan Ness, the most easterly point on the mainland. There is a pleasant 19th-century character in the older parts of Boddam, though it is hard to believe they once boasted 85 herring drifters and 13 curing yards. All the fishing boats now operate out of Peterhead.

Peterhead

Peterhead, originally called Peterugie, is a couple of miles (3km) north near the mouth of the River Ugie and is known locally as the 'Blue Toon'. It is the most easterly town on the Scottish mainland. The first harbour was built in 1593 and the town has always been linked with fishing, from early times when the first fishermen used lines to catch cod and ling. Whaling began in 1788 and Peterhead quickly became the leading whaling port in Britain, until herring fishing took over in 1818. By 1836, 260 boats fished out of Peterhead, rising to over 400 by the middle of the century. During this time extensive, deep-water harbours were built, so that when fishing boats grew larger and could no longer use the smaller ports, Peterhead flourished. Although herring fishing is dying fast, the town continues to prosper, with white fish as its main catch. It is now the largest white fish port in Europe with over 400 highly sophisticated boats. It was also ideally placed to cope with the influx of sea traffic during the oil-boom of the 1970s.

Peterhead was a popular spa town in the 17th, 18th and 19th centuries and the remains of a mineral well and some baths can still be seen by the lifeboat shed. Burns was one of the many people who took the waters here. Surrounded by sandy beaches, golf courses and dunes, it is the largest town in the northeast, after Aberdeen. Many of the houses are built of local pink granite.

The Harbour with its three main basins is an energetic place, with boats coming and going; vessels being refitted, repaired, repainted; chandlers and all the clutter of a seafaring port. The **Fishmarket**, as in Aberdeen, is a place to visit early in the morning when the boats are landing their catches in up to 14,000 boxes. Business starts at 8.30am except on Sundays, but you are best to go well before this to get the full flavour of this salty industry. Catches include whiting, haddock, sole, cod, mackerel and herring.

Town House, built in 1788, has a spire 125 feet (38.5m) high. The statue in front is of Field Marshal Keith, born in Peterhead, who became Frederick the Great of Prussia's most trusted general, killed in battle in 1758.

Deer Abbey (officially open Thurs–Sun, but the caretaker is usually there and will let people in) is 9 miles (14.5km) west of Peterhead. This insubstantial ruin was a Cistercian monastery founded in 1219 by Comyn, Earl of Buchan. It thrived until the late 16th century and you can see the ground plan quite clearly, though most of the masonry was taken away for other uses.

Aden Heritage Centre (pronounced 'Adden') is a mile (1.5km) west of Mintlaw, near Deer Abbey (open daily May–Sept and at weekends in April and Oct: adm). The semi-circular farm steading, recently restored from almost total dereliction, was inspired by the French wife of a former laird. Reconstructions show past and present farming life in this agricultural area—you can almost smell the oatcakes, cooking on the griddle. Audio-visual shows and exhibitions give further information on the life of estate staff at the turn of the century. There is a shop, a café, a picnic area and separate camp site. Aden stands in a country park around the consolidated ruin of the old mansion, with nature trails and all the trimmings, open all year.

Back to the coast, the villages along this northeast corner are unspoiled and soaked in seafaring history, their deserted sands a hermit's dream. Many of the original fisher cottages remain, sturdy and low, their gable-ends to the sea, to take the full force of winter storms. In some of the villages, the old tradition of painting the houses with oil paint to protect them from the weather has become a competitive attempt to produce the most striking colour.

Rattray is a wild, unfrequented area south of Loch of Strathbeg, about 6 miles (9.5km) north of Peterhead. Once a thriving fishing port and Royal Burgh, its records go back to the 12th century, to the days when the loch was open to the sea. In 1720, a great storm caused the dunes to shift, cutting off the loch and silting up the harbour. Today, all that remains is a ruined chapel, said to have been built in the 13th century in memory of the son of the Earl of Buchan who drowned in a well there, and the remains of a Comyn fortress in the process of excavation by Aberdeen University.

Loch of Strathbeg Nature Reserve covers 2300 acres including the loch, with over 180 different birds recorded, including such rarities as the Caspian tern with its black crown and heavy orange-red bill, the pied-billed grebe from North America—such a rare visitor to Scotland that only five have been seen since 1963—and the red-footed falcon with bright red patches round its eyes as well as its legs. There are two hides and entry to the reserve is by written permission only; write to The Warden, Loch of Strathbeg Nature Reserve, Crimonmogate, Fraserburgh.

Crimond, just west of the loch on the main road, has two claims to fame. Its clock shows 61 minutes to the hour—a slip of the clockmaker's hand—and the Crimond version of the 23rd Psalm was composed by Jessie Seymour Irvine, daughter of the local manse.

On the southern slopes of **Mormond**, the hill to the west of the main road and the highest point in this area, at 768 feet (236m), the glittering white quartzite horse and stag were cut out of the hill in the 18th century by a Captain Fraser, possibly as memorials. Fraser built the now ruined hunting lodge above the horse.

Cairnbulg and Inverallochy, one either side of the B9107 about 3 miles (4.5km) north of Loch of Strathbeg, are among the oldest coastal settlements in the area with their original fisher cottages. One of these, known as 'Maggie's Hoosie', was to be restored and fitted out to show life in a 19th-century fishing community but the Community Council are now debating whether this plan is feasible.

Fraserburgh

Across Fraserburgh Bay from Cairnbulg Point, Fraserburgh stands on the shoulder of Grampian at Kinnaird Head, a great slate rock thrusting into the North Sea and the Moray Firth. It is not a beautiful town but an unmistakable tang of the sea lurks in its bones, giving it great character, and its 3 miles (4.5km) of dune-backed beach has won international awards for cleanliness. Known locally as the Broch—Scots word for burgh—the town began as a village called Faithlie. The Frasers bought the lands of Faithlie in 1504 and began developing the town. The first harbour was built in 1546 and in the 1570s Sir Alexander Fraser built a castle on Kinnaird Head. At the peak of the herring boom, during the last 30 years of the 19th century, more than 1000 drifters would land their fish during the season which ran from July to September. Today the town is a major white fish port and the harbour is an increasingly busy commercial port.

Kinnaird Head Lighthouse is the oldest in Scotland and the original was built on to the castle in 1787. Admission by appointment: ✆ 0346 28175. **The Wine Tower**, overlooking the cove beside the lighthouse, is thought to have originally been a chapel dating from the 16th century and then perhaps a watch tower. It is a strange building with three floors which have no connecting stairs. Six carved pendants attached to the arched room have been acclaimed as the finest examples of late 16th-century three-dimensional heraldry in Scotland. Access is by arrangement with the Tourist Board.

The **Mercat Cross** in Saltoun Square is dated 1736 but thought to have been carved around 1603, as it is the only one in Scotland to show the royal arms of both the old Kingdom of Scotland and the new United Kingdom. The carved **Moses Stone** inside the South Church, dated 1613, is all that remains of the University of Fraserburgh, a short-lived establishment that attracted many students for a brief time when there was a cholera epidemic in Aberdeen.

Rosehearty about 4 miles (6.5km) west of Fraserburgh, is one of the oldest ports in Scotland. A party of Danes is said to have been shipwrecked here early in the 14th century. They were absorbed by the crofting community whom they taught to fish, an industry that was to swell to vast proportions along this coast. In the mid-19th century, Rosehearty rivalled Fraserburgh as a fishing port but when the herring fishing declined, Fraserburgh's railway link and larger harbour drew the new steam drifters and Rosehearty's industry dwindled.

Pitsligo Castle (always accessible: free), half a mile (1km) to the south, was built by the Frasers in 1424 and is now a large and impressive ruin with 9-foot (3m) thick walls. Originally the square keep had three rooms, one on top of the other: a vaulted kitchen, a vaulted banqueting hall and at the top, a sleeping apartment with 24 beds. It was extended into a courtyard castle in the 1570s.

The last laird was Alexander Forbes, 4th and last Lord Pitsligo, a fervent Jacobite who was forced into hiding when his lands were forfeited after Culloden in 1746. He dressed in rags and hid in caves or in the houses of his tenants for 46 years until he died at the age of 84. He is remembered for his generosity to the poor. The castle was bought by one of his descendants, an American multi-millionaire, Malcolm Forbes, who is said to have plans for turning it into a heritage centre.

New Aberdour, a mile (1.5km) inland from Aberdour Bay, west of Rosehearty, was built in 1798 to succeed an earlier village on the bay. Saints Columba and Drostan are said to have landed here around AD 597 and founded a Celtic monastery at **Old Deer**, some 10 miles (16km) southeast as the crow flies. *The Book of Deer* came from here—one of the most precious literary relics of the Celtic church—a 9th-century Latin manuscript of parts of the New Testament, with Gaelic notes in the margin. It is now in the Fitzwilliam Library in Cambridge.) Ruined **Old Aberdour Church** stands above the Dour Burn on the road down to the bay. It was founded by the two saints and part of it is Norman. The old font is said to have held the miracle-working bones of St Drostan and the oldest readable gravestone is dated 1440.

The broad sweep of Aberdour Bay is popular with holidaymakers, with rock pools and caves. At low tide you can get away from the crowds by walking round the headlands to more deserted stretches of clean sand. Everyone has heard of Grace Darling, but not so many of Jane Whyte whose memorial can be seen on the ruin of a woollen mill, where she lived, on the bay. In 1884, this brave lass saved the lives of 15 men, shipwrecked when their steamer ran aground during a storm. She struggled through raging seas to carry a line out to the ship along which the seamen could escape.

Dundarag Castle is a ruin on the cliffs above Aberdour Bay to the northeast. Dun Dearg—Red Fort—was probably Pictish before it was turned into a monastery by St Drostan. It later became a Comyn stronghold and was destroyed by Robert the Bruce in 1308. Quickly refortified, it was as quickly re-demolished, this time in the 16th century by the English. It is now privately owned and can be visited with permission from the owner who lives in the gatehouse.

Rocky **Ceard's Cove**, west of Aberdour Bay, has a hermit's cave, where an anti-social retired sailor lived in the 1920s and 1930s.

Pennan, on the western side of Aberdour Bay, is a picturesque village on a ledge below high red sandstone cliffs with a pebbly beach running down to the sea. You have to be practically on top of the village before you see it. If it seems familiar to filmgoers, it was one of the settings for *Local Hero*, including the public telephone box from which the central character made his reports to his American boss. (Other settings were at Arisaig and Morar.) The smuggling of liquor and silk ran a close second to fishing as the main industry here, with lots of secret coves and caves in which to evade the exciseman.

Bronze Age **Fort Fiddes**, on a promontory above sandy **Cullykhan Bay**, west of Pennan, is said to be the earliest industrial site in Europe. Beads from the Rhine region are among the artefacts excavated from the ruins by archaeologists, suggesting that the inhabitants traded with the Continent as far back as 700 BC. It's an impressive site, overlooking the sheer face of Lion Head and the deep gash in the cliff called Hell's Lum (chimney).

Troup Head is a massive red sandstone headland beyond the bay, separating Pennan from **Crovie**, which is reached either by a narrow footpath along the bottom of the cliff or by a steep, zigzag road with a 1 in 5 gradient. It clings to the foot of the cliffs, its cottages with one gable-end practically in the sea and the other tucked into the cliff. There is only a narrow footpath between the cottages and the sea. This tiny village once had nearly 100 fishermen and over 60 boats. A tremendous gale in 1953 drove many of the villagers to seek a more sheltered home and Crovie was temporarily deserted.

Gardenstown, a mile (1.5km) to the west, is larger, built on the cliff that rises from Gamrie Bay in a series of narrow terraces. The road through the village descends steeply in a series of hair-raising bends dropping from roof level behind a house to run level with the door in front. The original Seatown is at the bottom with narrow footpaths and huddled, whitewashed cottages. This lower bit, severely threatened by the gale that depopulated Crovie, was saved by the newly built seawall.

There were no inland villages in Buchan before the 18th century. Between 1750 and 1850 local landowners built a succession of 'planned' villages, to house and employ displaced tenants during a period of 'enclosures' for estate improvement. These little inland villages have down-to-earth names: Auchnagatt, Longside, Maud, Mintlaw, Stuartfield, Cuminestown, Fetterangus, New Blyth, New Leeds, New Pitsligo, Strichen. Dotted over the hinterland, each of them retains a strong community spirit and many of the traditional trades continue to flourish.

Central Buchan Tourism Group publish a leaflet, 'Walks Roon Aboot Buchan', giving 33 walks that take in places of interest on the way.

Macduff

Macduff is a fishing town about 6 miles (9.5km) west of Gardenstown, at the foot of the Hill of Doune beside the Deveron estuary. It developed as a spa when **The Well of Tarlair**, a mineral spring just east of the town, was found in 1770 to have healing properties. Health fanatics used to flock to drink the waters until the well dried up. (It was blown up by a mine in the last war and is now a derelict swimming-pool.) Macduff stands around a four-basin harbour, with a thriving fish market and a customs house. Next to the Doune Church there is an anchor, 13 feet (4m) long, weighing more than 3 tonnes. It is believed to be from an 18th-century sailing ship and was dragged up in a fishing net. It was placed here by the Town Cross to symbolize the town's long association with the sea. The Harbour Master organises tours of the harbour on Wednesday afternoons and Friday mornings in July and August. If you climb the hill to the 70-foot (21m) high octagonal War Memorial Tower, you get splendid views of the rugged coastline.

Banff

Banff, less than 2 miles (3km) west of Macduff, is an old county town looking across the Deveron Estuary and Banff Bay. From the 16th to the 18th century, the landed gentry built themselves elegant town houses in Banff, to retreat to during the winter months, when their castles became too cold and draughty. The town's history goes back to 1120 when it was one of the Hanseatic trading towns sending ships as far afield as the Mediterranean and the Baltic, carrying hides, wool, sheepskin and salted salmon. Smuggling was rife. Banff was an important herring fishing port, with 90 boats and an annual export of 30,000 barrels of herring, until the harbour silted up after a storm and caused the Deveron to change course. The fleet then moved across the bay to Macduff.

Duff House, beside the golf course, is due to reopen in 1995 after extensive renovation. The Duff family, later Earls of Fife, made a considerable fortune buying up land from impoverished lairds just before the Union in 1707. The house is among the finest works of Georgian Baroque architecture in Britain and could accurately be described as unique. Its original design included flanking pavilions, which were never built, hence its rather tall stark appearance. In its time, it has been a hotel, a hospital and a prisoner of war camp. It can be viewed from the outside, until it reopens, and you can walk in the park.

Banff Castle, now a municipal building, was designed by William Adam, built on the site of a medieval fortress of which the moat remains.

Banff Museum (open daily except Thurs, June–Sept: free) has a collection of armour, costumes, burial urns, silver and local natural history.

Plaques have been put up on many of Banff's finest old buildings and you can get a *Royal and Ancient Banff* booklet from the tourist information centre, giving details of a town walk. They also do a 'Walkman Tour of Banff', on tape. Every July there is a yacht race to or from (alternate years) Stavanger in Norway. Banff Golf Week is in September.

A 2-mile (3km) walk south along the river from Duff House takes you to **Bridge of Alvah**, a single-arched bridge built high across a gorge of the Deveron: not for vertigo sufferers.

Whitehills, just west of Banff, is the smallest village to retain its own fishing fleet and daily fishmarket. It is another place where the 19th-century cottages, built gable-end to the sea for protection from storms, are unchanged. In the *New Statistical Account of 1845*, the Rev A. Anderson wrote of a prosperous fishing village whose villagers were 'cleanly in their habits', so that 'fish cured by them has a superior reputation'. He also noted that the women of Whitehills were dominant over the men, claimed the entire proceeds of the white fish market, and were of a 'superior comeliness'.

Whitehills is built round **Knock Head**, said to be where grey rats first came ashore in Scotland from a wreck. There is a sandy beach to the east, at Boyndie Bay. **The Red Well**, near the shore past the caravan park, is a beehive-shaped house built by the Romans to protect a spring with a high iron content. At the spring and autumn equinox, the first rays of the sun, rising over Troup Head 10 miles (16km) away, illuminate the interior of the well while the surrounding area is still in complete darkness. It is thought the well must have been some sort of calendar.

Boyne Castle is a ruin in a wooded valley above the Burn of Boyne, not far to the west. It was built by the Ogilvy family in 1580 and in those days was a great complex with four corner towers, four storeys high. The Ogilvys lost their estate after Culloden and the castle eventually fell into ruin.

Portsoy is a fishing town, less than five miles (8km) west of Whitehills, built round a 17th-century harbour. Many of the 17th- and 18th-century buildings were restored in the 1960s, and a large part of the town is preserved as a conservation area. Among the buildings to look out for are **The Old Star Inn** dating from 1727, and **Soy House**, possibly built in 1690 and the oldest house in the town. Green and pink Portsoy marble was cut from a seam of serpentine which runs across the hills west of the harbour, and provided two chimney pieces for Louis XIV's palace at Versailles. The **Portsoy Marble Workshop and Pottery** (open daily except Sun: free) continues to make things out of the local marble and sell small samples in the form of paperweights and knick-knacks.

Fordyce, 3 miles (4.5km) southwest of Portsoy, nestles under Durn Hill. This cluster of cottages, among narrow streets, with a small late 16th-century tower and quaint church, has won many conservation awards.

Sandend, a couple of miles (3km) north on the coast, is a 19th-century fishing village much painted by artists and said to have the smallest harbour in Scotland. It stands on the western arm of Sandend Bay, one of the most popular beaches in the area.

Findlater Castle is a spectacular three-storey ruin built into a rock face beyond Sandend, its windows overlooking a sheer drop of 50 feet (15m) to the sea. Built as a fortress by the Ogilvys in 1455, it was unsuccessfully besieged by Mary, Queen of Scots when she was trying to subdue the powerful Gordons in 1562. Although easy to get to, the castle is highly dangerous and children should be tethered.

Cullen, about 3 miles (4.5km) further west, is tucked in under a steep hill overlooking Cullen Bay—a sweep of white sand on which are curious red sandstone rocks called the 'Three Kings of Cullen'. The small harbour, once busy with herring boats, is now mainly used for pleasure craft. One of the things you notice here is the series of railway viaducts which divide the sea town from the upper town. They were built in 1886 because the Countess of Seafield refused to allow the railway line to cross the grounds of Cullen

House. The village specialized in smoked haddock and the local delicacy, 'Cullen Skink', is a fish stew based on smoked haddock. George Macdonald, a 19th-century Congregationalist minister who was rejected by his congregation and had to support his family of 11 by writing, set two of his novels in Cullen, *Malcolm* and *The Marquis of Lossie*. He is better known, however, for being the author of *The Princess and the Goblin.*

Portknockie, 3 miles (4.5km) west of Cullen, had to be built on the clifftop because there was no room between the water and the foot of the cliff, and has wonderful views across the firth to the hills of Sutherland and Caithness. Its harbour is the only one in the area that is accessible at lowest tides. An archaeological dig revealed the remains of an Iron Age fort on the promontory.

Findochty, a couple of miles (3km) further west, is a striking example of villages whose houses are painted in brightly coloured oil paints, vying with each other for effect. The old smugglers' route to Buckie ran along the edge of the Strathlene Golf Course and beach. In the old days, the pack ponies of the nightriders, with their hoofs muffled, would not have had the footbridges and steps.

Buckie

Buckie is another 2 miles (3km) on, taking the A942 round the coast, overlooking **Spey Bay**. This long town is an important fishing base with all the attendant maritime establishments: chandlers, boat builders, ice works, fish market and the largest scampi-processing factory in Scotland. It's a solid, unpretentious town with the fisher houses typical of the area, some are restored, with external stone steps going up to what used to be the net loft on the upper floor. **Buckie Drifter**, to be opened some time in 1994, will be a 'hands-on' experience of the fishing industry.

The mouth of the River Spey is about 3 miles (4.5km) to the west. A footbridge crosses the river on the old railway viaduct and you can walk an invigorating 8 miles (13km) along the beach to Lossiemouth. Spey Bay is also the beginning—or end— of the Speyside Way, which goes south to Ballindalloch and Tomintoul, via Tugnet.

Lossiemouth

Lossiemouth is a popular resort with a pretty harbour and two good beaches. It is also a busy fishing port. It developed as the port for Elgin, 5 miles (8km) to the south, after sand and shingle silted up the previous port at Spynie. Ramsay MacDonald, Britain's first Labour Prime Minister, was born here in 1866 and his house is marked with a plaque. There is a reconstruction of his study in the **Lossiemouth Fisheries and Community Museum** (open daily except Sun, May–Sept: free), as well as exhibits relating to the fishing industry of the area.

This stretch of windswept coast has great sweeps of sand, rich in wildfowl. The peace is frequently shattered by low flying planes from RAF Lossiemouth.

Burghead

At Burghead, 7 miles (11km) west of Lossiemouth, there are traces of both Iron Age and Norse forts. In the Iron Age fort you can go down steps to what is called the 'Roman Well', probably an early Christian baptistry, fed by a natural spring. In common with many communities, Burghead re-enacts ancient ceremonies that were performed to scare away evil spirits. In a ceremony called 'Burning the Clavie', a lighted tar barrel is carried through the streets every 11 January—the old-style New Year's Eve—unless it falls on a Sunday when the ceremony takes place a day earlier.

Findhorn Bay

Findhorn is a village, 7 miles (11km) on along the coast, on the eastern arm of Findhorn Bay, a large expanse of tidal flats which dry out at low tide. If the name is familiar it may be because of the local sailing club's challenge for the America's Cup in 1991.

Findhorn Heritage Centre is in two salmon fishery huts by the Culbin Sands Hotel. One hut is a reconstructed salmon fisher's bothy and the other traces Findhorn's history.

In the huge caravan park, there is the Findhorn Foundation, an international community of some 200 members, founded in 1962, as a centre for 'spiritual and holistic education'. The inhabitants stroll about, smiling politely and somewhat vacantly, and you will need determination to get through their apparent unwillingness to communicate with strangers.

In the village of **Kinloss**, on the southern edge of Findhorn Bay, the small overgrown ruin of Kinloss Abbey was once an important Cistercian centre. It was founded by David I who was led there by a dove after he had lost his way in the forest.

Much of this coastline has changed dramatically over the years, as a result of the storms that batter it. **The Culbin Sands**, stretching away to the west of Findhorn Bay, were built up over the years by wind-blown sand until 1694, when a mighty storm finished the job, engulfing all the farmland and buildings in its path. The sands now cover 3600 acres of dunes and marram grass.

Forres

Forres, a scant 3 miles (4.5km) southwest of Kinloss, has a long history going back to before the mythical day when Shakespeare's Macbeth and Banquo met the witches on the blasted heath, on their way to the town to attend the court of King Duncan. The location of the heath is fairly flexible, including Macbeth's Hillock, 5 miles (8km) west, and Knock of Alves, 8 miles (13km) east. The town preserves its medieval layout with the main street widening to form the market place, linked to parallel streets by a series of narrow lanes. Forres has well-kept parks, especially Grant Park, at the foot of Cluny Hill, which is a riot of colour in summer, with amazing floral sculptures. The town won a certificate of commendation in the European 'Entente Florale', in 1990. **Nelson Tower**, on top of the hill, is a landmark for miles and is open to the public.

The Crimean Memorial Obelisk, at the west end of the High Street, stands on the site of Forres Castle, where King Duncan held his court. **The Falconer Museum** (opening

Caithness Tourist Board, Whitechapel Road, Wick, Caithness, ✆ 0955 2596.

Fort William and Lochaber Tourist Board, Cameron Centre, Cameron Sq., Fort William, ✆ 0397 3781.

There are also a number of seasonal information offices, usually open from Easter to the end of September or October.

Inverness

As the capital of the Highlands and the junction of many routes, Inverness is a good place from which to explore the Highland area. The River Ness flows through the heart of the town, converging with the northern end of the Caledonian Canal. Although not outstandingly beautiful, parts of Inverness have a certain sturdy charm and the riverside is most attractive. Perhaps the best view is from the bridge below Bridge Street. Fishermen stand thigh-deep in the fast-flowing River Ness, flanked by well-proportioned houses and churches. When the sun shines, it is a curiously continental picture.

Its sheltered position beside the sea made Inverness a natural place for trade to develop and it has been an important centre from earliest times. In the Middle Ages it developed as a port and ship-building centre, with trade links with Europe. It was often the focal point of clashes between Highland and Island Chiefs who ruled their lands like kings, and the Scottish Crown, ever trying to subdue them. It is now the communications and administrative centre for the north of Scotland.

St Columba is recorded by his biographer, St Adamnan, as having visited the Pictish King Brude in a castle somewhere near the River Ness in AD 565 and converted him and his people to Christianity. This could have been on Craig Phadrig, the small hill just west of the town which still has the remains of a 4th-century vitrified fort. It is more likely, however, that Brude's stronghold stood on the site of Macbeth's castle on Auld Castle Hill, east of today's Castle Hill.

Historical fact and poetic fiction have become so inextricably interwoven around the story of Macbeth and his bloodstained journey to the throne that there are several different claims for thetrue setting for King Duncan's murder. The most reliable sources say the deed was done in a house near Elgin, in 1039, not in Macbeth's castle in Inverness, but it is believed that Malcolm Canmore destroyed **Inverness Castle** in revenge for Duncan's death. A new castle was built in the 12th century on the site of the present one, and was much abused in subsequent years. The English occupied it in the War of Independence and Robert the Bruce destroyed it. Its successor became the hub of conflict between Highlanders and those trying to subdue their wild ways. Mary, Queen of Scots hanged its rebellious governor from the ramparts when he refused her entry in 1562. Jacobites occupied it in 1715 and 1745 and blew it up in February 1746 to keep it from government hands. The present castle was built in the 19th century and looks brand new, its pinkish walls rising from the small hill exactly like a toy fort. It houses the law courts and local government offices. There is a small exhibition (open Easter–Oct: free) telling the history of the castle.

The centre of the town is compact, with the Station Square in the middle, dominated by a splendid war memorial statue of a Cameron Highlander, erected in 1893 to mark the centenary of the Camerons—the local regiment. (They were amalgamated with the Seaforths to become the Queen's Own Highlanders, who are now fighting a losing battle against amalgamation with the Gordon Highlanders.) There are some excellent shops in a hideous new indoor shopping complex.

Inverness stages a Folk Festival in March, Highland Games in July, a Festival Week and Cadet Tattoo in August. The Northern Meeting Piping Competition is in September, when the finest pipers of the day compete for prestigious awards.

Inverness Museum (open weekdays: free) in Castle Wynd, between the castle and the town hall, has displays of social and natural history, archaeology, the culture of the Highlands and Jacobite relics. There are often exhibitions, talks and slide shows.

St Andrew's Episcopal Cathedral is to the south. An imposing, pinkish building on the banks of the river, it was built between 1866 and 1874, with an octagonal chapter house and an elaborate interior.

Eden Court, beyond the cathedral, is a glass edifice built in 1976, incorporating the 19th-century house of Bishop Eden. It is an 800-seat multipurpose theatre, conference centre and art gallery, with an excellent restaurant. Ambitious programmes are laid on throughout the year: concerts, ballet, drama, the latest films and many art exhibitions.

Ness Islands, up-river away from Eden Court, form a public park spread over a series of small islands in the River Ness. They are linked by foot-bridges, with views down the river towards the town.

Tomnahurich—Hill of the Yews, sometimes called Hill of the Fairies—is the small, boat-shaped hillock to the southwest. Two wandering fiddlers, Thomas and Farquhar, were lured to Tomnahurich by the Fairy Queen, to play for a night's dancing. In the morning they found the town and its people strangely altered and everyone laughing at them. The 'night' had lasted a hundred years. They crept into a church for refuge—and crumbled into dust. Tomnahurich is now the town's cemetery, with many elaborate monuments clinging to the steep, wooded sides and a splendid viewing point from the top. Below lie the environs of Inverness, with neat villas, well-kept gardens and an air of respectability.

The northern entrance to the **Caledonian Canal** is in the western suburbs. It was constructed in the 19th century by Thomas Telford, and much used in the old days by boats wishing to avoid the long and often hazardous slog round the north coast. Still used by fishing boats, it now offers a perfect way for sailors to explore the Great Glen. Cabin cruisers can be hired from the marinas just down from the entrance, and passenger cruises operate in the summer.

The 19th-century **Cameron Barracks** stands on a ridge high above Millburn Road on the eastern edge of Inverness—a wise old sentinel guarding the town. From here, many a brave young Cameron Highlander walked out, newly trained, to give his life so that his Highland home should remain free.

Inverness to Nairn

The south side of the Moray Firth is flattish open farmland with views across to the Black Isle and the hills of Easter Ross.

Culloden

Taking the back roads, east of the A96, Culloden is about 5 miles (8km) east of Inverness. Start at the first-class new visitor centre on the edge of the battlefield (open daily, Easter–end Oct: adm for audio-visual show and cottage). The audio-visual show gives details of the battle, on 16 April 1746, when Prince Charles Edward Stuart and his 5000 exhausted, starving and ill-equipped Highlanders were defeated by the Duke of Cumberland, son of George II, and his 9000 well-trained and well-equipped men. During that battle 1200 Highlanders fell; many more were butchered by order of the Duke as they lay wounded. Accounts of the Prince's reaction to the failure of his dreams vary: some say he tried to rally his Highlanders; some that he had to be held back from galloping forward to a hero's death; others are less starry-eyed. Whatever is true, one thing is sure: he was led away and hidden by loyal Highlanders for five months, with a price of £30,000 on his head, until he returned to the Continent in a French frigate, to live out the rest of his life in wretched, debauched exile.

As well as exhibitions and displays, the visitor centre has a study room for school parties, with a library and Jacobite relics. In addition there is a coffee shop and restaurant and a very good bookshop with a comprehensive range of Scottish publications.

The old cottage, outside, is the only building to survive the battle. It was still inhabited at the beginning of the 20th century and is now a folk museum. It still has its old furnishings and domestic equipment; taped music and Gaelic add an authentic touch.

On the battlefield (always open: free), wooden plaques tell which clan fought where, and how the battle progressed. There are clan graves: communal burial sites with headstones bearing clan names, and a memorial cairn, erected in 1881. On the edge of the bleak battle site is the Well of the Dead where wounded Highlanders were slain as they drank water to revive themselves. A single stone bears the inscription 'The English were buried here'. The flat stone beyond the visitor centre is called the Cumberland Stone, thought to have been the vantage point from which the Duke viewed the battle.

The Clava Cairns are signed, a mile (1.5km) east of Culloden. These form a remarkable Stone Age and Bronze Age burial site, possibly dating from 2000 BC. Three large burial cairns in a glade of beech trees take you back to the prehistoric rituals that would have accompanied the internment of those farmers and herdsmen so many years ago. Two of the cairns have passages leading into them; the third has curious stone strips radiating from it like the spokes of a wheel. Each is surrounded by a circle of standing stones, some inscribed with cup-and-ring symbols. Excavations revealed traces of cremated human bones, pottery and other remains: memorials of people who were alive nearly 4000 years ago.

Kilravock Castle (pronounced Kilrawk) is 5 miles (8km) northeast of Culloden, still keeping to the back roads (open Wed afternoons, April–Sept, or by appointment, © 06678 258; grounds open daily except Sun: adm). Dating from the 15th century, this castle has been preserved almost intact because the owners never had enough money to mess about with its original design. In 1190, a Norman called Rose came north, married into a local family and settled on these lands. Kilravock has been the home of the Rose chiefs ever since. Among its relics are two reminders of Culloden—a punch bowl and a pair of leather thigh boots. Rose of Kilravock entertained Prince Charles before the battle and offered punch from this bowl. He was not a Jacobite, but the Prince had ridden over to call on him and no true Highlander refuses hospitality. Shortly afterwards, Cumberland came blustering up, flushed with celebration of his 25th birthday: 'I hear, sir, you've been entertaining my cousin!' Rose explained and was excused. Cumberland, for some inexplicable reason, left his boots behind. These two relics are an ironic reflection of the two people associated with them: Prince Charles, merry and charismatic, who later drowned his failure in alcohol; Butcher Cumberland, brash, gross and cruel—very much a jackboot image. The gardens and grounds are lovely, especially in spring. Prince Charles walked here with his host and watched young trees being planted. He remarked on the contrast between this peaceful scene and the commotion that was going on all round, preparing for the battle. Some of the beautiful old trees today must be the ones that were being planted. (Kilravock is now a hotel: *see* 'Where to Stay', below.)

Cawdor

Cawdor (pronounced Cawder), 8 miles (13km) northeast of Culloden, is familiar to anyone who has read Shakespeare's *Macbeth.* **Cawdor Castle** (open daily 1 May–1 Oct: adm) dates from 1372, when the central tower was built. Domestic buildings were added in the 16th century and later remodelled. Protected by a gully on one side and a dry moat on the other, the castle, floodlit at night, has a walled garden, ablaze with colour in the summer.Entry is over a drawbridge, and it feels like a living home, rather than a museum, probably because the Cawdors still live here. It is easy to imagine it in medieval times, with its winding stairways and massive walls. Among the things to see are Flemish tapestries, paintings, weapons, household equipment and family heirlooms. Carbon dating has confirmed that the scrap of an ancient tree, railed off in the basement, is older than the castle, thus authenticating an old story. The original founder, Thane William, was granted a licence to build himself a fortress. He was told in a dream to load a donkey with panniers of gold and build a castle wherever it stopped. He obeyed and the donkey stopped for a rest in the shade of a thorn tree round which Thane William built his castle.

Outside there are nature trails, a nine-hole mini-golf course, putting green and picnic spots, as well as a licensed restaurant and souvenir shop.

In a conservation area, Cawdor village, straggling round the castle grounds, is not at all typical of Scotland: its peaceful cosiness matches that of the castle. The church is 17th-century, built in thanksgiving by the twelfth Lord Cawdor after he was saved from a shipwreck.

Fort George

Fort George (open daily: adm) is about 8 miles (13km) northwest of Cawdor on the B9006, on a windswept promontory jutting out into the Moray Firth. It is the most unspoilt example of an artillery fort in Europe. Built between 1748 and 1769, to replace 'Old' Fort George in Inverness, destroyed by Prince Charles in 1746, it is a classic 18th-century fortress. The defences include the traditional outer works: ravelin, ditch, bastion and rampart, designed by William Skinnor who was in his day the leading expert on artillery fortification. The government contractor who built it was John Adam, oldest son of architect William Adam, and brother of Robert.

Passing through the forbidding fortifications, one is brought to a delighted standstill by the mellow pink sandstone garrison buildings, their impeccable 18th-century proportions mercifully unscarred by Victorian or later 'improvement'.

The fort was built to house a garrison large enough to overawe Jacobite support in the Highlands, but by the time it was completed the Jacobite threat was finally dead, so it has never had a history of conflict. It became a base where a long series of regiments were mustered and equipped and whence they embarked for service in America, the West Indies, the Middle East, India and South Africa. In 1881, when each British infantry regiment was allocated its own territorial recruiting area and home base, Fort George became the depot of the Seaforth Highlanders. Generations of Highland soldiers trained there for colonial service, for two World Wars and for modern Cold War campaigns.

The regiments of the garrison change over every two years, and they have the privilege of living in barracks that are the oldest in the world still occupied by a battalion of British infantry.

The **Regimental Museum of the Queen's Own Highlanders** (open daily except some Sat, April–Sept; weekdays, Oct–March: free, donations welcome) is in the fort.

Formed in 1961 by the amalgamation of the Seaforth Highlanders and the Queen's Own Cameron Highlanders, they are the present-day descendants of the two historic regiments of the northern Highlands. In the building formerly used by the Lieutenant Governor, the Queen's Own Highlanders preserve a superb collection of uniforms, pictures, medals, weapons, colours, artefacts and treasures, representing nearly every major campaign fought by the British Army over the past 200 years. The splendour of red coat and tartan, the glitter of gilt plate and dirk, the glint of steel broadsword and bayonet, cannot fail to stir the imagination and make hearts beat a little faster. With its history, its atmosphere and its garrison, Fort George is unique as a 20th-century military base where the 18th century lives on.

Nairn

Nairn, not quite 9 miles (14.5km) east of Fort George, is a seaside holiday town, sometimes called the Brighton of the North. On the mouth of the River Nairn, it has sandy beaches along the Moray Firth, two golf courses and a reputation for a high average of sunshine. (In Victorian times, a Dr Grigor put Nairn on the map by recommending it to his patients as 'one of the healthiest spots in Britain'.) Imposing houses built by retired Victorian Empire-builders and trim villas with neat gardens give it an aura of old-fashioned gentility. The Nairn Highland Games are in August. There is a Holiday Week and a Vintage Car Rally in July. The Fairground Fortnight and the Farmers Show are also in August.

Originally called Invernairn, the old fishertown is a collection of restored cottages. **Nairn Fishertown Museum** (open afternoons except Sun, May–Sept: adm) is in Laing Hall, King Street. Here you can see photographs and articles relating to the Moray Firth and the herring fisheries during the steam drifter era. There are also displays of domestic life in a fishing community. (Nairn now has a yacht marina, but no longer any local fishing boats.)

The Little Theatre, also in Fishertown, is a small theatre with a repertory company who perform every Wednesday in the summer and there is a thriving Nairn Performing Arts Guild.

See Grampian for Brodie Castle (p.167) and Pluscarden Abbey (p.152), nearby, both well worth a visit during this tour from Inverness.

Where to Stay

expensive

Caledonian Hotel, Church Street, Inverness, © 0463 235181, is convenient, in the centre backing on to the river, but huge and soulless with cabaret most nights.

Culloden House Hotel, 4 miles (6.5km) east of Inverness, © 0463 790461, is a Georgian mansion built round a Jacobean castle. Prince Charles made it his headquarters for two months before the Battle of Culloden, when it was the home of Duncan Forbes, the Lord President. (He and his officers managed to get through 60 hogsheads of the Lord President's claret—3150 imperial gallons—so perhaps the outcome of the battle was inevitable.) The hotel is luxurious, with an Adam dining room, four-poster and curtain-framed beds, ornate plasterwork and attractive grounds. The food is worth staying in for.

moderate

Drumossie Hotel, on the A9 to Perth, 3 miles (4.5km) out of town, © 0463 236451, is modern, with views over the Moray Firth. The food isn't too bad. **Bunchrew House Hotel**, Bunchrew, © 0463 234917, is a much better bet, though bordering on expensive. A 16th-century mansion in 15 acres of gardens on the shores of the Beauly Firth, about 5 miles (8km) west of Inverness, it has turrets and towers and tremendous atmosphere. There are only six bedrooms. **Dunain Park**, Inverness, © 0463 230512, is a country house on the western outskirts, in six acres of lovely grounds. Comfortable and well-run, but bordering on the expensive.

Newton Hotel, Nairn, © 0667 53144, has five crowns and is well recommended as one of Nairn's best; friendly, quiet and with excellent food. **The Clifton Hotel**, also in Nairn, © 0667 53119, is highly recommended as one of the best in all the good food guides. **Carnach Country House Hotel**, Inverness Road, Nairn, © 0667 52094, is at the lower end of this price bracket, comfortable and peaceful, in eight acres overlooking the Moray Firth. Also overlooking the Firth, close to the golf course, at the top end of the bracket, **Golf View Hotel**, Nairn, © 0667 52301, has tennis courts, outdoor swimming pool, sauna, games room and regular entertainment.

inexpensive

Glendruidh House, Old Edinburgh Road, Inverness, © 0463 226499, is a delightful, family-run hotel overlooking the Moray Firth and the town. **Heathmount Hotel** in Heathmont, Inverness, © 0463 235877, has a good reputation, a nice pub atmosphere and five comfortable bedrooms.

Kilravock Castle, Croy, © 06678 258 (*see above* for description), is a great experience for anyone who is an abstemious Christian. Pronounced 'Kilrawk', this historic old castle is where Prince Charles dined before Culloden. It stands in peaceful grounds near the river and the emphasis is very much on God: grace before meals, Bible readings and comment at breakfast and dinner; no drink—though naughty guests have been known to smuggle bottles into their cells and smoke up the chimney. Country-house bedrooms in a wing of the castle are cheap, while historic rooms in the castle proper cost a few pounds more.

Eating Out

For a night out, go to **Culloden House**, © 0463 790461, and don't look at the prices. (An Adam dining room adds to the occasion.) Or try **The Longhouse** in Nairn, which is expensive but has seriously good food.

Inverness to Kingussie

The Spey, Scotland's second-longest river, is born high in the hills above Loch Laggan, 40 miles (64km) south of Inverness, and cuts across the southeast corner of the Highland region. Beginning as a mere stream, it gathers momentum as it flows east and then north to the sea near Buckie in Grampian region, fed by many burns that drain from the hills on either side, turning it into a rushing tumult of water. Running between the great Cairngorms in the east and the Monadhliath Mountains to the west, the Spey is famous for astonishing natural beauty. In spring, fresh green shows through winter brown and snow still caps the mountains; in summer it is a patchwork of mulberry heather, emerald bracken, sparkling water and grey granite; in autumn, snow already dusts the hills making a backdrop to the splendour of the turning leaves; in winter, a white Alpine world dazzles and enchants. Leave the main roads and explore any of the minor roads and tracks.

Grantown-on-Spey

About 26 miles (41.5km) down the A9 from Inverness, branch left at Carrbridge on the A938. Grantown-on-Spey, 10 miles (16km) east and 6 miles (9.5km) south of the Grampian border, is one of Speyside's tourist centres, a Georgian town at the junction of several routes. On the banks of the River Spey and surrounded by trees, the town was founded in 1776 by Sir James Grant, one of the Highland's 'improving lairds'. With the development of skiing in the hills, this area is popular all the year round for holidays. The Grantown-on-Spey Highland Games are held in June.

The Loch Garten Nature Reserve, 8 miles (13km) south of Grantown-on-Spey, is known for its breeding ospreys. Americans, accustomed to seeing these 'fish-hawks' in countless numbers nesting in their rivers and estuaries, are amused by the security surrounding Scotland's few pairs, but it must be remembered that before the mid-1950s (when one pair set up their nest in a tree at Loch Garten) they had not been seen in Britain for almost 50 years. When an over-enthusiastic egg thief robbed this precious nest in 1958, precautions had to be taken. Now, it is not so unusual to see the slow, flapping flight of one of these brown and white birds, or hear its shrill, cheeping cry. The nature reserve has a lot more than ospreys for any one who will stand still and observe. Its bird life includes blackcock, capercaillie and crossbills, and among the animals are red squirrels and deer. In winter the haunting cry of geese and the eerie honk of whooper swans float across the waters of Loch Garten.

Boat of Garten, west of the loch, is so called after the ferry that operated here until a bridge was built in 1898. It is the home of the **Strathspey Steam Railway Association**, which has its own station and some remnants of the old Highland railway (closed in 1965). It was reopened in 1978 and enthusiasts can travel to Aviemore in a steam train. There is a museum of railway memorabilia. While you are in the area, visit the Tomatin Distillery, Scotland's largest malt whisky distillery and the first to be acquired by the Japanese, in 1985, with guided tours and a free dram (open weekdays, Easter–Oct: Sat mornings, May–Sept: free). Tomatin is derived from a Gaelic word meaning 'the hill of the juniper bushes'—curious for a whisky distillery.

Also nearby, award-winning **Speyside Heather**, 6 miles (9.5km) from Granton (open daily except Sun, Nov–March: free), grows over 300 different heathers: its visitors centre will give advice on growing them at home.

Aviemore

Aviemore, about 14 miles (22.5km) southwest of Grantown-on-Spey, is a thriving tourist centre and dormitory for the Cairngorm ski resort, teeming with energetic holidaymakers. Dominated by the Cairngorms, with several peaks over 4000 feet (1230m), this area has some of Scotland's grandest scenery.

Aviemore has every sort of accommodation, cafés and restaurants, bistros and bars, gift shops, craft shops, souvenir stalls, amusement arcades and discos. It is just the place for gregarious people looking for action. Throughout the year the surrounding countryside is a kaleidoscope of anoraks and knapsacks, psychedelic skiing clothes, or shorts and tee-shirts. Within spitting distance of this hub of sporting activity lie heather-clad moors, mountains, valleys, tumbling burns and beautiful lochs.

The Aviemore Mountain Resort (open daily: adm for various attractions) offers a bewildering choice of activity. There is an ice rink and curling rink, theatre/cinema, ballroom, artificial ski slope, games room, squash courts, go-kart track, and children's outdoor amusements.

Rothiemurchus Visitor Centre (open daily: adm) gives an insight into everyday life on a working Highland estate. **The Cairngorm Reindeer Centre** (open daily: adm), at Glenmore, has Britain's only herd of reindeer, living free on the slopes of the Cairngorms.

Loch Morlich, 5 miles (8km) to the east, is a water-sports centre for gregarious aquarians—camping and caravanning included, not for the recluse. **Kincraig Highland Wildlife Park** (open daily, March–Nov: adm) is 6 miles (9.5km) southwest of Aviemore. Animals which once roamed free over the Highlands live here in a natural setting: boar, wolves, bears, bison and many more. You drive through the park and must leave pets in the kennels provided. There are also aviaries with indigenous birds such as capercaillie, eagles and hawks, and an exhibition on man and fauna in the Highlands.

Loch Insh, a mile (1.5km) southeast of Kincraig, is formed by a widening of the river and is surrounded by blue hills and trees. **Loch Insh Watersports and Skiing Centre** offers courses in canoeing, wind surfing, sailing, swimming and skiing— all the ingredients necessary for an excellent action holiday.

The white 18th-century church on a rocky point at the northern end of the loch was built on a site said to have been used by Druids, and used continually for Christian worship since the 6th century. Inside is an 8th-century hand-bell, shaken to call the faithful to worship, before the days of bells in steeples. The **Rock Wood Ponds**, southeast of the loch, teem with wildlife.

The gaunt shell of **Ruthven Barracks** (pronounced 'Rivven') stands on a hillock east of the A9, 5 miles (8km) southwest of Kincraig, dramatically floodlit at night. On the site of a stronghold of the Wolf of Badenoch (notorious son of Robert II), it was built after the 1715 Jacobite uprising to discourage further rebellion and extended by General Wade in 1734. Prince Charles captured it from government troops during his ascendancy and it was here, after Culloden, that some 1500 surviving Jacobites assembled, awaiting their Prince. They waited in vain, until they received the message that the cause was dead and they must now fend for themselves. On the day after the battle, Lord George Murray sat down in the barracks and wrote a long, bitter letter to the Prince, resentfully listing all the blunders that had contributed to their defeat. Prince Charles never forgave him. Before disbanding to return to the homes they had so eagerly left, the loyal Highlanders, abandoned by their leader, blew Ruthven up to save it from the enemy.

Kingussie

Kingussie, a mile (1.5km) to the west and by-passed by the A9, is another popular holiday resort. Derived from the Gaelic *cinn giuthasich*, meaning 'at the head of the first', and pronounced 'King-yewsie', it has one main street, backed by lovely Highland scenery. The Badenoch and Strathspey Music Festival is held here in March.

The Highland Folk Museum (open daily, April–Oct; weekdays, Nov–March: adm) is a must for anyone interested in Highland life and folklore. It was founded in Iona in the 1930s and later moved here under the control of the universities of Glasgow, Edinburgh, St Andrews and Aberdeen. Beautifully arranged, both indoors and outside, it includes an authentic black-house from Lewis, built by someone who was bought up in one, a clack mill (named from its 'clacking' noise), and many exhibits of farming and domestic life, including a salmon smokehouse.

At Newtonmore, **Waltzing Waters** (open daily except from 5 Jan to 20 Feb: adm) is an indoor 'water, light and music spectacular' that defies description: go and see it.

From Kingussie, south to the Tayside Border, the A9 runs through Glen Truim to Dalwhinnie, backed by hills, forest and moor, crossing the border through the Pass of Drumochter. Very isolated and unpopulated, this is not an area for running out of petrol on a winter's night.

The A86, west from Kingussie to Glen Roy and Spean Bridge, runs through glens flanked by steep hills, the road dipping and climbing beside Loch Laggan. Cars should be abandoned to walk up valleys into the hills, past secret lochans and hidden glens.

Where to Stay

See also previous section.

moderate

Carrbridge Hotel, © 047984 202, is an old-established, rambling, easy-going establishment. Also in Carrbridge, **Dalrachney Lodge Hotel**, © 047984 252, has four crowns, and **Fairwinds Hotel**, © 047984 240, has three crowns.

In Grantown-on-Spey, **Grant Arms** in the town centre, ✆ 0479 2526, is an old-fashioned grey pile. A bit cheaper, **Garth Hotel** in Castle Road, ✆ 0479 2836, is a white and black building just off the square, dating from the 17th century, in four acres of landscaped garden.

In Aviemore, **Stakis Badenoch**, ✆ 0479 810261, and **Stakis Four Seasons**, ✆ 0479 810681, offer comfort and all mod cons. **Stakis Coylumbridge Resort Hotel**, 3 miles (4.5km) out of Aviemore, is much the same. **Freedom Inn** in Aviemore Centre, ✆ 0479 810781, is modern, with a cheerful staff. **Red McGregor Hotel**, ✆ 0479 810256, on the main road in the village, is attractive and comfortable.

Muckrach Lodge Hotel, Dulnain Bridge, ✆ 047985 257, is an old family home in attractive grounds, with a good reputation for comfort and food.

inexpensive

Struan House, in the middle of Carrbridge, has log fires, tennis and a small dry ski slope and putting green. In the same village are **Feith Mhor Country House**, ✆ 047984 621, and **Cairn Hotel**, ✆ 047984 212. **Seafield Lodge Hotel,** in Woodside Avenue, Grantown-on-Spey, ✆ 0479 2152, is a fishing hotel and runs fishing courses.

Boat Hotel, Boat of Garten, ✆ 047983 258, is a country house near the loch with 6 miles (9.5km) of fishing on the Spey, and a good reputation for food.

In Kingussie, **Columba House Hotel**, Manse Road, ✆ 0540 661402, and **The Osprey Hotel**, ✆ 0540 661510, are both good value with no frills.

Eating Out

For local colour and good value, try **Tomatin Inn**, at Tomatin, ✆ 08082 291.

Craggan Mill Restaurant on the Grantown–Dulnain Bridge road, ✆ 0479 2288, is in a converted mill: the food is good and not too expensive.

Inverness to Glencoe via the Great Glen

Some 400 million years ago, the landmass of Scotland split apart along what is now the Great Glen, the fissure being eroded by glaciers in the Ice Age until the final retreat of the ice as recently as 10,000 years ago. The Caledonian Canal, a waterway through the glen, was surveyed by James Watt in 1773. Thomas Telford started work on construction in 1803, and completed it in 1821. Of its 60-mile (96km) length, 22 miles (35km) is true canal; the rest takes advantage of the natural lochs and rivers in the rift. The Great Glen, starting with Loch Ness, is spectacular and the best way to enjoy it is by boat. Caley Cruisers, Canal Road Inverness, ✆ 0463 236328, hire boats sleeping from four to eight. Passenger cruises include: Jacobite Cruises, ✆ 0463 233999 and Loch Ness Cruises (Drumnadrochit), ✆ 04562 395.

Loch Ness

Loch Ness is world famous, thanks to Nessie: it is also extremely beautiful. Long and narrow, its steep wooded banks form a wind-funnel, causing surprisingly rough waters at times. Depths of 900 feet (278m) have been recorded. Feelings run high over Nessie—the Loch Ness Monster—known to the cognoscenti as *Nessiteras rhombopteryx.* Sceptics may scoff, but St Adamnan, not given to telling fibs, records a sighting of her in his biography of St Columba, when they were sailing up the loch to convert Inverness. Columba, it seems, had a calming effect on her when she threatened one of his monks, and she has never been troublesome again. Setting aside whisky-induced hallucinations, and wishful-thinking sightings, many eye-witness accounts of Nessie come from people whose honesty and integrity are beyond doubt. A 16th-century chronicle describes 'a terrible beast issuing out of the water early one morning about midsummer, knocking down trees and killing three men with its tail'. A monk who was organist in Westminster Cathedral saw her in 1973, and several of the monks at Fort Augustus Abbey have seen her. Thirty hotel guests saw two humps appear in an explosion of surf and cruise half a mile before sinking, in 1961. Bertram Mills was sufficiently convinced to offer £20,000 to have Nessie delivered alive to his circus. However logical one is, it is impossible to drive down Loch Ness without scanning the dark waters hopefully. Anyone who spends a night at anchor in a boat on the loch will find themselves starting up in the darkness, every time a ripple slaps the hull. If you are feeeling really adventurous, for a mere £70 you can take a submarine trip beneath the waves to see what really goes on in Loch Ness.

There are two roads down Loch Ness from Inverness: the A82 is the main road down the west side, with views of the loch and quite a lot of traffic in the summer. The B862/852 is much less frequented, very attractive, but with not so many views of the loch, some sections of it being inland.

The Loch Ness Monster Exhibition Centre is at **Drumnadrochit**, 15 miles (24km) down from Inverness on the A82 (open daily: adm). Here is all the information known about Nessie: documents, photographs, possible explanations, models, a sonar room, etc, all presented objectively—a study for sceptic and credulous alike. In summer there is also a tartan shop and a house of heraldry, where people can check up on their origins. There is a glass blower, too, and a Hollywood-style model of Nessie for family photographs.

Urquhart Castle (open daily: adm) is just beyond Drumnadrochit on the southern tip of Urquhart Bay, overlooking Loch Ness, with free off-road parking from where there is an overview of the whole layout. A jagged keep rises from crumbling walls against a backdrop of loch and hills beyond. This was once one of the largest castles in Scotland, dating from the 14th century. Built on the site of a vitrified fort, it was given to John Grant of Freuchie in 1509 by James IV. In 1692 it was blown up to save it from Jacobite hands. Romantics say that Nessie lives in a subterranean cave below the castle.

At **Balbeg**, about 4 miles (6.5km) on, is the memorial cairn to John Cobb who was killed in 1952, trying to break the world water speed record on Loch Ness's measured mile. The memorial is inscribed in Gaelic: 'Honour to the brave and to the humble'.

Fort Augustus

Fort Augustus, on the southern end of Loch Ness, is the halfway halt down the Great Glen, a popular tourist centre with an ancient history. There is a pre-Christian crannog, Cherry Island, just to the north in Loch Ness.

The town's original name was Kilcumein (burial place of Cumein who was one of St Columba's followers). After the Jacobite rising in 1715, barracks were built in the town to quell further rebellion and there are still traces of the old buildings behind the Lovat Arms Hotel. General Wade made his headquarters here in 1724, and in 1729 began the building of the fort beside the loch. It was named Augustus after William Augustus, Duke of Cumberland, at that time the fat, eight-year-old schoolboy son of George II, who was to go down in history as Butcher Cumberland. Jacobites took the fort in 1745 and held it until after Culloden. Lord Lovat bought the ruins and presented them to a Benedictine community in 1876, for the founding of an abbey which became a public school until it closed in 1993. Much of the old fort was incorporated into the ground floor. The Great Glen Gala is a lively occasion in Fort Augustus in July.

To complete a circular tour of Loch Ness, rather than go on down the Great Glen, take the B862 from Fort Augustus back up the east side, which is prettier and quieter. Part of the way is one of General Wade's military roads.

Just after Whitebridge, 10 miles (16km) from Fort Augustus, the road forks. The left fork goes to **Foyers**, where there are woodland walks and a spectacular waterfall. From Inverfarigaig, about 3 miles (4.5km) northeast of Foyers, back to Inverness, there are a number of excavated remains of burial chambers, forts and cairns, some in good condition, including a vitrified Iron Age fort, at **Ashie Moor**, west of Loch Duntelchaig.

Going on down the Great Glen from Fort Augustus, **Tobar nan Ceann** is the 'Well of the Heads' monument beside the road on the western shore of Loch Oich. An obelisk supports the bronze heads of seven men, held together by a dirk through their hair. Beyond, steps lead through a damp tunnel to a sinister well underneath. This is where Iain Lom MacDonell, poet of his clan, washed the severed heads of the murderers of his chief, Alasdair MacDonell, 12th Chief of Keppoch, in 1663. He presented the washed heads to MacDonell of Glengarry, who had refused to help him avenge the murder. It was the 15th Chief MacDonell of Glengarry who erected the monument in the 19th century. Inscribed in English, Gaelic, French and Latin are the words: 'this ample and summary vengeance'.

Nearby, three days before the raising of the standard at Glenfinnan, two companies of government troops surrendered to a handful of Jacobite Macdonalds. They had heard a great din of pipes and noise and believed themselves to be in the midst of a mighty army. The two companies were from the Royal Scots, in garrison at Fort Augustus, ambushed at High Bridge and retreating with ignominious haste back to barracks: the engagement was commemorated by the pibroch 'The Rout of the Lowland Captain'.

A little further down, at **Laggan** between Loch Lochy and Loch Oich, there was a ferocious clan battle between the Frasers and the Macdonalds in 1544. It was called

Blàr-na-léine—the Battle of the Shirts, because it was so hot: they all threw off their cumbersome plaids and fought in their shirts. Of the 1000 men engaged, only 12 survived. The casualties included the entire Fraser hierarchy, leaving Clan Fraser leaderless: fortunately, 80 of the gentlemen's wives had been left pregnant and each one produced a male heir.

Several routes meet at **Spean Bridge**, about 12 miles (19km) south down Loch Lochy. Just short of the village is the much-photographed **Commando Memorial** by Scott Sutherland, erected in 1952. A bronze group of commandos stand on a high promontory looking out over the view towards Ben Nevis and Lochaber, surrounded by the harsh terrain where they trained during the Second World War.

Highbridge, 2 miles (3km) from Spean Bridge, is one of Wade's most remarkable bridges, completed in 1736. It crosses the gorge of the River Spean, 100 feet (31m) below.

Glen Roy is a slight detour from Roy Bridge, 3 miles (4.5km) east of Spean Bridge on the A86. At first it seems just another glen, with the River Roy tumbling down through wooded gorges to flatten out and meander at a more stately pace across the valley floor, bare hills rising on either side. Stop at the large observation car park some way along and look down the valley. A number of horizontal lines run across the hillside, quite high up, each line exactly matched by one on the opposite side of the valley. These 'parallel roads' are terraces left by the receding glacier that once filled the valley. They are geologically famous because of their clarity, and date from a late Ice Age build-up about 11,000 years ago. Glen Roy used to be well populated but like so many others in this area it is now virtually empty.

Several secret glens lie beyond the end of the track. Tucked away up in the hills, the source of the Roy, about 6 miles (9.5km) from the end of the road, is very close to the source of the Spey, gathering courage for its long trek to the sea.

Northwest of Spean Bridge, at Achnacarry, **The Clan Cameron Museum** (open afternoons, mid-April–mid-Oct: free) covers Clan Cameron, Lochaber, the Jacobite risings and the use of the estate for Commando training in World War II, and has a section on the Cameron Highlanders.

On the western route down the Great Glen (B8004), Strome is the site of Bonny Dundee's headquarters where he mustered the clans loyal to James VII before Killicrankie.

At **Erracht** close by, tucked away up a track, a cairn was unveiled in 1993 by Colonel Sir Donald Cameron of Lochiel, to commemorate Alan Cameron of Erracht, the founder of the 79th Highlanders, raised in 1793. He was born in the little house above the cairn.

Continuing on down the Great Glen from Spean Bridge on the A82, **Inverlochy Castle** stands by the road about 8 miles (13km) to the southwest and is being restored by Historic Scotland as a consolidated ruin. Dating from the 13th century, it has a walled courtyard and round corner towers, one of which was the keep, and a water gate. The castle was once a stronghold of the Comyns and scene of several battles, including one in 1645 in which Montrose defeated a Covenanter army under Argyll with a loss of 1500 men. This was one of the greatest feats of arms in Scottish history. The first Argyll knew of Montrose's presence was the sound of the pibroch: *Sons of the dogs, come out and get flesh.* Legend tells of a Pictish settlement on this site, where King Archaius signed a treaty with Charlemagne in 790.

Fort William

Fort William is 10 miles (16km) southwest of Spean Bridge and is the southern gateway to the Caledonian Canal. It is a tourist resort, the epitome of a West Highland town, shopping centre for the whole of this area and hub of several routes. It lies in the lee of Ben Nevis, Britain's highest mountain, 4406 feet (1356m)—an ugly lump, with several routes to the top depending on expertise and physical fitness.

The fort for which the town was named was demolished in the 19th century to make way for the railway. It was first built by General Monk in 1655, an earth construction that proved to be of insufficient strength when put to the test by rebellious Highlanders later in the century. It was then rebuilt in stone, withstanding Jacobite attacks in 1715 and 1746. The town was named Maryburgh after the wife of King William III, before being named in honour of the king himself. It grew up around the railway and is Victorian and sturdy, with a cheerful holiday atmosphere. For Gaelic speakers its official name is still An Gearasdan—the Garrison

Steam trains run from Fort William to Mallaig from May to October, past many historic sites, through glorious scenery. Special trips linked with a visit to Skye are arranged every Sunday from the end of June to mid-September. It is essential to book in advance: © 0397 703791.

Don't miss the **Great Glen Sheepdog Trials** at the end of June or beginning of July. The Highland Games are also in July and the Lochaber Agricultural Show is in August.

The West Highland Museum (open daily except Sun: adm), in Cameron Square, is crammed with interesting historical, natural history and folk exhibits. There is a crofter's kitchen, just as it was in the old days with all the original equipment, as well as agricultural implements. Montrose's helmet and many Jacobite relics are displayed. The most fascinating exhibit is the 'secret' portrait of the prince, used in the days when loyal Jacobites toasted 'the king across the water', a meaningless blur of paint until you view it from the right angle through a cylinder, when it is transformed into a recognizable portrait.

You can pass a sunny hour or so leaning over the rails beside the long ladder of locks that bring the Caledonian Canal down to the level of the sea. The locks are used by fishing boats and pleasure craft and the gates are hydraulically operated, the water boiling through sluices until the level is equal either side. Eight of the 11 locks that link Loch Linnhe with the canal are called **Neptune's Staircase**, a rise of 80 feet (24.5m) which presented Telford with an enormous problem when he built the canal. Loch Linnhe is always busy with pleasure boats in the summer.

There is a new skiing complex 4 miles (6.5km) north of Fort William on **Aonach Mor**, close to Ben Nevis. Nevis Range, the operators, anticipate more people using the gondola system lifts in the summer than in the winter.

A fast road runs along the east side of Loch Linnhe to the new Ballachulish (pronounced Balla-hoolish) Bridge, 13 miles (21km) to the south. The bridge spans a narrow constriction between lochs Linnhe and Leven, where not so long ago a small car ferry used to slither and slide on the fast current. Look out for the stark, stone memorial to James Stewart, with its bitter inscription, beside the road. Stewart was falsely hanged for the 'Appin Murder' in 1752, on which Robert Louis Stevenson based *Kidnapped* and its sequel, *Catriona*. The staunchly Jacobite Stewarts of Appin had to forfeit their lands after Culloden. The Crown factor, Colin Campbell of Glenure, known as the Red Fox, took delight in evicting Stewarts in favour of Campbells. He was assassinated during one of his forays and James Stewart was unjustly used as a scapegoat, tried before the Duke of Argyll at Inverary by a jury of 11 Campbells, found guilty and hanged. The rough stone on top of the monument came from his farm. A memorial cairn marks the site of the Red Fox's murder in the Wood of Lettermore, about a mile (1.5km) west of Ballachulish, near the road.

Ballachulish was the centre for Scotland's biggest slate quarry, still full of slate but no longer used because slate is now imported. Some of the slate workers' cottages have been converted into a teashop and craft shops.

Glencoe

Glencoe is 4 miles (6.5km) to the east. This dramatic pass with raw peaks reaching up on either side is slashed by white scars of cascading water. In good weather, away from the road, Glencoe is staggeringly beautiful, with creaming burns and falls, glistening rocks and hidden lochs and glens. But when the weather closes in, there is an unmistakable aura of doom, enhanced by its well-known history. *Glen Coe* means 'Glen of Weeping', and many tears were shed on 13 February 1692. Macdonald of Glencoe, late with his oath of allegiance to King William III, provided the government with an excuse to get rid of his troublesome clan. It was an affair of the greatest possible dishonour. Campbell of Glenlyon billeted himself and 128 soldiers with the Macdonalds for several days, living as guests and accepting the generous hospitality that was such an integral part of Highland life. Glenlyon's company, acting on higher authority, rose one dawn and massacred their hosts as they slept. Tradition has it that the Glenlyon's piper, who was called MacKenzie, played to warn the Macdonalds. The Massacre Memorial, in the village of Glencoe, is a tall, slender cross—a poignant reminder of senseless slaughter.

Glencoe and North Lorne Folk Museum (open daily except Sun, May–Sept: adm) is in Glencoe village. It contains many Jacobite and historic exhibits, domestic implements, weapons, costumes, photographs, dolls and dolls' houses, tools, and much else, all housed in a group of thatched houses. **The National Trust for Scotland** has a visitor centre, 2 miles (3km) east of the village, full of information.

Clachaig, 2 miles (3km) east of Glencoe village, is a hotel/hostel which always seems to be peopled by cold, wet climbers sitting about looking miserable. Here a resident warden will advise about good walks and climbing in the glen. This is a centre for some of the most challenging mountaineering in the country, much of which is not suitable for amateurs. There is a chairlift and T-bars for skiers at the head of the glen, and good skiing on Meall a Bhuiridh, when conditions are right.

Loch Ossian is about 17 miles (27km) northeast of Glencoe, tucked into a valley surrounded by hills and inaccessible by road. There is a youth hostel and the train stops at Corrour Station, but the energetic should get out the map and attack it on foot. It is a lovely 10-mile (16km) tramp from Black Corries Lodge, over the shoulder of Stob na Cruaiche, round the eastern end of Blackwater Reservoir and beside the railway.

Beyond Glencoe, Rannoch Moor stretches away to the east, a vast swampy wasteland, unpopulated except by birds, bleak even in summer. Plans to extend the West Highland Line across this most desolate of moors in the last century, so it could link up with Perthshire, were abandoned after a group of top railway executives set out over the moor to survey it, got lost, had to spend the night out in the bog and nearly died of exposure.

Kinlochleven, at the head of Loch Leven, was a big iron ore smelter, founded to bring employment at the beginning of the century and now closed. Most of the houses were built for the workers.

Where to Stay and Eating Out

expensive

The grandest is the Victorian mansion, **Inverlochy Castle Hotel**, at Torlundy, 3 miles (4.5km) north of Fort William, © 0397 702177. It is so exclusive it doesn't publish its prices.

Knockie Lodge Hotel, Whitebridge, © 04563 276, in an old family house, set amidst remote scenery high above Loch Ness, is comfortable, with fishing.

moderate

Alexandra Hotel, Old Fort Parade, Fort William, © 0397 702241, is old-fashioned, not wildly exciting but dependable.

Ballachulish House, © 08552 266, is an 18th-century laird's house overlooking Loch Linnhe and the Morven Hills. It has a great atmosphere and you feel welcome as you walk through the door. **Ballachulish Hotel**, © 08552 606, has a marvellous position overlooking the water and the food is excellent.

Corriegour Lodge Hotel, Loch Lochy, near Spean Bridge, © 039781 685, has good views over the loch and reasonable food. Slightly more expensive, **Spean Bridge Hotel**, © 039781 250, is old-fashioned, comfortable and jolly.

Glengarry Castle Hotel, at Invergarry, © 08093 254, is a rather grim-looking pile but should suit those who hanker for ghosts. Not historic itself, it has in its grounds the ruins of Invergarry Castle, where the seven severed heads were presented to the chief of the MacDonells of Glengarry (*see* Tobar nan Ceann, p.185). The hotel is comfortable, in a lovely position overlooking Loch Oich. It is only open from April to October.

For Nessie-spotters, **Loch Ness Lodge Hotel** at Drumnadrochit, © 04562 342, has a lot to offer. Perched above Loch Ness, the hotel is comfortable and friendly and includes a visitor centre with interesting exhibits of local history and culture and a 200-seat cinema with simultaneous translations in six languages.

Lovat Arms Hotel, Fort Augustus, © 0320 6206, is comfortable, overlooking Loch Ness and the abbey. Good food.

inexpensive

Kings House Hotel in Glencoe, © 08556 259, claims to be Scotland's oldest inn. Whether it is or not, it is cosy, in dramatic surroundings.

Roy Bridge Hotel, © 039781 201, is at the entrance to Glen Roy, a pleasant, well-run hotel with passable food. **Invergarry Hotel**, © 08093 206, is nice, cheap, and recently completely refurbished.

Another one for monster-spotters is **Drumnadrochit Hotel** at the Exhibition Centre, © 04562 218. Surrounded by monsterabilia, this is slightly tawdry.

Lewiston Arms Hotel, near Drumnadrochit, © 04562 225, is a charming, 200-year-old inn in a pretty garden. **Glenmoriston Arms Hotel**, © 0320 51206, is a traditional Highland inn, with comfortable rooms, good food and a choice of 170 malt whiskies.

West of the Great Glen to Kyle of Lochalsh

There is a detour from Invermoriston or from Invergarry, 13 miles (21km) to the south, off the A82. The two roads join up and go west of the Great Glen to Kyle of Lochalsh, the stepping stone to the Isle of Skye. The A887 from Invermoriston goes 16 miles (25.5km) through Glen Moriston to meet the A87 from Invergarry. Some 12 miles (19km) from Invermoriston, look out for the cairn beside the road beyond Achlain. It is in memory of a brave man, Roderick Mackenzie, an Edinburgh lawyer, who had the dubious honour of being a Bonnie Prince Charlie look-alike. Hoping to deflect government troops from their quest for the Prince's head after Culloden, Mackenzie allowed himself to be captured. He lost his life for his gallantry and his head was presented to Butcher Cumberland in triumph at Fort Augustus.

The A87 is an excellent new road along the north side of Loch Garry, over high moorland with sweeping views. Five miles (8km) west of Invergarry, a narrow single-track road goes out to **Kinloch Hourn**, Loch of Hell. This, despite its name, is another glorious sea loch, snaking out towards the western isles, steep sided and treacherous for sailors in certain winds. The Glengarry Highland Games are held in July.

After the two roads join, the A87 runs north of Loch Cluanie, through mountain passes that are a patchwork of heather and scree, with rich wooded glens where the many rivers and burns cascade down from the surrounding hills. The Five Sisters of Kintail dominate Glen Shiel.

At **Shiel Bridge** on Loch Duich, 10 miles (16km) west of Cluanie, a narrow, twisting road branches left and climbs over the **Mam Ratagan Pass**. This was the route taken by the drovers bringing cattle and sheep from Skye, down to trysts at Falkirk and Crieff. It follows the course of the military road out to **Fort Bernera**, 8 miles (13km) west of Shiel Bridge. Johnson and Boswell travelled along this road in 1772, when soldiers were still working on it. The ruins of the Bernera Barracks are north of Glenelg, just before the ferry across to Kylerhea in Skye. They were built in 1722 and used until after 1790.

Glen Beg runs east off a narrow road 2 miles (3km) south of Glenelg. Here are two of the most splendid examples of the Iron Age brochs built to provide shelter and refuge for the chiefs and their people: **Dun Telve** and **Dun Troddan**. Their double walls are honeycombed with galleries, and pierced by a single small entrance, easily defended. At the end of the road a track leads to Dun Grugaig, an earlier fort, on the brink of a steep gorge.

Not far south of Glen Beg is Sandaig. The house where Gavin Maxwell lived with his otters was on the beach below Upper Sandaig—it was burnt to the ground. In his books, *Ring of Bright Water*, *The Rocks Remain*, etc., Maxwell miscalls the place Camusfeàrna (bay of the alders), in order to preserve its remoteness and isolation. There are many other, genuine Camusfeàrnas in Scotland, causing some confusion.

This rough road goes right on down to Arnisdale and Glen Corran on Loch Hourn, 10 miles (16km) or so to the south.

Back on the main road round Loch Duich, stop at Morvich, 2 miles (3km) beyond Shiel Bridge at the head of the loch. There is a National Trust for Scotland visitor centre here, with an audio-visual exhibition giving an excellent picture of the surrounding Kintail estate, with its many walks and climbs. They have details of the route out to the spectacular Falls of Glomach, 3 miles (4.5km) further on by road to the northeast and then about a 4-mile (6.5km) walk and climb. The 370-foot (114m) falls are among the highest in Britain, falling in two spectacular cascades over a projecting rock, into a breathtakingly deep chasm. The air is full of the sound of water and the sides of the gorge are hung with lush green ferns and foliage.

Eilean Donan Castle (open daily, Easter–Sept: adm) is 10 miles (16km) northwest of Shiel Bridge, one of the most photographed castles in Scotland and familiar to anyone who saw the film *Highlander*. Standing on a rocky island reached by a causeway, on the edge of Loch Duich, it was built in 1230, on the site of an ancient fort, and was the seat of the MacKenzies, Earls of Seaforth. What you see today is almost entirely Victorian—a loose 19th-century reinterpretation of a medieval castle, not entirely accurate. It was garrisoned by Spanish troops in 1719, supporting one of the Jacobite attempts to regain the throne for the Stuarts: in reprisal it was bombarded by English warships. It is open to the public and dedicated as a war memorial to the Clan Macrae, who held the castle as Constables to the Earls of Seaforth. Among other things are interesting Jacobite relics.

Kyle of Lochalsh is 7 miles (11km) west, terminus for the railway from Inverness and the ferry to Skye. This busy little holiday resort has several shops, a swimming pool and is usually full of a cheerful crowd of holidaymakers. Cars wait to catch the ferry to Kyleakin, a 24-hour service that takes only a few minutes. A new bridge across to Skye is planned. There are plenty of good walks round here.

Where to Stay

See also previous and following sections.

expensive

Lochalsh Hotel, © 0599 4204, stands right on the water at Kyle of Lochalsh, a huge hotel, worth every penny for position alone, but also for comfort and good food.

moderate

A lot cheaper and just as nice in a different way, **Balmacara Hotel** nearby, © 059986 283, looks across Loch Alsh. **Kintail Lodge Hotel**, Glenshiel, © 059981 226, has a pleasant atmosphere. **The Castle Inn**, Dornie, © 059985 205, has a reputation for being particularly kind and hospitable to weary travellers. The food is good, they offer trout fishing and you can hire their motor launch.

inexpensive

Loch Duich Hotel, Ardelve, Dornie, © 059985 213, is good value. **Cluanie Inn** Cluanie, Glenmoriston, © 0320 40238, is a welcome haven in a remote landscape and reasonable.

The Southwest Corner

The southwestern corner of the Highland Region is Jacobite country and still remains a very Catholic pocket of the mainland. It is an enchanted land, full of beauty as well as history. Cars should be abandoned whenever possible and sailors should put to sea.

The **Corran Ferry**, 9 miles (14.5km) southwest of Fort William, crosses Loch Linnhe at the Corran Narrows, a frequent service taking 5 minutes. Several districts occupy the peninsula to the west and south: Ardgour, Moidart, Sunart, Ardnamurchan, Morvern and Kingairloch. Rugged, mountainous and beautiful, deeply cut by lochs and glens, this is one of the most magical corners of Scotland.

The road south from Corran goes down Loch Linnhe, branching left after 7 miles (11km) to become the B8043. Keep on southwest through Morvern, cut by lush green glens alive with the sound of water and bird song. **Lochaline**, on the southern shore of the peninsula, means 'the beautiful loch'. It faces across the Sound of Mull to Fishnish Point, linked by a fairly frequent car ferry taking 15 minutes. Silica sand is mined at Lochaline, used for making optical glass.

There is no road to **Ardtornish Castle** on a point a couple of miles east of Lochaline. Built in 1340, it was for many years a stronghold of the Lords of the Isles. The ruined keep and ramparts are custodians of a stirring past when proud, independent chiefs ruled over this territory with a total disregard for the authority of the Crown.

Fiunary is 5 miles (8km) west of Lochaline along the coast, the home of George Macleod, the left-wing Presbyterian who re-established a community on Iona in 1938 and took the name Lord Macleod of Fiunary when he was made a life peer in 1967. There are lovely views across the sound from this road, which peters out after 8 or 9 miles (14km).

Strontian, north of Lochaline on the A884, is at the head of Loch Sunart. From Strontian Lead Mines, opened in 1722, came the discovery of the element strontium. These mines, manned by French prisoners of war, provided bullets for the Napoleonic Wars. There is a well-stocked yacht chandler here and an inn where groups of holidaymakers often create their own spontaneous *céilidhs* in the summer months.

The Floating Church

It was just off Strontian, in Loch Sunart, that the 'Floating Church' was anchored in 1843, during the 'Disruption', when the Free Church broke away from the Church of Scotland. The local laird refused members of the breakaway church land on which to build their kirk, so they bought an old ship on the Clyde, fitted it up as a church and towed it to Loch Sunart; the congregation rowed out to worship in it.

Loch Sunart is a perfect, safe anchorage for boats. For sailors, there can be few more enjoyable experiences than to sail out of Loch Sunart early on a fine morning, the wind on your quarter, the sun on your back, watching the whole of the island-studded Minch open up ahead.

Halfway along the north shore of Loch Sunart, the B8007 is a cul-de-sac branching west to **Ardnamurchan**, a rugged, windlashed peninsula, familiar to west-coast yachtsmen as the most westerly point on the mainland of the British Isles. The ruin of **Mingary Castle**, about 16 miles (25.5km) along, was once the stronghold of the MacIans of Ardnamurchan. The castle stands on a rock cliff, its walls rising sheer with the cliff on the seaward side, guarding the entrance to Loch Sunart and to the Sound of Mull. James VI came to Mingary to receive the homage of the Lords of the Isles, and was disappointed by their lack of enthusiasm. The castle was taken by Montrose's men in 1644 and garrisoned in 1745 by government soldiers, who built a barracks within the walls.

Ardnamurchan Point, about 22 miles (35km) from Salen, is wild, heather-clad rock with a lighthouse at its tip, at present closed to the public and a good 5-mile (8km) walk from the road. The lighthouse is a listed building. Although it was restored not so long ago when visited by the Queen, it is already at risk again. This dramatic headland takes the full force of westerly gales and can present quite a challenge to small boats, even in lighter winds.

Moidart, north from Salen, has a Jacobite legend in every glen, hill and loch. **Acharacle** (difficult to pronounce: the 'ch' is guttural) is a scattered village at the western end of **Loch Sheil**, 3 miles (4.5km) north of Salen. With plenty of kit houses, this is a very typical 20th-century Highland community. From here, **Ardtoe** is another 3 miles (4.5km) west on **Kentra Bay**. This sheltered, sandy haven has been turned into a vast seawater reserve for white fish farming. Ardtoe is a delightful place, popular with artists.

Castle Tioram

Just north of Acharacle, an unmarked lane to the left twists and turns out to the South Channel of Loch Moidart, and one of the most stirring, romantic ruins in Scotland. Castle Tioram, pronounced 'tiram' and meaning 'dry land' in Gaelic, stands high on a rocky promontory overlooking Eilean Shona, reached on foot by causeway at low tide. This 13th- to 14th-century castle was the seat of the Macdonalds of Clanranald. It was burnt in 1715 by the staunchly Jacobite chief, to prevent it from falling into government hands while he was away fighting at Sheriffmuir. The tower dates from 1600; the walls enclose an inner court yard, with several chambers.

In 1984 these ancient walls became the fine setting for a gathering of Clanranald Macdonalds from all over the world. They were entertained by their chief, in the roofless banqueting hall, roasting whole lambs in the old hearth, and for a few hours the castle lived again. The darkness was vibrant with pipe music and laughter. The next day an open-air Mass was celebrated in the courtyard to rededicate the Clanranald banner, said to have survived from Culloden.

It was at **Kinlochmoidart**, 5 miles (8km) north of Acharacle, that Prince Charles waited while the clans were rallied to his cause, and it was here that his charm won over the chiefs who were reluctant to take part in his rebellion. Seven oak trees here, some replanted after a gale, are called the Seven Men of Moidart, in memory of the Prince's followers.

The road twists up through Moidart and follows the zigzag of **Loch Ailort** to its head. Here turn left on the A830 (another cul-de-sac) for about 6 miles (9.5km) to **Loch nan Uamh** (Loch of the Caves). Here, on 25 July 1745, Prince Charles landed from Eriskay, with only seven companions, at the start of his campaign to restore the crown to the Stuarts. A cairn, on a crag overlooking the loch beside the road, commemorates the event. A year later, broken and defeated, the Prince embarked from this same place, to return to France, effectively ending what became known as *Bliadhna Teàrlach* (Charles's Year). The knobbly hills of South Morar, to the northeast, mottled sepia-greyish, are rather gloomy but the view across to Eigg and Rum is splendid.

Arisaig, about 7 miles (11km) west of the cairn, has a sheltered anchorage and is a peaceful holiday village from which boat cruises run to the islands. Around the bay, where trawlers lie at anchor, attractive houses cling to the hillside. The prominent tower of the Catholic church was erected in memory of Alasdair MacMhaigstir Alasdair, one of the greatest of the Gaelic poets, who took the Jacobite side in 1745. The tower is a landmark for boats. Arisaig has its Highland Games in July.

Morar, about 7 miles (9.5km) north of Arisaig, stands on a sheltered bay with glorious silver sands. **Loch Morar** runs 9 miles (14.5km) eastwards, the deepest inland loch in Europe at over 1000 feet (308m). North Morar, on its far shore, and Knoydart, beyond Loch Nevis to the north, are wild and roadless, accessible only by boat or on foot.

Mallaig

Mallaig is about 10 or 11 miles (17km) north of Arisaig on the western tip of North Morar. The road to it from Fort William is one of the most scenic in Scotland and under heavy pressure, being the only route to the rail and ferry terminus. This bustling little fishing port is unspoilt, in spite of being a favourite for holidaymakers. The quays are a jumble of fish-curing sheds and all the clutter of fishing: stacks of creels and fish boxes, piles of netting and gear. If you want to take a box of kippers home with you, this is the place to buy them. Cruises run to many of the islands, and there is a steam train to Fort William. The Mallaig and Morar Highland Games are held in August and there is a **Marine Life Centre**, covering the fishing tradition.

Glenfinnan

From Mallaig it is necessary to backtrack. Glenfinnan is 14 miles (22.5km) east of Lochailort. The road twists and is very steep, with lovely views, between banks of rhododendrons, until it drops into Glenfinnan. A column, topped by a Highlander, rises from a marshy plain at the head of Loch Shiel, where three glens meet against a backdrop of layers of blue-grey hills. The Glenfinnan Monument, another milestone in *Bliadhna Teàrlach*, was erected in 1815 to commemorate the raising of Prince Charles's standard on 19 August 1745.

It is easier to recall the past if you turn your back on this Victorian folly, and look down the loch and up into the hills. This was where the Prince stood on that summer's day, so full of hope, surrounded by those of the clans who had already committed themselves to his cause, waiting to see if Cameron of Lochiel would join them, a man whose great influence would sway the decisions of other clans. This powerful chief had not been enthusiastic about the uprising, but he was a brave man and a loyal one. 'I'll share the fate of my Prince', he had said, and now, in the still afternoon, the waiting clans heard the skirl of pipes. They turned to watch Lochiel, at the head of 700 clansmen, marching down from the hills to join Prince Charles's cause. The well known 'March of the Cameron Men' was composed by Mary

Maxwell Campbell, in 1829, to commemorate this event. Lochiel's action quickly brought in other clans and later in the afternoon the great red and white silken banner was unfurled: the Prince's father was proclaimed King James III of Britain, with Prince Charles Edward his Regent.

Whatever misguided folly may have influenced this final Jacobite rising, no one with a shred of romance in their veins can stand here, remembering that day, and not feel staunchly Jacobite. However, many wise, clear-sighted chiefs remained neutral, without dishonour, and it was those men, ruled by their heads rather than their hearts, who did more for Scotland's subsequent survival than the impetuous Jacobites.

The Gothic-style Catholic church above Loch Shiel, with the hills behind, must be the most beautiful Catholic church in Scotland. It contains another monument to the Prince. The **Glenfinnan Viaduct** is an impressive landmark and a great engineering feat, carrying the railway westwards.

The **National Trust for Scotland Visitor Centre** (open daily, April–Oct: adm) is across the road from the monument. It provides excellent maps showing the progress of the Prince's army, and traces his wanderings after Culloden out to the islands and finally back to Loch nan Uamh.

The Glenfinnan Games are held every August on the nearest Saturday to the 19th.

Where to Stay

What hotels lack in mod cons and sophistication in this area, they make up for in hospitality and courtesy.

expensive

Glenborrodale Castle, near Ardnamurchan, © 09724 266, is a restored Victorian pile in 850 acres overlooking Mull and Loch Sunart. Open from May to October, it has a quirky Highland character, with unreliable plumbing in beautifully fitted-out bathrooms, and a half-size billiard table.

moderate

The Arisaig Hotel is a delightfully warm, friendly coaching inn, with glorious sea views and reasonable food. Another nice one is **Arisaig House**, highly recommended, with terraced gardens and views to sea, and with good food and wine.

Stage House Inn, Glenfinnan, © 039783 246, is fairly sophisticated, on Loch Shiel. Open April to October, it has good food.

West Highland Hotel, Mallaig, © 0687 2210, is a splendid family-owned hotel, overlooking the islands, oozing with hospitality. Open April to October.

Ardgour Hotel, ✆ 08555 225, is very good, and right on the water at Ardgour with glorious views.

Salen Hotel, Acharacle, ✆ 096785 661, has a friendly atmosphere and serves delicious salmon sandwiches for lunch. **Clanranald Hotel**, Acharacle, ✆ 096785 662, is a homely little hotel with not too many frills and masses of character. The six bedrooms share two bathrooms. Open from Easter to October.

Kilchoan House Hotel, near Ardnamurchan, ✆ 09723 200, is an attractive Highland lodge with one bathroom between eight bedrooms. The food is good.

Glenfinnan House Hotel, Glenfinnan, ✆ 039783 235, is a splendid old mansion overlooking the Glenfinnan Monument, with glorious views of Loch Shiel. Open April to October. You might get pipe music if you are lucky.

Morar Hotel, ✆ 0687 2346, is a good, family hotel, with very friendly staff, in a lovely position overlooking the Silver Sands of Morar. Open April to October.

Glenuig Inn, near Lochailort, ✆ 06877 219, is a dear little inn on a secluded bay with a sandy beach and freshwater trout lochs nearby. The food is first class, especially the seafood. Open April to October.

Kyle of Lochalsh to Inverness via the West Coast

The coastal route back to Inverness opens up more wonderful scenery. Take the narrow road to the left in Kyle of Lochalsh and follow the coast (and the railway) round for about 7 miles (9.5km) to **Plockton**. The views are across to Applecross and Torridon in the north and west to Skye. Plockton is an unexpected holiday village, its neat stone cottages all painted and trim, with velvet lawns and palm trees, lush shrubs, birches and pines, all grouped most attractively round a sheltered bay. Built in the 18th century as a fishing village, it is now unashamedly given over to up-market holidaymakers, with craft shops and pleasure boats, surrounded by picture-postcard scenery. This is an artist's haven. From Plockton the road follows the southern shore of Loch Carron, to the narrows at Stromeferry (no ferry now), and up to Strathcarron at the head of the loch.

It is interesting to reflect that there were virtually no roads in this area until General Wade's military roads were constructed in the first half of the 18th century. When the Highlands were so devastated by the potato famine in the middle of the 19th century, Destitution Committees were set up to send supplies of meal and provisions to the starving Highlanders. Some of the 'Destitution Funds' collected were used to build access roads to remote communities, making it easier to send help and providing work for the people. Some of these roads became known as 'Destitution Roads.'

Applecross Peninsula, round the head of Loch Carron and west from Lochcarron village, is another area of striking Highland scenery. Spectacular *Bealach-nam-Bo*, Pass of the Cattle, is a steep, narrow road across the southern end of the peninsula with hairpin bends that make the adrenalin flow. The scenery is almost alpine, fringed by cliffs and rock spurs, dotted with glinting lochans and burns, with the distant hills of Skye ever present to the west. Cattle were driven over this pass from Applecross *en route* for the lucrative markets on the east coast. Records in 1794 tell of 3000 cattle leaving the district.

Don't miss the excellent **Carron Tweed Factory** at Lochcarron.

There is a sandy beach at Applecross, on the west coast of the peninsula, in a sheltered bay. An Irish monk, Maelrubha, founded a monastery north of the village, in 673. It became an important centre of Christianity until it was destroyed by Norsemen. A cul-de-sac runs to the south of the peninsula. It is possible to drive right round the north coast from Applecross beach, along the southern shore of Loch Torridon, Loch Shieldaig and Upper Loch Torridon to Torridon village.

The 26,000-acre **Torridon Estate** was acquired by the National Trust for Scotland in 1967. There is a visitor centre at the road junction at the head of Upper Loch Torridon, with an audio-visual presentation on the area. There is a deer museum and enclosures, a programme of guided walks and advice on where to go. The 750-million-year-old red sandstone mountains dominate the whole of this part of the region with their distinctive white quartzite peaks.

The Beinn Eighe National Nature Reserve is northeast of Torridon on the A896, and was the first in Britain established for the preservation and study of the remains of the Caledonian Forest. The wildlife in the area includes deer, wild mountain goat, wild cat, pine marten, and eagles. For those who like leaflets and posters and illustrated information, there is a visitor centre at **Aultroy Cottage,** just northwest of **Kinlochewe**, with advice on walks, an illuminated model of the district and details about the work done on the reserve.

The drive west along the northern shore of Loch Torridon goes through scattered crofting townships, with sea views, backed by massive hills, as far as Lower Diabaig, about 8 miles (13km). A track goes further round the coast to a youth hostel. From here it is a lovely walk up the rocky coast to Redpoint.

The A832 goes northwest from Kinlochewe along the south shore of beautiful **Loch Maree**, dominated by **Slioch** on the opposite side. Loch Maree is 12 miles (19km) long, its name derived from St Maelrubha, the monk who founded the monastery at Applecross. He spent some time as a hermit on one of the islands on the loch and is, according to tradition, buried there.

About 8 miles (13km) along is the **Loch Maree Hotel**. Nothing seems to have changed here since Queen Victoria visited it in 1877 and stayed for six days. A rock on a bank in front of the hotel, inscribed in Gaelic, commemorates the queen's visit. This is a fishing hotel, with an impressive log of catches on the hall table.

The A832 leaves Loch Maree soon after the hotel and goes west towards Gairloch. At **Kerrysdale**, about 10 miles (16km) beyond the hotel, the River Kerry dashes towards the sea, through mossy glades and silver birches, with a few gnarled oaks and feathery rowans. Carpeting the dappled turf are a profusion of wild flowers: lousewort, milkwort, primroses, bluebells, wood anemones, orchids, and many more.

Take the very minor cul-de-sac left from Kerrysdale, past the sheltered anchorage of **Shieldaig**, and the attractive bay at **Badachro**. This was once a large fishing station where curers bought herring, cod, ling, etc., from local fishermen. Now the community life is centred on a tiny, friendly shop-cum-post office. The road, which was built with money from the Destitution Fund, goes on to **Redpoint**. Heather-carpeted moorland runs down to rocky cliffs and crescents of red-gold sand. The views are across to South Rona and Raasay, with the island of Skye beyond. An otter swims in the sea and builds its cone of fish-remains on the turf. Wheatears, ringed plovers, linnets and skylarks fill the air with song. Colonies of seabirds mass on the rocks.

Back at Kerrysdale, turn left to **Gairloch**, a well-developed holiday resort with excellent sandy beaches and several hotels. The hub of this community seems to be the Wild Cat Stores, purveyors of fresh milk, fresh baps and local chat. Opposite is the award-winning **Gairloch Heritage Museum** (open daily, Easter–Sept: adm), easy to miss and well worth a visit. In only a few rooms one can learn a great deal about life in the western Highlands. The exhibits range from Pictish stones and relics to Victoriana. There is a portable pulpit for outdoor preachers of the Free Church; an old ice-making machine; stuffed birds and wild animals; an illicit still; spinning wheels with the various wools and natural dyes; a wash house; a school room, with Gaelic on the blackboard; a village store; and a fisherman and his gear. The highlight is the replica of the inside of a croft house. This is imaginatively set up with press buttons to illuminate it, set the spinning wheel in motion, and animate the old woman in front of the peat fire. She sings a haunting Gaelic lullaby to the baby, rocking in a cradle. An annex contains interesting history displays and old photographs of the area.

Poolewe is 7 or 8 miles (12–13km) northeast of Gairloch. Stop on the bridge to watch the mighty force of water from Loch Maree, thrusting its way out into Loch Ewe, forming the pool that gave the place its name.

Inverewe Garden (open daily: adm) at Inverewe, half a mile from Poolewe, is famous to horticulturists all over the world. It was created by Osgood MacKenzie, a Victorian who had spent much of his early life on the Continent. Son of the Laird of Gairloch, he was given the estate at the head of Loch Ewe in 1862: a peninsula of red Torridonian sandstone, pocked by peat-hags and bare of vegetation except for heather, crowberry and dwarf willows. It is hard to believe, now, what this enterprising man achieved from such unpromising beginnings in an era when there were few roads and soil was carried in wicker creels. He planted an outer windbreak of Corsican and Scots pine, behind deer- and rabbit-proof fences. Plants were introduced from all over the world. Now, there are some 2500 species, in 50 acres of woodland, covering a steep hillside that juts into the loch, sheltered by hills behind. This exotic, sub-tropical paradise lies only a little to the south of the latitude that runs through Cape Farewell, in Greenland. The proximity of the

Gulf Stream is responsible for making this garden so fertile. Palm trees, rock gardens, peat-banks, ornamental ponds, all display a profusion of blooms from Japan, Chile, South Africa, the Pacific, and many other places.

An attractive cul-de-sac drive down the west side of Loch Ewe goes as far as **Cove**. Cove Cave is so deep and sheltered it was once used as a place of worship.

Gruinard Bay, about 11 miles (17.5km) north of Poolewe, has sandy beaches surrounded by hills, and views out to the Summer Isles. It is a magnificent spot, with a campsite right on the beach at **Mellon Udrigle**. Gruinard Island, in the bay, was infected with anthrax during the last war and was forbidden territory for years. It is now decontaminated, and has been restored to its original owner.

Sand

A small sign beside the road, not far east of **Laide** on the bay, points the way down a cliff path to two caves. The largest was a meeting place for hundreds of years and was used as a church for Presbyterians, as late as 1843. The smaller cave was lived in by an old woman and her girl companion in 1885. Families evicted from their crofts during the Clearances used to take shelter here. It is a magic place: at the entrance to the larger cave, with its protective wall in front, it is intriguing to picture it when perhaps several families were huddled together inside, with what they had saved of their possessions and livestock. The fire would be burning, children and dogs playing, and people making do with whatever fish and game they had managed to catch.

The A832 skirts Little Loch Broom (stop and look at the spectacular **Ardessie Falls** about two-thirds of the way along), and cuts across the moors. The part of the road from Dundonnell, by Feithean, to Braemore Junction, was built with funds raised during the potato famine and so is called the 'Destitution Road'. The name is misleading: it's lovely.

Braemore Junction is where the A832 meets the A835 to Ullapool, about 28 miles (45km) from Gruinard. It is also at the confluence of the rivers Broom, Cuileig and Droma, known locally as 'The Valley of The Broom'. Stop at the large observation car park just before the A835. It is a staggering view down into the junction of the three valleys, the steep wooded banks ablaze with colour in the autumn. Less than a mile (1.5km) further on, a sign on the left marks the Corrieshalloch Gorge and the Falls of Measach. It is only a short walk from the road and there is an alternative approach from round the corner, where there is another car park and signs, on the A835.

Corrieshalloch

Corrieshalloch is unforgettable: a mile-long (1.5km) box canyon, 200 feet (60m) deep, its sheer rock sides festooned with ferns and mosses, saxifrage, sorrel, tufts of grasses and wood-millet. Miraculously rooted wych elm, birch, hazel, sycamore, Norway maple and beech trees cling to the sides, with goat-willow, bird-cherry and guelder-rose. There is an observation platform from which to look back at the Falls of Measach, a single cascade of 150 feet (46m) that seems to hang in the air like smoke. There is an even better view from the suspension bridge that spans the gorge, but this is not for vertigo sufferers. The deep pools below are rich in trout, and, above the roar of the falls, the angry 'pruk' of the ravens can be heard, as they nest on a ledge opposite the viewing platform.

The drive back to Inverness from here is attractive, through open moor, past lochs and glens. See the Inverness to Durness section for things to look at on the way.

Where to Stay

moderate

Gairloch Hotel, © 0445 2001, is a huge Victorian pile overlooking the sea, open from April to October. You expect to see pitchers and bowls in the bedrooms but actually it is reasonably modern and comfortable and, rare in this part of the world, all 66 bedrooms are en suite. **Shieldaig Lodge Hotel**, near Gairloch, © 044583 250, is a Victorian country house, right by the water and backed by trees, with good food. **Kinlochewe Hotel**, © 0445 84253, is cheaper and reasonably comfortable. **Pool House Hotel**, at Poolewe, © 044586 272, is a small family-run hotel by the bridge where Loch Maree pours out into Loch Ewe, within walking distance of Inverewe Garden. **Loch Torridon Hotel**, © 0445 791242, is a Victorian mansion with lovely views in 56 acres, open April to October. **Ocean View Hotel** at Sand, © 0445 731385, has a marvellously friendly atmosphere.

inexpensive

Aultbea Hotel, © 0445 731201, is a small hotel on the eastern shore of Loch Ewe, quiet and comfortable with good food. **Drumchork Lodge Hotel** close by, © 0445 731242, is slightly bigger, slightly more expensive, with the same stunning views. **Badachro Inn**, © 044583 255, is a whitewashed inn with a small garden on the edge of the bay. It has two bedrooms only, and one bathroom. The food is unpretentious and very cheap.

Inverness to Durness

The first part of the drive to Durness goes through farmland backed by hills, rapidly turning to moor and rugged mountain as the road crosses to the west. From Loch Broom north it is all mountains and vistas of loch, mountain and sea.

Beauly is 10 miles (16km) west of Inverness at the head of the Beauly Firth. This is Lovat country. The Lovat family came to Britain with the Normans and it was their French influence that inspired the name Beauly, *Beau Lieu.* (Romantics prefer to attribute the name to Mary, Queen of Scots, fresh from her French chateau, exclaiming '*Ah, quelle beau lieu!*')

The centre of Beauly is a widening of the main road, making an attractive rectangular market place with the ruin of Beauly Priory (open daily: free) at the north end, beyond the old cross. Founded in 1230 for Valliscaulian monks, the priory is now a roofless shell. In the south wall are three fine triangular windows embellished with trefoils dating from the original building. It fell into ruin after the Reformation.

The monument in the Square commemorates the raising of the Lovat Scouts for service in South Africa, by Simon Joseph, 16th Lord Lovat. Perhaps the most colourful member of the family was Simon, Lord Lovat, born in about 1667. His many notorious escapades included the attempted abduction of a nine-year-old heiress and his subsequent marriage by force to her mother, a deed that left him convicted of high treason and outlawed. Having come into the title, by devious means, he became a Jacobite agent, involved in conveying false information to the enemy. Outlawed once more, he turned government man and received a full pardon. Swearing loyalty to the Crown, he sent his son to fight for Prince Charles in 1745. He was beheaded, finally, in London, meeting his end with humorous dignity. 'You'll get that nasty head of yours chopped off, you ugly old Scotch dog,' taunted a Cockney woman in the crowd. 'I believe I shall, you ugly old English bitch,' he replied. Hogarth painted a portrait of him in hideous old age, just before he was helped up the steps to the scaffold—bloated, villainous, with satanic eyebrows and a cruel mouth, racked by gout. Known as 'The Old Fox of the '45', he was indisputably a rogue, traitor and hypocrite. Alternative, more kindly, reports also credit him with intelligence, charm and Celtic wit.

Moniack Castle Winery and Wine Bar (open on weekdays) is an excellent staging post a few miles southeast of Beauly. They serve their own home-produced country wines, meads and a variety of delicious jellies, in converted out-buildings in an ancestral setting. The food is excellent and the wine is for sale.

Before continuing north, make a detour to visit the glens of Farrar, Glass, Beauly, Cannich and Affric. From Beauly, take the A831 southwest down Strathglass to Glen Affric, through wooded glens following the River Beauly and then the River Glass. The remains of two Iron Age forts lie off to the right from **Kilmorack**, 2 miles (3km) from Beauly. Here, and at **Aigas,** 3 miles (4.5km) further on, are hydroelectric dams where visitors can watch salmon being 'lifted' on their way upstream to breed. **Tomich** is an attractive estate village built in the late 19th century. The home farm up on the hill has been converted as a holiday centre with swimming pool, accommodation and some chalets.

There are lovely walks in this area where the three glens of the Farrar, Glass and Beauly meet; the scenery is gentler than that of the western Highlands but just as magnificent, enhanced rather than spoiled by the hydroelectric developments that have changed the landscape. Steep, pine-clad rocks rise from peaty lochs in broad, green valleys.

At **Glassburn**, look out for the **Holy Well of St Ignatius**, beside the road: an intriguing old headstone in a modern cairn, with ingravings that include references to: saints Columba 563, Bean 1015, and Margaret 1070, as well as Pope Leo XIII. There is also a poem which could be the marching song of the Temperance League:

'Water bright water, pure water for me,
the drink of the wise, the wine of the free ...'

and a lot more in that vein.

Stop off at the chapel of St Mary's, in **Eskadale**, a mile (1.5km) beyond Aigas. This pretty, early Victorian church was once the main Catholic centre for this area. In the graveyard is a memorial to an almost-forgotten episode in Scotland's history: the graves of the 'Sobieski Stuarts'. These two brothers, John Sobieski Stolberg Stuart, 1795–1872, and Charles Edward Stuart, 1799–1880, conned Victorian society into accepting them as grandsons of Prince Charles Edward Stuart. They claimed that their father, Lieutenant Thomas Allen, Royal Navy, was Prince Charles's son. They called themselves Counts d'Albanie and there is a splendid book, *The Sobieski Stuarts*, by H. Beveridge, about them. They lived at Eskadale House, further down the valley, and at Eilan Aigas House, where they kept deer hounds and invented several tartans with which further to impress their gullible friends.

More lovely scenery is at Cannich, 17 miles (27km) southwest of Beauly, where the River Glass meets up with the Rivers Affric and Cannich. There is a youth hostel here. About 3 miles (4.5km) southeast, the Corrimony Cairn is a Stone and Bronze Age burial cairn, its passage still roofed and surrounded by a stone circle.

Although it is far nicer to walk, it is possible to drive the 12 miles (19km) up Glen Farrar to Loch Monar; it is a private road so permission must first be asked. A road runs 8miles (13km) up Glen Cannich to Cozac Lodge, and another up Glen Affric (one of the most beautiful glens in Scotland) to a car park, 2 miles (3km) short of Affric Lodge. Each glen has its own charm, with tumbling burns, lichen-hung trees, glinting sheets of water, all sheltered by hills. From Affric Lodge there is a good hike, 10 miles (16km) west, to the youth hostel at Alltbeath. Another 10 miles (16km) or so reaches Loch Duich.

Contin, 11 miles (17.5km) north of Beauly, has an old coaching inn, on the west side of the River Blackwater, from which passengers used to depart on the tortuous journey west to Poolewe and Ullapool, after the roads were built in the 18th century. Telford built the first bridge here, later swept away by flood water. Dealers used to come up from England to the Contin Horse Fair, to buy sturdy Highland ponies for work in the coal mines. Fair days were festive occasions, drawing people in from far afield, to jostle and gossip over the braziers, among the peddlers' stalls and animal pens.

Strathpeffer

Strathpeffer, a couple of miles northeast of Contin, was a famous spa town until the First World War. People came from overseas, including foreign royalty, to the sulphur and chalybeate springs. The springs were used as early as 1770, but it was not until the first pump room (now derelict) was built in 1820 that Strathpeffer's fame spread over the border. Lying in a sheltered hollow among wooded hills, the town is a popular holiday centre, with plenty for the visitor to do, including climbing Ben Wyvis, the great bulk a few miles to the north. Houses and hotels rise in neat terraces from the heart of the town, whose gently refined atmosphere has won it the title 'Harrogate of the North'.

Strathpeffer Highland Games are held in the grounds of Castle Leod in early August, with all the traditional events such as tossing the caber, putting the shot, piping and dancing.

The **Eagle Stone** stands 3 feet (1m) high on a hillock to the east of Strathpeffer, reached by a lane near Eaglestone House. A Pictish symbol stone with an engraved angel and a horseshoe, it was the subject of one of the Brahan Seer's prophecies: if the stone should fall three times then ships would tie up to it. Setting aside a tidal wave, this seems improbable. However, the seer had an uncanny eye and it is said that the stone has already fallen twice (hence its having been cemented into place and surrounded by wire) and that on the second occasion the Cromarty Firth flooded up to the old county buildings in Dingwall.

Strathpeffer Craft and Visitor Centre (open in the summer: free) has craftsmen and women at work in what was the Victorian station.

Highland Museum of Childhood, in the Old Station (open daily Feb–Nov except closed Mon in Mar and Nov; closed Dec–Jan: adm), brings to life the story of childhood in the Highlands.

At the **Water Sampling Pavilion** in The Square (open daily, Easter–Oct: adm), you can hold your nose and sample the sulphur waters that made Strathpeffer famous as a Victorian spa.

To the south, on a ridge called **Druim Chat**, meaning 'cat's back', there is a well-preserved vitrified fort, **Knockfarrel**, one in a line of three great Pictish defence sites, the other two being at Craig Phadrig in Inverness and Ord Hill in Kessock. You can see the foundations clearly—a vast place, extending to some 810 feet (250m). This is believed to have been a stronghold of Fingal and his warriors, and many are the legends told about it.

A terrible clan battle took place to the southwest, at **Kinellan**, between the Macdonalds and the Mackenzies, in the 16th century. The Macdonalds, seeking vengeance after an alleged insult, lost the fight and were later punished by James IV who deposed them as Lords of the Isles.

Rogie Falls are just over 2 miles (3km) northwest of Contin, well signposted and only a short walk from the car park. It is a delightful picnic spot among birches, rowans and gnarled old oaks, carpeted in heather, bracken and mossy crags. It is possible to watch salmon leaping up a series of falls, from a suspension bridge over the river. They often achieve astonishing heights.

Five miles (8km) on, the road divides, beyond **Garve**. The A832 to the left goes southwest along attractive Strath Bran, past Loch Luichart (where there is an excellent knitwear shop) and out to Achnasheen, a lonely, scattered hamlet where the railway widens to provide a passing place for trains. Here the road divides again, southwest to Loch Carron and Applecross (*see* p.197) or northwest to Loch Maree (*see* p.198).

Ullapool

Ullapool is 32 miles (51km) northwest of Garve, a pleasant drive through moorland and river-filled glens, backed by hills including massive Beinn Dearg, 3547 feet (1090m), to the north. The **Lael Forest Garden Trail** is further on, with over 150 different species of trees and shrubs, all labelled. There are good views across Loch Broom, fringed with beaches and nice picnic spots. The town is a popular holiday resort as well as an important fishing port and the ferry terminus for boats to Stornoway in Lewis. Freshly painted houses line the sea front, their upper windows sharply gabled, looking down on the jumble of quays and slipways, cluttered with small boats and fishing gear, creels, spars, nets and fish boxes. The town was developed as a fishing port by the British Fishery Society in 1788, Loch Broom providing an excellent deep-water anchorage for the boats. There are often east European and Russian fishing boats at anchor in the bay in the anchorage, usually scruffy-looking tubs, bringing a gabble of foreign languages to the streets. It is not unknown to find a female skipper in these boats. Locals will tell intriguing tales of shady people coming and going from the boats with very little interference: splendid material for a spy thriller. The town has a good range of shops, boutiques, restaurants, cafés, bars and every sort of accommodation. Some of the street names are written in Gaelic.

The Loch Broom Highland Museum (open daily except Sun, April–Oct: free) gives insight into the history of Wester Ross, the life of a fishing village and the story of the Clearances. It also has displays of geology, wildlife, military and farming history.

Ullapool Museum, in West Argyle Street (open weekdays, April-Oct: adm), tells the life of the community over the past 200 years, including crofting, fishing, education, religion and emigration.

The tourist information office will give information on sea fishing, boating, pony trekking and cruises. There is a youth hostel and the surrounding countryside is perfect for walking.

Drumrunie is about 8 miles (13km) beyond Ullapool on the A835. Turn left here on to a minor road that skirts the **Coigach** peninsula, winding through land and sea-lochs in some of Scotland's loveliest and wildest scenery. **Achiltibuie**, about 13 miles (21km) round, well signposted, is a honeymooners' paradise and a perfect holiday base. Boats run to the Summer Isles, scattered a few miles off the Coigach Peninsula.

Horticulturists should visit the **Hydroponicum**, at the **Summer Isles Hotel**, in Achiltibuie (open daily, March–Oct: adm). Created by Robert Irvine, it has 'hi-tech soilless growing houses'—an amazing place, with three distinct climates: Hampshire, Bordeaux and the Canaries. Strawberries are picked fresh every day from April to October and bananas flourish. Figs, lemons, passion fruit, vines, vegetables, flowers and herbs all grow luxuriantly without soil. One-hour lecture tours are given in the summer; these include information on the use of solar energy. For details © 085482 202.

At **Achiltibuie Smokehouse** (open weekdays, Oct–April; daily except Sun, May–Sept: free), the process of curing and smoking meat, fish and game can be watched and there is a retail shop. For details © 085482 353.

Back on the A835, the road runs northwards through the Inverpolly National Nature Reserve, a remote, lonely stretch of moorland dotted with lochs, burns and great jagged red sandstone peaks. These include Stac Polly, 2009 feet (618m), Cul Beag, 2523 feet (776m) and Sul Mor, 2786 feet (857m), all very popular with climbers. There is a Nature Conservancy Council visitor centre at Knockan, less than 5 miles (8km) up the road with full information about this area.

Ledmore is less than 8 miles (13km) beyond Drumrunie. Here, an alternative route southeast runs 30 miles (48km) through Strath Oykel to Bonar Bridge, leaving the mountains and running through moorland and attractive wooded valleys.

Ardvreck Castle

Ardvreck Castle (always accessible: free), about 6 miles (9.5km) north of Ledmore, is a jagged fang of a ruin, three storeys high, on **Loch Assynt**. Dating from 1597, it was one of the few castles to be built in this area where lack of roads in the old days made it difficult to maintain large establishments. The Community Council is hoping to consolidate the ruin. It was a Macleod stronghold, and carries in its stones a poignant echo of the last days of Montrose. There are several conflicting stories but it is certain that gallant Montrose, fighting for Charles II, fled to Assynt in 1650 after his final defeat at Carbisdale, near Bonar Bridge. Some say he threw himself on the mercy of the Macleod laird of the time, who responded by selling him to the government for £25,000. Others say Macleod found him and took him prisoner honourably. Whatever the story, Montrose was imprisoned in this grim fortress, on its rocky peninsula jutting into the loch. From here he was taken ignominiously to Edinburgh, tied, back-to-front, on his horse, and abandoned by the king to whom he had given his loyalty.

Inchnadamph Caves, 2 miles (3km) south of Ardvreck, yielded evidence of occupation by early man and also bones of late Pleistocene animals, going back at least 10,000 years.

Lochinver is 10 miles (16km) to the west on the A837, along the north shore of Loch Assynt, a large-ish village and the only place of any size between Scourie and Ullapool. It is a delightful place on one of the most beautiful stretches of coastline in Scotland, with heart-stopping views all round. Two-hour wildlife cruises run from Lochinver, in the summer, with a chance to see some of the many birds and the colonies of seals basking on the rocks.

Dramatic sugar-loaf **Suilven**, 2,399 feet (738m), is 5 miles (8km) to the south in **Glencanisp Forest**, with **Canisp**, 2,779 feet (855m), 2 miles (3km) beyond to the east. Both are well worth climbing on a clear day. The coast road on round from Lochinver is another stunner, about 35 miles (56km) in all, back to join the A894 near **Kylestrome**, where a bridge replaces the small ferry that used to hold up traffic for hours in the holiday season. Boats run from Unapool, down Loch Glencoul to the southeast, to see Britain's highest waterfall, Eas-Coul-Aulin, a fantastic sight, 658 feet (202m) high in a wild, melancholy setting that seems appropriate for such a giddy cascade.

Yet another beautiful drive of nearly 10 miles (16km) reaches **Scourie**, a popular holiday village in a sheltered bay with a sandy beach and rocky pools. Several varieties of orchid thrive in the mild climate here; boats run to the nature reserve on **Handa Island**, a mile (1.5km) off the sandy beach north of Scourie. Here you will see a great variety of sea birds, including razorbills, guillemots, puffins, kittiwakes and skua.

The road north goes inland a few miles to **Laxford Bridge**. An alternative route goes southeast from here to **Lairg** (*see* p.215), through rocky mountains that tower threateningly over the road, with sharp turns and terrifying blind summits. On a sunny day, with the sparkling waters of Loch More, Loch Merkland, and Loch Shin, it can be beautiful, but on a grey, sullen day of mist and rain, it is an awe-inspiring route.

Four miles (6.5km) north of Laxford Bridge, at **Rhiconich**, a good new road goes 4 miles (6.5km) west to **Kinlochbervie**, on **Loch Inchard**, an important west-coast fishing port. Strong currents around the northern headland make swimming very dangerous here. For the most beautiful beach in Scotland, drive 5 miles (8km) on past Kinlochbervie to the end of the road and then walk on round the coast, about 4 miles (6.5km) over abandoned crofts, to **Sandwood Bay**. Entirely remote, it is outstandingly beautiful, with sand, cliffs and columns of rock rising from the sea.

The drive north from Rhiconich is through a bleak wilderness of rock-strewn glens, forbidding mountains and dark, sombre lochs.

Durness

Durness is about 15 miles (24km) northeast of Rhiconich, perched on the north coast, built to withstand the fury of the elements. It is a good base for exploring this northwestern corner and has plenty of places to stay. Durness Highland Gathering is in July.

Durness Old Church, on the bay and dating from 1619, is a roofless shell on the site of an older church. Look for the skull and crossbone carving on the wall; this is thought to mark the site of the grave of a notorious highwayman, Donald MacMurchov, who hoped to buy his way into the afterlife by making substantial contributions to the building of the church. The previous church on this site appears in records in the Vatican as having contributed to one of the Crusades in the 12th century. There was a summer palace for the Bishops of Caithness where the farmhouse now stands, opposite the church.

Smoo Cave is signposted from the road, about a mile (1.5km) to the east. This vast limestone cavern has three compartments, two of which are difficult to get to. The main chamber is 200 feet (61m) long and 120 feet (37m) high, with holes in the roof. Consult the Durness Information Centre for advice on how to reach the inner sections and the dramatic 80-foot (25m) waterfall, where the Alt Smoo River pours down from the cliffs into the caves.

Balnakeil Craft Village, in a former Ministry of Defence Early Warning Station camp, just along the track that runs west from Durness, stands on a lovely white sand bay. Sixteen or so non-local hippy-type craftsmen and women display and sell their astonishingly overpriced handiwork. The crafts include weaving, jewels, candles, rag dolls, bookbinding, painting, woodwork, pottery. In 1981 the Regional Council sold the buildings to the craftsmen and they then formed a Community Co-operative, which also runs the visitor centre.

Cape Wrath

A passenger boat runs across the Kyle of Durness in the summer to link up with a minibus that goes out to the Cape 10 miles (16km) northwest. Check times from local shops. It is worth walking one way, with binoculars and a good bird book: the promontory is an ornithologist's paradise.

Cape Wrath (pronounced 'Raath') got its name from the Viking word *hvarf* meaning 'turning place'. It was not named after the furious sea which pounds at the 523-foot-high (161m) cliffs. These cliffs have veins of rich pink pegmatite running through the gneiss. On a clear day you can see the Orkney Islands to the east, some 60 miles (96km) away, 45 miles (72km) west to the Butt of Lewis, and 80 miles (128km) southwest to Harris.

To the north lies the island of North Rona, with Stack Skerry and Skule Skerry further east. Turn your back on the great fort-like lighthouse and look across the bleak moor, **The Parbh**, that stretches away to the south. Wolves once roamed here in great numbers—an eerie thought as the mist comes creeping in across the desolate wasteland and you look around to make sure that the minibus hasn't left without you.

Where to Stay and Eating Out

See also Inverness.

expensive

Near Ullapool, the best is **Altnaharrie Hotel**, © 085483 230, an old drovers' inn on the shores of Loch Broom, reached by private launch from Ullapool. Small and very select, its bedrooms are pretty, and the food is sublime. This is the only place in Scotland to have been awarded two Michelin stars.

moderate

Unquestionably, the next two are the pick of the bunch. **Summer Isles Hotel**, Achiltibuie, © 085482 282, open Easter to October, is run by Mark and Geraldine Irvine and has been in the family since the 1960s. Wonderfully remote, in a spectacular setting overlooking the Summer Isles and beyond to the Hebrides, it is almost entirely self-sufficient. It has its own smokehouse, the Hydroponicum (*see above*) which provides fresh fruit and vegetables, and its own dairy, veal, quails, duck, fish, etc. There is everything here for lovers of solitude and beauty and it is exactly like going to stay with friends in a special place. In fact, once you've been there, that's what it becomes, except that you get a bill. It's worth every penny.

The other top choice is **Inchnadamph Hotel**, Loch Assynt, © 05712 202, known as the 'Anglers' Retreat'. This is another genuine Highland establishment where homely comfort is more important than double glazing, trouser presses and 'hospitality trays' in the bedroom. In the most glorious surroundings at the head of the loch, this hotel has been in the hands of the Morrison family for 71 years, which is probably why you feel completely at home the moment you arrive. It offers free fishing for salmon, grilse and brown trout, and excellent home-cooking.

Aigas Field Centre, Beauly, © 0463 782443, is a Victorian-Gothic mansion on a working estate in a magnificent setting. Guests are offered optional field study programmes. Very friendly and ancestral, it's open April to October. **Contin House,** © 0997 421920, is a Highland fishing lodge built in 1794, on a 35-acre island in the River Blackwater, in idyllic scenery surrounded by hills. They cater for parties of from six to ten, and it is like going to stay with very special old friends, except you don't do the washing up. **Coul House Hotel**, Contin, © 0997 421487, is a splendid 19th-century pile looking across to the Strathconon hills, with an excellent reputation for good food. **Cozac Lodge**, Cannich, © 04565 263, is an Edwardian shooting lodge in rugged Glen Cannich, furnished like a country house, warm and friendly with excellent food. **Ledgowan Hotel**, Achnasheen, © 044588 252, was originally built as a private shooting lodge, but has been now converted into a comfortable country-house-type hotel. Open Easter to November. **Inchbae Lodge**, Garve, © 09975 269, is a small country-house hotel with good food, quite comfortable. **Ben Wyvis Hotel**, Strathpeffer, © 0997 421323, is a huge, rather daunting Victorian pile in six acres of attractive gardens, open from March to November. The food is patchy.

In Ullapool, **Royal Hotel** in Garve Road, © 0854 612181, right on the shore of Loch Broom, is quite big, fairly sophisticated and has reasonable food. **Four Seasons Hotel**, also in Garve Road, © 0854 612905, is a modern monster on the shores of Loch Broom; very friendly with good seafood.

Eddrachilles Hotel, Badcall Bay, Scourie, © 0971 2080, is in a beautiful position overlooking the bay and islands, with good-ish food. Open March to October.

Scourie Hotel, © 0971 2396, is comfortable with good home-cooking, and very friendly. Open March to October. **Kinlochbervie Hotel**, © 097182 275, is highly recommended as a family hotel, with excellent food, overlooking Kinlochbervie harbour and Loch Clash. It's comfortable and friendly. **Cape Wrath Hotel**, Durness, © 097181 274, is an easy-going, comfortable hotel on this far northern coast, open March to January.

inexpensive

The Céilidh Place, in West Argyle Street, Ullapool, © 0854 612103, is mildly eccentric, rather hearty, and fun (if you like that sort of thing), comprising: hotel, clubhouse, restaurant, coffee shop, bookshop, live shows of jazz, classical and folk music, and all sorts of other jollifications. You could do a lot worse, as long as you are gregarious. **Ferry Boat Inn** on Shore Street, Ullapool, © 0854 612366, is a cosy, family-run inn looking across Loch Broom; it's rather noisy. **Morefield Motel**, also in Ullapool, © 0854 612161, purpose-built in the middle of a housing estate, is not what you would expect from its appearance. It's seafood has been acclaimed—it was voted 'Fish Pub of the Year' by the *Good Pub Guide*. It's well worth a journey to eat here.

Kylesku Hotel, © 0971 2231, is a delightful little place on the loch at Kylesku in lovely scenery, with good seafood caught in their own boat. Open April to

October. **Culag Hotel**, Lochinver, © 05714 270, is on the shore of Loch Inver with glorious views; an excellent place. **Parkhill Hotel**, Durness, © 097181 209, is a temperance hotel—and cheap.

Inverness to John o' Groats

The A9 north from Inverness crosses the Kessock Bridge, where the Beauly Firth meets the Moray Firth, in the lee of the Black Isle. Until 1982 this narrow neck of water was crossed in a small car ferry, known to side-slip in violent currents. The bridge, opened by the Queen Mother, won a design award. This east coast route to the top right-hand corner of Scotland crosses the fertile Black Isle and then hugs the coast almost all the way. The worst of the Highland Clearances took place in Sutherland and Caithness, and the scattered ruins of abandoned crofts can be found in deserted glens. Long straths run inland through vast tracts of moor and fen, linking the east with the north and west coasts. This, in Caithness, is the Flow Country, the biggest blanket bog in the world, coveted by forestry kings. Conservationists are struggling to stem the huge plantations already eating up this amazing concentration of wildlife. It is a fragile living surface of floating peat, with heather and sedges over a carpet of sphagnum mosses. Among the threatened victims are 55 species of birds related to Arctic tundra, including 70 per cent of Britain's greenshanks, meadow pipits, red-throated divers with their primitive whale-like cries, peregrines and merlins. Among the many plants threatened is the rare insect-eating sundew. Dubh lochans, black from peat, speckle the land.

The Black Isle

The Black Isle is joined to the mainland between Beauly and Dingwall and has its own unique, soft, sing-song dialect. It is made up of rolling farmland, wildfowl beaches and attractive fishing villages. The new main road seems to rip through it in a few moments, showing little of its charms. It would be a pity to dash through it without noticing. Take the first turning right after the bridge to explore it properly—a hidden turning, easy to miss.

Munlochy Bay, about 3 miles (4.5km) up this twisting minor road, is vibrant with the cackle of geese in winter, targets for sportsmen who like to see their wildfowl at the end of a gun. **Avoch** (pronounced 'Auch'), about 4 miles (6.5km) further on, is a picturesque fishing village with a small harbour. There are miles of bracing walks on the tidal sandflats, with good views across the firth.

Fortrose, a couple of miles on, is a pleasant, no-nonsense resort town, sheltered by Chanonry Point and excellent for small boat sailing. **Fortrose Cathedral** (open daily: free) is a mere fragment of the great church founded by King David I in the 12th century. All that remains is the south aisle of the nave and the sacristy. There are memorials here to Lord Seaforth and his family—an interesting confirmation of the Brahan Seer's prophecy about the downfall of the House of Seaforth (*see* p.46). In 1880, a hoard of silver coins was dug up from the green, dating from the reign of Robert III. Cromwell recycled much of the fabric of the cathedral for building a fort in Inverness. Look out for the memorial stone on **Chanonry Point** east of Fortrose. It marks the site where the Brahan Seer was burned in a barrel of tar.

Rosemarkie, a mile (1.5km) beyond the town on the northern side of Chanonry Point, is a popular beach in summer, with golden sand and rock pools. St Moluag founded a school and a church here in the 6th century, and tradition holds that he is buried below the Pictish stone in the churchyard.

Groam House Museum (open daily, June–Sept: adm) in Rosemarkie has local and archaeological exhibits: carved stones found in the vicinity of the church, indicating the importance of Rosemarkie in early Christian times; fragments of cross-slabs, and grave stones and a fine Pictish slab, all well displayed and explained. There is an audio-visual show and the curator is extremely knowledgeable.

Golf enthusiasts can enjoy an invigorating game within spitting distance of the sea on the 18-hole Fortrose and Rosemarkie golf course.

Cromarty

Cromarty, on the northeastern tip of the Black Isle, about 23 miles (37km) northeast of the Kessock Bridge, is an 18th-century fishing town and port, a Royal Burgh for seven centuries. Some of its old merchants' houses are important examples of domestic architecture of the period. Sheltered by the great headland of the South Sutor at the mouth of the Cromarty Firth, rows of terraced cottages stand gable-end-on to the street, hunched against the wind, forming rope walks where the fisherwomen used to stretch out the new ropes from the rope factory. The town was bought in 1772 by George Ross, some of whose descendants still live there. He built the harbour, founded a cloth factory, the rope factory, a nail and spade factory, a brewery, and a lace industry and built a Gaelic chapel for the Highlanders who came flocking to the town for employment. Cromarty has been skilfully and imaginatively restored. The old brewery is now Cromarty Arts Centre, with accommodation, and can be hired by groups for seminars and residential courses. Part of the old ropeworks is now housing and a restaurant. The sheltered bay was used as an anchorage for destroyer flotillas in the First World War.

Cromarty Courthouse (open daily: adm) is a visitor centre and museum, with video, animated figures, a reconstructed trial, cells, shop and displays.

Hugh Miller's Cottage (open daily, Easter–Sept, excluding Sun until June: adm), in Church Street, offers a nostalgic journey into the past. This long, low, thatched cottage with crow-stepped gables, its tiny upper windows half-buried in the eaves, was built in 1711 by the great-grandfather of Hugh Miller (1802–56). He rose from simple beginnings to become a famous geologist, stonemason, naturalist, theologian and writer. (Among other things, he wrote about the Brahan Seer in *Scenes and Legends of the North of Scotland.*) Restored by the National Trust for Scotland, the cottage contains a museum devoted to collections of his writings, personal belongings, geological specimens, and such endearing memorabilia as the wooden chair in which his mother sat to nurse him.

In four restored cottages near the seafront, the work of resident craftsmen and women is displayed and sold: pottery, silver, printed hangings, jewellery, etc. There is also a small art gallery with exhibitions of local paintings.

North and South Sutors guard the entrance to the Firth like two massive sentinels: the view north, to the oil installations at Nigg, is rather marred these days, but there are foreshore walks and long expanses of sand lining Cromarty Bay. Charles II landed here on his way to be crowned at Scone in 1650. A car ferry runs between Cromarty and Nigg, one way of getting on to the north.

Continuing round the Black Isle, the B9163 runs down the coastal plain south of the firth 17 miles (27km) to **Conon Bridge** and across the neck of land that joins the Black Isle to the mainland, about 4 miles (6.5km) to **Muir of Ord**. The Black Isle Show is held just outside Muir of Ord in August.

To complete a circular tour of this attractive peninsula, a one-track road skirts the northern shore of the Beauly Firth, 10 miles (16km) back to the Kessock Bridge. It hugs the shore for the last stretch, where the tidal flats are rich in wildfowl, backed by blue-grey hills to the north. The ruined castle (private) behind a wall at the western end of the firth is Redcastle, originally built by William the Lion in 1178. The original castle, Edradour, is claimed to be the oldest inhabited house in Scotland and passed through several hands before it was annexed by the Crown after the fall from power of the notorious Douglas family. The Mackenzies held it for 200 years from 1570. According to stories they resorted to sorcery and human sacrifices in an attempt to save the land from a cattle plague. This illicit activity backfired, and the family was henceforth under a curse.

North Kessock, an attractive village straggling along the shore of the Beauly Firth, used to be the ferry terminal. Surnames such as Patience and Skinner are said to date from when Cromwell's soldiers were here. You get good bar lunches in the listed pub.

Dingwall

Dingwall, at the southwestern corner of the Cromarty Firth, is at the junction of several main routes. It is a busy little market town, its curious name being derived from the Norse words *thing* (parliament or council) and *volle* (place). Macbeth was born here, presumably in the castle that once stood in Castle Street. A few stones are all that remain. It is hard to believe that Dingwall was a thriving port, before the waterway at the mouth of the River Peffery became silted up. The canal at the end of Ferry Road was built by Telford, in an attempt to cut through the encroaching mudflats. Dingwall has always been an important cattle and livestock market, and even today you may hear a few exchanges in Gaelic, around the market square any Wednesday. The Dingwall Highland Gathering is in July.

The Town House (open Easter–Sept: adm), dating from 1730, is a museum. A special exhibition relates to General Sir Hector Macdonald (1853–1903), popularly known as 'Fighting Mac'—a local man who rose from the ranks to become a distinguished soldier. He served in the Second Afghan War, the Egyptian Police and the Egyptian Army and was given command of troops in Ceylon in 1902. He surpassed himself at the Battle of

Omdurman. There is an impressive monument to him on Mitchell Hill, the local cemetery, a battlemented tower that serves as a landmark for miles around.

The surprising **Indian temple**, on the hill above Evanton, known as Fyrish Monument, was a folly erected by General Sir Hector Munro (1726–1805), as a philanthropic gesture, giving work to the unemployed in the area. It is modelled on the gateway to Negapatam, an Indian town captured by Sir Hector in 1781. It is clearly seen from the road, but much more fun close to and not an exacting climb.

The Tain Peninsula

Although the exploitation of North Sea oil fields has inevitably changed the character of the hammerhead peninsula jutting eastwards between Nigg Bay and Tain in the north, there are plenty of attractions to tempt the traveller to make a detour.

Invergordon

Invergordon, 14 miles (22km) northeast of Dingwall, is a busy industrial centre on the western tip of Nigg Bay, dominated by all the surrealistic constructions built for the oil industry. The Cromarty Firth is one of the finest deep-water anchorages in the world and is now one of the most important European centres for the repair and maintenance of the exploration rigs. There is something curiously beautiful about some of these giant skeletons whose fragile-looking girders are built to withstand the full force of a North Sea gale.

Fearn

Fearn, 11 miles (17.5km) northeast of Invergordon, is the hub of the peninsula, with cottages and pretty gardens grouped round a green. In restored 13th-century **Fearn Abbey**, the nave and choir are still used as the parish church. Fearn Abbey was the seat of the first martyr of the Scottish Reformation, Abbot Patrick Hamilton, who was burned at St Andrews for heresy, in 1528. The Reformation was responsible for the decay of the original abbey. In 1742, after it had been partly rebuilt to accommodate the parish church, the soaring voices of the parishioners had a disastrous effect on the stone-vaulted roof, which crashed down and killed 44 of them.

Tarbat Ness, about 9 miles (14.5km) beyond Fearn, on the northern tip of the peninsula, has one of the highest lighthouses in Britain, warning ships of the dangerous sandbanks threatening the entrance to the Dornoch Firth. The Norsemen called them Gizzen Briggs and were no doubt among their earliest victims. The views are stupendous and there are sometimes seals basking on the rocks below.

Portmahomack is a popular resort with a nine-hole golf course, a couple of miles (3km) south of the lighthouse. The small harbour once supported a fishing fleet.

Shandwick is halfway down the east coast, 8 miles (13km) south of the lighthouse. Fossil hunters may be rewarded if they search below the red sandstone cliffs and in the caves here. The 9-foot-tall (3m) stone cross slab above the village was erected in memory of one of three Norse princes who were shipwrecked on one of the reefs.

Tain

Tain, like Dingwall, is derived from the Norse word *thing*—a meeting place or parliament. It is a sturdy town on the south side of the Dornoch Firth, 11 miles (17.5km) north of Invergordon. It is a holiday resort and market centre for the surrounding area and has an aura of antiquity.

St Duthus was born in Tain, in about 1000 and his bones were brought back here after his death in Ireland. **St Duthus Chapel** (always accessible) is an overgrown ruin in the cemetery between the town and the 18-hole golf course. It was built in the 11th century on the saint's birthplace and is the repository for his bones. It was built as a 'prayer cell' with the resident hermit guarding the sacred relics. Elizabeth de Burgh, wife of Robert the Bruce, and her children, took refuge here when fleeing to Orkney, relying on its status as a sanctuary for fugitives. This was violated by the Earl of Ross, who ignored the safety zone and captured her in 1307—an act Scotland did not forget. The chapel was burnt down by a smuggler, McNeill of Creich, in 1427, to destroy an enemy he had chased inside.

St Duthus Collegiate Church was built in 1360 on the site of an earlier church, traces of which can be seen in the chapter house. It is now a show place and memorial, no longer used for worship. When the chapel was burnt down, the relics of St Duthus were transferred to this church: they disappeared in 1560. James IV came on an annual pilgrimage for 20 years, but not entirely out of religious fervour. He liked to keep in touch with his subjects all over Scotland and he had established his favourite mistress, Flaming Janet Kennedy, in Darnaway Castle in Moray, giving him an excellent stopping-off place on the way. Don't miss the stained-glass windows, showing Malcolm Canmore and Queen Margaret bestowing a royal charter on the town, and an assembly of the Scottish parliament in 1560, adopting John Knox's Confessions of Faith.

Tain and District Museum (open Easter–Sept, Mon–Sat: donation box) in Castle Brae, off the High Street, is well worth a visit. It is full of a large variety of items: relics, manuscripts, photographs, archaeological remains, etc. The museum was founded as an exhibition for the visit of the Queen Mother in 1966, and became permanent. It includes details of St Duthus and of the patronage of James IV—though not of Flaming Janet—and good displays showing what life was like in 18th and 19th centuries in a thriving market town. This is also the Clan Ross Centre.

The Tolbooth is a fine example of many built in the 16th and 17th centuries, a tall, castellated keep with angle turrets and the original curfew bell of 1616.

The Highland Fine Cheeses Factory (open weekdays: free) shows how cheeses are made and allows sampling (✆ 0862 892034/892734). North of the town is the Glenmorangie Distillery, founded in 1843, where whisky is produced using water from the burn.

The A9 now sweeps across the **Dornoch Firth**, cutting the journey north considerably. The drive along the southern shore of the Firth to **Struie** is attractive but far the most scenic approach from the south is on the B9176 due north, 3 miles (4.5km) beyond Evanton. This road goes up over the moors and down to the Firth. Stop at Struie, at the **Stone Viewpoint**, about 10 miles (16km) up the road, for panoramic views over the **Kyles of Sutherland**. There is a view indicator, and a board explaining about the glacial action that created this beautiful spot. Windswept heather and pines fringe a road that zigzags down through dramatic ravines.

Croick Church

Turn left at Ardgay (pronounced Ardguy as in Guy Fawkes), 14 miles (22.5km) west of Tain, at the head of the Firth. Drive 10 miles (16km) up Strath Carron, along a burn bordered by lichen, bracken and birches. Little **Croick Church** lies in a walled churchyard, surrounded by a few wind-bent trees in a pocket of desolate moorland. This is one of the most poignant places in Scotland. In the spring of 1845, families who had been evicted from their crofts in Glencalvie and who had nowhere to go camped here in an improvised shelter made of tarpaulin, rugs and plaids stretched over poles. They scratched memorials on the diamond panes of this simple kirk, which can still be read today: 'Glencalvie people was in the church here May 24 1845 . . .' 'Glencalvie people the wicked generation . . .' and one rather tart comment '. . . this place needs cleaning'. Inside, it is plain with unadorned walls, an iron stove, benches and table and a big pulpit. There is an interesting display board with contemporary newspaper cuttings from *The Times.*

Bonar Bridge

Bonar Bridge, a mile (1.5km) north of Ardgay, is so called after the bridge that spans the Kyle of Sutherland. It is a good base from which to explore Sutherland and has excellent fishing, walking and boating. **Carbisdale Castle Youth Hostel**, high above the river at **Invershin**, a couple of miles northwest, is near the site of Montrose's final disastrous battle, from which he fled to Assynt. This is a pleasant detour, up the River Shin, to Lairg. The **Falls of Shin**, on the way, are a popular beauty spot, complete with attendant café, gift shop, carpark and people.

Lairg, at the southern end of Loch Shin, is a fisherman's haven and a good base from which to explore the rugged hinterland of Sutherland. For those who don't want to spend their holiday on the end of a fishing rod, there are lovely walks.

Returning along the northern shore of the Dornoch Firth, the A949 passes several prehistoric remains: Dun Creich, a vitrified fort, on the promontory 3 miles (4.5km) out of Bonar Bridge; traces of a chambered cairn at Clashmore, west of the school; another cairn at Everlix; and a standing stone on the outskirts of Dornoch, 10 miles (16km) east of Bonar Bridge. These remains indicate what a large number of Pictish and Norse settlers populated this area.

Dornoch

Dornoch, isolated enough to retain its old-world dignity, though more accessible with the new bridge, remains unspoiled by its popularity as a holiday resort, a charming, higgledy-piggledy town, full of character. Long famous as a golfing centre, its links have been played on since at least 1616. On the same latitude as Hudson Bay and Alaska, it is the most northerly first-class golf course in the world. Excavations have dated settlements here at least as far back as 1000 BC.

Dornoch Cathedral (always open: free) dates from 1224 when the town became a bishopric. It must be the cosiest cathedral in the country: small and cruciform with colourful windows illuminating its warm, mellow walls. It was burnt in a clan dispute between Murrays and Mackays in 1570, when only the tower and spire survived. Restored in 1616, it was then further, and tastelessly, restored in Victorian times. In 1924, it was again restored to celebrate its 700th anniversary and much of the Victorian work was stripped away to reveal the original 13th-century stonework. It is now the parish church.

Dornoch Craft Centre and Town Jail (open daily, except winter weekends: free) is worth a visit. The restored jail gives a graphic example of what it would have been like to be imprisoned in the last century, and the crafts include the weaving of tartan on power looms, and kilt making. There is a book shop and coffee shop.

Dornoch is flanked by miles of clean sand, ideal for holidaymakers but not so good for the evicted crofters who, during the Highland Clearances, were expected to settle here and farm the infertile dune land. Small wonder so many of them emigrated.

Embo, about 3 miles (4.5km) north along the sands, has two Stone Age burial chambers dating from 2000 BC, at the entrance to the caravan site. When these were excavated it was discovered that two later cist tombs had been built into the originals.

On the shore of **Loch Fleet**, a couple of miles (3km) further north, there is the scant ruin of 14th-century **Skelbo Castle** on a grassy mound. It was here, in an earlier, wooden castle, in 1290, that emissaries of Edward I waited to greet the little Princess Margaret, Maid of Norway, whose marriage to Edward's son was to solve the problem of sovereignty in Scotland. Whether it would have done so or not was never to be known, for it was here that they heard of the child's death caused by sea sickness on the voyage. This triggered off the Scottish Wars of Independence and Edward's ruthless hammering of the Scots.

Golspie, 9 miles (14.5km) north of Dornoch, is the farming centre for the area. There is an 18-hole golf course. Seventeenth-century St Andrew's Church has a splendid old canopied pulpit, some fine panelled walls and carvings. The great statue on Ben Vraggie, behind Golspie, is to the first Duke of Sutherland, a man who was, on the one hand, blamed for his harshness to crofters during the Clearances, and on the other, praised for sponsoring many social improvements in the area.

Dunrobin Castle

Dunrobin Castle (open daily, June–mid Sept: adm) stands high on a natural terrace overlooking the sea, a mile (1.5km) north of Golspie. Built in the 13th century on the site of an ancient broch, this seat of the Dukes of Sutherland was considerably restored in Victorian times. The huge white extravaganza, standing on a massive plinth, is more like a château than a castle. Its towers and turrets are a flamboyant pastiche of French and Scottish architecture. Formal gardens, bordering a long terrace, are a riot of colour in summer. The castle contains some fine paintings, including two Canalettos, as well as magnificent furniture, tapestries, and family heirlooms. There is also a museum in a summerhouse in the park, with archaeological exhibits, Victoriana, crafts and natural history.

Brora

Brora, 5 miles (8km) up the coast from Golspie, is a small tourist resort with good salmon fishing and an 18-hole golf course. The harbour, once used by fishing boats, is now a haven for pleasure craft. In the middle of the 19th century, crofters sailed from here to New Zealand, to start fresh lives away from the threat of eviction during the Clearances. **Hunter's of Brora** (open weekdays) are woollen mills, renowned for their yarn and tweed in many parts of the world.

There are two brochs, one either end of Brora, the best being about 3 miles (4.5km) north between the road and the sea. It has domed chambers in the walls and outworkings. Two headless skeletons were excavated from the site in 1880. There is hardly a hill or hummock in this area that is not crowned by some sort of fort or broch. As you go north, you will find fewer Gaelic-derived names and more with Nordic origins.

Helmsdale

Helmsdale, 10 miles (16km) north of Brora, is a fishing and holiday town where road and railway part company. The ruin of 15th-century **Helmsdale Castle** (always accessible) overlooks the natural harbour. It was within these innocent-looking walls, in 1567, that Isobel Sinclair poisoned the Earl and Countess of Sutherland, so that her son might inherit the earldom. This somewhat drastic solution failed, however, because her son drank the poison and died with them.

The castle was rebuilt in the early 19th century by the Duke of Sutherland who, having evicted the crofters from his lands, tried to make amends by resettling them. The streets are laid out in neat geometric parallels, named after the Duke's estates.

Timespan Heritage Centre (open daily, Easter–Sept: adm), left and left again off the main road into the village, is a gem. It traces the history of man in the Kildonan area from the stone circles, cairns and brochs of prehistory, through Norse invasion, the Clearances, herring fishing, gold rush and crofting to the present—including local celebrity Barbara Cartland, who has a holiday house in the area. It is extremely well done in film and animated tableaux and supplies many good aids to the imagination.

The River Helmsdale is rich in salmon and trout and there is a nine-hole golf course.

Suisgill

An alternative route north from Helmsdale goes inland on the A897, 38 miles (61km) up to Melvich on the north coast. This route through **Strath of Kildonan** is a windswept, treeless moorland, broken by delightful river valleys. Suisgill, 10 miles (16km) from Helmsdale, was the centre of a mini gold rush towards the end of the 19th century, and a considerable amount of gold was panned from the rivers. Ask in the Helmsdale Tourist Information Centre for details of the Goldrush Heritage Tour. Kildonan lost four-fifths of its population in the first half of the 19th century, during the Highland Clearances. Now it is sparsely populated with shooting lodges and sheep farms along the Helmsdale—one of Scotland's top fishing rivers. Several years ago, there was a bout of 'lodge burnings', thought to be the work of drunks or Scottish Nationalists, which left a number of smoking shells. Suisgill Lodge was one of the victims: all that is left is one end of the house while a complete wilderness replaces what was once a beautiful garden. **Strath Halladale**, running north from Strath Kildonan on this road, is green and fertile, fed by many rivers and burns—attractive farmland for the invading Vikings so many years ago.

Ord of Caithness

Going on up the A9 from Helmsdale, the scenery becomes more dramatic, with ravines and steep cliffs as the road climbs to a high plateau with spectacular views from the Ord of Caithness about 4 miles (6.5km) beyond Helmsdale. No superstitious Sinclair has crossed the Ord on a Monday since that Monday in 1513 when the men of the clan passed this way to fight with James IV at Flodden, from which not one of them returned. There are often red deer up here, especially in the early morning or at dusk.

There is a broch at Ousdale, a couple of miles beyond the Ord, where the main road runs inland for a while. Take the track out to the old hamlet of Badbea, 2 miles (3km) east on the cliffs. Crofters took refuge here during the Clearances and stories are told of the beasts and the children having to be tethered to prevent them being blown into the sea.

The 15th-century castle visible from the road at **Dunbeath**, 5 miles (8km) north (private), was captured by Montrose in 1650. Six miles (9.5km) to the west, at **Braemore**, a monument was erected after the air crash here that killed the Duke of Kent in 1942. The Dunbeath Highland Games are held in July.

Laidhay Croft Museum, 2 miles (3km) north of Dunbeath (open daily Easter–Sept: adm), shows a typical Victorian croft house, looking cosier, perhaps, than it was in reality. These interiors are excellent for displaying domestic detail, but not so good at conveying the damp, cold, smoky atmosphere, when rats ran around the floor and animals shared the living space. There is also a collection of farm implements in an outhouse, some of which, like the peat-cutters, are still used today.

Clan Gunn Museum and Heritage Centre (open June–Sept, Mon–Sat: adm) is in the old parish church, a couple of miles further north, beyond **Latheron** with its picturesque harbour. The A895 is an alternative but less spectacular route north to Thurso, which goes inland from Latheron.

Turn off the broad thoroughfare, flanked by sturdy, dignified houses, in **Lybster**, 4 miles (6.5km) north of Latheron. Dip down to the harbour, scooped out of rock to provide a perfect haven for the large fishing fleet that once plied from here in the 19th century. The fleet is reduced now to a few lobster boats and a number of pleasure craft, but the atmosphere is still very much that of a fishing community, with piles of creels and fishing gear, and the salty tang of the sea.

Inland from Lybster a minor road joins the A895 north to Thurso. A few miles further on is the **Achavanich Standing Stone Circle**. This ritual site in the form of an unusual truncated oval may once have contained as many as 60 stones. Less than a mile (1.5km) west of here, on the main road up from Latheron, is Rangag Broch, dating from 150 BC, once 40 or 50 feet (12–15m) high.

Five miles (8km) to the east, on the minor road north from **Clyth**, beyond Lybster, the **Grey Cairns of Camster** date from around 2500 BC. They have been restored and there are explanation boards. The smoothly rounded cairn is one of the best of its kind on the mainland. Its original entrance passage is still intact. Both animal and human remains were excavated from this site.

A couple of miles' (3km) walk to the east reaches the **Hill o' Many Stanes**, dating from the early Bronze Age. This fan of stones has ribs, each containing about eight or more stones, numbering some 200 in all. This could have been a ritual site for burials, like other henges, or some form of astronomical calculator, lined up with the stars. Whatever its purpose, it is eerie to stand on this lonely, windswept moor and try to picture how it must have been for those early settlers, once so numerous in this northern corner.

In **Ulbster**, 7 miles (11km) up the A9 from Lybster, a flight of 365 stone steps twists steeply down the cliff to the old harbour. Now disused and overgrown, it was once used by fishing fleets to moor and unload their catches, among the cheerful bustle and raucous banter of the fishermen and the teams of women working at the gutting. The steps are only for the sure-footed; they can be extremely slippery.

Wick

Wick, so called from the Viking word *vik* meaning 'bay or creek', is a substantially built seaport and tourist centre, stretching round the sweep of Wick Bay, 15 miles (24km) northeast of Lybster. There is a harbour, airport and railway terminal. Norse pirates were drawn to Wick by the shelter of its bay at the mouth of the river and by the magnet of the rich farmland that beckoned from the west. Created a Royal Burgh in 1140, it was only properly developed in the 19th century, by the British Fisheries Society, who commissioned Telford to design a model village for them at Pulteneytown. It is difficult to believe, now, that 1,122 herring boats once plied from the complex of three harbour basins, before the decline of the herring stock and the development of vast factory ships. White fish trawlers still use the harbour.

The Heritage Museum (open Mon–Sat, June–Sept: adm), near the harbour, tells the fishing story of Wick. Its collections include a fishing boat, working lighthouse, kippering kilns, blacksmith shop, coopering shop and fishing gear.

Caithness Glass Factory (open daily, Easter–Oct: free) is on the north side of the town. Visitors can watch craftsmen fashioning molten glass, shaping it and engraving it. This factory was established in the slump of the herring industry to offer alternative employment for the fishermen. It is interesting to notice that in this land so full of echoes of the Norse occupation, the designs of the glass are distinctively Scandinavian.

Also south of the town is the shell of **Old Wick Castle** (always accessible), three storeys high on a rock promontory, and known to seamen as the 'Auld Man o' Wick'. Having no water supply, the castle was unable to withstand lengthy sieges and was abandoned in the 16th century.

Look out for the **Brig o' Trams** nearby, a spectacular natural rock arch formed by the erosion of sea and weather.

There are more spectacularly shaped rocks 3 miles (4.5km) to the north along the cliffs, at **Noss Head**. It is possible to drive but it is also a glorious walk, buffeted by the wind.

From the point it isn't far to walk to **Sinclair and Girnigoe Castles** (always accessible). These two dramatic ruins extend from a keep and were lived in as one dwelling by the Sinclairs, Earls of Caithness, for 200 years. The eastern part is 15th century, the western, 17th century. The jagged ruin seems to grow up out of horizontally layered rock on a cliff above a sheltered cove. Ghosts lurk in these history-soaked walls: in 1570 the 4th Earl of Caithness, suspecting his son of plotting to kill him, imprisoned him in the dungeons for seven years till he died of 'famine and vermine'.

The great sandy sweep of **Sinclair's Bay** leads north along coastland believed to be among the earliest inhabited in Scotland. Excavations revealed that Middle Stone Age man existed here in large numbers, on the fertile hinterland.

The tall, slender tower on top of the cliff at **Keiss**, 8 miles (13km) north of Wick, is all that remains of Keiss Castle, home of William Sinclair, founder of the first Baptist church in Scotland.

Northlands Viking Centre (open daily, June–Sept: adm), in the former schoolhouse at **Auckengill**, beyond the north arm of Sinclair's Bay, deals with the fascinating archaeology of this area.

The ruin of 12th-century **Bucholie Castle**, a mile (1.5km) north, was the stronghold of Sweyn Aslefson, a Norse pirate featured in the old Norse sagas. A 10th-century Viking settlement is in the process of excavation, a mile (1.5km) further north at **Freswick**.

John o' Groats

Although it is neither the most northerly nor the most easterly tip of Britain, John o' Groats, 17 miles (27km) north of Wick, is loosely accepted as the northeastern extremity, linked diagonally to Land's End, 876 miles (1402km) away in the southwest, which is in fact neither the most southerly nor the most westerly tip of the country.

Stop on the summit of the final curve of the moor and look down. It is a bleak, scattered village, washed by the Pentland Firth whose islands sometimes appear so close you could almost jump the gap. It is a marvellous vista—the edge of the world. But it has to be said that John o' Groats itself is often a disappointment to tourists—little more than an uninspiring coach park, a few ugly buildings and a flat, dreary landscape.

The small settlement, given over to supplying the needs of the dozens of tourists who come here, got its curious name from a Dutchman, Jan de Groot, who established a ferry link with the newly acquired Orkney, in 1496, under the rule of James IV. There are several explanations for the octagonal house he built, with eight doors, no longer standing but represented by the octagonal tower on the hotel which is believed to stand on the site of de Groot's house. One explanation is that he wanted to provide shelter from every point of the fierce wind for his waiting passengers. A nicer theory is that when his eight sons squabbled over who should take precedence at the dinner table, he decided to settle the dispute by having an octagonal table and eight doors, so that each son had his own entrance and no one, or everyone, sat at the head of the table.

Duncansby Head

Boat trips run from the harbour to Duncansby Head, 2 miles (3km) east, the true 'top right-hand corner' where many different species of seabirds throng the dramatic cliffs. A road runs out to the lighthouse on the cliffs: in clear weather the only limit to the view over the Pentland Firth is the keenness of your eye. The 12-knot tide rip here is a notorious hazard to shipping: over 400 wrecks have been recorded in only the last 150 years.

Once away from the inoffensive blemishes of tourism, this coastline is perfect for those who like wild and lonely places and extremes of weather.

Where to Stay

moderate

Ord House Hotel, Muir of Ord, © 0463 870492, is an old family house, a listed building in 20 acres of garden and woodland. It's hospitable, comfortable and friendly. **Marine Hotel**, Rosemarkie, © 0381 20253, overlooks the sea with terraced lawns running down to a sandy beach.

Royal Hotel, Tain, © 0862 2013, right in the middle of the town, is quite comfortable, though the decor in some of the public rooms is a bit overpowering. The food is quite good. **Morangie Hotel**, Tain, © 0862 2281, has a good reputation for comfort and is more secluded.

Dornoch Hotel, Dornoch, © 0862 810351, is an imposing seaside hotel overlooking the golf course; solid, old-fashioned and comfortable. **Dornoch Castle**, © 0862 810261, is very special. This 400-year-old castle was formerly the Bishop's Palace and reeks of history. Its restaurant is one of the best in the area and the cellar is good. There is a sunny terrace and formal garden, and a 16th-century panelled bar overlooking the Square. **Royal Golf Hotel**, Dornoch, © 0862 810283, is on the golf course; large and comfortable, with reasonable food.

Links Hotel, Brora, © 0408 21225, is close to the golf course, serves decent food and is comfortable.

Forsinard Hotel, © 06417 221, perhaps the most remote hotel in Britain, right in the heart of the Flow Country, is a haven of peace and a paradise for nature lovers. Comfortable and relaxed, it is open mid-April to mid-October.

inexpensive

Royal Hotel, Fortrose, © 0381 20236, stands prominently on the corner of Union Street. It's rather central but the food is all right and the staff are friendly.

Royal Hotel in Dingwall, © 0349 62130, is not very peaceful but the comfort and service are reasonable. **Conon Hotel**, Conon Bridge, © 0349 61500, is an attractive inn by the River Conon, renowned for its fishing. The staff are friendly and obliging and the food isn't bad.

Castle Hotel, Portmahomack, © 086287 263, is a friendly hotel with panoramic views over the Dornoch Firth. **Bridge Hotel**, Bonar Bridge, © 08632 204, is friendly.

Burghfield House Hotel, Dornoch, © 0862 810212, has been run by the same family since 1946. It is known for its good food. **Golf Links Hotel**, Golspie, © 04083 3408, is another good refuge for golfers. It's right on the golf course, and only 300 yards (275m) from the beach.

John o' Groats House Hotel, © 095581 203, is the most northerly hotel on the mainland. What it lacks in sophistication, it makes up for in fresh air.

Portland Arms Hotel, Lybster, © 05932 208/255, is early 19th century, attractive and comfortable, with friendly staff and good food.

Eating Out

If you want a meal out on the Black Isle, **Le Chardon** in Cromarty, © 03817 471, is a gourmet restaurant with a bistro-style atmosphere. Very reasonable.

John o' Groats to Durness

This is an end-of-the-world highway, with detours into great tracts of barren wasteland to the south.

Castle of Mey, 7 miles (11km) west of John o'Groats, was built around the middle of the 16th century for the Earl of Caithness and bought by the Queen Mother in 1956. The gardens are open on certain days in the summer in aid of charity.

Dunnet Head, 9 miles (14.5km) further on, is the most northerly point of Scotland's mainland. Walk out to the tip on a carpet of pink thrift, laced with tormentil, trefoils, wild thyme, yellow saxifrage, purple butterwort and many other wild flowers. You'll see lots of puffins, those endearing birds with comic tuxedo garb and vivid striped beaks, burrowing in the turf. The view from Dunnet Head is memorable particularly at sunrise or sunset. The village is a scattering of houses near the vast sweep of Dunnet Bay.

The tower of the charming little white church, with its saddle-backed roof, dates from the 14th century, a pre-Reformation survivor adding continuity to a place where nothing seems to have changed much over the years.

The fishing is good, both sea, river and loch. A halibut weighing 210lbs (93kg) was caught here with rod and line in 1975.

Castlehill Harbour, 6 miles (9.5km) south of Dunnet Point, was the main centre for the Caithness flagstone industry. Some stone is still produced today but a major scheme is under way for the renovation of the harbour and the construction of an Interpretive Museum and Heritage Trail, based on the flagstone industry.

Thurso

Thurso, 20 miles (32km) west of John o' Groats, is a large, thriving holiday resort and an important fishing port, built on the River Thurso. Elegant 18th-century houses built of brown sandstone surround a central square, with a long, narrow harbour. The name stems from the Norse *Thorsa*—meaning 'river of the God Thor'. This important Viking stronghold reached its zenith in the 11th century under Thorfinn, who defeated King Duncan's nephew in 1040 in a mighty battle at Thurso. The town was the chief trading port between Scotland and Scandinavia in the Middle Ages.

Thurso Folk Museum (open June–Sept, daily except Sun: adm), in the High Street, has a good collection of exhibits of local interest, including a reconstruction of a croft house kitchen, whose homely equipment was often just as efficient as its modern counterparts. The Pictish 'Ulbster Stone' is in the museum, with intricate carved symbols.

St Peter's Church, near the harbour, dates from the 12th or 13th century. It was restored in the 17th century and used for worship until 1862. Some of the original stone can be seen in the curious choir—a semicircular apse within a square end.

Harald Tower, just over a mile's walk along the coast to the northeast, was built in the early 19th century as a burial place for the Sinclairs. It stands on the grave of Harald, Earl of Caithness, a mighty war lord who ruled over half Caithness and Orkney and was killed in battle nearby in 1196.

There are good shops in the town, plenty of places to stay, an 18-hole golf course, and splendid walks all around.

Scrabster Harbour, 2 miles (3km) round the bay, is the terminal for the car ferry, *St Ola*, to Stromness in Orkney. It is an invigorating two-hour trip and on Mondays and Thursdays in the summer it links with special bus tours to make a pleasant day excursion, returning to Scrabster in the evening.

St Mary's Chapel, at **Crosskirk**, 6 miles (9.5km) to the west, dates from the 12th century, a simple little kirk with its chancel linked to the nave by a small doorway.

Dounreay

The tourist office in Thurso arranges tours of Britain's prototype Fast Reactor Power Station at Dounreay, 8 miles (13km) west of Scrabster. There is a visitor exhibition here for anyone with a scientific turn of mind. In a strange way this vast modern complex is not offensive to the eye in a land of such contrasts.

A few miles west, the A897 branches off south back to Helmsdale through Strath Halladale and Strath of Kildonan, into the heart of the Flow Country.

Just outside **Melvich**, a couple of miles (3km) on round the coast, is the **Split Stone of Melvich**. An old woman was returning from a shopping trip when she was chased by the devil. She ran round and round this stone and escaped: the devil was so furious he split it in two. Parts of **Portskerra Fort**, a mile (1.5km) or so beyond Melvich on the point, rise 80 feet (25m) sheer from the shore.

At **Strathy Point**, 12 miles (19km) west of Dounreay, the sea has carved fabulous arches and caverns in the cliffs. The variety of the coastal scenery is amazing; there are many types of rock, sandy beaches, sheltered bays and the restless sea, licking the feet of the cliffs. There is good birdwatching here and lots of wild flowers.

To the west is **Armadale Bay**, with a lovely sandy beach, and between the next two points, **Ardmore** and **Kirtomy**, the sea has carved out a natural tunnel from the cliffs. On **Farr Point**, 3 miles (4.5km) west, **Borve Castle** was a stronghold of the Clan Mackay in medieval times. It was destroyed by the Earl of Sutherland's army in 1515.

Bettyhill

Bettyhill, 10 miles (16km) on, named after Elizabeth, first Duchess of Sutherland, is at the top of Strath Naver. The **Strath Naver Museum** (open June–Sep, daily except Sun: donation) is in a converted church. It gives a fascinating insight to the Strath Naver chapter of the Highland Clearances. The museum is extremely well laid out, and it is interesting to think that the minister may have read out eviction notices from his pulpit here.

The B873, to the south, runs through **Strath Naver**, where many croft houses went up in flames during those troubled times and where people died of exposure, huddled against the ruins of their homes. This too is Flow Country. About 5 miles (8km) down and accessible only on foot, there is a particularly attractive wooded gorge.

Invernaver National Nature Reserve, 2 miles (3km) south of Bettyhill, is a gold mine for nature lovers. It is situated around the mouth of the River Naver, with the finest collection of mountain and coastal plants in the north. Among the rarer birds that breed here are greenshank, ring ouzel and twite. On the edge of the reserve, on a plateau, is **Baile Marghait**, once a Neolithic community, with graves, hut circles and a broch.

Tongue

Tongue, 12 miles (19km) west of Bettyhill, is held by some to be the most attractive place on this northern coast; it has a very special charm. The ruin of **Castle Varrich** dominates the town, once a Norse stronghold in the days when the Vikings occupied these lands.

The **Kyle of Tongue**, crossed by a causeway, is a long, shallow inlet from the wild sea outside, so shallow that at low tide you can walk out to Rabbit Island at its mouth. The lane up the west side winds among sandy bays, cliffs, weirdly shaped rocks and islands, remote and lovely.

The **North Coast Adventure Centre** in Tongue organizes watersports and hill walking. This includes climbing Ben Loyal, 2504 feet (770m) high, its four jagged peaks dominating the skyline 5 miles (8km) to the south.

From Tongue, the A836 goes south through the heart of the Flow Country, past Loch Loyal, 38 miles (61km) to Lairg.

Loch Eriboll, 10 miles (16km) west of Tongue, is a sea loch running 10 miles inland, very deep and beautiful. This was one of the subjects of a prophecy by the Brahan Seer, early in the 17th century. He named Loch Eriboll as a place where a war would end one day. In 1945, German submarines came into the loch to surrender, at the end of the Second World War.

There are the remains of several ancient settlements around here. About a mile north of Laid School on the west side of the loch, there is a souterrain, complete and untouched, with curved steps leading down to a round chamber. You need a torch for this earth house, which floods after heavy rain.

Durness is the gateway to Cape Wrath and the top left-hand corner (*see* p.207).

Where to Stay and Eating Out

moderate

Farr Bay Inn, Bettyhill, © 06412 230, is an early 19th-century inn with good views and near a sandy beach. **Borgie Lodge Hotel**, Skerray, © 06412 332, is a well-established fishing hotel in a nice old family house in attractive grounds. **Tongue Hotel**, © 084755 206/7, is a family-run Victorian hotel which has kept its original character, including a paucity of bathrooms. Nice views and reasonable food.

inexpensive

Northern Sands Hotel, Dunnet, © 084785 270, is on the coast, five minutes from the sandy beach and friendly. Each of the nine rooms has a bathroom. **Ulbster Arms Hotel**, Halkirk, © 084783 206, stands on Thurso River, 5 miles (8km) south of Thurso in Flow Country. The bad news is that there are only five public bathrooms between 31 bedrooms. The staff are amiable and it's beautifully remote. A bit more expensive, **Forss Hotel**, © 084786, about 5 miles (8km) west of Thurso, is quite nice, in extensive woodland overlooking the river. **Berriedale Arms Hotel**, Mey, © 084785 244, is an attractive old inn near the Queen Mother's castle, with one bathroom between four bedrooms. **Royal Hotel**, Traill Street, Thurso, © 0847 63191, is in the town centre, and not over-endowed with style. However, it offers game and sea fishing and the staff are obliging.

Bettyhill Hotel, © 06412 202, has panoramic views of the sea and the hills, and wonderfully old-fashioned hospitality. Bathrooms are scarce, but it is a lovely place. **Ben Loyal Hotel**, Tongue, © 084755 216, overlooks Kyle of Tongue and Ben Loyal. The staff are very pleasant.

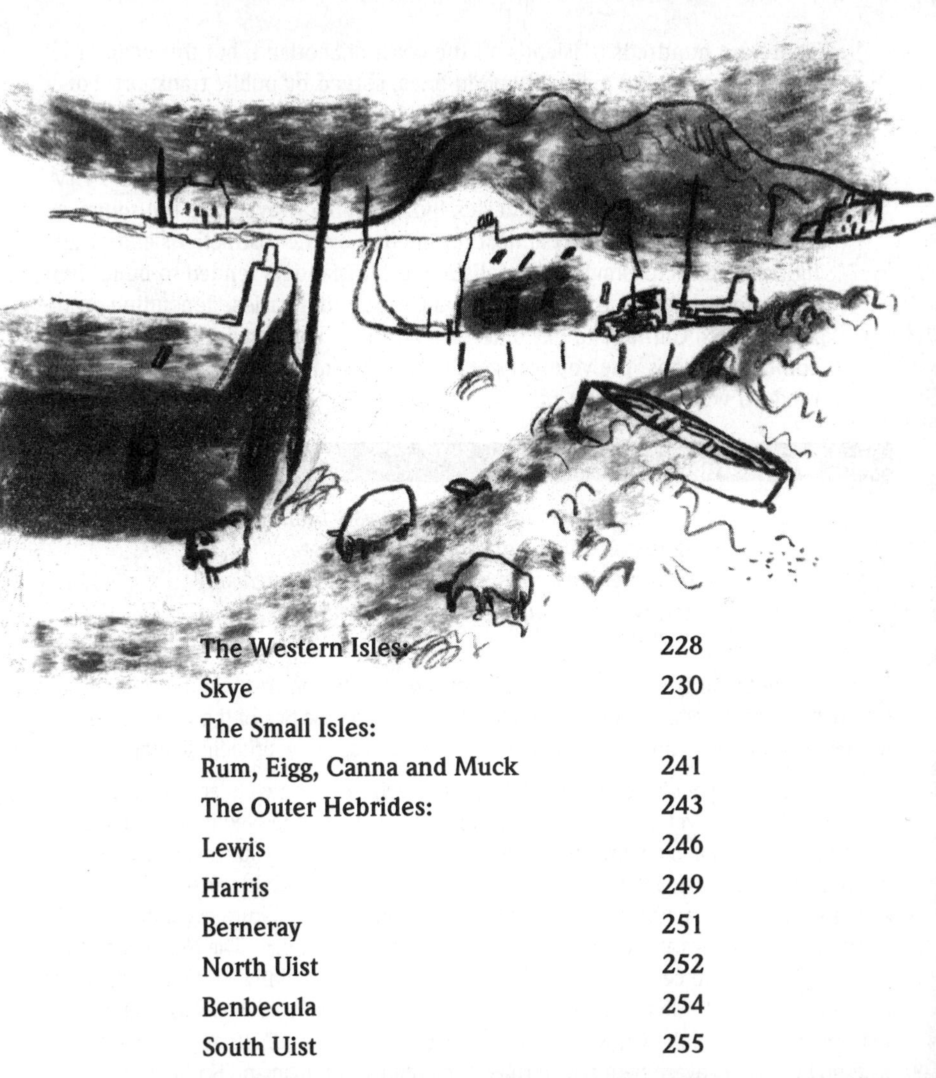

The Islands

There are hundreds of islands off the coast of Scotland, but this chapter only deals with the main inhabited ones, served by public transport. For the rest you need your own boat, a good knowledge of seamanship and navigation and many years of leisure. Each one has its own, special magic, each one is 'intire of it selfe'. (*See* also 'Strathclyde Islands', pp.72–94.) A native of Eriskay can feel homesick living a mile away across the sound in South Uist. Until recently almost untouched by the distractions and bright lights of an increasingly materialistic world, islanders tended to build their lives around God and the Church—a Church that varies, depending on the island, from Catholic to extreme Presbyterian. Today, with improved communications, the younger generations are more in tune with the modern world.

The Western Isles

From the lone shieling on the misty island
Mountains divide us, and a waste of seas
Yet still the blood is strong, the heart is Highland
And we, in dreams, behold the Hebrides.

Canadian Boat Song

Skye and the Small Isles lie close to the west coast between Ardnamurchan Point and Gairloch. They are separated from the Outer Hebrides by the Sea of the Hebrides and the Minch, a notoriously capricious channel treated with respect by prudent mariners.

First known to be populated around 3800 BC, the Hebrides are rich in archaeological sites, many of which are yet to be dug. Mesolithic man gave way to Neolithic, who came in boats made of animal hide, bringing skills and culture and leaving burial cairns as evidence of his existence. Gaelic immigrants from Europe arrived, with Celtic arts, building brochs and stone circles, practising a Druid religion and worshipping nature gods, until the first Christian missionaries arrived from Ireland early in the 6th century. The Norsemen arrived at the end of the 8th century and remained until the defeat of King Haakon by Alexander III at Largs in 1263. After this the islands were ceded to the Scottish Crown. But stronger than the authority of the Crown was the Lordship of the Isles. Chiefs as powerful as kings paid no heed to a government which ruled from the east of mainland Scotland.

A succession of Stewart kings tried to whip in the arrogant clans of the Western Isles, but they clung to their own traditions. A patriarchal clan system existed, with every member of the clan family being independent and equal in status, looking to their chief for guidance and justice but not for oppression. This was the foundation of that proud independence that still endures in Hebrideans today, a truly classless pride that endured even the suppression of the clans after Culloden, and, in the 19th century, the appalling depopulation of the Highland Clearances.

The islands to the south of Benbecula rejected the Reformation, in favour of the Gaelic-speaking monks who came over from Ireland to keep the faith alive. They reconverted, with the help of the Clanranalds, Macneils and Macleods of Skye, who had political influence (the Macleods later defaulted). These islands are now almost entirely Catholic. North Uist, Harris and Lewis, and Skye embraced the Reformed Church with such enthusiasm that even today visitors must be careful not to offend their strong Sabbatarianism.

Most island families have their own croft, or smallholding, their tenancy carefully controlled by the Crofters Commission, brought about in 1886 as a result of public indignation after the Highland Clearances. But crofting is a hard life in the islands. With only a few acres, poor markets and expensive freight, few can exist solely on its returns. Crofting is therefore usually an auxiliary occupation, during weekends and days off from more lucrative employment such as building, fishing, and public works.

The old thatched croft houses have mostly been replaced by modern houses, but some are still occupied. In the old 'black houses', the byre was usually part of the dwelling, with the peat fire on a raised platform in the middle of the room, its smoke escaping through a hole in the roof. Black houses are only seen now as folk museums, restored and authentic in design, but probably misleadingly cosy in atmosphere. No museum can duplicate the reality: the vermin, the pervading damp, the smell from the byre and heavy pall of smoke.

Electricity transformed living conditions, but it brought with it the television, which has effectively killed the *céilidh* tradition. In the old days, when a crofting township was totally communal, the day's work was done on a co-operative basis and in the evenings communities gathered together round the fire in one of the black houses, to listen to music and poetry and to tell the old sagas. Attempts have been made to capture some of this ancient folklore and imprison it on paper, but it was a living thing, passed verbally from generation to generation, embroidered and altered year by year; its true spirit cannot be appreciated except by ear. Gaelic is still the first language for most people in the Outer Hebrides, but an influx of non-Gaelic speakers means that the children of today are growing up speaking English.

Those who go to the islands for their holidays enjoy outdoor life: walking, climbing, bird-watching, wild flowers, boating, fishing. Whatever the weather, and it is often good, each day is an adventure. Walk 5 miles (8km) to an isolated beach, collect driftwood and make a fire using dried heather twigs as kindling. Cook sausages on the stones and wash them down with peat-coloured water from a burn. Collect mussels from rocks below the high tide and rake cockles out of the white sand. Have a quick swim, diving into deep water as clear as glass (whatever people may say about the proximity of the Gulf Stream, the waters of the Minch are icy). Pick wild mushrooms from the grassy hillsides.

In the outer isles, there are few smart shops, only general foodstores which stock most things from boots to butter. There are a few craft shops and weavers, and a post office here and there. Portree and Stornoway have more sophisticated shops, but on the whole, people who enjoy shopping tend to stay on the mainland. For public entertainment, in the outer isles, there may be a local *céilidh* or concert in the village halls to mark a particular occasion, and there are games in the summer on most of the islands. Otherwise, evenings are spent in front of a peat fire with a good book, or the television, or listening to the tales of local people, who can still tell much of the old folklore, and who will often make music for you, or in the pub. Skye, being more accessible, has a much more modern culture.

Speed bonny boat, like a bird on the wing,
'Onward' the sailors cry;
Carry the lad that's born to be king
Over the sea to Skye.

from the 'Skye Boat Song' by Sir H.E. Boulton

On the map, Skye looks like a great, misshapen lobster claw, its pincers being lumpy peninsulas, separated by fiord-like inlets, surrounded by many islands. From the distance, Skye's outline is dominated by the Cuillins in the middle, a massive range of pointed peaks, training ground for international climbers, and by Macleod's Tables, two distinctive, flat-topped hills further north. It contains unique geographical features such as the Quiraing and the Old Man of Storr.

Skye is the most touristy of the Western Isles, but tourism has not yet spoiled it. However, in 1991 the Scottish Office approved a long-disputed plan to build a half-mile (700m) toll bridge between Kyle of Lochalsh and Kyleakin—the longest single-span bridge outside Australia. This is due to open in 1994 and will improve communications dramatically for the locals. Whether they will appreciate this in a few years' time, when Skye has become a Bonnie Prince Charlie Theme Park, remains to be seen. Off the main road there are still rural communities quite untouched by the influx of knapsacks and campers. Gaelic is no longer the first language, though it is still spoken, and road signs are bilingual. Attempts are made in certain parts to revive the old language, with Gaelic teaching, a Gaelic College in Sleat and Gaelic playgroups opening all over the island. Portree is the only town on the island, a lively little place, busy in the summer. The island now has arts centres, theatre shows, opera, traditional music and even reasonable restaurants.

Getting to Skye

by sea

Boats run frequently between Kyle of Lochalsh and Kyleakin in Skye from 7.30am to 9.45pm, taking only a few minutes to cross. Outside these hours there is a half-hourly service subject to demand. There is a daily ferry service from Mallaig to Armadale, taking half an hour, and a limited service from Glenelg to Kylerhea. Ferries also run from Uig to the Outer Isles.

by train

Trains run from Inverness to Kyle of Lochalsh—the Kyle Line, one of the most beautiful in Britain. Just as scenic is the West Highland Line, from Glasgow to Mallaig, connecting with the ferry to Armadale.

by road

Once on the island, there is a limited bus service and you can hire cars at Broadford and Portree. Broadford has a 24-hour petrol station.

15km
10 miles
N
Flodigarry
Kilmuir
Staffin
Loch Mealt
Uig Bay
Trumpan
Vaternish
Loch Snizort
Rona
Sound of Raasay
Trotternish
Borreraig
Loch Dunvegan
Dunvegan
Colbost
Isle of Skye
Portree
Raasay
Macleod's Tables
Orbost
Bracadale
Loch Bracadale
Loch Harport
Loch Sligachan
Sconser
Scalpay
Kyle of Lochalsh
Kyleakin
Sligachan
Loch Ainort
Luib
Broadford Bay
Broadford
Minginish
Cuillin Hills
Loch Coruisk
Camasunary
Strathaird
Loch Slapin
Kylerhea
Glenelg
Kilmarie
Loch Eishort
Isle Ornsay
Isle of Ornsay
Soay
Loch Scavaig
Elgol
Tarskavaig
Knock Bay
Armadale
Aird of Sleat
Mallaig
A855
A856
A850
B885
A863
A881
A851
1 Armadale Castle
2 Prince Charlie's Cave
3 Old Man of Storr
4 Kilt Rock
5 Duntulm Castle
6 Prince Charlie's Cave
7 Dunvegan Castle
8 Kildonnan Church
9 Kinloch Castle
Canna
Rhum
Laig Bay
Eigg
Muck
Isle of Skye and Surrounding islands

Tourist Information

Tourist Information Centre, Meall House, **Portree**, Isle of Skye, © 0478 612137. Open all year.

Open May–September: **Broadfor,** © 0471 822361; **Kyle of Lochalsh**, © 0599 4276; **Shielbridge**, © 0599 81 264.

Ferry Information: Caledonian MacBrayne Ltd, Uig (for Western Isles), © 047042 219; Kyleakin (for Kyle of Lochalsh), 0599 4482; Armadale (for Mallaig), © 047 14248.

Kyleakin, the ferry terminal, stands round a small bay overlooked by a fragment of a ruin on a knoll; a jagged double tooth, familiar from postcards. The 12th-century relic was once a Mackinnon stronghold: **Castle Maol** or Moil, or Dunnakyne. (Kyleakin and Dunakin are said to be so named from King Haakon, who passed through on his way to Largs.) A story is told of one of the castle's earliest inmates, Saucy Mary, a Norwegian princess, who somehow managed to stretch a barrier across the Kyle in order to levy tolls from passing ships. There are several hotels and a shop, and a constant flow of traffic using the ferries. From Kyleakin, the road runs west along the coast. About 4 miles (6.5km) along, a very minor road leads southeast across moorland to **Kylerhea** (pronounced 'Kile-ray') and the ferry back to Glenelg.

A couple of miles on past the turning to Kylerhea, the A851 leads south to the **Sleat Peninsula** (pronounced 'slate'), Macdonald territory. **Isleornnsay** is an attractive hamlet, on the east coast of the peninsula, 9 miles (14.5km) across heather-carpeted moor, looking across the Sound of Sleat into the mouth of Loch Hourn. There is an excellent hotel and a bar, whose landlord encourages his staff to speak Gaelic. There is also an art gallery and shop. The Isle of Ornsay is just offshore from the hotel with a lighthouse and a ruined chapel dedicated to the Columban monk, Oran.

Sabhal Mór Ostaig (big barn of Ostaig) is a Gaelic college in a former Macdonald home farm, so popular and successful that they have just completed a great new extension.

Knock Bay is 3 miles (4.5km) on. Knock Castle (always accessible), an overgrown ruin on a rocky peninsula, was held by the Macdonalds on condition they were always ready to receive the king or one of his representatives. Watch out for the *glaisrig* who haunts this ruin—a female sprite who graciously accepts libations of milk.

Armadale Castle, another 3 miles (4.5km) south, was built by Gillespie Graham in 1815. Much of it was demolished, some has been left as a 'sculptured ruin' and the rest has been imaginatively restored. It is now the **Clan Donald Centre** (open daily, April–Oct: adm), with an excellent Museum of the Isles exhibition, telling the story of Clan Donald and the Lords of the Isles. It stands in lovely grounds with a mature arboretum and a children's play area. Rangers take guided walks round the estate. The former coach house/stable block has won prestigious awards for its restoration and conversion to a well-stocked book and gift shop, and a restaurant.

A ferry runs from Armadale Pier to Mallaig, in the summer, taking half an hour: book ahead through Caledonian MacBrayne.

The road goes on another 5 miles (8km) to **Aird of Sleat** with glorious views across the sound. A couple of miles' walk reaches the lighthouse on the southern tip of the peninsula where there is a sandy beach and more good views. Returning on the same road, take the narrow, twisting lane to the west, a mile (1.5km) north of Armadale. It runs for 5 miles (8km) through woodland and moor, past lochans and mossy glades among silver birches, out to the west coast of Sleat.

Tiny settlements cluster round coves and sandy beaches. The road goes north from **Tarskavaig** about 2 miles (3km) to **Dunsgiath Castle** (always accessible). This is one of the oldest fortified headlands in the Hebrides, home of the Macdonalds until the late 16th century. Little remains now but stacks of stones on a rock 40 feet (12m) high, overlooking Loch Eishort. Celtic legend tells of Scathac the Wise, Queen of Skye in the Dark Ages, who held court here and preached the arts of peace and war to Cuchullin, an Ossianic hero. Cuchullin went off to a foreign land to practise his newly learned arts, leaving his beautiful wife, Bragela, weeping in vain at Dunsgiath, on 'The Isle of Mist'.

Another 2 miles (3km) north, at **Ord**, the views, particularly of the Cuillins across Loch Eishort, and southwest to the Isle of Rum, are magnificent, especially at sunset.

From here, it is 15 miles (24km) or so to **Broadford**, rejoining the road a couple of miles short of Isleornsay. Broadford, a straggling settlement, is a busy place on a crossroads with hotels, shops and a baker who makes delicious bread and cakes.

Take the narrow, cul-de-sac road 14 miles (22.5km) southwest to Elgol. **Elgol** is a scattered village with more splendid views and from here you can get a boat across Loch Scavaig to **Loch Coruisk**. This was a popular stop for Victorian tourist steamers and was painted by Turner. A half-hour stop gives time to walk across ice-smooth rocks to the inland loch, long, deep and dark, surrounded by the peaks of the Cuillins. In the evening, the sun goes down behind the hills sending up great shafts of colour, made more dramatic by the proximity of the hills. For the energetic, another way is out along the Camasunary track, from **Kilmarie**, about 3 miles (4.5km) before Elgol. It is an easy walk over stony ground through bracken and heather, with just one tricky bit—The Bad Step.

Anyone fortunate enough to be exploring by boat should put into the perfect natural harbour on the island of **Soay** off the entrance to Loch Scavaig. The remains of a shark factory can be seen on the quay, established after the Second World War by the author Gavin Maxwell. His subsequent book, *Harpoon at a Venture*, is a compelling read, telling about these waters in the days when sharks and whales were so plentiful in the Minch that at times the water was literally black with them.

Continuing round the island from Broadford, the road follows the coast, looping round long inlets, zig-zagging up the hills. In a thatched cottage at **Luib**, 7 miles (11km) northwest on Loch Ainort, **Old Skye Crofter's House** is a folk museum (open daily except Sun, Easter–Sept: adm) furnished in the style of a croft house 100 years ago, with an 'on the trail of Bonnie Prince Charlie' exhibition. From Luib there is an easy 4-mile (6.5km) walk due south following the river along Strath Mor, between the rounded paps of the red Cuillins and mighty Blaven, an isolated black Cuillin.

Continuing north, the main hazard for golfers on the nine-hole course at **Sconser**, 6 miles (9.5km) further on, is sheep. The ferry for **Raasay** sails from here, five times a day.

The Cuillins

Beyond the lochs of the blood of the children of men,
beyond the frailty of plain and the labour of the mountain,
beyond poverty, consumption, fever agony,
beyond hardship, wrong, tyranny, distress,
beyond misery, despair, hatred, treachery,
beyond guilt and defilement; watchful
heroic, the Cuillin is seen
rising on the other side of sorrow.

This is the final lyric from 'The Cuillin', by Somhairle Macgill-Eain (Sorley MacLean), Skye's greatest contemporary poet.

There is a delightful hotel at the head of **Loch Sligachan**, 5 miles (8km) west of Sconser. It sits on the junction of the east and west routes to the north and is popular with fishermen and anyone planning to climb in the Cuillins. Here, surrounded by the sound of falling water, the Cuillins reign supreme. Whether capped with snow, their lower slopes mottled and smeared like camouflage jackets; or elusive and eerie in mist; or shrouded by swirling cloud; or brilliant against a postcard-blue sky, they always present a challenge. Only experienced climbers, with proper equipment, should attempt to conquer these mountains, which have claimed many lives over the years.

The road up the east coast, 9 miles (14.5km) from Sligachan to Portree, runs through valleys, pine woods and moorland past fast-flowing rivers and burns. Just south of Portree, a minor road goes out to Braes overlooking the Sound of Raasay, with lovely views and sheltered bays below the cliffs.

Portree is a busy little tourist resort. During the summer, bus excursions run from here to many of the island's beauty spots. It is an attractive town, built round a natural harbour with the houses rising steeply from the water's edge, neat and brightly painted. The name Portree is derived from the Gaelic for King's Port, after a visit by James V in 1540 when he came to subdue the islanders.

Coming into Portree from the south you will see **Aros Heritage Centre** (open daily: adm) with exhibitions of life in Skye from the 18th century, an excellent audio-visual display and commentary in six languages. Don't pass this one by. There is also a restaurant, a shop and forest walks from the car park.

It was in a room in what is now the Royal Hotel that Prince Charles took his leave of Flora Macdonald. He repaid her the half-a-crown she had lent him, gave her a miniature of himself, and said: 'For all that has happened, I hope, Madam, we shall meet in St James yet.' He bowed and kissed her hand—a fugitive with a bundle of clean shirts, a chicken, a bottle of whisky and a bottle of brandy tied at his waist, and £30,000 reward on his head. Such is the romance of Scotland.

Portree is the stage for Skye Week in June, with every sort of Scottish entertainment both indoors and out, the Portree Show in July, Portree Folk Festival in mid-August, the Skye Highland Games also in August, and the Portree Fiddlers Rally in September.

The Skye Woollen Mill has excellent cashmere and lambswool products at reduced prices, as well as a coffee lounge. Fishermen should visit **North West Fishermen**, down by the pier, for fishing tackle, flies and fishing permits.

The Old Man of Storr

The Old Man of Storr is about 7 miles (11km) north of Portree, to the west of the road and is another of those landmarks made familiar by cameras. Geographically part of Quiraing or Trotternish Ridge, the easiest walk up is through the forestry woods along maintained paths, rather than up the steep, southerly grass slopes. The Old Man is the tallest of a group of mighty towers and pinnacles of basaltic rock. He is over 180 feet (55m) high and 40 feet (12m) in diameter: a great weathered stack, undercut and pointed at the top, like a giant fir cone.

In 1891, on the shore below the Old Man of Storr, a hoard of treasure was unearthed—a remarkable collection of silver neck rings, brooches, bracelets and beaten ingots, together with many 10th-century coins, some from Samarkand. It is believed they must have been left there by a Norseman, who presumably died before he could return to claim them. These treasures are now in the Antiquities part of the Royal Museum of Scotland, in Edinburgh.

There is good trout fishing in the stocked **Storr Lochs**, from bank or boat.

Loch Mealt

The road twists and turns up the east coast, with views across the islands of Rona and Raasay, to the Highland skylines of Dundonnel, Torridon and Applecross on the mainland, south to the Cuillins and west to the Quiraing ridge. Stop at the car park at Loch Mealt, 7 miles (11km) north of the Old Man of Storr where the road comes to the brink of the cliff. The loch drains in a sheer 300-foot (92m) white cascade, plummeting into the cobalt sea. **Kilt Rock**, on the north side of Loch Mealt, has vertical columns of basalt over horizontal strips of grey and white oolite like the pleats and pattern of a kilt.

The Quiraing is 2 miles (3km) west of Staffin and you must scramble up quite a slope to get into it through a steep narrow gorge in the rocks. Great pillars of basaltic rock surround an emerald-green grass amphitheatre, like a surreal Gothic cathedral. Cattle used to be driven here for safety during raids in the old days. It is hard to find and difficult to get to, but once there it is a magical place with stunning views.

Flodigarry, about 3 miles (4.5km) north of Staffin, is where Flora Macdonald lived for eight years, after her marriage to Captain Allan Macdonald of Kingsburgh in 1751. Five of her seven children were born here. **Flora Macdonald's Cottage** is adjacent to the Flodigarry Country House Hotel which has a Moorish-style bar in what was probably the billiard room of the house.

Duntulm Castle

This is a jagged ruin, less than 5 miles (8km) to the west. The castle, with a water gate, stands in an easily defended position on a precipitous cliff on the northwest coast. Built on the site of an earlier fortress, it was a stronghold of the Macdonalds of Sleat, under the authority of James VI during his attempts to discipline the Hebridean chiefs at the turn of the 16th century. Sir Donald Gorme Macdonald was ordered to maintain his fortress in good condition, to restrict his household to six gentlemen, to limit his consumption of wine to four tuns (1008 gallons) a year, and to produce three of his kinsmen, annually, as surety for his good behaviour. The family left the castle after a nursemaid dropped the laird's infant son out of a window into the sea. The luckless nursemaid was punished for her carelessness by being cast adrift in an open boat full of holes.

Kilmuir

One of Scotland's most endearing heroines, Flora Macdonald is buried below a simple white Celtic cross in the windswept churchyard at **Kilmuir**, a couple of miles further south. They say her shroud is a sheet on which Prince Charles slept when he was hidden at Kingsburgh House. Flora smuggled the Prince, disguised as her maid Betty Burke, from Loch Uskavagh in Benbecula to Skye. For this act of courage she was briefly imprisoned. She lived with her family in North Carolina for some years but returned to Kingsburgh for the last decade of her life, dying at the age of 68. A portrait of her by Allan Ramsay shows a woman with large eyes and a calm, fine-boned face of classic Scottish beauty.

From the churchyard you can look westwards across the entrance to Loch Snizort, to where Flora and the Prince came on their daring voyage. Kilmuir has a popular agricultural show in August.

The Skye Cottage Museum (open daily except Sun, April–Sept: adm) is close to the churchyard. It consists of a group of cottages with a 'black house', farming and domestic implements and a collection of documents and photographs, giving a good idea of what life was like in the old days of crofting. The green plain stretching away to the south is known as the Granary of Skye and was once a loch until drained by the Macdonalds.

Monkstadt House

Monkstadt House, 4 miles (6.5km) south of Kilmuir, is now virtually a ruin, though the owner plans to restore it. This was the home of Sir Alexander Macdonald of Sleat who supported the Hanoverian cause. Flora and Prince Charles landed here while the house was occupied by Hanoverian troops. Fortunately Macdonald was away ingratiating himself with the Duke of Cumberland at Fort Augustus and his wife, Lady Margaret, was a staunch Jacobite. The Prince hid in the grounds where he was served by Macdonald of Kingsburgh who brought him food and wine under the noses of the soldiers. (Sir

Alexander is reputed to have made a fast buck by shipping Highlanders to the Caribbean as slaves but in fact he seems to have been honest, if naive, and only sanctioned the removal of undesirables such as thieves from his lands. He certainly resisted attempts to cook the books to disguise the fact that some of the 'criminals' were small children. It is said that Macleod of Dunvegan and Macdonald of Boisdale were much more deeply involved.)

Uig Bay

Uig Bay, 3 miles (4.5km) to the south, lies below a green amphitheatre of hills, its long pier cutting across it like an outflung arm. The hamlet of Uig is busy with ferry traffic, for this is the terminal for the steamer to the Outer Isles. If you are lucky, one of the fishing boats that use the pier may have berthed with a load of scampi and may agree to sell a bagful, scooped up off a great pile on deck. Anyone with a portable camping stove should boil these for just a few moments and eat them while still warm, accompanied by a slice of locally baked brown bread from the village shop.

Loch Snizort Beag

At Borve, 11 miles (17.5km) south of Uig, take the right turn (west) and stop in **Skeabost**, about 3 miles (4.5km) along, a pretty hamlet at the head of Loch Snizort Beag. Below the stone bridge the river branches round an island, now reached by a bridge. (Take the road to the village hall; by the stone bridge on the right, a path leads to the new bridge.) This was the site of an ancient Christian settlement, probably founded by St Columba, whose name it bears, with the ruin of a Celtic chapel and a collection of old gravestones carved with effigies. This was a burial place around the Cathedral Church of the Bishops of the Isles, certainly from 1079 (except for about 60 years when it was transferred to St Germain's on the Isle of Man) until the bishopric moved to the Benedictine Monastery of Iona in 1498 after the eclipse of its patrons, the Lords of the Isles. The small cruciform church dates from the 13th century and the 16th-century mortuary chapel is said to contain the remains of 28 Nicolson chiefs. Information plaques give some of the history of this site. **Skeabost Hotel** offers salmon fishing and lays on an excellent eat-as-much-as-you-want buffet lunch.

Annait

Annait is the site of the oldest Christian settlement in these parts. The wall and foundations of a small chapel and the monks' cells are scattered across a green promontory between two deep gulleys. In this wild and lonely place the only sounds are the piping of skylarks, the chatter of running water and the wind.

At **Trumpan**, the scant remains of a church have an unholy history. In 1579, the Macleods were attending a service in the church when they were attacked by their bitter enemies, the Macdonalds of South Uist, who massacred them, setting fire to the church and burning the congregation. One woman, cutting off a breast in order to escape through a window, managed to get away and warn the remainder of the Macleod clan. When the Macdonalds returned to their boats they were massacred by the alerted Macleods.

Dunvegan

From the road south towards Dunvegan, the outline of Macleod's Tables dominates the horizon 10 miles (16km) away to the southwest. It is said that when Alasdair Crottach Macleod went to the court of King James V at Holyrood in Edinburgh in the 16th century, he was asked somewhat patronizingly whether he was impressed by the grandeur of the palace. He replied that he saw nothing to compare for grandeur with his own domain in Skye. When James V then visited Skye, trying to rally support from the Hebridean clans, Macleod gave an open-air banquet for him, on the lower of the two 'tables', lit by his kilted clansmen, each holding aloft a flaming torch. 'My family candlesticks', he told the king, with a sweep of his hand. One can only hope it was a fine day and that the monarch was supplied with a good horse or some stout walking shoes.

Dunvegan Castle (open daily, Easter–mid-Oct; winter by arrangement: adm) is 5 miles (8km) southwest of the Fairy Bridge. Seat of the Macleods since at least 1200, it is a massive castle on a rock, with Georgian sash windows added later which soften its otherwise fortress-like appearance. From every angle it seems to show a different face, each one grey, formidable and impressive. Today it is approached by a bridge over a ravine which once formed a dry moat. In the old days the only way in was from the sea through a watergate on to the rocks.

The Fairy Flag

The castle contains family heirlooms, pictures, arms, original furnishings, documents and relics. The history of the Macleods can be traced back 30 generations to their Norse ancestry. The *pièce de résistance* is the Fairy Flag, a frail scrap of faded and worn silk, shot with gold thread and marked with crimson 'elf spots'. Legend tells of the Macleod who fell in love with a fairy, hundreds of years ago. The lovers were forced to part (at Fairy Bridge, to the north) and the fairy left the flag as a coverlet for their child. This flag had the power to save the Macleod Clan from destruction three times, but only if waved in a genuine crisis. It has been used twice: once at Trumpan (*see above*), helping the Macleods to massacre the marauding Macdonalds of South Uist, and once during a famine, caused by cattle plague.

Boat cruises run from the jetty below the castle to the little islands where seals bask on the rocks. Dunvegan has a Gala Day in August and the Dunvegan Show, also in August. Look out for the excellent craft shop just outside Dunvegan on the Portree road. Drive a few miles on past the castle to see seal colonies and swan lochs. At Claigan, follow the path to the coral beaches.

The Durinish Peninsula

The Durinish Peninsula, topped by Macleod's Tables, stretches away west of Loch Dunvegan. Macleod's Maidens, only visible if you walk or go by sea, are off the southern tip 8 miles (13km) south of Dunvegan. These three basalt stacks are called after the wife and daughters of a Macleod, who drowned here in a shipwreck.

The Orbost Art Gallery

The Orbost Art Gallery, 3 miles (4.5km) south of Dunvegan on the east side of the peninsula, has modern exhibitions in the summer. Five miles (8km) further north, the **Colbost Folk Museum** (open daily except Sun, Easter–Sept: adm) is a thatched 'black house' with peat fire in the middle of the room and all the implements and furnishings of the 19th century. There is also an illicit whisky still, once common all over the Highlands. The museum includes a watermill, 3 miles (4.5km) to the west at Glendale. Also on this road, 2 miles (3km) north of Colbost, is the Piping Centre at Borreraig. Here, a cairn marks the site of the piping school where the hereditary pipers to the Macleods, the MacCrimmons of Durinish, lived and taught piping for 300 years.

Carry on west to Loch Pooltiel, with its sheltered anchorage, and then on to **Neist Point**, the most westerly point in Skye. Park at the top and walk down to the lighthouse.

Going south on the main road from Dunvegan, after about 8 miles (13km) look carefully up to the left as you drop down into Bracadale. **Dun Beag** (always accessible), one of the best brochs in Skye, seems to grow out of the hillside and would be easy to miss. It is only a few minutes' climb over springy turf and stones to this 2000-year-old relic, which once stood 40 or 50 feet (12–15m) high. This refuge, once used by farmers and herdsmen, has double walls braced by a honeycomb of chambers and galleries, with cells, passages and stairways and traces of outbuildings.

To complete a circular tour of Skye, take the road that runs southeast along the northern edge of the Cuillins, dappled with brown, tan, grey, blue and ochre, 14 miles (22.5km) back to Sligachan and the route to the mainland.

A detour west from Drynoch takes you to **Talisker**, home of Skye's malt whisky, with daily tours on weekdays. To the south are glorious sands and coastal and hill walks at **Glen Brittle**. This is the base for exploring the Cuillins and there is a campsite and a hostel here.

Raasay

The island of Raasay can be reached by ferry from Sconser (daily except Sundays). It is a 15-mile (24km) strip, sheltered and fertile, once the hiding place of the fugitive Prince Charles, who spent a couple of nights in a shepherd's hut. Dr Johnson visited the island during his tour of the Hebrides with Boswell and was lavishly entertained at Raasay House, built by the Macleods in 1746. The house and land were badly neglected by an absentee landlord in the 1970s. It now houses the Raasay Outdoor Centre.

Castle Brochel

Castle Brochel—Caisteal Bhrochail—(always accessible) is a ruin on a rock on the eastern shore overlooking a bay, with the hills of Torridon massing on the eastern horizon. The danger notices are justified.

There are two carved Celtic crosses within easy walking distance of Kilmaluag.

The island has a ruined chapel dedicated to St Moluag of Lismore, with a carved Celtic cross, and the remains of a ruined broch, Dun Borodale. A nice walk goes up the Inverarish Burn to the flat-topped volcano-like Dunn Caan, then west along the track to join the coastal road.

Where to Stay and Eating Out

moderate

Broadford Hotel, Broadford, © 04712 204/5, is on the edge of the village. The food isn't too bad.

Cuillin Hills Hotel, © 0478 2003, overlooks Portree Bay. **Portree Hotel**, Somerled Square, © 0478 2511, has three crowns. **Rosedale Hotel**, Portree, © 0478 2531, is on the waterfront overlooking the harbour. **Royal Hotel**, Portree, © 0478 2525, is not quite as it was the day Prince Charles took his leave of Flora Macdonald in one of its parlours, but the older part has plenty of character. **Viewfield House Hotel**, © 0478 2217, is on the outskirts of Portree as you come in from the south. Run by the family for whom it has always been home, it still feels more like a welcoming, comfortable country house than a hotel. Open from May to mid-October, it is not expensive.

Sconser Lodge Hotel, © 047852 333, was a Victorian shooting lodge, at the mouth of Loch Sligachan, looking across to Raasay. **Kinloch Lodge**, Isleornsay, © 04713 214/333, is another Victorian shooting lodge overlooking the sea, owned and run by Lord and Lady Macdonald. The magic touch of Lady Macdonald, who writes cookery books, is very evident. Open from March to January. **Hotel Eilean Iarmain**, Isle Oronsay, © 04713 332, is right on the water. It is a lively place and has art exhibitions in the adjoining Céilidh Hall.

Torvaig House Hotel, Knock Bay, Sleat, © 04713 231, is on the bay, and serves good food.

Isle of Raasay Hotel, © 047862 222/226, overlooking the Sound of Raasay, is comfortable. **Uig Hotel**, © 047042 205, is highly recommended—especially for its breakfasts.

inexpensive

Duntulm Castle Hotel, © 047052 213, stands high above Score Bay, looking across to the Outer Isles. Open April to October. **Dunringell Hotel**, Kyleakin, © 0599 4180, is reasonably comfortable.

The Isles Hotel in Somerled Square, Portree, © 0478 2129, has three crowns. You might also try: **Bosville Hotel & Restaurant**, Bosville Terrace, © 0478 2846; **Kings Haven**, Bosville Terrace, © 0478 2290, two crowns; and **Tongadale Hotel**, Wentworth Street, © 0478 2115.

Flodigarry Country House Hotel, at Staffin, © 047 052 203, is cheapish and historic (*see above*), beneath the Quiraing, with fine views across to the Ross-shire coast and an 'eastern-style' bar. The food is excellent. **Sligachan Hotel**, © 047852 204, is easy-going, ideally placed for the Cuillins. **Ferry Inn Hotel**, Uig, © 047042 242, is a charming old inn with atmosphere and not too many frills.

Of the many **bed and breakfast** places, two are specially recommended. Mrs Flora Cumming, Eilean Dubh, Edinbane, © 047082 218, is so welcoming and hospitable it is like going to stay with an old friend. At Mrs B. La Trobe's house in Fiordham, Ord, © 04715 226, the sea laps below the dining room whose picture windows look west to the setting sun. Take your own wine if you want dinner.

One of the nicest **self-catering** houses is at Braes, high above the Narrows of Raasay south of Portree. This is a cosy, family house, sleeping six to seven people, looking across Isle of Raasay to the mainland and is very reasonable. Book c/o Mrs Bengough, White Lodge, Church Street, Sidbury, Devon EX10 0SB, © 03957 214.

The Small Isles: Rum, Eigg, Canna and Muck

Getting There

Caledonian MacBrayne run a service to all four islands from Mallaig daily except Sundays. The round trip takes seven hours. For details write to Caledonian MacBrayne, The Ferry Terminal, Gourock, Renfrewshire, PA19 1QP, © 0475 34531. Murdo Grant runs regular cruises from Arisaig at Easter and from May to September, less frequently out of season. His boat, *MV Shearwater*, is fast and comfortable and takes 130 people. He will also charter; © 06875 224.

Tourist Information

Fort William and Lochaber Tourist Board, Cameron Square, **Fort William**, © 0397 3781.

Rum

Rum is a squashed-diamond-shaped island, rising to a series of peaks; an unmistakable landmark for sailors, 8 miles (13km) west of Sleat in Skye. Inhabited since the Stone Age, its population of over 400 was reduced to one family in 1826, to make way for one sheep farm of 8000 sheep. Deer were then introduced and it became a private sporting estate until the Nature Conservancy acquired it in 1957. It is now an 'outdoor laboratory', trying to discover how the Hebrides can best support wildlife and human beings.

The name Rum is thought to come from the Greek *rhombos*, referring to the rhomboid shape. The 'h' that sometimes creeps into the spelling of Rum was added by the Bulloughs, *see below*, who hoped thus to give a Gaelic flavour to the name, not realising that in Gaelic, 'r' is never aspirated. The island's chief interest is its geology: special permission must be obtained from the Scottish Natural Heritage warden to visit most places.

The half-wild golden-brown ponies on Rum are said to be descended from the survivors of a Spanish galleon, part of the Armada, which was wrecked off these coasts in 1588. There are also wild goats, golden eagles and plenty of red deer.

The red sandstone castle that looks across the bay is Kinloch Castle, built in 1901 by the owners of the estate, the Bulloughs of Lancashire. It is said they offered extra wages to employees who would work in kilts, despite the fact that Rum is notorious for its midges. It is now a hotel with the atmosphere of a baronial seat and all the original furnishings. The hotel is owned by Scottish Natural Heritage and gets written up in quality magazines. One of the features is the extremely rare electric 'orchestrarian', a Heath Robinson contraption whose parts represent a full orchestra, activated by a vast library of pre-set cylinders, each programmed with a well-known tune. All the working components can be seen in action, in a huge glass chamber in the hall. For further information about the Kinloch Castle Hotel, ring 9687 2037.

Eigg

Eigg, privately owned, is an idyllic holiday island about 4 miles (6.5km) southeast of Rum, with chalets and cottages to let. Shaped like an upturned boat, or a crouching lion, surrounded by clear, sparkling water, it is a magic place, both in sunshine, or in storm. About 6 miles by 4 (9.5 by 6.5km), it is dominated by the huge black hump of the Sgurr.

Walk up from the little harbour in the southeast, east round the bay to the ancient burial ground at Kildonnan Church. This is the resting place of Macdonalds, who were once holders of the island. A broken Celtic cross, a scattering of grave stones and a roofless ruin are all that remain.

An aura of tragedy still hangs over *Uamh Fhraing*, a cave southwest of the pier, easily reached by a path from Galmisdale—torch advised. In 1577 some Macleods were forced to shelter from storm on Eigg. Owing to constant feuding over disputed land, the Macdonalds were not hospitable. The Macleods left and returned later to take revenge. The Macdonalds took shelter in this cave and the landing party found one old woman, whose life they spared. But as they were putting out to sea, they saw a scout, sent from the cave to see if they had gone. They rushed back, found the cave and lit a fire in the mouth of it, suffocating the 398 inhabitants. Sir Walter Scott is said to have found bones here in 1814 and taken a souvenir away with him. Several people have seen ghosts here.

Palm trees and flame trees thrive on this paradise island in the garden surrounding the lodge and there are lovely walks. Go up to the northwest corner, the glorious Bay of Laig, with 'Singing Sands'. The sands make a curious keening sort of song in certain conditions. Cattle wander on the beach and the views across to Rum are glorious on a clear day.

Where to Stay

inexpensive

Both the following are friendly and hospitable: **Laig Farm Guest House**, © 0687 82437, is a farmhouse overlooking Rum and Skye near the Singing Sands, and

Seaview Guest House, ✆ 0687 82433, is a working croft overlooking the Sgurr and Laig Bay. For information about self-catering places, write to: Eigg Holiday Bookings, Maybank, Udny, Ellon, Aberdeenshire, ✆ 06513 2367.

The café on the pier is the meeting place for the island, there being no pub. Locals and visitors mingle and enjoy delicious home cooking and exchange island news.

Canna

Sometimes called 'the Garden of the Hebrides', Canna lies less than 5 miles (8km) off the west coast of Rum. The highest point of this long thin island is only 690 feet (212m) above sea level. Compass Hill, 458 feet (141m), in the north, is so called because of the magnetic rock in it that can distort the true readings of a ship's compass. Canna is charming—serene and lonely, with a good harbour. The remains of a Celtic nunnery that once flourished here can still be seen. The ruined tower near the harbour was owned by a Lord of the Isles, who is reputed to have imprisoned his beautiful wife in it, suspecting her of infidelity. Canna is owned by the National Trust for Scotland. A tiny fragile Hebridean community survives here—just.

Where to Stay

The National Trust for Scotland has a guest house on the island; members get priority. Apply to National Trust for Scotland, 5 Charlotte Square, Edinburgh, EH2 4DU, ✆ 031 226 5922.

Muck

Muck, 7 miles (11km) south of Rum, is the smallest of the group known as the Small Isles, its strange name being derived from the Gaelic *muc*, a pig. It is a green, pretty little island with lovely sandy beaches. Bed and breakfast can be had from Mrs Martin, Godag House, ✆ 0687 2371.

The Outer Hebrides

Of all Scotland's islands, the Western Isles seem to evoke the deepest nostalgia; its exiles suffer the strongest pangs of homesickness. There is no specific explanation. The distinctive tang of peat-smoke, the Gaelic, the wild flowers on the machair, the cry of the curlew, the fundamental faith, the humour; these and many other things cast an unbreakable spell.

The Western Isles run about 130 miles (208km) from the Butt of Lewis in the north, down to Barra Head in the south. The main islands include Lewis and Harris, Berneray, North Uist, Benbecula, South Uist, Eriskay, Barra, Scalpay, Vatersay and Mingulay.

Each is unique, with dialects that differ even between the moorlands of Lewis and the mountains of Harris. Gaelic still lives, the first language for many and fighting to remain so.

North of Benbecula the islanders are almost entirely Presbyterian, and south almost entirely Catholic. The islanders are famous for the warm hospitality and friendliness they offer to strangers.

The scenery is made up of miles of white sand; acres of machair, rich in wild flowers; rugged hills and moorland carpeted with heather. The east coast is indented by long sea lochs that provide shelter for boats in bad weather. An aerial photograph reveals a land broken up by a vast number of lochs and lochans, which once provided waterways throughout the islands. The climate is unpredictable.

Tourists should note that all road signs are now only in Gaelic, except in Benbecula where they are bilingual, and are often difficult for strangers to pronounce and to translate into the more familiar Anglicized version. For example, if you saw *Taobh a Deas Loch Aineort,* you might not realize you had reached South Locheynort. In this guide, the Gaelic translation is given where it differs from the Anglicized name. The Western Isles Tourist Board have published an excellent leaflet with all the names in both English and Gaelic, well worth arming yourself with.

Getting to the Outer Hebrides

by sea

Ferries run from Ullapool to Stornoway in Lewis daily except Sundays; the crossing takes 3 hours 30 minutes. From Uig in Skye boats run to Tarbert in Harris and Lochmaddy in North Uist daily. There is no crossing between Uig and Tarbert on Sundays.Both trips take 1 hour 45 minutes. Boats run daily from Oban via Castlebay in Barra to Lochboisdale in South Uist. The trip takes 7 hours. A ferry is planned soon from Mallaig to Lochboisdale. The timetable changes for winter and summer and is constantly under review. Apply to Caledonian Macbrayne, The Ferry Terminal, Gourock PA19 1QP, ✆ 0475 34531. Local boats run between the smaller islands. Their timetables are sometimes subject to tides and sometimes they do extra runs to connect with other services. Details of these times are available locally and through the tourist information centres.

by air

British Airways operate a daily service (except Sundays) from Glasgow/Inverness to Stornoway, Lewis, and from Glasgow to Benbecula. Apply to British Airways, Buchanan Street, Glasgow, ✆ 041 889 1311. Loganair operate a daily service from Glasgow to Barra, and a Glasgow to Stornaway service, Mon–Fri. They also operate an inter-island service between Stornoway, Lewis, Benbecula and Barra. Charter flights can be arranged. Write to Loganair Ltd, Glasgow Airport, Abbotsinch, Renfrewshire, ✆ 041 889 1311.

Public transport in the islands is operated through local garages, supplemented by the Post Bus Service. For visitors wanting to explore at random, a car is essential. Cars can be hired locally; consult the tourist office for more information.

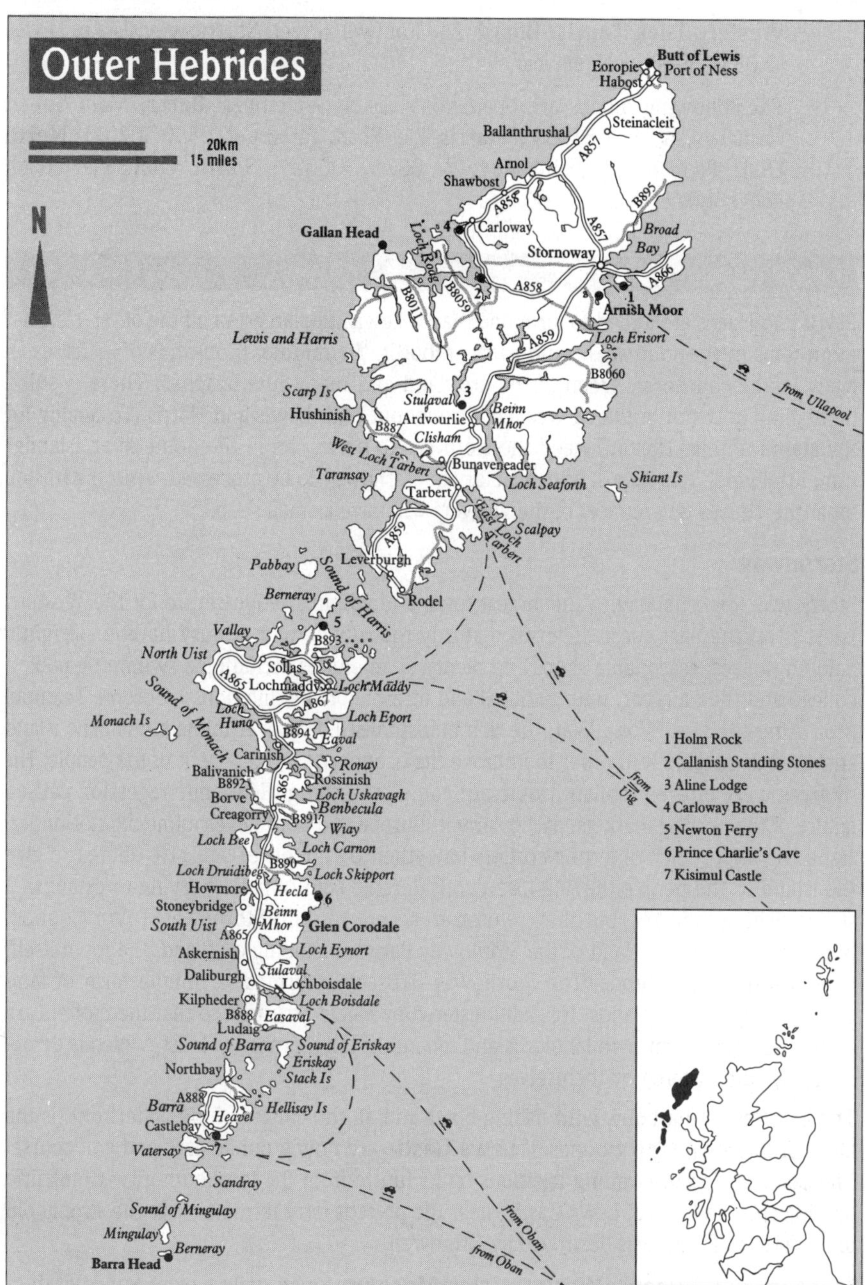
Outer Hebrides
20km
15 miles
N
Butt of Lewis
Eoropie
Port of Ness
Habost
Steinacleit
Ballanthrushal
Arnol
Shawbost
Gallan Head
Carloway
Loch Roag
Stornoway
Broad Bay
Arnish Moor
Lewis and Harris
Loch Erisort
from Ullapool
Scarp Is
Stulaval
Hushinish
Ardvourlie
Beinn Mhor
Clisham
West Loch Tarbert
Bunaveneader
Taransay
Tarbert
Loch Seaforth
Shiant Is
East Loch Tarbert
Scalpay
Pabbay
Leverburgh
Sound of Harris
Berneray
Rodel
Vallay
North Uist
Sollas
Lochmaddy
Loch Maddy
Sound of Monach
Loch Huna
Loch Eport
Monach Is
Eaval
Carinish
Ronay
Balivanich
Rossinish
Borve
Loch Uskavagh
Creagorry
Benbecula
Wiay
Loch Bee
Loch Carnon
Loch Druidibeg
Loch Skipport
Howmore
Hecla
Stoneybridge
Beinn Mhor
South Uist
Glen Corodale
Askernish
Loch Eynort
Stulaval
Daliburgh
Lochboisdale
Kilpheder
Loch Boisdale
Easaval
Ludaig
Sound of Barra
Sound of Eriskay
Eriskay
Northbay
Stack Is
Barra
Heaval
Hellisay Is
Castlebay
Vatersay
Sandray
Sound of Mingulay
Mingulay
Berneray
Barra Head
from Uig
from Oban
from Oban
1 Holm Rock
2 Callanish Standing Stones
3 Aline Lodge
4 Carloway Broch
5 Newton Ferry
6 Prince Charlie's Cave
7 Kisimul Castle

Tourist Information

Western Isles Tourist Board, 26 Cromwell Street, **Stornoway**, Isle of Lewis, ✆ 0851 3088, open all year.

The following offices are open from Easter–September: **Barra**: Main Street, Castlebay, ✆ 0871 810336; **Harris**: Pier Road, Tarbert, ✆ 0859 502011; **North Uist**: Pier Road, Lochmaddy, ✆ 0876 500321; **South Uist**: Pier Road, Lochboisdale, ✆ 0878 700286.

Lewis (Eilean Leòdhas)

Lewis and Harris are joined to form one island. Lewis, the largest of all the outer isles, has mountains in the southwest, undulating moor in the middle, thousands of lochs, especially in the southeast, green fertile croftland and many fine beaches. There is still a flourishing network of tweed weavers throughout both Lewis and Harris. To qualify for the stamp of pure Harris Tweed the cloth has to be woven in the home of an islander from local wool. It is then sent to a factory in Stornoway to be processed. Visitors can stop off at the houses where most of the weavers will have a small shop.

Stornoway

Stornoway (Steòrnabhagh), the largest town and administrative centre for the Western Isles, is on the east coast. It forms a sturdy metropolis with a busy harbour, brightly painted houses, reasonable shops and plenty of amenities including a swimming pool, a college and the Laintear, with national and international exhibitions—Europie Teampul Mor. After the First World War, the rich industrialist Lord Leverhulme bought the island and tried to develop it in order to improve the economy for the benefit of the people. His motives were entirely philanthropic but came to nothing. Economic recession caused failure of the herring markets, particularly in Europe and Lord Leverhulme did not understand the importance of letting crofters have their own plots of land. He offered to give the island to the people, having lost a considerable sum of money trying to establish a strong fishing industry, but they refused to accept his gift. Stornoway Town Council, however, accepted the land of the Stornoway Parish, including croftland, the town itself, Lews Castle and grounds. The Stornoway Trust was formed, a unique form of land ownership in the Highlands. It is administered by elected trustees so that the crofters are at the same time their own landlords and tenants of the Stornoway Trust, which is democratically administered by themselves.

The picturesque harbour, with fishing boats and all the clutter of the waterfront, is the focus of the town. The grounds of **Lews Castle** are now a public park and golf course. The castle is closed, awaiting decisions on its future from the local authority, Comhairle nan Eilean. The original Lews Castle, near the present ferry terminal, was the stronghold of the Macleods and was destroyed by Cromwell.

Museum nan Eilean—Western Isles Museum (open daily except Sunday; afternoons only in winter: free) is in the Old Town Hall, with good local history displays. Also in the town hall, open daily except Sunday, is the award-winning **An Lanntair Gallery**, with exhibitions by local artists and themes of local interest.

About 4 miles (6.5km) south of the castle, on the edge of Arnish Moor, a cairn commemorates the night Prince Charles spent here, while trying to negotiate for a boat during his fugitive days after Culloden. (Such was rumour in those days that when one of his three companions, Donald Macleod, went ahead of him into Stornoway to make arrangements, he found large numbers of armed Mackenzies preparing to fight off the Prince and an estimated army of 500 Highlanders.)

On New Year's Day 1919, a troop ship, the *Iolaire*, hit Holm Rock on the other side of the harbour and sank, drowning 200 men returning from the war.

East of Stornoway, past the airport, a narrow neck of land connects **Point** (an Rubha) to the rest of Lewis. It is also called the Eye (or Ui) Peninsula, after a Norse word meaning narrow ford or isthmus. The 14th-century **St Columba's Church**, at the western end of Point, is the burial ground of the Macleod chiefs. There is some fine carving in the church which was last used in 1828.

North of Stornoway, **Back** (Am Bac) and **North Tolsta** (Tolastadh) have fertile croft land, steep cliffs and large white beaches, unique on the east coast of the Western Isles. At the end of the road is Lord Leverhulme's 'bridge to nowhere', the beginning of the road he hoped to build between Tolsta and Ness to complete the coastal road.

The Butt of Lewis (Rubha Robhanais) is a bleak headland on the northern tip of the island, 27 miles (43km) from Stornoway by road, and topped by a lighthouse. This is a birdwatcher's dreamland: shags, cormorants, puffins, razorbills, guillemots, terns, kittiwakes, fulmars, gulls, oystercatchers, plovers, redshanks, greenshanks are just a few of the birds whose calls echo among the cliffs.

The 'Ness' (Nis) district just to the south has a hotel, a tearoom (open in the summer), and a very active football and social club. There are good beaches here, particularly the one near the harbour at Port of Ness. On the road out to the lighthouse, the old *feannagan* or inappropriately named lazy beds can be seen clearly, characteristic of the old type of agriculture practised throughout the islands. There was nothing lazy about the hard work that went into digging these strips and fertilizing them with seaweed carted from the shore in heavy creels.

At **Eoropie** (Eoropaidh), the hamlet southwest of the lighthouse, is the restored 12th-century **St Moluag's Chapel**, known as Teamphull Mholuidh and built on the site of an early Christian chapel. The key for this charming little place is in the shop. Episcopal services are held occasionally and there is a strong feeling of the simple, uncomplicated faith that keeps such a remote church alive.

About 10 miles (16km) down the A857, the 20-foot (12m) monolith, the **Thrushel Stone** (Clach an Truiseil), is the largest single stone in Scotland, a relic from prehistoric settlers. This and the burial cairn within a stone circle surrounded by bleak moorland at **Steinacleit**, about a mile (1.5km) or so away, have a marvellously primal atmosphere.

About 8 miles (13km) further on, at **Arnol**, there is the **Black House Museum** (open daily except Sun: adm). It illustrates how crofting families lived until as recently as the Second World War. At **Bragar**, a mile (1.5km) beyond Arnol, look for a gateway beside the road made of the massive jaw bone of an 80-foot (24.5m) blue whale that came ashore in the bay in 1920 after being harpooned. The harpoon hangs from the centre of the arch.

Shawbost (Siabost) Folk Museum (open daily except Sun: donation box) is a couple of miles further on. Here there is an exhibition covering the old way of life in Lewis. It includes a restored Norse watermill about a mile (1.5km) to the west. The entire museum was set up by pupils of the school. There is a modern Harris Tweed Mill, open to visitors, in Shawbost.

Between Shawbost and Carloway (Carlabhagh), there are beautiful sheltered beaches at **Dalbeg** (Dail Beag) and **Dalmore** (Dail Mor), down two turnings off the A857.

In **Carloway**, 5 miles (8km) southwest of Shawbost, drive out to the end of the Gearrannan road. Here is a typical village street of black houses in traditional style, one of which has been renovated and is a Gatliff Trust Hostel. Stop on the way to watch John MacGregor at work in his weaving shed and buy a length of his Harris tweed.

Carloway Broch, on the northern shore of East Loch Roag, a couple of miles south of the village overlooking the sea, is the best-preserved broch in the Hebrides. Its only rival for age and quality of preservation is Mousa Broch in Shetland. Part of it rises to about 30 feet (15m), forming a reassuring shelter for those families who 2000 years ago crowded inside the massive walls to take refuge from invaders.

Callanish (Calanais) Standing Stones

The Callanish Standing Stones are 5 miles (8km) southeast of Carloway along the northern shore of East Loch Roag. They rank in importance with Stonehenge, being one of the most complete prehistoric sites in Britain. The stones are laid out to depict a Celtic cross with a burial cairn at the centre, approached from north and south by avenues of pillars. Traces of cremated bones were found in the cairn. The central pillar casts its shadow along the entrance passage into the grave only at sunset on the days of the equinox. It is a dramatic place, in moorland overlooking the loch. It stirs the imagination, conjuring up the burial of some priest-king with the elaborate ritual practised in the centuries before Christianity. A mini-museum, open in the summer, gives details of the stones. There is also a tea room in a converted thatched house. On a clear day the **Flannan Islands** lighthouse can be seen, 15 miles (24km) to the west. In 1900 a gale raged at Christmas and all three of the lighthouse-keepers vanished without trace.

After Callanish, the B8011 branches south at **Garynahine** (Gearraidh Na H-Aibhne) for **Bernera** (Bearnaraigh) and **Uig**. The island of Bernera is reached by a 'bridge over the Atlantic', built in 1953.The men of Bernera were agitators in the period leading up to the 1886 crofters' revolt, when they marched with their grievances to the landlord, Sir James Matheson, in his castle in Stornoway. **Bosta Beach**, on the northern tip, is well worth a visit. Go on down the B8011 and explore the district around Uig, which has some of the most beautiful scenery in the islands.

The famous **Lewis Chessmen**, made of walrus ivory, were discovered in 1831, in the sands of **Ardroil** (Eadar Dha Fhadhail), a few miles south of Gallan Head. Of Norse origin, they are thought to have been buried here to save them from plunder by nuns living in a Benedictine convent at Brenish at the end of the road. Replicas can be bought all over the islands. The original chessmen are divided between the British Museum and the Scottish National Museum.

This is grand walking country—along the coast to the Uig Hills and south to the hills of Harris. Going south from Stornoway towards Harris, the road goes through the 'Lochs' area and a detour east on the B8060 leads down to **Lemreway** (Leumrabhagh). The land is split by deep sea lochs and masses of little lochans, surrounded by heathery hills.

Harris (Na Hearadh)

Aline Lodge, at the head of Loch Seaforth (Shiophoirt), marks the boundary between Harris and Lewis. Harris is divided into north and south by a narrow isthmus at Tarbert (Tairbeart), between East and West Loch Tarbert. North Harris has outstanding mountain scenery and the west coast of South Harris has machair and huge white sandy beaches. The east coast of South Harris is a complete contrast, with a rugged landscape so rocky you could be on the moon. Although geographically one island, Lewis and Harris are effectively divided by the high range of hills along the border and are always referred to as separate islands. The inhabitants are conscious of their very different Gaelic dialects and marked character differences.

The moors of Lewis give way to the hills of Harris, dominated by Clisham, at 2600 feet (800m) the highest mountain in the Western Isles. Although not as impressive as the mainland Munros, these hills and their glens offer wonderful walks. There is a controversial plan to form a huge quarry in one of the hills, virtually removing it entirely, for rock infill by Redlands Quarrys. It will provide much needed employment and Harris can easily spare one rocky mountain, but it could bring less welcome developments.

Tarbert (An Tairbeart)

Tarbert, Harris's main village, at the head of East Loch Tarbert on the east coast, is a thriving centre with good shops and the ferry terminal for Skye and North Uist. It is a good base for fishermen, both for salmon, sea trout and trout, and for sea fishing. There are local tweed suppliers who welcome visitors to watch Harris Tweed being woven.

Scalpay (Scalpaigh), at the entrance to East Loch Tarbet, was where Prince Charles stayed whilst trying to arrange a boat from Stornoway. He and his three companions spent four nights here as guests of the tenant, Donald Campbell. It was here that the only recorded attempt to betray the Prince for the £30,000 reward offered for his capture was made. John Macaulay (grandfather of the historian Lord Macaulay) was the Presbyterian minister in South Uist. A zealous Whig on a Catholic island, he sent word to his father, Aulay MacAulay, who was minister in Harris. He warned him of the Prince's arrival and urged him to contact Colin Mackenzie, the minister in Stornoway, and arrange to have the fugitive arrested. A boatload of armed men led by Aulay duly landed on Scalpay 'with a determined resolution to seize the Chevalier and secure the bribe offered by the Government'. They reckoned without Donald Campbell who, although not a Jacobite, was deeply aware of his obligations as a Highlander and a host. He refused the offered bribe and dismissed the invaders with bitter scorn; they slunk away, ashamed. Donald Campbell's house is now the Free Church Manse.

The footpath east from Tarbert to Scalpay road was until now the only access by land to the little village of Rhenigadale (Reinigeadal). The new road down from Maraig will transform the lives of this community.

When weather permits, boat cruises run from Tarbert to the **Shiant Islands**, 12 miles (19km) to the east, a wild cliff-land with a natural sea arch and a huge colony of puffins as well as other sea birds. Compton Mackenzie wrote some of his books here.

North of Tarbert is **Ardvourlie Castle**, once a shooting lodge and now a guest house, on the west side of the loch. It was here that Prince Charles Edward Stuart landed to walk the rest of the way to Arnish.

The road to the west from Tarbert runs through 14 miles (22.5km) of lovely scenery with views out to sea, among hills sliced by burns and carpeted in heather. There was a whaling station along this road, at **Bunavoneadar** (Bun Abhainn Eadarra), built by Norwegians in 1912, when whales were plentiful in these waters. About 8 miles (13km) further on, you can see literally hundreds of salmon jostling about in the sea, waiting to jump the falls where Loch Leosaidh pours down a cliff into the sea. **Abhainnsuidhe**—pronounced Avensooey—is a jewel of a castle on the road into the village, built in 1868 by the Earl of Dunmore. James Barrie began his novel *Mary Rose* here. The beaches at **Hushinish** (Huisinis), another 5 miles (8km) on, at the end of the road, are magnificent. **Scarp**, the island off the tip at Hushinish, is best known because in 1934 it was to be the recipient of a very advanced method of postal delivery: mail was to be sent by rocket. A special stamp was issued, coveted by philatelists, and the first rocket was fired. Unfortunately it exploded, as rockets tend to, destroying the mail and the project.

The roads down the east and west coasts of South Harris are so different it is fun to travel them both. The east coast road is a tortuous single track through a bleak, stony landscape. The tiny cultivated patches were painstakingly nurtured by people evicted from the fertile west coast who were forced to live here and try to make a living from fishing. Many of the inhabitants are now weavers. Stop at **Plocrapool** (Plocrabol) to see Marion Campbell spinning and handweaving tweed in the old way. There is a youth hostel at Stockinish (Stocinis), open in the summer, and a guest house halfway down at **Lickisto** (Liceasto).

At **Rodel** (Roghadal), on the southern tip, the Church of St Clement's dates from the 12th century and is the best piece of architecture in the outer isles, with some intriguing carved kilted figures on its tower. It was restored in the 19th century. Among the tombs there is one of Alasdair Crottach, the Macleod chief from Dunvegan who entertained James V at Macleod's Tables (p.238). The 18th-century harbour is wonderfully secluded, overlooked by the **Rodel Hotel**, part of which is now closed and dilapidated, although the atmospheric bar still operates.

On the main road round the west side, the first expanse of coast is the huge **Luskintyre Beach** (Losgaintir)—one of the most beautiful beaches in Britain—and from here on there are beaches and sea views all the way down to Leverburgh.

Leverburgh (An T-ob/Tob), on the south coast, a couple of miles northwest of Rodel, was developed by Lord Leverhulme after his plans for Stornoway had collapsed. He put a great deal of money into improving the harbour, building a large pier, houses, kippering sheds, roads and lighthouses. But he died a year after the local fishing industry began to flourish and with him died the drive and energy needed to keep things going. A passenger ferry runs from Leverburgh to North Uist and Berneray.

Where to Stay in Lewis:

moderate

Caberfeidh Hotel, Manor Park, Stornoway, © 0851 2604, is modern and purpose-built, at the upper end of the price range; comfortable if characterless. **Seaforth Hotel**, Stornoway, © 0851 2740, is cheaper, friendly and comfortable.

inexpensive

Baile-Na-Cille, Timsgarry, Uig, © 0851 672242, is a converted 18th-century manse in a superb position overlooking Uig Sands. Closed in January, it is simple but very comfortable with good country cooking. **Cross Inn**, Ness, © 085181 378, is an attractive old inn with lovely views, very cheap and friendly.

For a recommended bed and breakfast, try Mrs C. Mackay, Blackburn, 109 Newmarket, Stornoway, © 0851 705232.

Where to Stay in Harris:

expensive

Scarista House, Scarista, © 0859 550238, is a Georgian manse backed by hills and overlooking a sandy beach. This is unquestionably the pick of the bunch. It is very comfortable, with peat fires and a good library, interesting food and an extensive wine list.

inexpensive

Harris Hotel, Tarbert, © 0859 2154, is a comfortable, friendly and relaxed place. **Ardvourlie Castle Guest House**, © 0859 2307, is a splendid, rather gaunt house overlooking the loch where Prince Charlie landed after his narrow escape from the avaricious minister, Macaulay, on Scalpay.

Berneray (Eilean Bhearnaraigh)

As well as the ferry from Leverburgh, a car ferry runs to Berneray from Newton Ferry in North Uist. It is a lovely, fertile island, its people living by crofting and fishing.

North Uist (Uibhist a Tuath)

North Uist is about 17 miles (27km) long and 13 miles (21km) wide and a great deal of it is water. Wild peat moors cover the eastern side and the centre, with gentler green farmland to the west and glorious sandy beaches.

Lochmaddy (Loch Na Madadh) is the island port, a sprawling village with a sheltered harbour. It has a court house, hospital, church, several shops, a bank, hotel, and guest houses. Some say the three rocks at the harbour entrance look like crouching dogs and, indeed, the port's name comes from the Gaelic for dog—*madadh.*

Uist Outdoor Centre, on the outskirts of Lochmaddy, is a new adventure training establishment where groups or individuals can indulge in sub-aqua diving, watersports of all kinds, climbing, walking, wildlife watching, environmental and field studies— and a lot more. The accommodation is good. For details contact Niall Johnson, Uist Outdoor Centre, Cearn Dusgaidh, Lochmaddy, Isle of North Uist, PA82 5AE, ✆ 08763 480.

A road circles the island, an attractive drive through a series of crofting and fishing communities. Peat bogs flank the road with rows of neatly stacked peat bricks waiting to be transported to the houses. Almost all the outer isles use this free fuel, each croft having its own 'hag', supplemented by gas and, in recent years, electricity. The peat is cut in spring and stacked on the site until dry enough to cart. It is then built into piles beside the houses and used both on open fires and in stoves for the rest of the year.

There are several prehistoric remains to look at round the island. About 3 miles (4.5km) west from Lochmaddy going anti-clockwise, there are three standing stones on the slope of **Blashaval** (Blathaisbhal). These are known as the Three False Men, said to be three men from Skye who were turned to stone by a witch as punishment for deserting their wives.

Five miles (8km) west of Lochmaddy, a small road goes 4 miles (6.5km) north to **Newton Ferry** (Port Nan Long). In a loch on the right of this road, just before its end, is a well-preserved fortress, **Dun-an-Sticir**, reached by a causeway and occupied as late as 1601. A car ferry runs from Newton Ferry to Berneray and a passenger ferry to Harris.

Back on the circular road, **Eilean-an-Tighe** is a rocky islet in Loch-nan-Geireann, 2 miles (3km) west. It was the site of a Neolithic potters' workshop, the oldest to be excavated in western Europe. The pottery found here was of a very high quality, better than that of later times and there was so much of it that the factory must have supplied a large area.

In **Sollas** (Solas), 3 miles (4.5km) west, a medieval settlement is being excavated. This district was the scene of one of the episodes of the Highland Clearances. In 1849 Lord Macdonald, 4th Baron of the Isles, was faced with debts of around £200,000, due mainly to the decline of the kelp industry. Among other schemes to find money to pay off his creditors, he decided to evict some 600 people from the overcrowded, uneconomic area around Sollas and rent the land to sheep farmers. Since the potato famine in 1846, the people had been living well below subsistence level. However, they loved their land and resisted eviction physically during some extremely unfortunate skirmishes with the

Sheriff's officers and police. Eventually they were forced to give in, but for various reasons there was a three-year delay before they were shipped off to Canada—in a frigate carrying smallpox germs below decks.

Vallay (Bhalaigh), pronounced Varlie, is an island at the entrance to a wide, shallow bay running north and west from Sollas. Here stands a big Edwardian house sadly dying of neglect, inhabited only by birds and the occasional dead sheep. There are also the remains of an earlier house and outbuildings. You can walk out to Vallay at low tide but watch out for the flood tide: it is very easy to get cut off.

Follow the road about 4 miles (6.5km) round the coast westwards to **Huna**. Here, a foot-path goes 2 miles (3km) east across the moor, to a chambered cairn on **Clettraval.** This was built before peat covered the land, in the days when birchwood copses grew here. A fort was built over it in the Iron Age, from which pottery was excavated and found to be the same as that made in the factory at Eilean-an-Tighe.

At **Balranald** (Baile Raghaill), stretching out to the most westerly tip of the island at **Aird an Runair**, there is an important RSPB reserve supporting one of the highest densities of breeding waders in Britain. Altogether, 183 species of bird have been recorded on the reserve. Visitors are asked to report to the RSPB cottage on arrival.

Unival is a hill north of the road, 6 miles (9.5km) southeast of Huna. Walk across the moor, up its eastern flank, on the west side of Loch Huna to another chambered burial cairn with a small cist. A couple of miles further down, the road forks, south to the right and northeast to the left. The left-hand road completes the circuit of the island and takes in two of its greatest treasures.

Pobull Fhinn

Two miles (3km) along this road back to Lochmaddy, a track to the right is signposted to Langlass Lodge Hotel, less than a mile (1.5km) away. Park at the hotel and take the foot-path up behind it, a 10-minute climb through heather, bracken and bog-myrtle. On the hillside is an oval of standing stones called Pobull Fhinn (Finn's People), a prehistoric site deeply overlaid with mysticism. This may have been one of the sites where, hundreds of years before Christ, an annual ritual included the ceremonial sacrifice of the king.

Barpa Langass

Back on the road, continue less than a mile northeast. On the shoulder of Ben Langass on the right there is a grey lump, obviously man-made, shaped like a squashed beehive. This is Barpa Langass—a truly magnificent and amazingly well-preserved burial cairn, the tomb of a chieftain, thought to date from about 1000 BC. Visitors are asked not to crawl through the tunnel into the cairn, both for their own safety and for the preservation of the site. Great stone slabs line the interior and there are traces of where other cells may have led off the main chamber.

From here it is about 6 miles (9.5km) on to Lochmaddy, to complete the circuit of the island. Going back southwest to the fork, go left. **Carinish** (Cairinis) is 2 miles (3km) down the road, with some of the most interesting, though by no means the oldest, remains in North Uist.

Teampull-na-Trionaid (Trinity Temple) is a ruin on the top of a knoll on the Carinish promontory at the southern end of the island. A large building with a detached side chapel reached by a vaulted passage, this early 13th-century church was regarded as an important seat of learning for the training of priests.

The last battle to be fought in Scotland using just swords and bows and arrows was the Battle of Carinish, in 1601, between the Macdonalds of Uist and the Macleods of Harris. The cause of the battle appears to have been the insulting behaviour of one of the Macdonalds, who divorced his Macleod wife and sent her home. The Macleods descended on Carinish in a wild frenzy, but in the furious battle that ensued all but two of them were killed. **Feith-na-Fala** (The Field of Blood) marks the site of the battle, which is just north of the Carinish Inn.

Ben Lee, 896 feet (276m) high, southeast of Lochmaddy, gives a marvellous view of the island with its mass of lochs and great expanses of moorland, peat and hill.

Where to Stay

inexpensive

Langlass Lodge Hotel, Locheport, © 0876 580285, is a converted shooting lodge overlooking Loch Langlass, remote and peaceful. The food is first class. **Lochmaddy Hotel**, © 0876 500331, is convenient for the ferry terminal; a comfortable, old-established fishing hotel with friendly staff.

There are also quite a few bed and breakfast and self-catering places, listed in the tourist information brochure.

Benbecula (Beinn Na Faoghla)

Benbecula is linked to the south of North Uist by over 3 miles (4.5km) of causeway. The low-tide route across North Ford by foot, once the only way, is extremely dangerous for those who don't know the path. Locals tell hair-raising stories of lost travellers and quick-sands. Rocky bays and inlets surround the causeway, washed by the ever-changing tides.

The Gaelic name means 'the mountain of the fords'. The only mountain is Rueval in the east, a small round hillock only 409 feet (126m) high, but with good views from the top. The island is flat and waterlogged, with a fertile strip on the west side. The main road cuts through the middle with minor roads off to the east and a circular road round the west coast to the airport. Benbecula has an army base which runs the rocket range to the south. In the northwest corner there is a large army camp—a rash of utility buildings not designed to please the eye. The airport is just beside the army camp, at **Balivanich**. In contrast to the ugly military buildings there are white beaches and spectacular views and a landscape dotted with old stone houses. Near the airfield are the remains of St Columba's Chapel, dating from early Christian times. There is a well close by, now marked by a cairn, where people came to drink the holy water.

Benbecula was part of the patrimony of the Macdonalds of Clanranald from the 13th to 19th centuries, when the lands were sold off to pay impatient creditors. Most of the ruins are of Clanranald origin.

At **Nunton**, 2 miles (3km) south of Balivanich, there is a ruined chapel which belonged to a nunnery whose nuns were brutally massacred when the building was destroyed during the Reformation. The stones of a large-ish farmhouse by the road came from the nunnery. This is Nunton House, L-plan with a pavilion on each side of the entrance to a courtyard.

Borve Castle, a gaunt ruined keep near the road 4 miles (6.5km) south of Balivanich, was a Clanranald stronghold and scene of many a bloody skirmish. The scant remains of the castle chapel can still be seen nearby.

Wiay, an island off the southeast tip of Benbecula, is a bird sanctuary supporting snipe, duck, geese and swans.

It was from **Rossinish**, on the northeast corner, that Prince Charlie sailed 'over the sea to Skye' disguised as gawky Betty Burke, the servant of Flora Macdonald.

In 1988 a new Community School was built at **Liniclate** on the southern end of the island. It is a huge place with a swimming pool, superb sports facilities, restaurant, library and museum, serving children throughout the islands, some of whom previously had to board on the mainland for their education. It is also open to the public, and has been the cause of dispute between Presbyterians and Catholics over Sunday opening.

Keen shoppers must visit **D. MacGillivray and Co**, at Balivanich opposite the high cone-shaped water tank at the airport. Inside the unpretentious building is an Aladdin's Cave of tweed and woollen products, including some fantastic bargains. It's the sort of place you pop into to buy a pair of socks and stagger out of laden with parcels.

Where to Stay

inexpensive

Creagorry Hotel, Creagorry, © 0870 602024, is an old inn with a newish extention, known for its convivial bar. **Dark Island Hotel**, Liniclate, © 0870 602414/602283, is a modern hotel with very obliging staff and reasonable food. Prices range from cheap to moderate. **Inchyra Guest House**, also at Liniclate, © 0870 602176, is comfortable and gives a very warm welcome.

There is a self-catering bungalow, sleeping six, at Liniclate; apply to Mrs Shepherd, Heisker, Liniclate, © 0870 602235.

South Uist (Uibhist a Deas)

A straight causeway links Benbecula with South Uist, less than half a mile (0.8km) across South Ford, a white strand that yields an abundant harvest of cockles at low tide. When the tide is out there is usually at least one stooped figure scooping the molluscs into a bucket.

South Uist is about 20 miles (32km) long and 7 (9.5km) wide at its widest point, with mountains and long sea lochs to the east, sand and machair to the west, peat bog and moorland in between. Ben Mhor, less than halfway down in the east, is the highest peak at 2034 feet (626m). A roadside shrine to the Virgin Mary, just south of the causeway, seems to be a gentle reminder that you have left the Presbyterian north and are on the threshold of the Catholic south.

In **Iochdar**, just down the road to the west, look out for Mrs Johnson's amazing bus, completely decorated with shells, and her partly shell-covered house. The main road runs straight from north to south, part single track and part fast, new highway—this is somewhat unnerving as it narrows abruptly and often without warning, back to the old road. Lateral roads branch off like the veins of a leaf and lead to the many crofting townships that scatter the island.

The first road to the east, a mile (1.5km) south of the causeway, goes out 2 miles (3km) to **Loch Carnan**, a beautiful fiord-type sea loch with a pier for large boats.

Three miles (4.5km) to the south, the main road becomes a causeway and crosses **Loch Bee**, one of the largest swan reserves in Britain. The area of marshland to the east is a nature reserve, the breeding ground of many wildfowl including greylag geese. The hill on the left, just south of Loch Bee, is another **Rueval**, crested by a futuristic contraption which is an army range head. Rocket targets can often be seen off the west coast, and you will hear the muffled bang of firing.

On the western slope of Rueval, clearly seen from the road, there is a classically beautiful statue by Hew Lorimer of Our Lady of the Isles. Carved from white granite, it stands high on the hillside, the Child held up on His mother's shoulder. The clean-cut simplicity of the statue seems to embody the deep faith that exists in these islands.

The next road east, a mile (1.5km) south, runs 4 miles (6.5km) out to **Loch Skipport** (Loch Sgioport), another fiord-like sea loch where there is a deep-water anchorage, a salmon farm and a skeleton pier which used to be the main one for the island.

Less than 2 miles (3km) further south on the main road, beyond the road west to **Drimisdale** (Dreumasdal), there is a small loch with an island and a ruined castle. A submerged causeway runs out to the island. Beware! Some of its wobbly stones have been known to topple the unwary into the dark peaty water of the loch. The ruined castle is **Caisteal Bheagram**, a 15th- or 16th-century keep that was once a mighty Clanranald stronghold. Some years ago the present Captain of Clanranald tried to map out the original layout of the castle and discovered that its foundations cover almost all the island.

A mile south, the side road runs west a mile to **Howmore** (Tobha Mor), where there is an ancient burial ground and early Christian stones. The Church of Scotland still has its old central communion pew here.

Ormaclete Castle (Ormacleit) (always accessible), attached to a later farmhouse now being restored, is 3 miles (4.5km) to the south on the western machair between the main road and the sea. The castle was finished in 1704. It was built for Allan Macdonald of Clanranald whose wife Penelope refused to live there until a new house was built, since even her father's hens were better housed. Only eleven years after its completion it was accidentally burnt down, on the day of the Battle of Sheriffmuir in which the chief was killed.

Hecla, 1988 feet (612m), and **Beinn Mhor**, 2034 feet (626m), rise to the east of the road from which they can be approached over a wasteland of bog. The summits are dangerous in high winds, especially the sharp serrated edge of Beinn Mhor, with dizzying drops off the east side.

To the south a road runs east to Loch Eynort (Loch Aineort), another sea loch, cutting deep into the east coast and a starting point for good walks over the remote moorland between it and Loch Skipport. Beinn Mhor can also be reached from here, as can **Glen Corodale**, about 4 miles (6.5km) northeast of the end of the road. This wild country north of Loch Eynort, among the hills and glens surrounding Ben Mhor and Hecla, was where Prince Charles took refuge for a while in a forester's hut in a shieling, hiding in a cave when discovery seemed likely. The cave is not the one marked on the map, by a group of ruined houses by a burn. The real one is difficult to find, up on the rock face. This whole area is only accessible on foot or by boat.

Three miles (4.5km) south of the turning to Loch Eynort, a road runs west, signposted to **Milton** (Gearraidh Bhailteas) where a cairn marks the place where Flora Macdonald was born in 1722. Flora's father was a tacksman. She was tending her brother's cattle in the shieling about 3 miles from here when the Prince was brought to her in need of her help.

Askernish (Aisgernis), a mile (1.5km) south, has a nine-hole golf course on the machair where players must dodge sheep and plovers' nests among the dunes. The South Uist Games take place on the golf course in July, usually followed by a dance or a concert in the church hall. Everyone on the island turns out for the games, where, as well as piping, dancing and all the traditional sports, there are jovial gatherings of spectators among the parked cars and in the beer tent.

Daliburgh (Dalabrog) is a village on the crossroads west of Lochboisdale. There are three shops and a post office, a hospital and an old people's home The road to the west leads to the parish church of St Peter's, a large, simple building dating from the 1860s, weathered and unadorned. This is the living heart of the island, filled to capacity at every Sunday Mass and well attended throughout the week, as indeed are the other churches that support it to the north and south.

Northwest of St Peter's is what must be one of the most beautiful, lonely burial grounds in the country, on the edge of the machair, overlooking the wild Atlantic.

The road east from Daliburgh goes 3 miles (4.5km) to the port of **Lochboisdale** (Loch Baghasdail), with a hotel, bank, police station and harbour. It is at its busiest early in the morning and late at night, for then the Caledonian MacBrayne ferry comes and goes, turning the quay into a bustling place, with a babble of Gaelic voices. A few visiting yachts anchor in the small bay in the summer and the hotel overlooking the harbour, with its reputation for fishing and for food, attracts many visitors. Towering over the northern shore of Loch Boisdale is **Beinn Ruigh Choinnich**. There is a challenging race to its summit every year for the young men of the area, who may take whatever route they choose to the top.

A mile (1.5km) south of Daliburgh a small road runs about 2 miles (3km) west to **Kilpheder** (Cille Pheadair), from where a track leads out on to the machair to an Iron Age Pictish wheel house. This is a communal dwelling with a central hearth with cells radiating from it like the spokes of a wheel, elaborate drainage systems and storage places sunk into the floor.

Two miles (3km) south of Daliburgh, a road runs east for 2 miles, through **South Lochboisdale** (Taobh A Deas Loch Baghasdail), to a parking bay. From here a map is needed to follow a faint track over hills and moor, along lochs Kerrsinish, Marulaig and Moreef, a total of 5 miles (8km) southwest to the coast. **Bun Sruth** is a loch joined to the sea by a narrow passage of sheer rock, surrounded by hills. It is inaccessible except by boat or on foot, peopled only by sheep and birds and the ghosts of the people who once lived in the now-ruined croft houses that lie scattered over the valley. When the tide is out, the loch is higher than the sea, draining over a shelf of rock in the entrance passage and marooning boats until the next tide, which comes in through the passage fast and hard. Golden eagles can be seen, gliding on the wind above the hills north of Loch Marulaig.

All this southeastern foot of the island is good walking country, and the views from the summits of the hills are spectacular. On a clear day you can see Ardnamurchan Point on the mainland. The road out to the west, opposite that to South Lochboisdale, leads to a white beach with the gloomy remains of a once-flourishing seaweed factory, a ghostly shell of flapping corrugated iron and scrap. A few years ago any islander could cut seaweed—a laborious job—and sell it to this factory, where it was processed into alginates for use in a large number of products ranging from soap to cosmetics. Now, any seaweed that is harvested is collected in lorries and shipped to factories on the mainland. The white beach runs for miles in great sweeps of sand where keen eyes will spot tiny pink cowrie shells. The wide fringe of machair is famous for its carpet of wild flowers in the summer. Opposite the seaweed factory there is a small conical island called **Orosay**, accessible at low tide, with lovely views. In westerly gales, spray has been known to break over its top.

The road south climbs to the modern wedge-shaped church at **Garrynamonie** (Gearraidh Na Monadh), built in 1963 and rather bizarre in its setting. It has an enamelled mosaic behind the side altar and Stations of the Cross designed by a priest from Barra, Father Calum McNeil. Here, as in the other churches, you can hear Mass in Gaelic, with a haunting chant from the choir.

At the end of the road, 5 miles (8km) south of Daliburgh, is the **Pollachar Inn** (Pol A Charra) overlooking one of the most beautiful views in Scotland, across the sound to Barra and east to Eriskay. The inn used to be a great place for local atmosphere and stories of the past. It is now being enlarged and altered, not necessarily to its advantage, but you can still sit outside and enjoy your drink overlooking a standing stone and the Sound of Eriskay, across to the heart-shaped hills of Barra.

Ludag is a couple of miles east along the south coast, and ferries run from the pier here to Eriskay (cars) and Barra (passengers only). A lovely sandy bay beyond at **South Glendale** dries out at low tide and makes an excellent picnic spot, sheltered all round by turf-covered rocks. East of the bay, along the rocky shore and below the water, lies part of the wreck of the *Politician*, immortalized as the *Cabinet Minister* by Compton Mackenzie in his book, *Whisky Galore*. The true story was only slightly embroidered in the novel. The ship was carrying 20,000 cases of whisky to America in 1941, at a time when whisky was scarce in the islands. Magnetic minerals in the rocks distorted the compass readings and she went off course, riding over Hartamul, the rock at the entrance to the Sound of Eriskay, and finishing up against the cliff. The islanders made a valiant attempt to 'rescue' the whisky, thwarted by the bureaucracy of the customs and excise department, and not a few families still own a much-valued 'Polly bottle'. Stories are still told, with a twinkle and a knowing shake of the head, of animals reeling down the road, and of bottles dug up on the machair that had been buried for years. Recently the last of the bottles went up for auction and fetched nearly £100 each.

South Uist is littered with places where Prince Charles is said to have sheltered. He certainly hid for a time in the jagged, ruined castle on Calvay Island, at the entrance to Loch Boisdale, clearly seen from the ferry.

Eriskay (Eiriosgaigh)

For some, the island of Eriskay is the jewel of them all. A car ferry runs from Ludag in South Uist but as the road is barely 2 miles (3km) long it is hardly worth taking a car across. The boat runs a mile across the sound to **Haun** (Haunn), a smiling village of freshly painted white cottages with roofs of bright blue, pink, green and red, sheltered by hills. The church, perched high above the harbour, is the heart of the island. It was built in 1903 by Father Allan MacDonald who wrote down the folklore and many of the songs of the Hebrides and was a distinguished poet. The altar is shaped like the prow of a ship, worshipped at by a community whose existence has always been shaped by the sea. The ship's bell outside, beyond the church, was rescued from the *Derflinger*, one of the German ships that sank in Scapa Flow in 1919.

Just beyond the village on the western shore there is a crescent of sand called Prince Charlie's Bay. This was where the prince landed from France on 23 July 1745 and where he spent his first night on Scottish soil. The black house he stayed in was only pulled down in 1902. Its smoky interior drove him out into the fresh air several times during the night. It was a simple place like all the others of its kind, with cupboard beds, hens running over the earth floor and wooden trunks holding the family possessions. The pink convolvulus called Prince Charlie's Rose, in the machair round Prince Charlie's Bay, is said to have been introduced here from a seed dropped from his shoe.

The **Stack Islands** lie just off the southern tip of Eriskay. There is a rock creek on the main island where boats can moor in calm weather. It is then a scramble to climb the precipitous cliff to the Weaver's Castle at the top. Here a notorious Macneil lived, a much-feared wrecker and pirate. He built the castle as a hideout, and stole a girl from a shieling in South Uist to be his wife and the mother of a large number of sure-footed children.

Where to Stay

inexpensive

Borrodale Hotel, Daliburgh, South Uist, © 0878 700444, stands on the cross-roads in Daliburgh and provides the centre of island life. It is comfortable and friendly and the food is good. **Lochboisdale Hotel**, South Uist, © 0878 700332, looks over Loch Boisdale by the ferry terminal. It has always been a popular fishing hotel and has a reputation for good food. The 17th-century **Pollachar Inn**, Kilbride, South Uist, © 0878 700215, has one of the best views in Scotland, and has a convivial bar. (Five bedrooms share one bathroom.) It is open from April to October. **The Grianaig Guest House**, Garryhallie, South Uist, © 0878 700406, is just north of Daliburgh, not far from the golf course. It is a comfortable, modern house, well run with good food. At the north end of the island there is **Orasay Inn**, Lochcarnan, © 0870 700298, a small, family-run hotel with good food.

A number of houses offer bed and breakfast, listed in the brochure.

For those who prefer the freedom of self-catering, **Boisdale House**, South Lochboisdale, is good value—a family holiday house by the water, sleeping 12; © 09856 219.

Barra (Barraigh)

Barra, 4 miles (6.5km) south of South Uist at the nearest point, is ringed by a number of smaller islands. One road circles the main part of the island, with an arm running north to the airport and Scurrival Point. Beaches, croftland and a hilly interior make up this compact haven which took its name from St Barr of Cork, who converted its people to Christianity. Barra has seascapes and landscapes that have inspired many artists, writers and musicians.

No one arriving in the ferry forgets their first sight of Castlebay (Bagh A Chaisteil). **Kisimul Castle** (open May–Sept, Wed and Sat afternoons: adm) stands on a rock in the middle of the harbour. Some people claim that it originates from 1060 and is one of Scotland's oldest castles but there is no firm evidence that it existed before the 15th century. It is a splendid sight in any weather but most romantic when silhouetted against a half-dark sky on a summer night. The Macneils acquired the castle as a reward for fighting for Robert the Bruce at Bannockburn. This clan was famous for its lawlessness, piracy and arrogance: a clansman from Barra is said to have declared, 'The reason there was no Macneil on Noah's Ark is that the Macneil had a boat of his own.' Kisimul was virtually destroyed by fire at the end of the 18th century. It remained in ruins until the 45th chief of the Macneil clan, returning from his adopted homeland in America, restored it to its present excellent condition in this century.

Neat shops and houses line the road that climbs from the harbour in **Castlebay**, overlooked by a statue of the Blessed Virgin and Child, high on the southern shoulder of **Heaval**—at 1260 feet (388m), Barra's highest peak. The Virgin stands, the Child on her shoulder holding a star. The statue, carved from Carrara marble, was erected in 1954, to celebrate the Marian Year and in memory of the 58 men from Barra who died in the Second World War, mostly in the Atlantic convoys. This is another symbol of the deep faith that governs the lives of these islands.

Like all the islands, Barra has its ancient remains. Going clockwise, 2 miles (3km) west from Castlebay, the standing stones beside the road past the Isle of Barra Hotel are said to mark the grave of a Norse pirate. A mile (1.5km) inland from the chapel at **Gariemore**, a mile further north, is **Dun Bharpa**, a large chambered cairn beyond the hamlet, surrounded by standing stones.

On the eastern side of the peninsula at the north end of the island, 4 miles (6.5km) beyond Gariemore and past North Bay, the great sweep of white sand is the landing strip for the daily Loganair air service. Two square miles (5 sq km) of dazzling cockle-shell strand, the **Tràigh Mhór** is washed twice a day by the tide and provides a firm touchdown for the little plane that comes droning in like a bumblebee, its timetable tied to the tide.

The house at the end of this great strand was the home of Compton Mackenzie, the writer who caught the spirit of the Highlands more perceptively than anyone. He attracted a lively community of writers and Gaelic scholars when he lived here. He is buried in the graveyard at **Eoligarry** (Eolaigearraidh), just to the north. Here among the ruins of a chapel are burial slabs said to have arrived from Iona as ballast in an ancient galley.

Another famous name can be seen in the cemetery: that of John Macpherson, better known to lovers of Gaeldom as 'The Coddy', who died here on his native island in 1955. *Tales from Barra*, recorded in both Gaelic and English, is a large collection of folk tales told by the Coddy in his inimitable voice—a delight for exiled Scots all over the world and well worth getting.

A grassy mound is all that remains of Eoligarry House, a three-storey house built by the Macneils after Kisimul Castle burned down in 1795. It was a substantial ruin until recently.

Isle of Vatersay (Bhatarsaigh), just off the south of Barra, is now linked by causeway. The other islands off Barra are each a delight for anyone with access to a boat. Golden eagles and a number of black rabbits greet visitors to **Hellisay**, off the east coast. The birds are magnificent, the wild flowers a delight, the sea so clear that the bottom seems no more than a few inches away.

Where to Stay

moderate

Castlebay Hotel, © 0871 810223, is comfortable and friendly, with prices from cheap to moderate. **Isle of Barra Hotel**, Tangusdale, © 0871 810383, is purpose built overlooking a crescent of white sand. It is comfortable and has good food, an easy-going atmosphere and self-contained apartments.

Clachan Beag Hotel, Castlebay, © 0871 810279, is full of local atmosphere, with a friendly staff. **Craigard Hotel**, Castlebay, © 0871 810200, serves nice food and the staff are obliging.

There are a number of bed and breakfast and self-catering places.

St Kilda

St Kilda, consisting of four islands and a few great rock stacks, is the most westerly of the British Isles apart from Rockall. These lonely islands are owned by the National Trust for Scotland. A small detachment of gunners man a missile tracking-station, but otherwise they are unpopulated. **Outer Hebrides Yachts**, 33 Cromwell St, Stornoway, operate regular trips to St Kilda. The main island, the one on which the people lived, is called Hirta (possibly derived from the Old Norse for shepherd – *hirt*). The origin of the name St Kilda is disputed–there was no saint by that name. Kilda may have come from Hirta, which the islanders pronounced as Hilta, which then became Kilda.

The islands' history is one of decline brought about by isolation in a world increasingly obsessed by centralization and conformity. There is evidence of human occupation as far back as the Iron Age with the remains of a pottery and earth house. A small, patriarchal, strongly Presbyterian society subsisted here, paying its rent with meat, feathers and oil from seabirds. They were often cut off by storms. The population of about 200 in the 18th and 19th centuries remained fairly constant, except for a smallpox epidemic in 1727, kept in check by puerperal fever. The introduction of money and visitors from the mainland reduced their self-reliance and many of the younger ones left. In 1930 the able members of the community, attracted by the lure of the outside world and dragged down by hardship, persuaded the older ones to move to the mainland.

Some of the houses, at Village Bay on Hirta, have been preserved, with their cleits—beehive-shaped cells of rough stone that served as larders and storerooms. The careful design of these cleits allowed air and wind to circulate inside and preserve the meat of the sea birds. It also kept clothes and gear dry. *The Life and Death of St Kilda* by Tom Steel gives an excellent account of the islands' history.

The Northern Isles

Although separated by 60 miles (96km) or so of ocean and very different in character, Orkney and Shetland have a common history and tend to be bracketed together. Norsemen called them the 'Nordereys'.

Both groups—about 70 Orkney islands, and 100 Shetland islands—were inhabited in the Stone Age. The Picts colonized them in the 1st century AD and were subjected to continual harassment from the Vikings for centuries until the Norse King Harold Harfagri annexed them in 875. When Harold succeeded to the throne of Norway in about 860, large parts of his kingdom didn't recognize the authority of the Crown—like the Lords of the Scottish Isles. Harold was in love with a Princess Gyda, daughter of one of the rebel 'kings', and she refused to marry him until he had conquered all Norway. He vowed that he would not cut his hair or his beard until he'd done this. He claimed his bride 10 years later. All the dispossessed *jarls*, or minor kings, took refuge in Orkney and Shetland and from here proceeded to harass Norway with wild Viking raids. King Harold, exasperated, collected up a fleet and sailed down to put an end to their antics. He landed at what is now Haraldswick in Unst, Shetland, and declared all the islands to be a 'Jarldom'. The Norse occupation of these islands is recorded in romantic stirring sagas, handed down over the years. *The Orkneyinga Saga* is one of the best known.

By the 13th century, although still under Norse rule, the islands were presided over by Scots earls. When Princess Margaret of Norway and Denmark became betrothed to James III of Scotland, her father, King Christian I, pledged the islands to Scotland as part of her dowry in 1468. They were formally annexed in 1472 and since then they have been part of Scotland.

Norse placenames still predominate and the people of these northern islands are a blend of Norse and Scots, very different in character to the dreamy Celts of the Hebrides. They are extremely friendly, extrovert and stolid, industrious and mainly Presbyterian. Their accent is sing-song; the old 'Norn' language disappeared during the 18th century, although some phrases have remained, and when the islanders talk among themselves they use many words more akin to Norwegian than English.

The coming of the oil boom struck hard at established roots, bringing innovations that were not always popular and making Shetland relatively rich compared to the rest of Scotland. However, on the whole the islanders managed to retain their old way of life.

Orkney

Orkney's 70 or so islands are 6 miles (9.5km) off the north coast of Scotland on a level with Leningrad. They extend 53 miles (85km) from north to south and about 23 (37km) from west to east: Oslo is closer than London. Nineteen of them are inhabited, and when an Orcadian talks of the Mainland, he means Mainland Orkney—the big island. (The Mainland of Scotland is 'the sooth'.) Orkney means 'seal islands', the *ey* being Norse for islands: no one talks of the Orkneys, just Orkney.

First impressions are of emerald green plateaux of turf above sheer rock cliffs and sandy beaches, fertile farmland and a sparkling sea. Apart from Hoy, nothing is higher than 900 feet (278m). A great dome of clear sky seems to shed an ethereal greenish light. Sunsets in May and June are fantastic. At midsummer the sun is above the horizon for 18 hours and it is possible to read a book outside all through the night. This midsummer twilight is called 'Grimlins', from the Norse word *Grimla*, to glimmer or twinkle.

St Magnus Festival in Kirkwall in June is a week of music, drama and art, rapidly growing in popularity and attracting companies from many countries. The standard is high. For two weeks in July there is a **Craftsmen's Guild** in Kirkwall, with demonstrations of local craftwork. Stromness has a **Folk Festival** in May and a **Shopping Week** in July. Although there is plenty of accommodation, it is wise to book well in advance.

Birdwatching is almost compulsive. One in six of all seabirds breeding in Britain nests in Orkney. The long-eared owl is an endearing resident; its 'ears' are elongated head feathers and have nothing to do with hearing. Its low, moaning hoot is an eerie sound at night. There are short-eared owls, which hunt by day over the moors; red-throated divers, so graceful until they come in to land; razorbills with their fascinating courtship displays and refusal to build nests; puffins, whose brightly coloured bills are a weapon and a spade with which to dig burrows in the turf. For **botanists** the wild flowers are a joy: tiny Primula scotica, a survivor from the last Ice Age; grass of Parnassus, whose honey-scented white flowers litter the marshland; bog pimpernel, oysterplant, bog asphodel, and many more. For general **naturalists** there is the unique Orkney vole to look out for, a sweet little round ball of fur. There are otters—Kirkwall must be about the only town to display a red triangular road sign reading: 'Otters Crossing 100 yds'.

Fishermen leave Orkney with enough fishing stories to keep them happy till they return. The brown trout are the best in Britain and fishing is free, thanks to Norse law. Sea angling is also good. **Water sports** enthusiasts will find perfect waters for **sub-aqua** diving, especially wreck-diving around Scapa Flow. **Archaeologists** will find more prehistoric remains than anwhere else in Scotland, some in a remarkable state of preservation: brochs, standing stones, burial cairns—an average of three sites per square mile. It is beyond the scope of this book to describe each of the many hundreds of historic sites and antiquities that pepper Orkney. The Tourist Board's information office, in Broad Street, Kirkwall, has brought out a first-class free booklet on what to see.

Getting There

By sea: P&O operate a daily roll-on, roll-off car ferry service (except on Sundays) from Scrabster near Thurso to Stromness on Mainland Orkney; sailing time two hours. They also run boats from Aberdeen, three times a week in summer and twice a week in winter, taking eight to ten hours. Thomas and Bews run passenger boats from John o' Groats to Burwick in the summer; crossing time 45 minutes, no bookings. Orkney Ferries run a new roll-on, roll-off car ferry from Gill's Bay; crossing time 45 minutes, no bookings.

By air: British Airways operate a daily service from Glasgow, Inverness and Aberdeen to Kirkwall. Loganair operate a daily service from Glasgow, Edinburgh, Inverness and Wick. Flights from Aberdeen take about 40 minutes.

On arrival, there is an excellent inter-island air service (the shortest flight, between Westray and Papa Westray, taking only a minute in good conditions), as well as ferries. It is easy to hire cars and there are causeways to some of the islands. Careful planning is needed to make the best use of the transport available. The people in the tourist office are very helpful and will advise on the best tours to take, and give up-to-date opening times.

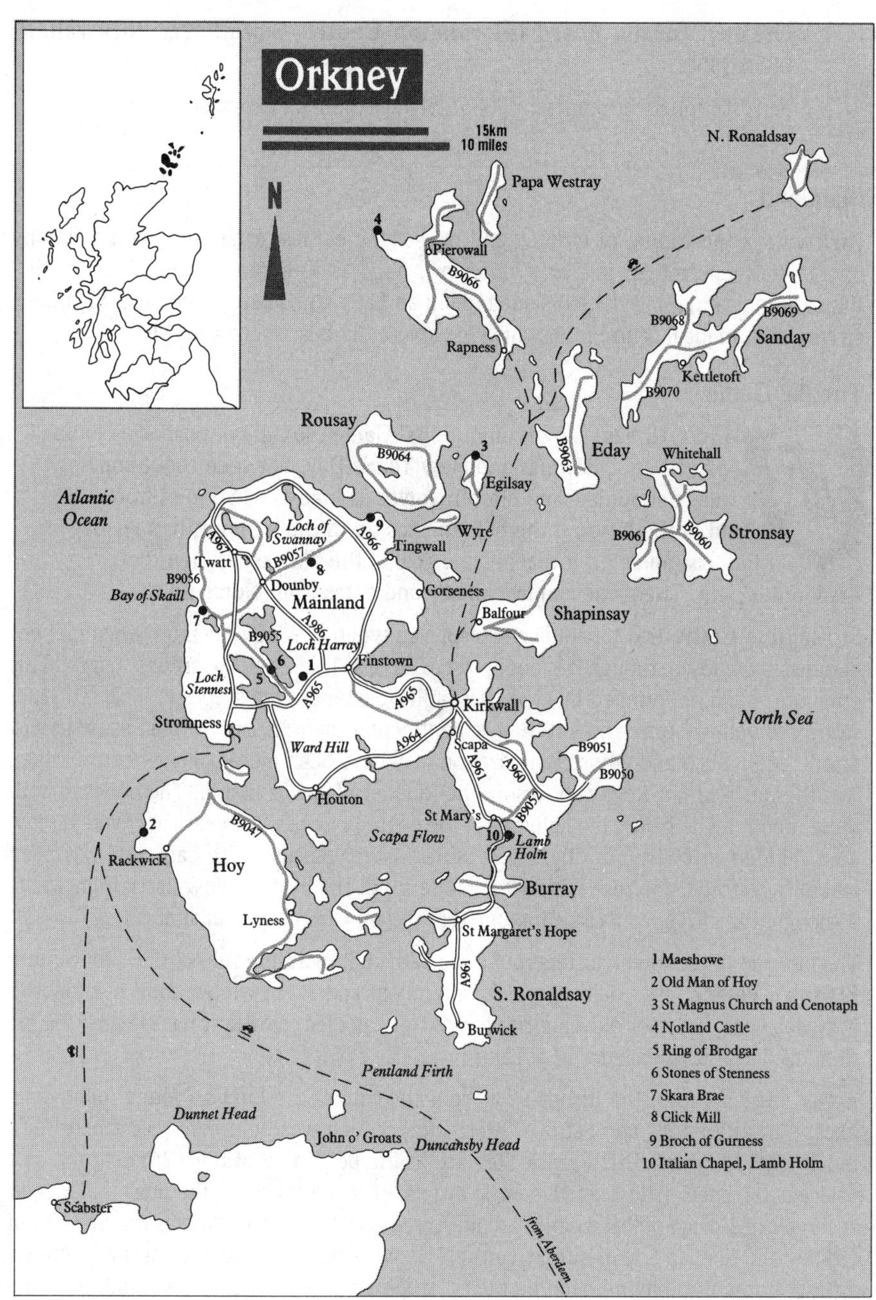
Orkney
15km
10 miles
N
N. Ronaldsay
Papa Westray
Pierowall
B9066
Rapness
B9068
B9069
Sanday
Kettletoft
B9070
Rousay
B9064
Egilsay
B9063
Eday
Whitehall
Atlantic
Ocean
Loch of
Swannay
A966
Wyre
Tingwall
A967
Twatt
B9057
B9061
B9060
Stronsay
B9056
Dounby
Gorseness
Bay of Skaill
Mainland
Balfour
Shapinsay
B9055
A986
Loch Harray
Finstown
Loch
Stenness
A965
Kirkwall
Stromness
North Sea
Scapa
Ward Hill
A964
B9051
A961
A960
B9050
Houton
St Mary's
B9052
B9047
Scapa Flow
Lamb
Holm
Rackwick
Hoy
Burray
Lyness
St Margaret's Hope
A961
S. Ronaldsay
Burwick
Pentland Firth
Dunnet Head
John o' Groats
Duncansby Head
Scabster
from Aberdeen
1 Maeshowe
2 Old Man of Hoy
3 St Magnus Church and Cenotaph
4 Notland Castle
5 Ring of Brodgar
6 Stones of Stenness
7 Skara Brae
8 Click Mill
9 Broch of Gurness
10 Italian Chapel, Lamb Holm

Tourist Information

Orkney Tourist Board Information Centre, Broad Street, **Kirkwall**, © 0856 2856.

Ferry Terminal, Stromness, © 0856 850716 (limited hours Oct–April).

Mainland

Kirkwall is the capital of Orkney and one of the earliest established Norse trading towns. It is referred to in *The Orkneyinga Saga* as Kirkjuvagr, 'Church-bay-of-the-Vikings', indicating that the Norsemen found an Early Christian church here when they arrived. It is an ideal centre from which to explore these fascinating islands.

The Ba' Game

Kirkwall has its own unique 'Ba' Game', loosely described as football, played on Christmas and New Year's Day, between the 'trsuppies' and 'trsdoonies' and often involves as many as 150 men from either end of the town. If the ball finishes up in the harbour, it is victory for the 'trsuppies': if it reaches the goal at the old castle, then the 'trsdoonies' win. The game can last all day and dates from Norse times.

St Magnus Cathedral (open daily except Sun when it is only open for worship: free) dominates the town, though it is not in fact as large as its clever proportions suggest. This cruciform building founded in 1137 was built up of alterating stripes of local red sandstone and yellow stone and looks more continental than British. St Magnus, who was murdered in 1116 and whose canonization may have been more political than spiritual, was the uncle of Jarl Rognvald Kilson, the founder of the cathedral. The bones of both these men now lie below the columns of the central bay of the choir. They were discovered, hidden in chests, during repair work in this century. The cathedral has been carefully restored; the rose window is modern but the east window dates from 1511. Although it is still called a cathedral, the services are Church of Scotland.

The old part of the town clusters round the cathedral, with the ruin of the 12th-century **Bishop's Palace** (open daily except Fri afternoons and Sat in winter: adm) next door to it. It was here that poor old King Haakon of Norway died, having struggled back this far from his defeat by Alexander III at Largs in 1263.

Across the road from the Bishop's Palace is the ruin of the **Earl's Palace** (open daily except Fri afternoons and Sat in winter: adm), which was built by forced labour for a much-loathed tyrant, Earl Patrick Stewart, at the beginning of the 17th century. The palace is L-shaped, with attractive angle-turrets, once described as 'the most mature and accomplished piece of Renaissance architecture in Scotland'. Earl Patrick was Steward of Orkney and Shetland, and entirely corrupt. He was finally executed for his awful crimes against humanity, having been granted a week's reprieve so that he could learn the Lord's Prayer.

Tankerness House Museum (open daily except Sun: adm) is in a very well-restored 16th-century merchant's townhouse, with an attractive courtyard and garden. The history of Orkney over 4000 years is displayed here.

The Library (open daily except Sun: free), founded in 1683, is the oldest public library in Scotland and has an excellent Orkney Room for anyone wanting to go more deeply into the history of the island.

Among the other things to visit in the town are the **Silver Works** and the two malt whisky distilleries, the **Highland Park Distillery** and **Scapa Distillery**, both of which welcome visitors, free, on weekdays.

Stromness, about 17 miles (27km) west of Kirkwall, is the only other proper town in Orkney. This pretty place, with a sheltered harbour and steep winding cobbled streets, has houses dating from 1716. It was once a principal port on the sailing route round the north of Scotland and base for the Hudson Bay Company ships. Many local men went to do contract work in Canada. The houses, many of them with their own jetties, seem to jostle each other aside, to get the best position along the mile of waterfront. Stromness is the terminal for the car ferry from Scrabster. There is a traditional Folk Festival in May and a Shopping Week in July, when all the shops compete for your custom.

Pier Arts Centre (open daily except Mon: free) is housed in well-restored 18th-century buildings and puts on exhibitions of modern paintings.

Stromness Natural History Museum (open daily except Thurs afternoons and Sun: small fee) has collections of birds, fossils, shells and butterflies. There are also exhibitions covering whaling, fishing, the Hudson Bay Company, Scapa Flow and the German fleet.

Scapa Flow is a great inlet to the south of Mainland, surrounded by protective islands. This perfect deep-water anchorage, up to 10 miles (16km) wide, was adopted as the main base of the Grand Fleet in 1912. At the end of the First World War, the German Navy sailed their fleet into Scapa, having surrendered. Then, on 21 June 1919, on the order of Rear Admiral Ludwig von Reuter, the whole fleet of 74 warships was scuttled. At the beginning of the Second World War a German U-boat crept through the defences and sank the *Royal Oak*, after which the Churchill Barriers were erected, making the anchorage almost impregnable. Scapa is popular with sub-aqua divers and its clear water offers great scope for wreck diving. There are good supplies of air obtainable locally.

The following is a small selection of the many historic and prehistoric antiquities to be seen in Orkney. Consult the tourist office in Broad Street, Kirkwall, for more detailed information and advice as to how best to fit in as much as possible.

Maes Howe

Maes Howe (open daily: adm) is 10 miles (16km) west of Kirkwall, just off the main road to Stromness. It is a huge Stone Age burial cairn, unquestionably the most outstanding in Britain. The passage into the cairn, made of huge single slabs of stone, is so aligned that a shaft of sunlight pierces its 36-foot (11m) length into the chamber on only one day of the year, that of the winter solstice. Burial cells lead off the main chamber, which has massive stone buttresses in each corner.

When Maes Howe was first excavated, in 1861, the cells were found to be empty and this fact, together with runic Viking inscriptions on the walls, misled archaeologists into thinking the tomb was Norse. Then it became obvious that the structure dates back many centuries before that and probably to around 3500 BC. The Vikings came much later, sacking the tombs and leaving their graffiti on the walls.

In fact the graffiti are just as fascinating as the much older cairn. There are references to treasure and to the Crusades, and a collection of sex slogans that are as modern as any today: 'Thorny was bedded, Helgi says so,' reads one; 'Ingigerd is the best of them all,' says another. There is an excellent guidebook on sale at the site. Beside the car park is **Tormiston Mill**, a restored 19th-century water mill with a restaurant and a craft centre.

The Ring of Brodgar

The Ring of Brodgar (always accessible) is on the narrow neck of land between Harray and Stenness Lochs, 4 miles (6.5km) northwest of Maes Howe. From the original 60 stones, 36 remain. They are precisely set, being 6° apart, with a surrounding ditch cut from bedrock, as much as 9 feet (2.75m) deep and 27 feet (8m) wide, crossed by two causeways. These stones date from about 1560 BC and are believed to be some sort of lunar observatory, a splendid reminder that those Stone Age men may have been primitive but they certainly weren't stupid.

The Stones of Stenness

The Stones of Stenness (always accessible) date from around the third millennium BC, and only four stones remain of the original circle. Excavations uncovered an almost square setting of horizontal stones, scattered with fragments of cremated bones, charcoal and shards of pottery, indicating that this must have been some sort of cremation and burial site. The two outlying stones, the Barnhouse and the Watch Stone, were probably associated with this circle, as must have been the many cists and cairns that have been unearthed in this area.

Skara Brae

Skara Brae (open daily: adm) is 5 miles (8km) northwest of the Stones of Stenness, on the west coast and on the southern arm of the sandy sweep of **Bay of Skaill**. This was a Stone Age settlement, hit by a massive storm that buried it in sand for about 4000 years. Another storm then blew away some of the sand to reveal the village to archaeologists. It is unique, giving an insight into the whole way of life of those prehistoric tribes, rather than just revealing a burial cairn, which only tells a fraction of their story. Careful excavation has uncovered about six of the original ten one-roomed houses, and a workshop, with covered passages from one to another and a communal paved courtyard.

Lack of wood meant they used stone for their furniture and the old bed platforms, cupboards, hearths, fish tanks and tables can still be seen, as well as a fascinating collection of tools and implements. Recent progress in carbon-dating means that more and more information is coming to light about those mysterious settlers and there is an excellent guide book with up-to-date findings. A small museum gives more details. Midden (rubbish heap) excavations have revealed that the inhabitants of this earliest fishing village in Scotland were also farmers.

The only surviving **Click Mill** is beyond Dounby, about 8 miles (12.5km) northeast of Skara Brae (always accessible). It is a horizontal water wheel, built in about 1800 from an earlier design and so called from the noise it makes as it turns. It is preserved in working order, although the pond has been drained.

Gurness

On the wild, windswept headland at **Gurness,** 5 miles (8km) northeast of the Click Mill, there is the best broch in Orkney (open daily: adm). A booklet describes the very complicated layout of the site. It was built as a broch and then added to over the centuries by the Norsemen, and includes many domestic buildings, Norse longhouses, partitioned chambers and a well.

Islands South of Mainland

Lamb Holm, linked by a mile (1.5km) of causeway, south of Mainland, has the heart-stirring little **Italian Chapel**. It was created out of two Nissen huts, corrugated iron, plasterboard, paint and cement by Italian prisoners of war during the Second World War. They were building the Churchill Barrier after the sinking of the *Royal Oak* and made the chapel in their spare time. It is a miracle of faith, with delicate wrought-iron tracery and frescoes. The artist, Dominico Chiocchetti, returned in 1960 to restore the original work.

South Ronaldsay, joined to Lamb Holm by 4 miles (6.5km) of causeway across Burray, has a picturesque village with a poignant memory—St Margaret's Hope. In 1290 the seven-year-old Princess Margaret, Maid of Norway, died of sea sickness in the ship bringing her from Norway to marry Prince Edward of England. (The marriage had been planned as a way of uniting Britain with Norway.) The ship, bearing the wasted body of the little princess, put in to St Margaret's Hope.

Hoy, the largest island apart from Mainland, about 3 miles (4.5km) south of Stromness, is the only one that is not flat. Its hills provide a good backdrop to views over the flat green farmland wherever you are in these islands. Ward Hill rises to 1500 feet (460m). **The Old Man of Hoy** is a rock stack, 450 feet (138m) high, on a promontory above the sea. This is a favourite challenge to serious rock climbers, a towering pinnacle of horizontally layered rock. **St John's Head**, on northwest Hoy, is part of a 1140-foot (350m) vertical cliff, teeming with seabirds and many rare plants. **Melsetter House**, not open to the public but visible from the road, was built on to an older house in 1898 by W. R. Lethaby for Thomas Middlemore, who inherited a fortune from a Birmingham leather business. New and old are kept distinct but the scale and materials used blend nicely into the Orkney landscape.

Islands North of Mainland

Birsay and **Brough of Birsay** are less than a mile off northwest Mainland; it is possible to walk out at low tide. There are the remains of early Christian and Norse settlements.

Rousay, a couple of miles (3km) northeast of Mainland, has a burial cairn at **Midhowe**. This cairn has a long chamber, 76 feet (23m) by 7 feet (2m), with 24 burial cells leading off it, in which the remains of 25 human bodies were found. Another tomb on Rousay, **Taversoe Tuick**, is unusual because it is two-storied. One tomb sits on top of the other, each with its own entrance passage. Rousay also has also a well-preserved broch, with a complex of cells, cubicles, passages, stairs and doorways, and outbuildings.

Wyre, a mile (1.5km) southeast of Rousay, has the ruin of a 12th-century stone castle, one of the oldest in Scotland, known as **Cubbie Roo's Castle** and probably the stronghold of a Norse robber baron. There is also a ruined 12th-century chapel, St Mary's.

Old Man of Hoy

Egilsay is 2 miles (3km) east of Rousay. **St Magnus' Cenotaph** marks the site of the murder of Jarl Magnus in 1116, after whom the cathedral in Kirkwall is named. The ruin of St Magnus' Church dominates this small, low-lying island, with a tall, tapering round tower at the west end. This design is of Irish origin, indicating close contact between Ireland and Orkney during Viking times. It was probably built in the 12th century, and its walls still stand to their full height. The tower, nearly 50 feet (15m) high, was once taller still and it seems to beckon from all round. Magnus was killed on the order of his rival, Earl Haakon, who wanted sole power over Orkney. Egilsay has a large proportion of southerners in its small population.

On **Eday**, 4 miles (6.5km) to the east of Egilsay, there are chambered tombs and an Iron Age dwelling that was once a roundhouse with radial divisions inside.

Westray, 7 miles (11km) north of Rousay, has the formidable ruin of **Noltland Castle**. This was built in 1560 by Gilbert Balfour who was implicated in the murder of Cardinal Beaton and served on a French galley beside John Knox in punishment. He was later Master of the Household for Mary, Queen of Scots. Its design is Z-plan, with all-round visibility and an extravagant provision of gun loops. It was burned by Covenanters in 1650.

Papa Westray, 2 miles (3km) off the northeast tip of Westray, is so called from the hermits who lived in the cells here. This island was part of an important Norse family estate in the 11th and 12th centuries and archaeologists discovered the remains of Neolithic settlements which have provided valuable clues to the lifestyle of those ancient inhabitants.

North Ronaldsay is the most northern island of Orkney, 15 miles (24km) east of Papa Westray and 32 miles (51km) northeast of Kirkwall. It is surrounded by a sea dyke designed to keep the unique breed of sheep off the grass, so that they feed from the rich seaweed on the shore. The meat of these small, sturdy animals has a distinctive flavour.

Where to Stay

moderate

Ayre Hotel, Ayre Road, Kirkwall, © 0856 3001, on the waterfront overlooking Kirkwall Bay near the main shopping area, is comfortable and friendly. **Kirkwall Hotel**, Harbour Street, © 0856 2232, overlooking the harbour, has good food.

inexpensive

Barony Hotel, Birsay, © 085672 327, is on the shores of Boardhouse Loch, with views of the village and the Brough of Birsay. Open from May to September, it has free trout fishing. **Merkister Hotel**, Harray, on the edge of Loch Harray, specializes in trout fishing holidays and is open April to October. **Merry Dancers Inn**, Eday, © 08572 221, is a cottage overlooking Calfsound and Calf of Eday. It only has three bedrooms and one bathroom, but it is cosy and has a licence and is ridiculously cheap.

There are plenty more, and dozens of bed and breakfast and self-catering places, all detailed in the brochure. For something a bit different, try **Wildabout**, Inner Urrigar, Costa, Evie, © 0856 75 307. Michael and Jenny Hartley run week-long 'Wildlife Environmental' Holidays with every day planned to take you round the sights of Orkney.

Shetland

Sixty miles (96km) north of Orkney and halfway to Norway, Shetland has its own character, very different from that of Orkney although they share much of their history. In spite of being on the same latitude as Greenland, Shetland's climate is mild, because of the Gulf Stream, with plenty of sunshine in early summer and less rain than the Western Isles. Of the 100 islands in the archipelago, only 15 are continuously inhabited.

According to Tacitus, when the Romans sailed round the north coast of Scotland and found Britain was an island, they 'discovered and subdued' Orkney but they left Shetland alone because of the wild seas that lay between them. He called Shetland *Thule*, that mythical island which the ancients believed lay on the edge of the world. Like Orkney, Shetland has long summer nights, the 'simmer dim' twilight of midsummer adding a touch of timelessness to holidays. The name Shetland is derived from the Norse word *hjaltland*, meaning Highland. Locals talk about Shetland, never the Shetlands. As in Orkney, when they talk about the Mainland, they are referring to the principal island. The terrain is mostly peat bog and rough highland hillside, carpeted with heather and turf and dotted with small lochs—not green and fertile as it is in Orkney. Ronas Hill, to the northwest of Mainland, is the highest point at 1475 feet (454m), and nowhere is more than 3 miles (4.5km) from the sea.

There is wonderful cliff scenery with long winding inlets, called 'voes', battered into arches, fissures and jagged stacks. Few trees survive the gale-force winds that lash the islands. Dairy farming and vegetable crops thrive in the south and central Mainland and sheep-farming is important, including the black and brown Shetland sheep. The Shetland cabbage is salt resistant and grown as a fodder crop. Shetland knitwear is world famous. In the old days the wool was plucked, or 'roo'ed' from the sheep's neck by hand, being too fine for shears, but this is no longer common except for some show animals. A true Shetland shawl should be so fine it can be pulled through a wedding ring.

Shetland ponies roam over the hills, originally mini draught horses on the crofts and then bred for work in coal mines, with 'as much strength as possible and as near the ground as can be got'. The skeleton of one found in the middle of Jarlshof Broch was smaller than the modern breed. They are not strictly wild as they are all owned. They feed on common grazing and efforts are made to improve the breed by introducing good Shetland stallions to run with them. Their tail hair was used as fishing line and it used to be illegal to steal hair from another man's horse.

The old life of crofting, fishing and knitting was greatly changed when the oil boom hit Shetland, but the oil depots are well confined to the Sullom Voe area on the Mainland. They have not spoiled the rest of the islands and have brought a new prosperity. The poet Hugh MacDiarmid said: 'It is indeed impossible to eke out a decent living in Shetland by crofting alone. That is the difference between Orkney and Shetland: the Orcadian is a farmer with a boat, the Shetlander is a fisherman with a croft.'

Up-Helly-Aa is held in Lerwick, on the last Tuesday in January and is a survival from Viking days. This pagan fire festival used to mark the end of Yuletide and symbolize the desire for the sun to appear again after the long winter nights. A Viking galley is carried to a park in the centre of the town amidst a forest of blazing torches and set alight while 'The Norseman's Home' is sung as a funeral dirge. In the old days, blazing barrels of tar were rolled through the streets and carried to the tops of the hills.

Because they were such good seamen, Shetlanders were vulnerable to press gangs. It was not unknown for a whole community of able-bodied young men to be snatched away in a furtive raid from the sea. The fiddle tune 'Jack is yet alive' was composed for a Shetlander

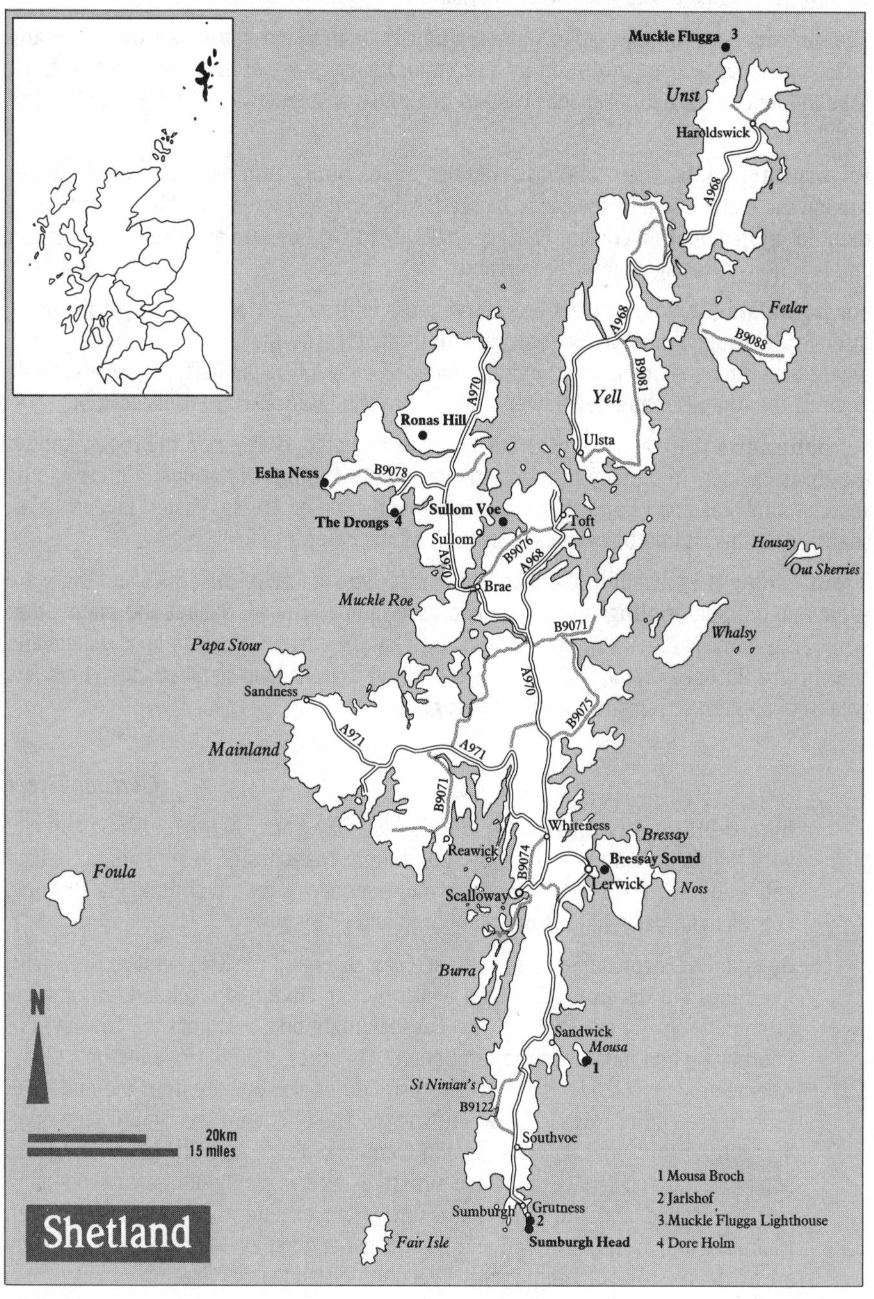

Shetland
Muckle Flugga
3
Unst
Haroldswick
A968
Fetlar
B9088
A968
B9081
Yell
Ulsta
A970
Ronas Hill
Esha Ness
B9078
The Drongs
4
Sullom Voe
Toft
Sullom
B9076
A968
A970
Housay
Out Skerries
Brae
Muckle Roe
B9071
Whalsy
Papa Stour
Sandness
A970
B9075
A971
Mainland
A971
B9071
Whiteness
Bressay
Reawick
B9074
Bressay Sound
Lerwick
Noss
Foula
Scalloway
Burra
N
Sandwick
Mousa
1
St Ninian's
B9122
20km
15 miles
Southvoe
1 Mousa Broch
2 Jarlshof
3 Muckle Flugga Lighthouse
4 Dore Holm
Sumburgh
Grutness
2
Fair Isle
Sumburgh Head

who had been press-ganged, served his time and returned to a family who had written him off long ago. Fiddle music is still very popular throughout the islands.

The seascapes are unforgettable: sudden glimpses of an island-dotted sea with dramatic rocks, cliffs and beaches, suffused by an extraordinary clarity of light. The colours must have influenced the natural shades used in the knitwear, particularly those in the Fair Isle designs.

For **ornithologists**, there are vast colonies of sea birds, both northern and migrant. Among the many hundred species to be seen is the Shetland wren, 'stinkie', even smaller than her more common cousin. Fair Isle, halfway to Orkney, has an observation station and is famous as a staging post for migrants.

For **botanists** the wild flowers are marvellous, with around 500 species of plants to discover. Because much of the pasture is untreated, many that have become rare elsewhere have survived, including the rather hideous large Australian daisy. There are Arctic flowers, the American mondey flower, and the tiny blue Caucasus from Asia Minor.

For **naturalists** there are vast quantities of seals to watch, basking on the rocks, known locally as 'selkies' (too many of them, in fact, due to culling restrictions). Otters can be seen, around small rocks and skerries in the remoter coastal areas. Whales, killer whales, sharks, dolphins and porpoises can all be seen off the coast.

Trout fishing is excellent in the lochs, of which there are more than 300, and there are some salmon. **Sea angling** is first class and fishermen catch cod, halibut and many other white fish. Porbeagle shark of up to 450lbs (200kg) have been caught in local waters and the current European record of a 226.5 lb (100kg) skate is held by Shetland. There is a wealth of prehistoric remains for **archaeologists**.

Getting There

By air: British Airways operate four flights a day from Aberdeen. These connect with flights to and from Glasgow, Edinburgh, Manchester, Birmingham, Belfast and London. They also operate a daily service from Inverness, via Orkney. Loganair run daily flights from Edinburgh and Glasgow.

By sea: P&O Scottish Services operate a passenger and car ferry service, overnight, five times a week from Aberdeen to Lerwick, including a weekend crossing via Orkney. From June to August, the Tuesday night boat also goes via Orkney. For information and booking write or phone P&O Ferries, PO Box 5, Jamieson's Quay, Aberdeen, ✆ 0224 572615. P&O Scottish Ferries also operate from the middle of June to the end of August, between Norway and Shetland, and Smyril Line operates during the same period between Denmark, Faroe and Shetland. There are good bus and taxi services from the airport, as well as plenty of hire cars. Shetland roads are good and the inter-island ferries are excellent. The ferries between Mainland and Yell, North Yell and Unst, Unst and Fetlar, Mainland and Whalsay are all roll-on, roll-off. There is also a good inter-island air service.

Tourist Information

Shetland Islands Tourism Information Centre, **Lerwick**, ✆ 0595 3434.

Mainland

Mainland is by far the biggest of the islands, its chief town being **Lerwick**, Britain's most northerly town, so called from the Norse *leir-vik* meaning 'clay creek'. Looking over sheltered Bressay Sound, Lerwick has always been a refuge for seafarers. In spite of its geographical isolation, it is a lot more up-to-date and cosmopolitan than many of the towns in the Highland region of Scotland. It was a stopping-off port for Norsemen: King Haakon reprovisioned his fleet here on the way to defeat at Largs in 1263.

Lerwick has always been important for fishing: the home waters are productive and it lies on the edge of the valuable northern fishing fields. Dutch fishing fleets were based here in the 17th century and by the 18th century the export of salt fish was thriving. In the 17th century the town became important as a base for the British Navy. Fort Charlotte was built in 1665 to protect the Sound of Bressay from the Dutch.

The buildings that grew up round the port were sturdy and compact, designed to withstand violent storms. Many of them were the town houses of Scottish lairds who succeeded the Norsemen and found winter conditions rather bleak.

The *Dim Riv* is a replica Norse longship, over 40 feet (12m) long, and she takes visitors on trips round the harbour in the summer. The harbour is a lively, bustling place with a picturesque waterfront, and charmingly haphazard, flagstoned Commercial Street, straggling up behind. This is the main shopping centre of the town, and the steep, narrow lanes around it are said to cover a network of secret tunnels and passages used by smugglers in the past. Boat trips run from Victoria Pier, to cruise round the coast in the summer. Look out for the distinctive Shetland sailing dinghy, a local design with the elegant double-prow effect of the Viking longboats. They can be seen in most of the harbours around Shetland and are raced in local regattas.

Fort Charlotte (open daily: free), built by Cromwellian troops, was partly burned by the Dutch in 1673. It was repaired and restored in 1781 and garrisoned during the Napoleonic wars. It is the only Cromwellian military building still intact in Scotland.

The **Town Hall** above Commercial Street in Hillhead is a Victorian-Gothic building, partly resembling a church with tower and rose window, four corner turrets, a central oriel window and stained-glass windows on the upper floor. These enclose the main hall and depict the history of Shetland, beginning with the Scandinavian conquest in 870. There are full-length figures of Norway's King Harald Harfagri, the conqueror of the islands, and Rognvald, Jarl of More, to whom Harald offered the first earldom. The windows cover all the main events in Shetland's story and include one of the Maid of Norway, who died at sea nearby.

The **Shetland Museum** (open daily except Sun: free) is opposite the town hall. It has four galleries devoted to the history of man in Shetland, from prehistoric times to the present. Look for the **Papil Stone**, dating from the 7th century, showing a procession of papas, or priests, one of whom is on a horse. Other exhibits include the history of Shetland knitting and the history of the islands' marine and fishing past. There are also replicas of the treasure found on St Ninian's Isle.

These beautiful islands are an inspiration to artists and there are exhibitions of local art and crafts in the **Shetland Workshop Gallery** (open daily: free) in Burns Lane.

Clickhimin Broch (always accessible) is on the western outskirts of the town, on an island in a loch, reached by a causeway. It is 65 feet (20m) in diameter, its walls 18 feet (5.5m) thick and 15 feet (4.5m) high, on a massive stone platform. Excavations on this site suggest that it may have been a late Bronze Age settlement.

A frequent car ferry crosses to the island of **Bressay** just east of Lerwick, and from here a boat crosses the 200 yards (185m) to the bird sanctuary on **Noss**. (It is only open to the public from mid-May to the end of August.)

Scalloway is Mainland's other town, in an attractive bay 7 miles (11km) west of Lerwick. It was the capital until 200 years ago and is still an important fishing port. It is much older than Lerwick and retains a quiet, old-fashioned atmosphere. There is a small local **museum** in the middle of the town, which has, among other things, a detailed history of the Shetland Bus. During the Second World War, small Norwegian fishing boats crossed to Nazi-occupied Norway to carry out sabotage or to land secret agents and bring back refugees. 'To take the Shetland Bus' meant to escape from Norway. **Lunna House**, in northeast Mainland, now a guest house, was the original headquarters of this Norwegian Resistance Movement, before it was transfered to Scalloway. *The Shetland Bus* by David Howarth, recently reprinted, gives a good account of the operation.

Scalloway Castle (always accessible) dominates the town, a forbidding ruin built by Earl Patrick Stewart in 1600. Stewart was the notorious despot who tyrannized Orkney and Shetland until he was executed. Built in medieval style, the roofless shell, with corner turrets and gables, stands on a narrow promontory by the water. The Earl is said to have hung his victims from an iron ring in one of the chimneys. The castle was, not surprisingly, left to rot after the Earl's death.

There are bridges across to the islands of **Tronda** and **Burra** just to the south. Scalloway is at the southern end of the agricultural valley of **Tingwall**, so called after the site of the old Norse parliament, or *thing*, at the north end of **Tingwall Loch**, reached by stepping stones.

At **Whiteness,** 7 miles (11km) north of Scalloway, the **Hjaltasteyn Workshop** (open weekdays: free) produces handmade jewellery, in silver, gold and enamel.

South of Lerwick

Mousa Broch (open daily: free, with a fee for ferry), on **Mousa Island**, is one of Shetland's main archaeological treasures. The boat runs, weather permitting, from **Sandwick**, 11 miles (17.5km) south of Lerwick. Mousa Island, a mile (1.5km) offshore, is inhabited only by sheep and ponies and its broch is the best preserved in existence. It is a thrilling experience to climb its steps, walking in the footsteps of its Pictish builders 2000 years ago. Over 50 feet (15m) in diameter, 45 feet (14m) high, with walls that taper from 12 feet (3.5m) to 7 feet (2m) in thickness, this was one of the smallest of the brochs and probably one of the latest. Galleries honeycomb its double walls and stairways lead to a parapet round the top. This broch illustrates clearly how the builders tapered the walls inwards to within about 10 feet (3m) of the top and then sloped them outwards, making it impossible for invaders to climb up.

Mousa appears romantically in two of the old sagas. In 1150, the Norwegian Prince Erland abducted a famous beauty and held her in the broch until her son, a Jarl, unable to storm the impregnable fortress, had to consent to their marriage. Another saga tells of a young man called Bjorn, who brought Thora, whom he had seduced, to Mousa in 900 and here they set up home together.

St Ninian's Isle is 4 miles (6.5km) southwest of Sandwick, off the west coast of Mainland. You can walk to it along a white crescent of sand, called a 'tombolo', that forms a causeway. Here are the foundations of a 12th-century chapel, buried by sand for many hundreds of years. In 1958, Aberdeen University began excavating the site and discovered not only the foundations of the chapel, but also a Bronze Age burial ground and the remains of a pre-Norse church.

Under a stone slab in the chapel nave they found a hoard of 8th-century Celtic silver, now in the Royal Museum of Scotland, in Edinburgh, with a replica collection in the museum in Lerwick. It is believed that this wonderful hoard was buried by the monks who lived here, probably during an invasion threat from Vikings. The treasure includes silver bowls, delicate brooches and a Communion spoon.

The Shetland Croft Museum (open daily, 1 May–30 Sept: adm) is at **Boddam** on the east coast of Mainland, 5 miles (8km) south of Sandwick. The museum is a restored croft house, typical of the mid-19th century. Inside the cottage is the original driftwood furniture and all the domestic utensils, giving a picture of how crofters lived in the last century. There is also the old watermill, down the hill by the burn. Recently restored **Quendale Mill** (open daily except Monday, May–Sept: adm) gives the history of a working 19th-century watermill.

Sumburgh, with the airport, is at the southern tip of Mainland, 27 miles (43km) south of Lerwick. The modern, clean-cut buildings at the airport present a remarkable contrast to the antiquity of Jarlshof, nearby.

Jarlshof (site always accessible: free; visitor centre open daily, April–Sept: adm) was a name invented by Sir Walter Scott in *The Pirate*. He visited the island in 1814, was impressed by the laird's hall and wrote his story around it. He was not to know how misleading this name was to prove because it was not until 1905 that a violent storm revealed that this was a site that had been occupied for over 3000 years, by seven distinct civilizations of which the Norse Jarls were by far the most recent.

The remains of these village settlements, from Bronze Age to Viking, are sprawled over a low green promontory by the sea. The first house dates from the early or middle part of the second millennium BC. It would be impossible to sort out the various ages and purposes of the conglomeration of stones without the excellent explanations displayed, and the very helpful guide book. The Bronze Age huts include cattle stalls and a metal workshop; the Iron Age settlement has two earth houses and a broch. The three 8th-century wheel-houses are thought to be family dwellings consisting of a number of individual recesses separated as if by the spokes of a wheel, all around a central hearth. A confusion of long-houses is all that is left of the Norse occupation. It was the now-ruined medieval farmhouse that Sir Walter used as his setting. A museum exhibits some of the artefacts that have been dug from the site as well as a good ground plan and an interpretive display showing the history of Jarlshof.

North of Lerwick

Sandness is about 25 miles (40km) northwest of Lerwick and boats run from West Burrafirth, nearby, to **Papa Stour**, a couple of miles off the coast. The boats go four times a week and day trips are possible on Fridays and Saturdays. The sea caves are believed to be the finest in Britain, but you will need to hire a boat locally to see them properly. The scent from the wild flowers on Papa Stour was said to be so strong that fishermen could fix their position from it if caught in fog out at sea.

Lunna is about 18 miles (29km) north of Lerwick as the crow flies, out on the east coast. When Lunna House, now a small hotel, was the original headquarters of the Norwegian Resistance, the barns and outhouses were used as an arsenal. Lunna Kirk is one of the oldest Shetland churches still in use. Built in 1753, it is a charming old building with a leper squint, through which lepers could listen to the service and receive Communion.

At **Brae**, about 23 miles (37km) north of Lerwick, a narrow neck of land called **Mavis Grind** prevents the northwest corner of Mainland from being an island. You can stand on this 'anchor cable' of land and throw a stone one way into the Atlantic and the other way into the North Sea.

Sullom Voe Oil Terminal (pronounced Soolem), with its complex of buildings and jetties, is on the peninsula of **Calback Ness**, 7 miles (11km) northeast of Brae, joined to Mainland by reclaimed land. The terminal is tucked away so discreetly that you are hardly aware of it, though you cannot miss the ugly buildings that house the oil workers—incongruous against the bleak landscape. **Firth**, nearby, was built to house the oilmen. **Toft** is 4 miles (6.5km) east of Sullom Voe and from here the car ferry crosses to **Yell**, 3 miles (4.5km) northeast.

This northern part of Mainland is dominated by **Ronas Hill**, Shetland's highest point, 1475 feet (454m) high, 10 miles (16km) north of Brae, and well worth climbing for marvellous views.

Eshaness, on the coast of Mainland, 15 miles (24km) northwest of Brae, has precipitous cliffs and breathtaking views of the **Drongs**, a collection of weird stacks carved by the force of the ocean. These stacks include a huge natural arch called the **Dore Holm**.

The island of **Yell**, to the north, is mostly peat moor. It was described by Eric Linklater as 'dull and dark and one large peat bog'. Although the second-largest of the Shetland islands, it has suffered from depopulation and can be rather depressing. It is one of the best places in Britain to see otters.

A Minister of the Kirk once said: 'Yell is Hell, but Unst—Oh! Unst!' **Unst** is Britain's most northern island, with the **Muckle Flugga** lighthouse on a rock just off its northern tip. The lighthouse was built by Robert Louis Stevenson's father and while he was designing and building it, his son stayed on Unst, dreaming up the story of *Treasure Island.* Unst supports a number of Shetland ponies and it has wonderful cliff scenery. Philatelists can get a special frank on their letters at Britain's most northerly post office in **Haroldswick,** in northeast Unst, the place where Harald Harfagri landed from Norway to subdue the troublesome Vikings.

Fetlar, east of Yell and much smaller, derives its name from the Norn name for 'fat land' and is the most fertile of the islands, with a large number of birds. Snowy owls bred on Fetlar until 1975, when the resident male died. Now, although they no longer breed there, visiting females can still be seen. They have a buzzard-like flight and distinctive white plumage. Another of Fetlar's rare visitors is the red-necked phalarope with a long, needle-like beak, which spins round on the water to stir up insects. The whimbrel, rather like a smaller curlew, usually a coastal migrant, nests on Fetlar and can be seen combing the shore for molluscs and worms with its long curved beak.

Whalsay, a couple of miles off northeast Mainland, is important for fishing and fish processing. On the pier there is a 17th-century Hanseatic trading booth. The Hanseatic League merchants came from northern Germany to Shetland to trade, buying fish and salting it for export, until salt tax was introduced in 1712. The traders set up booths like this one, from which they offered fine cloth, fishing tackle, exotic foods, tobacco, fruit and gin at a farthing a pint, in exchange for fish, butter, wool and fish oil. It is intriguing to look at this quiet, peaceful place and picture what it was like when the merchants haggled and bartered from their booths.

Whalsay has two prehistoric sites: the **Standing Stones**, at Yoxie, and the **Benie Hoose**, thought to have been the dwelling for the Druid priests who were responsible for the ceremonies performed around the standing stones.

Foula is an island 27 miles (43km) west of Mainland, with dramatic cliff scenery and a colony of skuas. Still inhabited, it is often cut off in bad weather. This was the last place where Norn was spoken, in the 19th century.

Fair Isle

Fair Isle is 24 miles (38km) southwest of Sumburgh on Mainland, and boats run to it from Grutness Pier, on Sumburgh Head. These aren't day trips: there is a three-day stay on the island before the next boat back. Alternatively, Loganair operate two flights from Tingwall Airport on Mondays, Wednesdays and Fridays, making a day's outing possible. Fair Isle, the 'Far Isle' of the Vikings, halfway between Orkney and Shetland, is a buffer between the Atlantic and the North Sea. It must be the most gale-battered island in Britain, presenting a tough challenge to the 60-odd people who live there. The bird population is enormous, preserved by the warden of the **Observatory**. Over 300 species have been recorded on Fair Isle; as well as resident colonies, it is a regular staging post for many migratory birds.

Although bleak, Fair Isle is magnificent, with needle-sharp rocks pounded by ferocious seas and sheer cliffs topped by green turf and wild flowers. Paying guests can stay at the Observatory in the summer.

Fair Isle knitting is internationally renowned. There is an island co-operative of men and women who work machines and hand finish 200 orders of Fair Isle jumpers, scarves, hats and gloves a year. These are only sold on the island. Each jersey takes seven hours to finish by hand. The designs date back to Viking times, possibly influenced by the Moorish patterns learnt from the survivors of a Spanish Armada shipwreck, in 1588, who were given shelter by the islanders.

Where to Stay

expensive

Kveldsro House Hotel, Lerwick, © 0595 2195, is highly recommended with four crowns, overlooking the harbour. **Lerwick Hotel**, © 0595 2166, 10 minutes' walk from the town centre, is a hideous modern building with a glorious view over Breiwick Bay and Bressay Island. What it lacks in style and character, however, it makes up for in comfort and service and it has four crowns. **Shetland Hotel**, Holmsgarth Road, © 0595 5515, is another modern horror, opposite the ferry terminal. It is comfortable and well run with a friendly staff and has five crowns.

Busta House, Busta, © 080622 506, is a large old country house, full of character, with four crowns, good food and wine and a selection of 120 malt whiskies.

moderate

Queens Hotel, © 0595 2826, with three crowns, is right on the water in Commercial Street, picturesque, old fashioned and comfortable, at the top of the price range. **Grand Hotel**, © 0595 2826, is in Commercial Street in the centre of the town, with an imposing castellated tower. It has three crowns and Shetland's only nightclub.

Sumburgh Hotel, © 0950 60201, close to the airport and next to Jarlshof, is an old laird's house, with lots of character and very friendly, with four crowns.

inexpensive

Westings Hotel, Wormdale, Whiteness, © 059584 242, is a family-run hotel with gorgeous sea views. It's easy-going and friendly, with three crowns. **St Magnus Bay Hotel**, Hillswick, © 080623 372/3, is a charming Norwegian-style hotel overlooking the bay, comfortable and hospitable.

For a really cosy, friendly bed and breakfast, try Mrs W. J. Hutchison, Orablaa, 3 Twageos Road, Lerwick, © 0595 3417.

Fair Isle Bird Observatory Lodge, © 03512 258, is idyllic. The building is modern and unbeautiful but it offers the perfect holiday for anyone interested in nature and hospitality. Open from April to October, its 12 bedrooms share one bathroom, its staff are relaxed and friendly and its outlook sublime. Full board.

83 Defeat of Picts at battle of Mons Graupius by Roman Agricola.

141–2 Building of Antonine Wall.

397 Founding of Christian church at Whithorn by St Ninian.

410 Departure of Romans from Britain.

500 Invasion of Scotland by Irish Scots, settlement of Dalriada.

563 Landing of St Columba in Iona, conversion of Picts to Christianity begins.

794 Invasion of Hebrides by Norsemen.

844–60 Kenneth Macalpine unites Picts and Scots.

1034 Whole of Scotland united into one kingdom under Duncan I.

1040 Duncan I murdered by Macbeth who is in turn murdered by Malcolm Canmore.

1057–93 Anglicizing of Scotland under Queen Margaret.

1102 Western Isles granted to Magnus of Orkney.

1124–53 David I founds many abbeys and burghs, grants land to Normans.

1174 William the Lion forced to acknowledge supremacy of Henry II.

1214 Alexander II, Golden Age of Scottish history.

1263 Battle of Largs, defeat by Alexander III of King Haakon of Norway. Annexation of the Hebrides.

1286 Death of Alexander III, succeeded by Margaret of Norway.

1290 Death of Maid of Norway at sea on her way to Scotland.

1291 Edward I arbitrates between Robert the Bruce and John Balliol. Balliol gets crown.

1296 Balliol renounces his crown in favour of Edward I. Scottish nobility agree to treaty of mutual assistance with Philip IV of France—the beginning of the Auld Alliance.

1297–98 William Wallace stirs up resistance, defeats Edward at Stirling Bridge, and is defeated at Falkirk. Goes into hiding.

1305 Capture and execution of William Wallace.

Chronology

1306 Robert Bruce slays John Comyn and is crowned at Scone.

1307 Edward I dies.

1314 Battle of Bannockburn, Bruce defeats English.

1320 Declaration of Arbroath.

1326 First Scottish Parliament at Cambuskenneth.

1328 By treaty of Edinburgh England recognizes Robert the Bruce as king of independent Scotland

1346 Battle of Neville's Cross. David II taken prisoner by English.

1371 Robert Stewart crowned Robert II, first Stewart King.

1406 James I captured, Duke of Albany become guardian of Scotland.

1414 Foundation of St Andrews, Scotland's first university.

1450–5 Struggle for supremacy between Stewarts and Douglases. Douglases crushed by James II.

1469 Orkney and Shetland pledged to James III as part of dowry of his wife, Margaret of Denmark.

1476 Overthrow of Lords of the Isles.

1488 James III defeated and killed by rebels at Sauchieburn

1491 Perkin Warbeck claims English throne, encouraged by James IV.

1503 James IV marries Margaret Tudor, daughter of Henry VII.

1513 Battle of Flodden, death of James IV.

1528 Burning of Patrick Hamilton, proto–martyr of Reformation.

1538 Marriage of James V to Marie de Guise-Lorraine.

1542 Defeat of Scots at Solway Moss, death of James V, accession of his infant daughter, Mary.

1544 Rough Wooing, devastation of Lowland Scotland by Henry VIII.

1546 Burning of George Wishart, murder of Cardinal Beaton.

1554 Regency of Marie de Guise.

1557 Signing of first Protestant Covenant.

1558 Marriage of Mary to Dauphin of France, later Francis II.

1559 John Knox returns to Scotland. Reformers destroy the abbey church at Scone.

1561 Mary, Queen of Scots returns to Scotland

1565 Marriage of Mary to Darnley. Moray's rebellion is suppressed.

1566 Murder of Rizzio. Birth of James VI.

1567 Murder of Darnley, marriage of Mary to Bothwell, defeat, imprisonment and abdication.

1568 Mary escapes to England and is imprisoned by Elizabeth.

1570 Moray is assassinated and Lennox becomes regent of Scotland.

1582 James VI is abducted in the Ruthven raid.

1587 Mary, Queen of Scots is executed.

1603 Accession of James VI to English throne making him James VI/I (VI of Scotland, I of England). Establishment of Episcopacy in Scotland.

1637 Riots of Edinburgh against Charles I's new prayer book.

1638 Signing of National Covenant to uphold Presbyterian worship.

1643 Signing of Solemn League and Covenant recognized by English Parliament.

1645 Battle of Philiphaugh. Defeat of Royalist Montrose by Covenanters under Leslie.

1646 Charles surrenders to the Scots.

1647 The Scots give Charles to the English.

1649 Execution of Charles I, Charles II proclaimed King in Scotland.

1650 Signing of Covenants by Charles II. Invasion of Scotland by Cromwell.

1660 Restoration of Monarchy.

1662 Renunciation of Covenants by Charles II and re-establishment of Episcopacy.

1666 Start of the Killing Times, persecution of Covenanters.

1688 James VII/II tries to restore Catholicism. He is deposed in favour of William and Mary.

1689 Highlanders, under Claverhouse, Bonnie Dundee, defeat King's army at Killiecrankie.

1692 Massacre of Glencoe.

1695 Bank of Scotland founded and Company of Scotland established to colonize Darien coast.

1699 Darien colony evacuated.

***c.*1700–**
***c.*1800** The Age of Enlightenment

1707 Union of Parliaments.

1715 Rebellion in favour of the Old Pretender.

1736 The Porteous Riots, Scots rebel against English domination.

1745/6 Final Jacobite rebellion. Defeat of Prince Charles Edward Stuart at Battle of Culloden. Repression of Highlands. Soon followed by the beginning of the Highland Clearances which lasted for over 100 years and depopulated the Highlands.

1760 Carron Ironworks starts production.

1845/6 Irish potato famine spreads to Scotland causing starvation and terrible hardship.

1947 Founding of Edinburgh International Festival, putting Scotland back on the cultural map.

1970s North Sea oil industry developed.

1979 Scotland rejects devolution in a referendum.

Kenneth Macalpine: 843–58
Donald: 858–62
Constantine I: 862–77
Aed: 877–8
Eochaid and Giric (joint kingship): 878–89
Donald II: 889–900
Constantine II: 900–43
Malcolm I: 943–54
Indulf: 954–62
Dubh: 962–6
Culen: 966–71
Kenneth II: 971–95
Constantine III: 995–7
Kenneth III: 997–1005
Malcolm II: 1005–34
Duncan I: 1034–40
Macbeth: 1040–57
Lulach: 1058
Malcolm III, Canmore: 1058–93
Donald III Bane: 1093–4 (six months)
Duncan II: 1094 (six months)
Donald III Bane: 1094–7
Edgar: 1097–1107
Alexander I: 1107–24
David I: 1124–53
Malcolm IV, the Maiden: 1153–65
William I, the Lion: 1165–1214
Alexander II: 1214–49
Alexander III: 1249–86
Margaret, Maid of Norway: 1286–90
John Balliol: 1292–6

Stewarts

Robert II: 1371–90
Robert III: 1390–1406
James I: 1406–37
James II: 1437–60
James III: 1460–88
James IV: 1488–1513
James V: 1513–42
Mary: 1542–67
James VI/I: 1567–1625
Charles I: 1625–49
The Commonwealth: 1649–60
Charles II: 1660–85
James VII/II: 1685–8
William and Mary: 1689–94
William (alone): 1694–1702
Anne: 1702–1714

Hanoverians

George I: 1714–27
George II: 1727–60
George III: 1760–1820
George IV: 1820–30
William II/IV: 1830–7

Saxe-Coburg-Gotha

Victoria: 1837–1901
Edward I/VII: 1901–10

Windsors

George V: 1910–36

Scottish Monarchs

Interregnum: 1296–1306
Robert I (the Bruce): 1306–29
David II: 1329–71

Edward II/VIII: 1936
George VI: 1936–52
Elizabeth I/II: 1952–

Clans and Families

The Gaelic *clann* means offspring, family, stock, race, derived from Latin *planta*—meaning 'sprout' or 'scion'.

When Robert the Bruce released Scotland from the English yoke in 1314, he opened the field for tremendous power struggles between the leading clans. Some became too powerful, others sank into obscurity. Many families, too weak to survive alone, sought the protection of stronger neighbours; some of these took the name of their adopted chief, others retained their own names. Thus many clans have 'septs' and dependants. Clans amalgamated for strength: the Clan Chattan Confederation consisted of a large number of clans who joined forces under Mackintosh hegemony. The chiefs of the Highland clans ruled with total disregard for the authority of the Crown, as did the powerful Border families. The final Jacobite rebellion, in 1745–56, resulted in the death of the old clan system. (See also 'Clans and Tartans', in 'Topics'.)

Today, although all that is left is the clan name, many still live in the area traditionally associated with their clan and there remains a pride and sense of loyalty so strong that people come from all over the world to visit the land of their ancestors. This is a list of the main clans and families, with the address (where there is one) of the clan secretary, or clan centre, who will send more information if required. Names not included will be those of septs, or clan branches. Anyone seriously seeking their roots should get hold of *The Clan Almanac*, by Charles Maclean, published by Lochar, a comprehensive little book which lists, among other things, the septs and dependants of the main clans: thus if you are called Abbot, for instance, you will find you are part of the Macnab clan. Mac and Mc mean son of, as of course does any name ending in son.

Anderson: son of Andrew, Highland version MacAndrew. They came from Badenoch and their motto is 'Stand Sure'. In the 15th century they were part of the Clan Chattan Confederation. Clan Chattan Secretary, Dyunmaglash, Westhill, Inverness-shire.

Armstrong: the original, armour-bearer to a King of Scots, saved his king, fallen in a battle, by lifting him on to his horse. He was given land as a reward and named Strong-arm. They were Borderers and their motto *Invictus maneo* means 'I remain unvanquished'. Clan Secretary, Brieryshaw, Langholm, Dumfriesshire.

Baird: from an old Scots word meaning sumptuous dress. They came from Aberdeenshire and their motto *Dominus fecit* means 'The Lord made'.

Barclay: derived from the Berkeley family who came over with William the Conqueror. They settled in Aberdeenshire and Kincardineshire and their motto *Aut agere aut mori* means 'Either action or death'.

Blair: from Gaelic *blar*—field, battlefield; motto: *Amo Probos*—'I love the righteous'. An ancient family, one branch having roots in Renfrew, Ayr and Wigtown; and another in Perth, Fife and Angus. The Barony of Blair, in Ayrshire, was granted by William the Lion in the 12th century. When the two branches competed for chieftainship, James VI settled the dispute by appointing the oldest man in either family to be chief. Thus the honour alternates, depending upon seniority. Clan Secretary, 15 Brompton Terrace, Perth.

Brodie: from their Norman ancestor, de Brothie. They settled in Morayshire and their motto is 'Unite'. Clan Secretary, Brodie Castle, Forres, Moray.

Bruce: from the French town Brix—Adam de Brus came over with William the Conqueror. They lived in Annandale, Clackmannan and Elgin and their motto, *Fuimus*, means 'We have been'. Robert the Bruce won independence for Scotland at the Battle of Bannockburn in 1314; Thomas Bruce, 7th Earl of Elgin and 11th Earl of Kincardine, 1766–1841, rescued the decorated sculptures on the Parthenon from vandalism and installed them in the British Museum.

Buchanan: from Gaelic *mac-a-Chanonaich*—son of the canon. They lived around Loch Lomond and their motto is *Clarior hinc honos*—'Brighter hence the honour'. Clan secretary, Brechin Robb, 24 George Square, Glasgow.

Cameron: from Gaelic *cam-shron*—crooked nose. They lived in Northern Argyll and Locheil. Their mottos, translated from Gaelic, are: 'Unite'; 'For King and Country'; and 'Sons of the hounds come here and get flesh'. The Cameron Highlanders, now amalgamated with the Seaforth Highlanders to become the Queen's Own Highlanders, were raised by Sir Alan Cameron in 1793. Their Clan Centre is at Aberchalder, Loch Eil, and the new Clan Cameron Museum is at Achnacarry. Clan Secretary, 78 Milton Road West, Edinburgh.

Campbell: from Gaelic *cam-beul*—crooked mouth. They came from Argyll, Cawdor, Loudoun and Breadalbane. Their various mottos are: 'Forget not'; 'Follow me'; 'Be mindful'; 'I byde my tyme'. The Duke of Argyll is their chief and the clan centre is Inverary Castle, Argyll.

Chisholm: means a water meadow which produces milk good for cheese-making. They lived in Roxburghshire and Berwickshire and later moved to Inverness-shire. Their motto *Feros ferio* means 'I am fierce with the fierce'. Clan Secretary, 21 Blytheswood Square, Glasgow.

Colquhoun (pronounced *k'hoon*): the name comes from the Barony, in Dunbartonshire and they lived around Loch Lomond. Their motto, *Si je puis*—'If I can', was said by one of their ancestors, to James I, when ordered to capture Dumbarton Castle. (He did.)

Cumming: the name derives from the herb cummin, which is thei the clan's emblem. Cummings come from Roxburghshire, Buchan, Badenoch and Altyre and their motto is 'Courage'. The Comyns came to Scotland during the reign of Malcolm Canmore in the 11th century, and it was Sir John Comyn—'The Red Comyn', who was murdered by Robert the Bruce in order to gain the Crown. Clan Secretary, House of Altyre, Forres.

Douglas: from Gaelic *dubh glais*—black water. They lived in Lanarkshire, Galloway, Dumfriesshire and Angus and were as powerful as kings in the Middle Ages. Their motto, *Jamais arrière*, means 'Never behind'. Archibald Douglas became known as Bell-the-cat, from his undertaking to kill the much-despised favourites of James III. Sir James Douglas was killed in 1330, while honouring his promise to take Robert the Bruce's heart to the Holy Land.

Drummond: derived from Drymen, near Stirling. They came from Perthshire and their motto is 'Gang (go) warily'.

Duncan: more properly Clan Donnachaidh—Brown Warriors. They came from Atholl and Lundie in Fife and their motto is *Disce parti*—'Learn to suffer'. Donnaichaidh Clan Secretary, 127 Rose Street, South Lane, Edinburgh.

Elliot (there are different spellings): probably derived from Old English *Aelfwald*—Elf Ruler, which became the Christian name Elward. They were one of the strongest of the Border families and their mottos are *Soyez sage*—'Be wise', and *Fortiter et Recte*—'With Strength and Right'. Clan Secretary, Redheugh, Newcastleton, Roxburghshire.

Erskine: from the Barony of Erskine in Renfrewshire. They lived around Alloa and their motto is *Je pense plus*—'I think more'. John Erskine, 11th Earl of Mar, was known as Bobbing John during the Jacobite rebellions because he kept changing sides.

Farquharson: the Gaelic *fearchar* means dear one, and they came from Aberdeenshire and Invercauld. Their motto is *Fide et Fortitudine*—'By Fidelity and Fortitude'. They were part of the Clan Chattan Confederation. Clan Chattan Secretary, Dyunmaglash, Westhill, Inverness-shire.

Ferguson: Fergus founded the Scottish kingdom of Dalriada and they inhabited the lands of Argyll, Perthshire, Dumfries, Galloway and Raith. Their motto is *Dulcius ex asperis*—'Sweeter after difficulties'. They are one of the oldest clans of Scotland. Clan Secretary, Pendle Cottage, Dunigoyne, Glasgow.

Forbes: from Gaelic *forba*—field or district. They were powerful in Aberdeenshire and their motto is 'Grace me guide'. Clan Secretary, Balforbes, Lonach, Donside, Aberdeenshire.

Fraser: of Norman derivation, from *fraises*—strawberry flowers. Originally they were in East Lothian, then Aberdeenshire. Their motto is *Je suis prest*—'I am ready'. Clan Secretary, Balblair House, Beauly, Black Isle, Ross-shire.

Gordon: from Gordon in Berwickshire, where they settled, as Anglo-Normans, in the 12th century. They became very powerful in the northeast in Strathbogie, Deeside and around Aberdeen, and their chief was called Cock of the North. Their mottos are *Animo non Astutia*—'By Courage, not Craft'; and *Bydand*—'Remaining'. Clan Secretary, Harlaw House, Harlaw Hill, Prestonpans, East Lothian.

Graham: Anglo-Saxon origin—*graeg ham*, meaning grey home. William de Graham came to Scotland with David I, who gave him lands and the family became prominent in the Wars of Independence. Their lands included those north of Glasgow,

Loch Katrine, part of Perthshire, and around Dundee and Montrose. Their motto is *Ne Oublie*—'Do not forget'. Among their greatest ancestors were Montrose, that gallant Royalist, and Graham of Claverhouse (Bonnie Dundee), hero of Killiecrankie in 1689. Clan Secretary, 23 Ardmillan Terrace, Edinburgh.

Grant: derived from the French *grand*—'great'. Their origins are disputed: some say the first Grant was a Nottinghamshire squire married into an Inverness-shire family, some that they are descended from Kenneth MacAlpine, some that they are descended from MacGregors. Their lands were Strathspey, Rothiemurchas, Glen Moriston and Loch Ness and their motto is 'Stand fast'. Clan Secretary, 18 Great Stewart Street, Edinburgh.

Gunn: possibly from Gunni, in the Norse sagas, or from Gaelic *guineach*, meaning fierce, or of Pictish descent. Their lands were in Caithness and Sutherland and their motto is *Aut Pax Aut Bellum*—'Either Peace or War'. Clan Secretary, 22 Muirhouse Gardens, Edinburgh.

Hamilton: derived from Hameldone, meaning crooked hill', in England, whence came Walter Fitz-Gilbert to lands in Renfrewshire and Arran during the Wars of Independence. Their motto is 'Through'. Patrick Hamilton, 1498–1528, was the proto-martyr of the Scottish Reformation. Clan Secretary, Lennoxlove, Haddington, East Lothian.

Hay: derived from La Haye, in Normandy, which stemmed from *haie*, meaning hedge. Their lands were Aberdeenshire and Tweedale and their motto is *Serva jugum*—'Keep the yoke'. Clan Secretary, 12 St Peter's Place, Edinburgh. Clan Centre, Delgatie Castle, Turriff, Grampian.

Henderson: in Gaelic, this clan is MacEanraig, anglicized as MacKendrick. Their lands were Caithness and Glencoe and their motto is *Sola Virtus nobilitat*—'Virtue alone ennobles'.

Home (pronounced Hume): derived from Gaelic *uamh*—cave. Their lands were the Borders and their motto is 'A Home, a Home!' Among their scions were David Hume, the great philosopher of the Scottish Enlightenment and Sir Alec Douglas-Home, Prime Minister of Britain.

Innes: meaning 'greens'. Innes was a town in Morayshire for which the family received a royal charter in the 12th century. Their motto is *Be traist*—'Be faithful'. Clan Secretary, 35 East Clarmont Street, Edinburgh.

Johnstone: derived from John's *toun*—homestead; the Gaelic for John is Iain, giving MacIain. There are various spellings but Johnson is uncommon in Scotland. They were a powerful Border family and also had lands in Aberdeenshire. Their mottos are *Numquam non paratus*—'Never unprepared', and 'Light thieves all'.

Keith: from the town of Keith in Banffshire. Their lands stretched from East Lothian to Caithness and they held the hereditary office of Great Marischal of Scotland from the 12th to the 18th centuries. Their motto is *Veritas vincit*—'Truth conquers'. Clan Secretary, North Dykes, Kilbirnie, Ayrshire.

Kennedy: from Gaelic *ceann éitigh*—grim-headed—or possibly from *ceann dubh*—black-headed. Their lands were in Ayrshire, Lochaber and Skye and their motto is *Avise la Fin*—'Consider the end'. The seat of their chief, the Marquess of Ailas, is Culzean Castle.

Kerr: pronounced *kar*, the name is derived from the Norse *kjarr* meaning 'brushwood'. They were an Anglo-Norman family who came to Scotland in the 12th century. Their lands were Roxburghshire and their motto is *Sero sed serio*—'Late but in earnest'. Legend has the Kerrs left-handed so they reversed the spiral of their staircases to allow space for the left sword-arm.

Lamont: derived from Lawman, Lawgiver; MacKeracher is the Highland version. Their lands were in Argyll and Cowal and their motto is *Nec parcas nec spernas*—'Neither spare nor dispose'. Clan Secretary, 17 Broomhall Loan, Edinburgh.

Leslie: taken from the barony of Leslie in Aberdeenshire which they adopted in the reign of William the Lion. Their motto is 'Grip fast'.

Lindsay: Lindsey means Linden (lime tree) Island. They came to Scotland with David I and became very powerful, with lands in the Borders and in Angus. Their motto is *Endure Fort*—'Endure with Strength'. Clan Secretary, 112 Corsebar Road, Paisley.

Livingstone: from Livingstone in West Lothian where they held land, as well as in the Trossachs and Lorne. Their motto is *Si je puis*—'If I can'. Clan Secretary, Bachuil, Isle of Lismore, Oban, Argyll.

Logan or **MacLennan**: Logan is in Lothian, with MacLennan as the Highland version. Their lands were in Lothian, Berwickshire and Easter Ross and their motto is 'The Ridge of Tears'.

MacAlister: son of Alasdair, Gaelic for Alexander, who was descended from the great Somerled. Their lands were Kintyre, Arran and Bute and their motto is *Fortiter*—'Boldly'. Clan Centre, Glenbarr Abbey, Kintyre, Strathclyde.

MacAlpin: Alpins claim descent from 9th-century King Alpin and Dunstaffnage was their traditional home, though the race had no land. Their motto is *Cuimhnich bas Ailpein*—'Remember the death of Alpin'.

MacArthur: the MacArthurs were the senior branch of the Campbell clan, taking their name from Arthur Campbell in the 14th century. Their lands were Argyll, Cowal and Skye and their mottos are *Fide et Opera*—'By Fidelity and Work' and *Eisd! O eisd!*—'Listen! O listen!' Clan Secretary, 14 Hill Park Road, Edinburgh.

MacAulay: son of Olaf, who was King of Man and the Isles in the 13th century. Their lands were Dunbartonshire, Isle of Lewis, Sutherland and Ross. Their motto is *Dulce Periculum*—'Danger is sweet'. Clan Secretary, Cameron Loch Lomond Ltd, Alexandria, Dumbartonshire.

MacBean: son of Beathan, or from the Gaelic *bian*—fair skin—or from King Donald Ban, from whom they claim descent. Donald Ban was the son of Duncan, murdered by Macbeth. Their lands were in Inverness-shire and their motto is 'Touch not the catt bot a targe' (without a shield). At Culloden, gallant Gillies MacBean breached a gap in a wall with his enormous body and killed 14 Hanoverians before he was himself slain.

MacBeth: derived from the Gaelic for 'Son of Life'. Their lands were in Morayshire and Perthshire and their most famous ancestor, King MacBeth 1040–57, was very different from Shakespeare's character: a wise, generous, pious ruler, the last of the Gaelic kings.

MacCallum: *calaman* is Gaelic for dove, implying a disciple of St Columba whose emblem was the Dove of Peace. Their lands were in Argyll and their mottos are *In ardua petit*—'He has tried difficult things' and *Deus refugium nostrum*—'God is our refuge'.

Macdonald: *Dòmhnall* is Gaelic for world ruler. Donald of Islay was grandson of Somerled, Lord of the Isles and Ragnhildis, daughter of King Olaf of Man. Clan Donald was the largest and most powerful of the clans, with a number of branches, reigning supreme in the northwest Highlands and Islands. There are a variety of spellings, including MacDonnell. (Mac was not used in the surname until the 16th century.) It is the commonest Mac name in Scotland. The main branches were: Sleat in Skye, Clanranald in Moidart, Glengarry, Keppoch in Lochaber, and Glencoe. They were staunch Jacobites and Royalists, fiercely claiming their position on the right wing of any battle, given them by Robert the Bruce at Bannockburn and still held at Culloden. Their mottos include: *Per mare per terras*—'By land and by sea'; *Fraoch eilean*—'The heathery isle'; 'My hope is constant in thee'; *Dh'aindeoin co'theireadh e*—'Gainsay who dare'; *Creag an fitheach*—'the Raven's Rock'; and *Dia's naomh Aindrea*—'God and St Andrew'. Clan Centre, Armadale Castle, Sleat, Skye. Clan Secretary, Ceadach, 39 Redford Road, Edinburgh.

MacDougal: from the Gaelic *dubh gall,* meaning 'dark stranger'. Their lands were Lorne and their motto is *Buaidh no bàs*—'To conquer or die'. They fought against Robert the Bruce in the Wars of Independence, and with the Hanoverians at Culloden. Clan Secretary, Dunollie Castle, Oban, Argyll.

MacDuff: from the Gaelic *mac dubh*—son of the dark one. Their lands were in Fife, Lothian, Strathbran and Strathbogie and their motto is *Deus juvat*—'God assists'. The MacDuffs spawned a number of other clans: a MacDuff earl was known as *Mac an tòiseach*—son of the chief, which became MacIntosh, for example. Clan Secretary, 5 Sidlaw Road, Glasgow.

MacEwan: son of Ewan, who flourished in the 13th century. Their lands were Cowal, Lennox and Galloway and their motto is *Reviresco*—'I grow strong'.

MacFarlane: son of Partholon, whose father, Sear, took over Ireland after the Flood. Their lands were around Loch Lomond, Tarbert and Arrochar and their motto is *Loch Sloigh*—'Loch Sloy'.

MacFie: derived from the Gaelic *Dubhsìth*, meaning 'peaceful dark one', the MacFies are a branch of the Clan Alpine. Their lands were Colonsay and their motto is *pro rege*—'for the king'. Clan Secretary, 120 Cockburn Crescent, Balerno, Midlothian.

MacGillivray: *gille breth* is Gaelic for 'servant of judgement' and the clan belonged to the Clan Chattan Confederation. Their lands were in Mull, Lochaber and Morven, and later in Inverness-shire. Their motto is Dunmaghlas, the name of the chief's castle. MacGillivray of Dunmaglass led the Clan Chattan at Culloden. Clan Secretary, Dunlichty, 7 Cramond Park, Edinburgh.

MacGregor: *Grioghair* is Gaelic for Gregory and they claim descent from Griogar, son of 8th-century King Alpin. Some prefer to claim Pope Gregory the Great as their forefather. Whatever the truth, they all claim royal descent. Their lands were in Argyll and Perthshire and their motto is *S'rìoghail mo drèam*—'Royal is my race'. Their name was first proscribed 'under pain of death' after a bloodthirsty massacre of the Colhuhouns in 1603, and again by William III. Many changed their names. Clan Secretary, 14 Lockharton Avenue, Edinburgh.

MacInnes: *aontaghais* is Gaelic for 'unique choice' and they were an ancient Celtic clan. Their lands were Morven and Ardnamurchan and their motto is *Irid Ghibht dhe Agus an Righ*—'Through the Grace of God and the King'. Clan Secretary, 35 East Claremont Street, Edinburgh.

MacIntosh: see **Mackintosh** and **MacDuff**.

MacIntyre: *an-t-saor* is Gaelic for 'son of a carpenter' and the clan is said to have taken this name from one who chopped off his thumb to stop a leak in a Macdonald chief's galley. Their lands were Kintyre, Glenoe and Badenoch and they were part of the Clan Chattan Confederation. Their motto is *Per ardua*—'Through difficulties'. Clan Chattan Secretary, Dyunmaglash, Westhill, Inverness-shire.

MacKenzie: *coinnich* is Gaelic for 'fair' or 'bright' and was a popular Celtic forename, anglicized as Kenneth. MacKenzie lands were in Ross and Cromarty and the Isle of Lewis. Their mottos include *Luceo no uro*—'I shine, not burn'; *Tulach Ard*—'The High Hillock'; and *Cuidich 'n righ*—'Save the King'. Traditionally they provided most of the men in the Seaforth Highlanders, now amalgamated with the Cameron Highlanders to form The Queen's Own Highlanders. Clan Secretary, 1b Downie Place, Musselburgh, Midlothian.

MacKinnon: Kinnon derives from 13th-century Fingan and the MacKinnons were the family of St Columba, part of the Clan Alpin. Their lands were Iona and North Mull, then Skye and Arran, and their mottos are *Audentes fortuna iuvat*—'Fortune favours the brave'; and *Cùimhnich bas Ailpein*—'Remember the death of Alpin'. Clan Secretary, 222 Darnley Street, Pollockshiels, Glasgow.

MacKintosh: *toiseach* is Gaelic for 'tribal leader' or thane and the clan descended from the MacDuffs, originally the leading family of the Clan Chattan Confederation. Their lands were Inverness-shire and their motto is 'Touch not the cat bot (without) a glove'. Brave, beautiful, Jacobite Lady Anne MacKintosh, known as Colonel Anne, masterminded the Rout of Moy, ousting 1500 of Cumberland's troops with a mere five men. Clan Secretary, Moy Hall, Moy, Inverness-shire.

MacLachlan: Lachlan was a Celtic forename derived from Lochlann, the Gaelic for Norway, and the clan claims descent from Niall of the Nine Hostages, High King of Ireland, who won land in Argyllshire. They later spread to Lochaber, Perthshire and Stirlingshire. Their motto is *Fortis et Fidis*—'Brave and Trusty'. MacLachlan of MacLachlan, Prince Charles' ADC, died at Culloden in 1746. Clan Secretary, Tigh-na-Croft, Enochdhu, Blairgowrie, Angus.

MacLaine of Lochbuie: *gille Eoin* is Gaelic for 'servant of John' and they claim descent from Lachlans and MacLeans. Their lands were Lochbuie and their motto is *Vincere vel mori*—'conquer or die'.

MacLaren: from the Gaelic, 'son of Lawrence'. Their lands were Strathearn and Balquhidder and their motto is 'The Boar's Rock'. Clan Secretary, 1 Inverleith Place, Edinburgh.

Maclean: *gille Eoin* is Gaelic for 'servant of John' and they claim descent from the Kings of Dalriada. Their lands were Morvern, Mull, Coll and Tiree and their mottos are *Bas no Beatha*—'death or life'; and *Fear eile airson Eachairn*—'Another for Hector'. Clan Secretary, 12 Elie Street, Glasgow.

Macleod: *liotr* was old Norse for 'ugly'; *leod* was Saxon for 'prince.' They claim descent from Olaf the Black, King of Man and the Islands in the 13th century, and their lands were Skye, Lewis and Harris. 'Hold fast' is their motto. Clan Secretary, 38 Ravelston Gardens, Edinburgh.

MacMillan: *maoilein* means 'bald one', meaning tonsured and therefore priest, so their origins were ecclesiastical. Their lands were Lochaber, Argyll and Galloway and their motto is *Miseris succurrere disco*—'I learn to succor the distressed'. John MacMillan, 1670–1753, founded the Reformed Presbyterian Church. Clan Centre, Finlaystone, Langbank, Renfrewshire. Clan Secretary, 21 Huntley Gardens, Edinburgh.

MacNab: from *aba* meaning 'abbot', the MacNabs are descended from the Abbot of Glendochart, in the time of David I. Their lands were Glendochart and Loch Tay and their motto is *Timor omnis abesto*—'Let fear be far from all'. Raeburn's magnificent painting of *The MacNab* was of the 12th chief, Francis, 1734–1816, a remarkable eccentric, described by one as 'a herculean Highlander'. Clan Secretary, Finlarig, Killin, Perthshire.

MacNaughton/MacNachtan: *neachdainn* is Gaelic for 'pure one' and they can be traced back to Pictish royalty. Their lands were Strathtay, Lewis and Argyll and their motto is 'I hope in God'. The Clan Centre is at Dunderaive Castle, near Inveraray. Clan Secretary, 2 Douglas Crescent, Edinburgh.

MacNeil: descended from the O'Neills who were High Kings of Ireland. Their lands were Barra, Gigha, Knapdale and Colonsay and their motto is *Vincere vel mori*—'To conquer or die'. Clan Secretary, 34 Craigleith Hill Avenue, Edinburgh.

MacNicol or **Nicholson**: sons of Nicol, trace their ancestry back to the dark ages. The clan's lands were Sutherland, Skye and Argyll and their motto is *Sgorra Bhreac*—Skorrybreck.

MacPherson: *phearsain* was Gaelic for 'parson'. They were part of the Clan Chattan Confederation and trace their ancestry to Ferchar, King of Lorne, who died in 697. Staunch Jacobites, they arrived too late for the Battle of Culloden. Their land was Badenoch and their motto is 'Touch not the cat bot (without) a glove'. Clan Secretary, 39 Swanson Avenue, Edinburgh.

MacQuarrie: *guardhre* is Gaelic for 'noble one' and they trace their roots to the Clan Alpine and Saint Columba's family. Their lands were Ulva and their motto, *An t-arm breac dearg*, means 'the red tartaned army'.

MacQueen: from the Norse *sweyne*, or Gaelic *siubhne*, meaning 'good going'. They were strong members of the Clan Chattan Confederation, with close Macdonald connections. Their lands were Skye, Lewis, Argyll and Lanarkshire and their motto is 'Constant and faithful'. Clan Chattan Secretary, Dyunmaglash, Westhill, Inverness-shire.

MacRae: means 'son of grace', probably of ecclesiastical origin. Known as the 'Wild MacRaes' and also as 'MacKenzies Coat of Mail,' they were hereditary Constables of Eilan Donan Castle for the MacKenzies of Kintail, now restored by one of their descendants. Their lands were Beauly and Kintail and their motto is *Fortitudine*—'With Fortitude'. Clan Secretary, 6 Gardiners Crescent, Edinburgh.

Malcolm: followers of St Columba. Their lands were in Argyll, Fife, Lochore and Dumfriesshire. Their motto was *Deus refugium nostrum*—'God is our refuge', and is now *In ardua petit*—'He aims at difficult things'. Clan Secretary, Duntrune Castle, Kilmelford, Lochgilphead, Argyll.

Matheson: *math-ghamhainn* is Gaelic for 'bear' and, traditionally, the Clan of the Bear helped Kenneth MacAlpin against the Picts in 843. Their lands were Lochalsh and Sutherland and their motto is *Fac et Spera*—'Do and hope'. Clan Secretary, Burnside, Duirnish, Kyle of Lochalsh, Ross-shire.

Maxwell: from Maxwell on the River Tweed, derived from Maccus's Wiel, they were a powerful Border family descended either from 11th-century Maccus, King of Man and the Isles, or from Norman settlers. Their lands were in Nithsdale and their motto is *Reviresco*—'I flourish again'.

Menzies (correctly pronounced *mingiz*): from Mesnières in Normandy. Although of Anglo-Norman origin they became Gaelicized. Their lands were Atholl, Weem, Aberfeldy and Glendochart and their mottos are *Vil God I Zal*—'Will God I shall'; and *Geal 'us dearg a suas*—'Up with the white and red'. Clan Secretary, 1 Belford Place, Edinburgh. Clan Museum, Castle Menzies, Aberfeldy, Tayside.

Moncreiffe: from Gaelic *monadh craobhe*—tree on the moor, descended from Maldred, brother of King Duncan. Their lands were in Perthshire and their lairds were traditionally archers of the sovereign's bodyguard. Clan Secretary, Easter Moncreiffe, Perthshire.

Montgomery: from Montgomerie, in Normandy, the family are descended from Anglo-Norman Robert de Montgomery, who came to Scotland in the 12th century. Their lands were Eglinton, Ardrossan and Kintyre and their motto is *Gardez bien*—'Look well'. Clan Secretary, c/o P.O. Box 6, Saltcoats, Ayrshire.

Morrison: *gille Mhoire* is Gaelic for 'servant of Mary', presumably of ecclesiastical origin, and they trace their ancestors to the MacLeods of Dunvegan in 13th century. Their lands were Lewis, Sutherland, Skye and Harris. Hebridean Morrisons are well-known pipers today. Clan Secretary, Ruchdi, by Loch Maddy, Isle of North Uist.

Munro: from the Gaelic *Rothach*—man from Ro, thought to be from the River Roe in Ireland. Their lands were in Easter Ross, their motto is 'Dread God' and their war-cry, 'Castle Foulis Ablaze!', refers to the beacon that used to be lit on the chief's castle to summon the clan to arms. They were Whigs, supporting the Government against the Jacobites.

Murray: from Moray, the placename meaning 'settlement by the sea'. They are descended from Pictish Mormaers, with lands in Morayshire and Perthshire. Their motto is *Tout pret*—'All ready'. Andrew Murray, who died in 1338, was Regent of Scotland; Lord George Murray was a Jacobite general, believed by some to have been a traitor at Culloden. Clan Secretary, 204 Bruntsfield Place, Edinburgh.

Napier: descended from the ancient earls of Lennox; legend has it that one, having been particularly brave in battle, was ordered by his King to change his name to 'Nae peer'! Their lands were Gosford, Fife and Midlothian and their mottos are *Sans tache*—'Without stain'; and *To vincula frange*—'To break bones'.

Ogilvie: from Brythonic *ocel fa*—'high plain'. Ogilvie Earls of Airlie descend directly from the Earls of Angus, and were granted lands in Angus by William the Lion. Their motto is *A fin*—'To the finish'. St John Ogilvie, 1579–1615, was a Scottish Jesuit martyr, canonized in 1976.

Ramsay: meaning 'wild-garlic island'. The family is descended from an Anglo-Norman, Simund de Ramesie, who was granted lands in Lothian by David I. Their lands were Dalhousie and Perthshire, and their motto is *Ora et labor*—'Pray and work'.

Robertson: the eponymous Robert was Robert Riabhach (Grizzled Robert) Duncanson, 4th Chief of Clan Donnachaidh, and the Robertsons of Struan are one of the earliest known families in Scotland. Struan was their land and their mottos are: *Virtutis Gloria Merces*—'Glory is the reward of valour'; and *Garg'n uair dhuis gear*—'Fierce when raised'. Clan Secretary, 29 Lauriston Gardens, Edinburgh.

Rose: descended from the Norman family de Rose and first recorded in Scotland in the reign of Alexander II. Their lands were Strathnairn and Ross-shire and their motto is 'Constant and true'. Clan Secretary, Kilravock Castle, Nairnshire.

Ross: the Gaelic *ros* means 'headland'; Brythonic *ros* means 'moor'. They are descended from Fearchar Mac-an-t-Sagairt of Applecross, created Earl of Ross in 1234. Their lands were Ross-shire, Ayrshire and Renfrewshire and their motto is *Spem successus alit*—'Success nourishes hope'. Clan Secretary, 57 Barnton Park View, Edinburgh.

Scott: the Scoti were the Irish tribe who gave Scotland its name. The family descend from

Uchtred, *filius Scoti*—'son of a Scot'—in the 12th century, and were one of the most powerful Border families. Their lands were in the Borders and Fife and one of their best-known scions is Sir Walter, the 19th-century writer.

Scrymgeour: from French *eskermisor*—sword-fencer or skirmisher. Their ancestor Alexander 'Schyrmeschar' was royal banner-bearer, hanged by Edward I in 1306. Their lands were in Argyll and Fife and their motto is 'Dissipate'. Clan Secretary, 21 Braid Farm Road, Edinburgh.

Shaw: possibly derived from the Gaelic *seaghdha*—pithy. Principal members of the Clan Chattan Confederation, they were probably descended from 14th-century Shaw Macduff, founder of the MacIntosh clan. Their land was Strathspey and their motto is *Fide et Fortitudine*—'By Fidelity and Fortitude'. Clan Secretary, Tordarroch House, Tordarroch, Inverness-shire.

Sinclair: from the French St Clair sur Elle, in Normandy, whence came William de Sancto Claro in the 12th century, receiving the barony of Roslin. Their lands were in Midlothian, Orkney and Caithness, and they were jarls of Orkney in 14th century. Their motto is 'Commit thy work to God'. Clan Secretary, 2 Shandon Road, Edinburgh.

Skene: from Skene in Aberdeenshire, they are descended from Robertsons of Struan. Their lands were in Aberdeenshire, granted by the king in 11th century. Their motto is *Virtutis regia merces*—'A palace the reward of bravery'.

Stewart: derived from High Steward. Walter Fitz-Allan, an Anglo-Norman, came to Scotland in the 12th century and was given land and the greatest office in the realm—Steward of Scotland. The family provided Scotland with 14 sovereigns, five of whom also reigned in England. Stuart was the French form of the name, adopted in England. Their lands were Renfrewshire, Teviotdale, Lauderdale, Appin and Ardshiel and their motto is *Virescit vulnere virtus*—'Courage grows strong at a wound'. Probably the best-known Stuart was the one who never got to the throne, Prince Charles Edward, 1720–88. Clan Secretary, 48 Castle Street, Edinburgh.

Sutherland: Sudrland was the Norman name for Sutherland, to the south of Caithness. The clan is descended from early inhabitants of Sutherland, which was granted to them in 1228. Clan Secretary, Donrobin Castle, Golspie, Sutherland.

Urquhart: derived from Brythonic *air cairdean*—at the woods, the name of the district where the family originated. William of Urquhart was hereditary sheriff of Cromarty during the reign of Robert the Bruce. Their lands were in Ross-shire and Inverness-shire and their motto is 'Mean, speak and do well'. Thomas Urquart, 1611–60, who claimed descent from Adam, was a brilliant translator of Rabelais and is said to have died of laughter, on hearing of the Restoration. Clan Secretary, Bigram, Port of Monteith, Stirlingshire.

Wallace: derived from Wallenses, the mediaeval word for the Welsh who peopled Strathclyde, from whom the Wallaces are descended. Their lands were Ayrshire and Renfrewshire and their motto is *Pro Libertate*—'For Liberty'. William Wallace fought for Scottish independence, paving the way for Robert the Bruce.

Note:
Emboldened page numbers indicate major entries and *italicized* page numbers indicate maps.

Index